"This book is a good resource for students and practitioners as it integrates strategic concepts with data-driven insights."

Krish Saha, *Dr, Birmingham City University, UK*

Data-Driven Strategic Management

This book provides a comprehensive and integrated understanding of contemporary concepts and practical frameworks in Strategic Management.

Emphasizing data-driven decision-making, this book incorporates quantitative tools, analytical frameworks, case studies, and critical-thinking exercises tailored to volatile business environments. Data analysis is supported by IBM SPSS, alongside a dedicated chapter on digital business and AI-based strategy. Real-world examples from firms of varying sizes and industries, across both developed and emerging markets such as India and China, illustrate how strategic decisions are made, both successfully and unsuccessfully. Each chapter is structured with clear learning objectives, while "data challenge" exercises, drawing on qualitative and quantitative data, help students develop practical analytical skills. End-of-chapter questions further reinforce understanding and application.

Designed as core reading for advanced undergraduate and postgraduate students in Strategic Management, Business Strategy, and Business Analytics, this book equips learners to make data-informed decisions, formulate competitive strategies, evaluate market expansion opportunities, identify competitors, and leverage AI effectively.

Online resources accompanying this book include PowerPoint slides, a test bank, additional case studies, and data challenge materials.

Arpita Agnihotri is a tenured Associate Professor of Management at Penn State Harrisburg, USA, with research spanning strategic marketing, international marketing, upper echelons theory, digital marketing capabilities, sustainability, and consumer behavior.

Saurabh Bhattacharya is a Reader in Digital Marketing at Newcastle University Business School, UK. His research focuses on digital marketing, consumer behavior, artificial intelligence, and international marketing strategy, with publications in leading international journals.

DATA-DRIVEN STRATEGIC MANAGEMENT

Quantitative and Qualitative Analysis

Arpita Agnihotri and
Saurabh Bhattacharya

Routledge
Taylor & Francis Group
LONDON AND NEW YORK

Designed cover image: Varijanta/Getty

First published 2027
by Routledge
4 Park Square, Milton Park, Abingdon, Oxon, OX14 4RN

and by Routledge
605 Third Avenue, New York, NY 10158

Routledge is an imprint of the Taylor & Francis Group, an informa business

British Library Cataloguing-in-Publication Data
A catalogue record for this book is available from the British Library

ISBN: 978-1-032-93893-6 (hbk)
ISBN: 978-1-032-93891-2 (pbk)
ISBN: 978-1-003-56810-0 (ebk)

DOI: 10.4324/9781003568100

Typeset in Times New Roman
by codeMantra

Access the Support Material: www.routledge.com/9781032938912.

This book is dedicated to our students—past, present, and future—whose curiosity, engagement, and critical thinking inspire continuous innovation in the teaching and practice of strategy. Their questions, insights, and willingness to challenge conventional wisdom have been a constant source of motivation in shaping both the content and the applied orientation of this book.

We also dedicate this book to the broader academic community, including fellow researchers, educators, and collaborators, whose scholarship, guidance, and constructive feedback have enriched our understanding of strategy and informed the development of caselets, data challenges, and applied exercises.

Finally, we dedicate this work to managers, entrepreneurs, and industry practitioners who navigate complex global business environments and strive to make thoughtful, ethical, and data-informed decisions. Their efforts to balance innovation, performance, and responsibility serve as a practical inspiration for the frameworks, examples, and cases presented in this book, bridging theory and practice in meaningful ways.

Contents

Preface

Strategic management is both an analytical discipline and a managerial craft. In an era characterized by volatility, uncertainty, complexity, and ambiguity, managers must not only understand foundational strategy frameworks but also interpret data, anticipate competitive responses, and make informed decisions under rapidly changing technological, economic, and institutional conditions. This book is designed to equip readers with the conceptual rigor, practical frameworks, and applied tools necessary to navigate these challenges effectively.

The primary objective of this book is to provide a comprehensive and contemporary understanding of business strategy that integrates classical theories with emerging perspectives. The chapters progress logically from analyzing the external environment and competitive dynamics to formulating and implementing strategies at the business, corporate, and global levels. In doing so, this book emphasizes how strategic decisions vary across industries, organizational forms, firm sizes, and national contexts.

A key feature of this book is its strong applied orientation, driven by caselets, full-length business cases, and data challenges. These practical elements allow readers to explore real-world strategic dilemmas, examine managerial decision-making, and understand the implications of these decisions for firm performance. Analytical tools such as SPSS are integrated throughout this book, with examples of outputs and their interpretation to show how data informs strategy. Readers learn how to translate insights from quantitative and qualitative analysis into actionable recommendations, enhancing both analytical and decision-making skills.

This book also addresses contemporary strategic issues, including hypercompetition, corporate governance, CEO activism, digitalization-driven growth, co-creation, blue ocean strategies, corporate venture initiatives, mergers and acquisitions, and strategic alliances. Cases and data challenges are primarily contemporary (2020 onward), enabling readers to evaluate both successful and failed strategies and understand the trade-offs, risks, and performance outcomes associated with managerial decisions.

Recognizing the increasingly global nature of business, this book adopts an international and comparative perspective. It highlights firms from emerging markets, such as India and China, and examines institutional environments, business groups, and cross-country differences in strategy. By covering entrepreneurial ventures and large corporations across B2B and B2C sectors, this book enables readers to understand how strategies are adapted to different organizational and environmental contingencies.

Each chapter is structured around clear learning objectives and practical exercises, making this book suitable for undergraduate and postgraduate courses in strategic management, international business, and business policy, as well as executive education programs. Practitioners and entrepreneurs will also find the frameworks, cases, and analytical tools valuable for diagnosing strategic challenges and making data-informed decisions in real-world contexts.

Pedagogical Features of this Book

Across all chapters, this book emphasizes:

- **Caselets and full-length business cases:** Contemporary, real-world examples demonstrating strategic decision-making and firm performance outcomes.
- **Data challenges:** Applied exercises using SPSS outputs, dashboards, and simulations to interpret financial, operational, and market data.
- **Performance interpretation:** Step-by-step guidance on analyzing the consequences of strategic decisions, including success, risk, and failure scenarios.
- **Global and comparative perspective:** Coverage of firms in developed and emerging markets, including institutional differences, market dynamics, and cross-country strategic variations.
- **Sector diversity:** Inclusion of manufacturing, services, B2B, and B2C contexts to illustrate differences in strategic approaches.

By combining conceptual rigor with applied exercises, readers develop the ability to analyze, interpret, and act on complex strategic data, bridging theory and practice.

Acknowledgements

We are grateful to our colleagues, students, the broader academic community, and industry partners who provided insight and feedback during the preparation of this book. Classroom discussions, executive sessions, and practitioner interactions were invaluable in shaping the applied caselets, data challenges, and SPSS exercises that illustrate how strategic decisions influence firm performance.

We would also like to acknowledge the contributions of current and past researchers whose work, collaboration, and guidance have informed the conceptual frameworks, empirical analyses, and pedagogical design presented in this book. Their scholarship has been instrumental in helping us bridge theory and practice.

Special thanks are due to the organizations and managers who generously shared their experiences and data, enabling the development of authentic, contemporary case studies. We also appreciate the support of our home institutions, which fostered research, collaboration, and pedagogical innovation. Finally, we thank the reviewers and editorial teams whose guidance enhanced the clarity, structure, and practical relevance of this book.

About the Authors

Dr. Arpita Agnihotri is a tenured Associate Professor of Management at Penn State Harrisburg, USA. Her research spans strategic marketing, international marketing, upper echelons theory, digital marketing capabilities, sustainability, and consumer behavior. She has published extensively in leading ABS-listed journals, including *Industrial Marketing Management, International Marketing Review, Journal of Business Research, Management International Review, Journal of World Business, Group & Organization Management, International Journal of Human Resource Management, International Journal of Contemporary Hospitality Management, Psychology & Marketing, and Journal of International Management.* Her current research agenda examines digital marketing capabilities, metaverse adoption, leadership values, sustainability-oriented innovation, and technology-enabled consumer and organizational outcomes.

Dr. Agnihotri serves as an Associate Editor of the EuroMed Journal of Business and regularly reviews for top-tier journals, including *California Management Review, British Journal of Management, Journal of Business Ethics, European Management Journal,* and *Management Decision.* She has secured competitive research funding from the British Academy, Penn State Harrisburg, and international collaborators, and currently leads externally funded projects on deepfakes, credibility, and ethical decision-making.

She provides academic leadership in teaching management, strategy, marketing, and innovation at undergraduate and postgraduate levels. Beyond academia, Dr. Agnihotri is a globally recognized case writer, having authored numerous award-winning business case studies published by Ivey Publishing and Sage Publications, which are widely adopted by leading business schools worldwide. Her work has earned multiple international case-writing awards, including recognitions from HEC Montréal, John Molson MBA, Emerald, Sage, and Oikos, and her expertise is frequently featured in international business media outlets.

Dr. Saurabh Bhattacharya is a Reader in Digital Marketing at Newcastle University Business School, UK. His research explores digital marketing, consumer behavior, artificial intelligence, and international marketing strategy, with publications in leading ABS-listed journals. His current research agenda addresses digital nudging, conversational agents, deepfakes, and the strategic role of top management in marketing and internationalization.

He is a Fellow of the Higher Education Academy (UK), a member of the American Marketing Association, and Associate Editor of the *EuroMed Journal of Business.*

He regularly reviews for top-tier journals and has secured funding, such as a BA/Leverhulme Small Research Grant and international collaborative awards. Dr. Bhattacharya is developing projects on digital infrastructure, social well-being, and AI ethics, and supervises doctoral researchers in AI-driven marketing and digital engagement.

Dr. Bhattacharya provides academic leadership in teaching, leading, and redesigning core undergraduate and postgraduate modules in digital marketing, digital consumer behaviour, and marketing research. Beyond academia, he is a co-consultant to Entrepreneurs Associates, a non-profit organization supporting micro-entrepreneurs, where his research has informed strategic decision-making and delivered measurable organizational impact. He is also a globally recognized case writer, having co-authored over 100 business case studies published with Ivey Publishing and Sage Business Cases. Many of these cases are bestsellers, award-winning, and widely adopted by leading universities and business schools worldwide.

CHAPTER 1

Macroenvironment Analysis Tools

Learning Objectives

After completing this chapter, students should be able to:

- Conduct Volatility, Uncertainty, Complexity, and Ambiguity (VUCA) environment analysis;
- Apply Porter's five forces for determining the attractiveness of an industry;
- Examine how a country gains a competitive advantage over other countries using the Porter's Diamond Model;
- To comprehend how firm strategies change over the industry life cycle.

VUCA ENVIRONMENT

The VUCA environment refers to the dynamics of the macroenvironment that affect the feasibility and sustainability of corporate decision-making.[1] The Volatility, Uncertainty, Complexity, and Ambiguity of the macro environment that characterizes the VUCA environment makes it challenging for CEOs to devise the most effective business strategies or predict their outcomes. *Volatility* refers to the speed and magnitude of change in a given environment.[2] As fluctuations in demand, supply chain disruptions, or financial instability increase, the market becomes more volatile. Volatility occurs due to changes in a country's macro environment, such as political instability, economic instability, or disasters like the COVID-19 pandemic or other natural disasters.[3]

Uncertainty implies that the present business environment is unclear, and the future is also uncertain.[4] Uncertainty arises when the cause-and-effect relationship between two variables is not well understood. Furthermore, managerial experience from the past may not be applicable or helpful in the current situation because managers do not have complete and sufficient information to make a decision.[5] Consequently, clarity on what to do is lacking, making forecasting the future a challenging task.[6] For instance, political landscapes create an uncertain environment, as changing landscapes make the future unpredictable, thereby increasing

DOI: 10.4324/9781003568100-1

uncertainty. When the 2016 Brexit referendum happened, in which the UK decided to leave the European Union, it created uncertainty regarding the changing nature of trade agreements and immigration policies.[7] Consequently, firms in the UK and the rest of Europe, which had been trading in the UK, found it challenging to make long-term strategic decisions due to uncertainty about the economic and political outcomes resulting from Brexit.

Complexity implies that several interconnected factors have complex casualty that create chaos and confusion.[8] Moreover, the volume of information could be overwhelming to process. A firm may need to process a significant amount of internal information, as well as data on global competition, market conditions, technological advancements, and supply chain disruptions, among other factors.[9] For example, during the COVID-19 pandemic, the complexity of the VUCA environment increased significantly as lockdowns globally disrupted the supply chain, and the cost of raw materials for firms rose due to supply chain shortages. At the same time, consumer buying propensity decreased owing to furloughs and layoffs during the pandemic.[10] Rising costs, a demand-supply gap, and decreasing purchasing power all made the firm's macro environment very complex. Similarly, if a firm is a global organization conducting business in several countries, then processing regulatory, economic, and cultural values information for each country to adapt business practices according to the given attributes of each country can be a complex task.[11] Managers can combat the complexity of a VUCA environment by seeking outside expert help and developing a culture of continuous learning, leveraging technological advancements such as data analytics to make informed decisions.[12]

Ambiguity implies a lack of clarity or awareness about situations.[13] Ambiguity arises when different sources provide conflicting and contradictory information regarding a specific issue, making strategic decision-making challenging. Organizations must become agile and flexible to navigate the ambiguity of the VUCA environment.[14] Companies like Amazon, Tesla, and Netflix have successfully navigated an ambiguous environment.[15] Amazon, for instance, when entering the online retail space, was uncertain about consumer behavior and whether they would adopt online shopping as a permanent change in behavior. To address this uncertainty, Amazon introduced innovative customer-friendly features, including one-click purchasing, free returns, easy comparison of reviews and prices, and the availability of a wide range of products that surpass those found on retail shelves, to encourage customers to engage in online shopping. Today, it holds the maximum market share in online retail.[16]

Combatting VUCA Environment

Companies can perceive VUCA as an opportunity by identifying various business opportunities within a VUCA environment. Companies can foster a culture of innovation, enabling them to develop unique solutions in response to uncertain environments.[17] When Hershey experienced rising commodity prices, such as cocoa, and changing consumer habits toward healthy food products, the company innovated in the chocolate segment by adding more healthy ingredients while reducing the proportion of cocoa to combat rising commodity prices.[18] Another company, Olipop, capitalized on growing health concerns among consumers to offer a healthy gut soda.[19]

Companies can also effectively combat a VUCA environment through effective people management, like hiring diverse teams that bring varied perspectives on the issue at hand, thereby navigating the hardships of a VUCA environment more smoothly. Then, statistical tools can be used, such as scenario planning. When in the US, in 2025, the Trump Administration announced a tariff increase on Mexico, Coke was not affected by the rising aluminum cost, which it primarily imported from Mexico. Coke already had scenario planning in place and devised a plan of alternative strategic actions that it may need to take if the cost of aluminum increases for any reason.

Companies may also deploy data analytics to forecast changing consumer trends or emerging market opportunities. Companies can also develop collaborative networks with competitors, suppliers, or research institutions for joint innovation, thereby reducing costs in a VUCA environment. Companies should conduct thorough risk assessments to identify areas of vulnerability and potential risks. In annual report, there is generally a section of "Risks Related to Our Business" where companies list all areas of vulnerability. In its annual report, Netflix mentions, "If government regulations relating to the internet or other areas of our business change, we may need to alter the manner in which we conduct our business or incur greater operating expenses."[20]

Tesla also experienced a VUCA environment, as the automotive sector was volatile owing to rapid technological changes, uncertainty associated with consumer acceptance of electric vehicles, complexity in developing new battery technologies, especially when other automotive companies have failed to create affordable EVs with batteries, and ambiguity around regulations and market trends, which could push or demotivate customers for electric vehicles.[21] The VUCA environment requires companies to transform their traditional business models as needed. Thus, companies need to have flexible, innovative, and sustainable business models. Flexible, so that a company can quickly adapt to changing market conditions. Innovative, so that a company can rapidly embrace new technologies and disruptive ideas. Overall, a continuous learning and open culture can help firms to combat a VUCA environment.

Industry Dynamism, Munificence, and Complexity

The VUCA environment is a more macro-environmental analysis tool, and dynamism, munificence, and complexity measure the impact of VUCA on each industry. *Dynamism* refers to the rate of volatility in an industry environment.[22] The rate at which unpredictable changes occur in market conditions, such as the introduction of new products or regulatory changes, characterizes it. Firms operating in dynamic or fast changing industry do not aim for very long-term plans and keep their planning horizon short.[23] The standard deviation of the average growth rate of an industry's sales measures industry dynamism.[24] The higher the standard deviation, the higher the volatility, and the more dynamic the industry. For example, sales growing at a compound annual growth rate of a certain percentage, even if that percentage is less (say 4%) is likely to give more leverage to a firm to devise long-term strategy, compared to a high growth industry that is very volatile (say a growth rate of 10% in a given year and then 2% in the following year). The cryptocurrency industry is highly dynamic, with price fluctuations being very high and market regulations evolving irregularly.[25]

Munificence implies abundance and availability of resources in an industry that could support organizational growth. These resources encompass not only financial resources but also market opportunities and talent availability. More available resources provide greater flexibility for firms to fulfill their strategic intent. However, if the availability of slack resources is limited, then the firms' revenue-earning potential also declines. For instance, if the market has reached a mature stage in terms of demand, then market slack will be less, and firms will struggle to attract new customers easily. Instead, competitive intensity will increase where all players would compete for the same segment of customers, rather than attracting new users. Low industry munificence in terms of market size or talent availability is accompanied by more intense competition between firms, be that for customers or potential employees.[26] The rate of growth of sales of firms in an industry determines the industry's munificence.[27] Suppose the sales growth rate is increasing for an industry. In that case, it is beneficial as most players in the industry are adding new customers, implying an expanding market, which results in overall industry sales growth.

Complexity implies comprehensiveness of information that managers need to consider for decision-making.[28] The more information processing required, the more complex the industry becomes. Generally, more competitive industries are more complex, as competitive strategies of different competitors and their strategic actions, informed by competitive intelligence, need to be determined. Similarly, the more dispersed the value chain activities of players in an industry, the more complex the industry's operations become. The pharmaceutical industry in the US is complex, not because of the complex technologies involved in the drug development process, but because of the dispersed global supply chain of most pharmaceutical companies.[29] The US automobile industry is also an example of industry complexity.

PESTLE ANALYSIS

A PESTEL analysis is a framework that helps to analyze the macro environment of a business. In PESTEL, "P" stands for political environment, "E" stands for economic environment, "S" stands for social environment, T stands for technological environment, "E" stands for ecological, and "L" stands for legal environment.[30] *Political* factors in PESTLE include government policies related to taxation, fiscal policy, and trade tariffs, among others.[31] In 2025, the Trump Administration imposed tariffs on several countries, including neighboring countries such as Mexico and Canada,[32] which raised supply chain costs for several corporations that had outsourced manufacturing to Mexico, as it was a low-cost country, or were importing products from Canada.

In the PESTLE framework, political factors significantly influence *Economic* factors. When the Trump Administration pushed for tax reductions in the US, it was likely to impact the US economic environment through inflation.[33] Apart from inflation, other economic factors include interest rates, foreign exchange rates, and economic growth patterns. Following the COVID-19 pandemic, when inflation occurred, governments globally had to increase interest rates to reduce borrowing.[34] GDP growth, as part of economic growth, is also part of the economic environment that may impact corporations. Following the pandemic, as interest rates increased, it became difficult for SMEs to obtain credit due to high interest rates. In fact, in emerging markets, average businesses were able to cover only 55 days of expenses with their cash reserves, and loans became expensive, thus threatening their survival.[35]

Social factors include the demographics of consumers, such as their age, gender, race, family size, and consumer attitudes, lifestyle, and buying patterns. Post-pandemic consumers became more health-conscious, paving the way for new businesses like Olipop and Poppy, which offered healthy and gut-friendly sodas and became one of the most successful and popular categories.[36] The *Technological* factors of the PESTLE framework include innovation occurring across various fields that impact either the work processes or product markets of the firm. For instance, AI has led to the automation of work processes, while advancements in non-gasoline-based engines have contributed to the evolution of electric vehicles.

PORTER'S FIVE FORCES

Michael E. Porter's *Five Forces Model* determines the *attractiveness of an industry*, i.e., its profit-earning potential, based on five dimensions of a given industry.[37] These dimensions refer to the power possessed by buyers and suppliers in comparison to the focal firm, competitive rivalry in the industry, the likelihood of new entrants entering the industry (i.e., potential competition), and the threat of substitutes (i.e., alternatives available to consumers). Porter identified these forces as the *bargaining power of buyers* and *suppliers*, *competitive rivalry*, the *threat of new entrants*, and the *threat of substitutes*.

As can be easily predicted, the more buyers and suppliers there are, the more likely they are to have power over the firm.[38] This power reduces a firm's strategic flexibility, negatively affecting its profit-earning potential. Thus, for a focal firm's manager, the industry becomes less attractive. If competitive rivalry is high, firms will need to invest more resources to combat competition, which will reduce their profitability and make the industry unattractive.[39] If new entrants, whether entrepreneurs or existing firms diversifying into a given industry, can easily enter the industry, then the profit-earning potential for the focal firm will decline, given potential competition from new players. Finally, if consumers can easily use substitutes to fulfill their needs, then demand will fall if the firm raises prices, making the industry unattractive. However, the role of a manager is to combat these forces and make even an unattractive industry attractive, rather than merely labeling the industry as attractive or unattractive or exiting from unattractive industries. These forces are discussed in detail below.

Bargaining Power of Buyers

According to Porter, when the bargaining power of buyers is high, it may adversely impact industry profitability, as the wide variety of choices available to buyers may pressure firms to lower their prices or enhance the quality of their products and services. Either way, the seller's margin is reduced owing to a low selling price or a higher cost of operations, respectively. The bargaining power of buyers is generally high when there is a wide number of sellers/ suppliers available in the market, or when the buyer's switching cost is low. Thus, when buyers do not incur any losses, such as contractual value or loss of warranty period, in switching to another seller for their next purchase, their bargaining power increases.

The bargaining power of buyers also increases when sellers' or suppliers' products are undifferentiated. In the absence of a unique positioning or a unique selling proposition, buyers are inclined to try products from different sellers, rather than remaining loyal to a particular supplier.

The bargaining power of buyers also depends on their price sensitivity and knowledge about available options. When buyers have high price sensitivity and are aware of available options at lower prices, their bargaining power also increases. For example, in the online travel agencies business, consumers can easily compare airline prices across different platforms such as Expedia, Agoda, or Skyscanner.[40] They can use any platform without incurring any switching cost. Moreover, the services of online travel agencies are also highly undifferentiated, with most platforms offering nearly the same services without any unique point of differentiation,[41] which further enhances consumers' bargaining power. However, in the software industry, for example, Microsoft, a leading player, the bargaining power of buyers remains low, as switching from MS Office to any other operating system is difficult due to the uniqueness of each operating system. Buyers are also locked in with Microsoft, owing to compatibility issues, training costs associated with learning a new operating system, and the risk of disruption, which limited their ability to negotiate better prices or terms.[42]

Bargaining Power of Suppliers

According to Porter, the bargaining power of suppliers is high when there are few suppliers and many buyers, thereby creating a demand higher than supply.[43] Then, when substitutes are unavailable, the buyer's choice is also reduced, which enhances supplier power. In a similar vein, if suppliers offer highly differentiated products, buyers may find incentives to remain loyal to a particular supplier, thereby increasing the bargaining power of suppliers, who can charge a premium price for the differentiated products they provide.[44] Moreover, suppose suppliers can integrate forward to bypass the buyer and serve the end customer directly. In that case, their bargaining power also increases, as buyers risk losing their customers to the supplier if they integrate forward.

If new suppliers find it difficult to enter the given industry, then the power of existing suppliers also increases as barriers to entry become higher. Again, if suppliers can generate economies of scale and thus offer products at lower prices, their bargaining power also increases, particularly if buyers are price conscious.[45] For example, in the commercial aviation industry, there are two major key players, namely Boeing and Airbus. Given the capital expenditure involved, new entrants find it difficult to enter this industry, thereby raising the bargaining power of aircraft suppliers. Similarly, flying an aircraft is a highly skilled job, and given the varying technical specifications of different aircraft manufacturers, airlines need to train pilots for specific aircraft types.[46] Given the cost of training, airlines find themselves locked into agreements with aircraft manufacturers, such as Boeing or Airbus. It is for this reason that, even after the recent crisis caused by Boeing due to its 737 Max quality issues, airlines did not switch to Airbus for aircraft deliveries. On the contrary, fast-food companies such as KFC, Pizza Hut, or McDonald's benefit from the availability of a plethora of suppliers for the raw ingredients needed for their respective food items, thus reducing the bargaining power of these suppliers.[47]

Threat of New Entrants

The threat of new entrants is high when barriers to entry in the industry are low, i.e., the capital investment needed to start a business in a given industry is not high. Again, when existing competitors do not offer any differentiated value in their products or services, new entrants find it easier to imitate the quality of existing products and services, making their entry into the market easier and decreasing overall industry profitability. In addition, if consumers are not brand loyal and can easily switch from one company to another, then new entrants find it easier to attract new customers, thus further lowering the entry barriers in the industry.

Furthermore, if new entrants find it easier to establish a supply chain with easy access to distributors and suppliers, then entry barriers are again lowered. Local services such as locksmiths or lawn care companies require less capital investment and offer commoditized services.[48] Thus, too many new entrants enter this industry, thereby lowering entry barriers. The oil and gas industry, on the other hand, requires high capital expenditure, and firms in this industry generally have proprietary technology, which gives them a differentiated advantage.

Threat of Substitutes

Firms face a high threat of substitutes when customers find it easy to switch to alternative product categories, making the industry less profitable and less attractive to existing customers. Similarly, if customers have too many substitutes available for a given product or service, then the threat of substitutes also becomes high. Specifically, if substitutes offer a better price-performance ratio and consumers are aware of it, then the threat of substitutes becomes high. When streaming services such as Netflix and Amazon Prime emerged, both cinemas and TV channels faced a significant threat from substitutes, as consumers found a better price-performance ratio with streaming services than attending movie shows or watching TV channels.[49] On the contrary, the healthcare industry faces less threat of substitutes, as substitutes for hospitals and medicines manufactured by the pharmaceutical industry are not present.

Competitive Rivalry

Competitive rivalry is high when there are either too many players in the industry or when there are few competitors, but they are equal in size, financial power, or performance. As a result of competitive rivalry, firms respond to each other's competitive moves to either attract customers from competitors or retain their own customers, thereby gaining or sustaining their respective market shares.

Competitive rivalry also increases when the industry's growth rate is slow or in decline, implying that the industry has reached a mature or declining stage. Under such circumstances, when firms are able to expand their market and hence gain access to new customers, they compete for each other's existing customers, which further intensifies competition. Similarly, if products are commodity-based in nature with low differentiation, then competition also intensifies as firms have nothing special or specific to attract customers. Again, when exit barriers are high, i.e., firms find it difficult to exit the industry and are forced to compete aggressively against each other to survive, which further increases rivalry and pushes industry profitability down, making it less attractive. The semiconductor or search engine industries, in which large players such as Nvidia and Google, respectively, are more attractive, as they face less competition.

PORTER'S DIAMOND MODEL

Porter's Diamond Model explains why certain nations or industries within those nations perform better on a global platform, i.e., why specific industries from certain nations have a competitive advantage compared to the same industries in other nations.[50] According to Porter, this occurs when certain nations achieve four success factors that enable specific industries to grow within those nations. These factors are demand conditions, factor conditions, supply conditions, and competitive rivalry.

Factor Conditions

Factor conditions imply both basic and advanced factor conditions. *Basic factor conditions* refer to natural endowments, such as land, climate, and natural resources like coal mines, as well as unskilled labor.[51] *Advanced factor conditions* refer to complex resources, such as an educated and highly skilled workforce, well-developed road, air, and water infrastructure, financial capital resources, and technological capabilities. Countries that are relatively rich in basic or advanced factor conditions perform better in industries that rely on these factor conditions. For instance, China has rich reserves of one of the basic factor resources—lithium—and this makes it a major supplier of lithium for electric car batteries.[52] Similarly, Western countries such as the US have an ample supply of a highly skilled workforce in the software industry, which makes them a global leader in software-related businesses.[53]

Demand Conditions

Demand conditions indicate the sophistication of the domestic market for products and services within a given industry. Sophistication is important because demanding local customers can successfully pressure firms to improve the quality of their products and services, which in turn increases the overall industry's competitiveness at the global level. Germany has gained a reputation in the automobile industry as its consumers are sophisticated and demand luxurious cars.[54] Over the years, this reputation has driven German companies to deliver superior technology cars, such as BMW and Mercedes.[55]

Related and Supporting Industry

Related and supporting industries refer to the presence of competitive supplier industries that help develop a robust supply chain for the focal industry. In Germany, apart from the automobile industry, the steel industry is also well established, and so is the presence of advanced electronics companies. These different kinds of suppliers help to enhance the productivity and competitiveness of automobile manufacturers in Germany. Similarly, the software industry in the US thrives because the related and supporting education industry is well established in the country, with several reputable universities generating a pipeline of well-trained engineers.

Competitive Rivalry

Competitive rivalry refers to the competition among domestic players in an industry that helps strengthen the competitive position of firms in a given industry of a nation at a global level. For instance, the Japanese automobile industry has a global reputation due to intense competition among Japanese automobile companies, such as Toyota, Mitsubishi, Nissan, and Honda, which drove these firms to develop advanced automotive engineering capabilities, helping them achieve a global reputation.[56]

INDUSTRY LIFE CYCLE

The industry life cycle refers to the evolution of an industry or business over time.[57] The industry life cycle comprises four distinct stages: introduction, growth, maturity, and decline, each with its own unique characteristics. Firms in an industry begin their journey with the *birth or introduction phase*, where they develop radically new products that give rise to a new industry altogether. Electronic appliances, such as refrigerators and mobile phones, all began their journey at the birth stage.[58] At this stage, consumers have limited information about the products and industry players. Thus, demand is also limited.[59] New entrants or firms in the industry in this phase generally focus on finetuning the product for commercial launch once the pilot stage launch has been successful.

In the *growth phase*, as players invest in raising consumer awareness about products, demand catches up rapidly. As demand increases, more players have begun to enter that industry. When Blue Apron introduced the ready-to-cook category of food in the US, demand rapidly caught up after the company's promotional activities. Soon, other players entered the meal kit industry, including HelloFresh, Home Chef, and Eat Clean.[60] At this stage, even after the entry of new competitors, firms are still able to earn a profit as the market expands and firms in the newly established industry are able to acquire new customers, rather than vying for each other's customers. However, to effectively compete against each other, firms invest aggressively in both marketing and R&D to develop newer versions of their products that can entice and serve the needs of even more customers.

In contrast to the growth stage, where firms experience rapid sales growth, the sales growth rate begins to decline in the *maturity stage* as market and customer demand have saturated. Finally, in the *decline stage*, the industry continues to experience a decline in demand and profitability, owing to newer technologies that have either replaced the need for a product with another substitute or led to technological advancements, such that newer and better versions of products are now more acceptable to customers. A firm can either opt for revival by adopting newer technologies or file for bankruptcy due to constant sales decline, despite making aggressive efforts to push their traditional products to customers. The film photography industry faced a similar scenario where players like Kodak filed for bankruptcy after the decline of the film photography industry.[61] The decline happened as newer technologies, such as digital technologies, became available and were widely accepted by customers. However, Kodak continued to push for film photography for a long time and later struggled to adapt to digital technology, ultimately resulting in its bankruptcy filing.

ASSIGNMENT QUESTIONS

1. Consider any industry of your choice. Explain how the four VUCA components were impacted pre- and post-COVID-19 pandemic. Recommend strategies that firms in the industry of your choice can use to combat the VUCA environment.
2. How has the PESTLE environment impacted the pharmaceutical industry post 2025? Consider the country where you reside for analyzing its environment. As a manager, how would you counteract negative forces and capitalize on positive ones?
3. An entrepreneur intends to enter the streaming service industry of your home country. How attractive is this industry to entrepreneurs? Explain using Porter's five forces. How can this entrepreneur address the negative forces impacting its entry and earn profits?
4. Asian countries, such as China and India, have a comparative advantage in the herbs and spices product category. Explain how this happens using the Porter Diamond model.

CASE STUDY **1.1**

Boeing

Struggling and Sustaining with Crisis

Learning Outcomes

By the end of the case study discussion, students should be able to:

- Examine how firms can rationalize their strategic assets;
- Evaluate the turnaround strategies of a firm;
- Explore reasons for the negative financial performance of a firm;
- Critically examine how firms survive in an industry despite poor financial performance.

Agnihotri, A., & Bhattacharya, S. (2026). *Boeing: Struggling and sustaining with crisis*. Thousand Oaks, CA: SAGE Publications. https://doi.org/10.4135/9798348853594

INTRODUCTION

By April 2025, Arlington, Virginia-based Boeing Co (Boeing) was experiencing severe financial and order-related distress (Isidore, 2024). Boeing's situation arose due to a series of crises the company has experienced since 2018. Between 2018 and 2019, Boeing's 737 Max aircraft was involved in two fatal crashes wherein 346 people on board these aircraft died. After the second crash, airlines globally grounded Boeing's 737 Max aircraft (from March 2019 to January 2021) (German, 2024) until the company resolved safety issues. Again, on January 5, 2024, a Boeing 737 Max 9 aircraft that Alaska Airlines operated met with a serious incident. As the Alaska flight (Flight No. 1,282) from Portland, Oregon, to Ontario, California, with 171 passengers and six crews on the flight, was climbing and was only 20 minutes into the flight, a door plug of the aircraft came off, startling passengers and crew (Sodhi, 2024). Though the pilots landed the aircraft safely, a subsequent investigation revealed loose hardware and connections on their 737 Max planes (Sodhi, 2024). After the Alaska incident, the US Federal Aviation Administration (FAA) grounded 171 Boeing aircraft in the US for inspection, most of which were operated by Alaska and United (Sodhi, 2024). See Table 1.1 for details of issues with Boeing 737 aircraft over the years.

TABLE 1.1 Timeline: Issues with Boeing 737 Aircraft

Month, Year	Issues	Source
July, 1970	United Airlines reported a non-fatal Boeing 737 accident in which a flight had to abort takeoff.	Aviation Safety Network. (n.d.). Boeing 737-222. Accident investigation report completed, and information captured. Asn.flightsafety.org. Retrieved from https://asn.flightsafety.org/asndb/331068
1991–1996	Three fatal crashes (United Airlines Flight 585, USAir Flight 427, and Birgenair Flight 301) happened due to a design flaw in the Boeing 737 rudder control system.	Prisco, J. (December 25, 2020). Boeing 737: How world's most successful airplane became its most troubled. *CNN*. Retrieved from https://edition.cnn.com/travel/article/boeing-737-story-behind-the-troubled-aircraft/index.html
October, 2018	Lion Air Flight 610 was involved in a fatal crash due to a Maneuvering Characteristics Augmentation System (MCAS) failure in the Boeing 737 Max aircraft.	Klee, M. (May 18, 2024). A complete timeline of the Boeing 737 Max disaster. *Rolling Stone*. Retrieved from https://www.rollingstone.com/culture/culture-features/boeing-737-max-disasters-timeline-1235007089/
March, 2019	Ethiopian Airlines Flight 302 crashed, killing all on board. The plane was a Boeing 737 Max, and the cause of the failure was the MCAS.	
2019–2020	Production halt of the Boeing 737 Max and investigation by the US FAA, followed by the fixing of issues in the 737 Max aircraft.	Rushe, D., & Reuters. (December 16, 2019). Boeing suspends production of 737 Max model involved in fatal crashes. *The Guardian*. Retrieved from https://www.theguardian.com/business/2019/dec/16/boeing-737-max-production-faa
August, 2023	Safety concerns with the Boeing 737 Max aircraft resurfaced due to improperly drilled holes in the plane by one of Boeing's leading suppliers, Spirit AeroSystems.	Insinna, V., & Shepardson, D. (August 24, 2023). New Boeing 737 MAX supplier defect to delay aircraft deliveries. *Reuters*. Retrieved from https://www.reuters.com/business/aerospace-defense/new-boeing-737-max-supplier-defect-delay-aircraft-deliveries-2023-08-23/
December, 2023	One of the airlines discovered a bolt with a missing nut on a 737 Max aircraft, prompting Boeing to request that other airlines inspect loose bolts in the rudder control system of their plane	Wright, G. (December 29, 2023). Boeing urges 737 Max inspections for possible loose bolt. *BBC*. Retrieved from https://www.bbc.com/news/business-67838424
January, 2024	There was a missing bolt in the emergency door panel on Alaska Airlines Flight 1282, which led to the door's ejection mid-flight.	Klee, M. (May 18, 2024). A complete timeline of the Boeing 737 Max disaster. *Rolling Stone*. Retrieved from https://www.rollingstone.com/culture/culture-features/boeing-737-max-disasters-timeline-1235007089/
March, 2024	The FAA conducts a detailed audit of Boeing 737 aircraft and finds several manufacturing lapses committed by Boeing and its supplier, Spirit AeroSystems.	

Source: Developed by the Authors.

Then, in September 2024, Boeing workers went on strike. The direct financial impact of the one-month strike turned out to be USD 5 billion per day in terms of loss of production days (Mazein & AFP, 2024). Supply chain issues and inflationary pressures also escalated the problem (Gil, 2024). Expressing bankruptcy concerns for Boeing, Tim Clark, CEO of Dubai, UAE-based Emirates airline, said, "Unless the company is able to raise funds... I see an imminent investment downgrade with a Chapter 11 (bankruptcy proceeding) looming on the horizon" (Mazein & AFP, 2024) Boeing also had approximately USD 20 billion locked in its non-strategic assets that could be potentially sold off (Mazein & AFP, 2024).

In April 2025, the US government imposed a tariff of up to 145% on Chinese goods. In retaliation, the Chinese government ordered its airlines to halt accepting Boeing aircraft deliveries. Further retaliatory tariffs of 125% imposed by China on US goods more than doubled the cost of Boeing aircraft for Chinese airlines (TOI Business Desk, 2025).

In August 2024, Boeing appointed Robert K. Ortberg as the new CEO. Ortberg replaced Dave Calhoun as the new CEO. What strategies does Ortberg need to opt for to ensure the survival of Boeing? Can strategic asset rationalization help? How was Boeing able to sustain operations despite so many crises?

BACKGROUND

William E. Boeing founded Aero Products Company in 1916 in Seattle. He changed the company's name to Boeing in 2017. In its early days (1920s and 1930s), Boing received several US Military contracts and built military aircraft like the popular B-17 Flying Fortress and the B-29 Superfortress (O'Connell, 2020). After the Second World War ended, Boeing began building commercial planes like the Boeing 707 commercial passenger jetliner (launched in 1957) (Bauer, 2024). By 2023, Boeing operated had three divisions: commercial (passenger and cargo aircraft), defense, space, and security management (manned and unmanned military aircraft and weapons systems for strike, surveillance, and mobility), and Global services (supply chain and logistics management, engineering, maintenance, and modifications) (Boeing, 2024).

The aerospace industry is a duopoly market, with Boeing and France-based Airbus SE (Airbus) as the major players. Customers (i.e., airlines) remain with either Boeing or Airbus aircraft. Pilots of Boeing aircraft require additional training to fly Airbus aircraft and vice versa (Boeing, 2024). By the end of 2023, Boeing employed 171,000 globally, representing 47 nationalities (Bowen, 2024).

BOEING'S CORE BUSINESS DIVISIONS

Boeing's core business divisions included Boeing Commercial Airplanes (BCA), which develops commercial jet aircraft and renders airline fleet support services (Boeing, 2015). Some key aircraft manufacturing models are the 737, 767, 777, and 787. Boeing's second division is Defense, Space & Security (BDS), which develops military aircraft, weapons, and strategic defense systems (Boeing, 2015). It also produces satellites and space systems for commercial

TABLE 1.2 Boeing Segment-wise Revenues and Loss (2021–2023)

	Revenue (USD Billion)				Loss from Operations (USD Billion)		
	2021	2022	2023		2021	2022	2023
Commercial airplanes	19.71	26.03	33.90	Commercial airplanes	−6.38	−2.34	−1.64
Defense, space and security	26.54	23.16	24.93	Defense, space and security	1.54	−3.54	−1.76
Global services	16.33	17.61	19.13	Global services	2.02	2.73	3.33
Unallocated items, eliminations and other	−0.30	−0.19	−0.17	Segment operating loss	−2.82	−3.16	−0.07
Total	62.29	66.61	77.79	Core operating loss	−4.04	−4.66	−1.83

Source: Boeing. (December 31, 2023). The Boeing Company: Form-10K: For the fiscal year ended December 31, 2023. Investors.boeing.com. Retrieved from https://s2.q4cdn.com/661678649/files/doc_financials/2023/q4/BOEING-10Q-Q42023-013124.pdf

and military customers. Boeing Global Services (BGS) is its third core division, offering aftermarket support and services to commercial and defense customers (Boeing, 2015). Although the commercial aircraft division contributes most of its revenues (i.e., 43%), BGS is the only profitable strategic business unit (Boeing, 2023). See Table 1.2 for division-wise revenues and losses of Boeing.

Boeing also operated ancillary units, including Boeing AnalytX, its technology services, HorizonX, the innovation and venture capital arm of BGS (international presence and partnerships), Government Operations, Advertising & Brand, and Licensing (Boeing, 2015).

BOEING CRISIS

Between 2018 and 2024, the stock price of Boeing nearly halved in value (Alpha Street, 2024). Boeing's stock has been dwindling since late 2018 after a 737 Max flight crash in Indonesia that killed all passengers (181 passengers) and crew (eight crew) on board. The flight belonged to Lion Air. Within six months, another 737 Max, operated by Ethiopian Airlines, also met a similar fate (Alpha Street, 2024). These two instances led to the grounding of 737 Max aircraft globally, with the FAA conducting the investigations (Alpha Street, 2024). Then, in January 2024, as Boeing was on the road to recovery, in yet another incident involving another 737 Max Alaska Airlines aircraft, the aircraft's door plug came off (Alpha Street, 2024). Subsequently, the FAA capped the production of 737, which was Boeing's largest source of cash (Supply Chain Brain, 2024). The FAA wanted Boeing to improve the quality of its production system. FAA limited the production of 737 Max to 38 aircraft units a month. Given that airline customers are supposed to make payment only after receiving delivery, Boeing's limited delivery ability also limited cash it could receive from its customers. Besides this, Boeing had to pay suppliers and fulfill debt obligations (Supply Chain Brain, 2024).

All this led to overall negative cash flow. Cash flow "refers to the net balance of cash moving into and out of a business at a specific point in time" (Stobierski, 2020). As the FAA mandated Boeing for production slowdown, Boeing leadership also initiated a program to review safety and quality measures and train employees to ensure quality standards across production lines (Alpha Street, 2024). By the first quarter of 2024, Boeing aircraft deliveries were lowest owing to the cap put by the FAA on production (Josephs, 2024).

Further, shortage of aircraft components also slowed deliveries of Boeing's 787 Dreamliners, a wide-body, twin-engine jet airliner. Several airlines, such as American Airlines and United, had to decrease international flights owing to delays in deliveries of 787 Dreamliner aircraft (Josephs, 2024). In 2023, the FAA also opened a probe into Boeing 787 Dreamliner after Boeing reported "misconduct" by some employees, where experts believed records to have been falsified by the employees (Josephs, 2024).

Boeing's defense and space division was also incurring losses. In the first three quarters of 2024, Boeing's defense and space division incurred losses of USD 3.1 billion (Thomas, 2024). Losses happened due to cost overruns in price-fixed contracts given to Boeing by the government through the bidding process (Gil, 2024). Brian West, chief financial officer of Boeing, commented on Boeing's struggles and share market performance, saying, "We have frustrated and disappointed our customers because of some of the production supply chain issues that we're up against" (Josephs, 2024). West added,

> And while I understand that frustration, the most important thing we can do for our customers and the supply chain in the industry is to focus on the actions that are underway as we speak so that we could stabilize this production system, improve quality, and get more predictable.
>
> (Josephs, 2024)

ASSET RATIONALIZATION

Boeing's partnership with NASA (The National Aeronautics and Space Administration) dates back to the 1960s, when Boeing supported Apollo missions. Boeing built five unmanned Lunar Orbiters that, between 1966 and 1968, mapped 99% of the Moon, helping NASA select future Apollo mission landing sites (Evans, 2024). Then, in 1993, NASA appointed Boeing as the primary contractor for the International Space Station (ISS) (Gil, 2024). ISS is a "permanently crewed on-orbit laboratory that enables scientific research supporting innovation on Earth and future deep space exploration" (Boeing, 2021). However, since 2014, SpaceX and Boeing have become a primary partner for NASA, especially for human spaceflight (Insinna, 2024).

Boeing's USD 6.7 billion revenues from defense and space business in 2023 were mainly attributed to military aircraft production rather than the space program (Fernholz, 2024). Boeing was facing several predicaments with its space division, including a satellite for Intelsat that stopped working and fell apart suddenly after suffering a technical issue in 2024 (Roth, 2024). Analysts also expected the Boeing-built ISS to be deorbited by the end of 2030 (Fernholz, 2024).

In 2024, Boeing is also considering selling its NASA contracts, such as Starliner. Starliner is a Boeing-developed spacecraft transporting people to and from the ISS. Parting with Starliner was expected to help Boeing get free of a deeply troubled program (Reuters, 2024). This has resulted in USD 1.8 billion charges (Reuters, 2024). Jeff Bezos-owned Blue Origin showed interest in acquiring the same (Gil, 2024). Over the years, Boeing fell far behind major technological leaps made in the space industry, such as by Elon Musk's SpaceX and other "new space" firms that mastered reusable rocket technology (Reuters, 2024). However, Boeing was not considering selling broader space operations. Ortberg, commenting on sales of the Starliner project, said, "We're better off doing less and doing it better than doing more and not doing it well." He added,

> Clearly, our core of commercial airplanes and defense systems are going to stay with the Boeing Company for the long run. But there's probably some things on the fringe there that we can be more efficient with or that distract us from our main goal here.
>
> (Roth, 2024)

BOEING'S TURNAROUND PLAN

Ortberg's strategic plan included workforce reduction and conservatively aligning production targets (TipRanks, 2024). Boeing, trying to become more efficient in its operations and to cut costs, decided to lay off 10% of its workforce (Laidley, 2024). As part of its turnaround initiatives, Boeing also signed an agreement to acquire a majority stake in its longtime supplier, Spirit AeroSystems, for USD 4.7 billion (Alpha Street, 2024). Experts believed this integration would significantly resolve Boeing's quality problems, as outsourcing component manufacturing was one of the major drivers of quality issues Boeing faced (Alpha Street, 2024).

Experts also accused Boeing of a lack of safety culture and preferring profits over safety. Commenting on the need to change Boeing's culture, Ortberg said that Boeing would implement "fundamental culture change" (Cabral, 2024). He added, "I know culture change starts at the top. Our leaders, from me on down, need to be closely integrated with our business and the people who are doing the design and production of our products."

Accordingly, as part of increasing its safety culture, Boeing launched a "Speak up" reporting system, wherein employees were encouraged to report quality issues. Reporting by employees increased by 220% from 2023 to 2024 (Catchpole, 2025). Additionally, Boeing managers other than those directly responsible for addressing the issues in question evaluated safety issues. Boeing also invested in machine learning to gauge quality problems in its supply chain (Catchpole, 2025).

Boeing was also trying to cut costs from its supply chain by establishing long-term relationships only with a few selected suppliers (Supply Chain 247, 2024). Chris Chadwick, chief executive of Boeing Defense, Space and Security, said, "There continues to be tremendous opportunity in the supply chain for efficiency, cost reduction." Chadwick added, "What we've found is that supplier who lean forward from a cost perspective, we do partner with them for the long term" (Supply Chain 247, 2024). Boeing was targeting to have a USD 6 billion cost reduction from its network of suppliers.

In April 2024, West forecasted Boeing to generate free cash flow "in the low single-digit billions" (Josephs, 2024). Accordingly, Boeing filed with US regulators to sell its bonds and shares to release USD 25 billion cash from the sale (Johnsson & Joshua, 2024).

INDUSTRY DYNAMICS

Financial analysts remained hopeful about Boeing's turnaround because Boeing was operating in a duopoly structure with limited competition. In more upstart-friendly industries, the crisis would have been ruinous (Laidley, 2024). Boeing since 2019 lost USD 32 billion without facing any bankruptcy issues (Isidore, 2024).

The industry dynamics is almost a duopoly with high entry barriers. Some of the emerging players, such as Boom and Spike Aerospace, were much smaller players in the aircraft manufacturing industry (Reed, 2024). Blake Scholl, founder and CEO of the Colorado-based Boom, said, "It's never been more obvious that the world is not well served by the duopoly that we have in commercial aviation" (Reed, 2024).

By October 2024, Boeing had a backlog of orders for more than 5,600 commercial jets valued at USD 529 billion. Additionally, the FAA's requirement for Boeing to reduce its manufacturing pace to address quality issues prevented it from producing enough planes to generate any profits (Isidore, 2024).

Moreover, Boeing's customers could not easily shift from Boeing to Airbus, given Airbus' backlog of more than 8,000 commercial jet orders, with a production rate of 800 planes per year and a booking Commitment for the next ten years. Furthermore, for any new aircraft manufacturer, it may take several years and billions of dollars in capital investment to compete against the two giant aircraft manufacturers. Finally, pilots without intensive training could not fly two different kinds of models, let alone fly two different aircraft companies planes (Isidore, 2024).

However, for non-commercial aircraft, customers had choices. Companies such as Bombardier, Embraer, and Gulfstream manufactured a range of smaller aircraft primarily used for military purposes (BlackJet, 2024).

Limited competition was believed to have saved the fate of Boeing. Richard Aboulafia, managing director at AeroDynamic Advisory, an aerospace and defense industry consultant, said, "Given the dynamics of their place in the industry and the industry itself, they have the luxury of time." "It's an industry with the highest possible barriers to entry and very strong demand for its products. But they've wasted a lot of that time" (Isidore, 2024).

Analysts expected the global aircraft manufacturing market to grow at a rate of 4.9% and reach USD 674.19 billion by 2034, from USD 420.30 billion in 2024. North America largely held a dominant market position, capturing 38.01% of the market share as of 2024 (Market.us, 2025). However, in this thriving market, Boeing, despite earning more revenue than Airbus, was an overall loss-making company. See Figure 1.1 for the net income of Airbus and Boeing between 2020 and 2024.

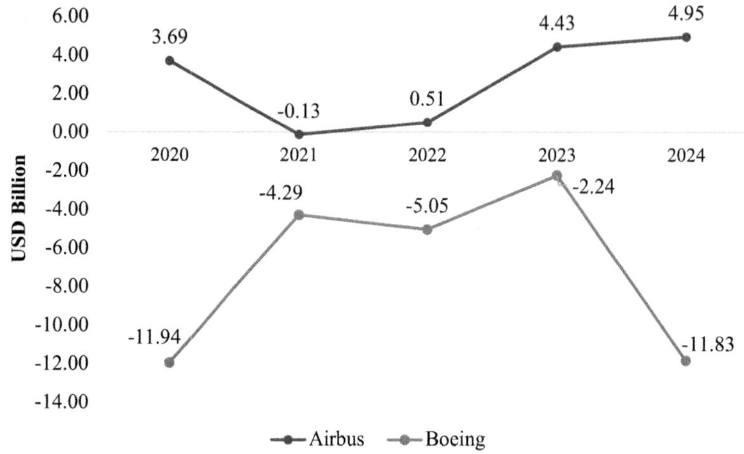

FIGURE 1.1 Net Income: Boeing Vs. Airbus (2020-2-204) (USD Billion)

Source: Nguyen, T. H. M. (July 8, 2025). Net income of Boeing from 2020 to 2024. *Statista*. Retrieved from https://www.statista.com/statistics/1515287/boeing-net-income/; Statista Research Department. (April 9, 2025). Airbus Group's net income/ loss between FY 2014 to FY 2024. *Statista*. Retrieved from https://www.statista.com/statistics/1471869/airbus-group-worldwide-income-loss/

THE ROAD AHEAD

Financial analysts appreciated Ortberg's strategy of focusing on core business sectors and expected that by 2025–2026, cash flow recovery could occur, with an estimated USD 9 billion cash flow by 2027 (TipRanks, 2024). Commenting on the liquidity of Boeing, Ortberg said, "Longer-term, we remain confident in our ability to achieve $10 billion of free cash flow" (Alpha Street, 2024). Explaining the issue of liquidity crunch, he added,

> However, given our continued focus on safety, quality, stability, we continue to expect that this goal will take us longer than we originally planned and later in the 2025, 2026 window primarily tied to the 737 and 787 production delivery ramps of 50 per month and 10 per month, respectively.
>
> (Alpha Street, 2024)

Boeing had also started making stronger-than-expected deliveries; these developments and potential divestitures were expected to generate a positive outlook for Boeing's financial health (TipRanks, 2024). Whether Ortberg will succeed in Boeing's turnaround remains to be seen.

DISCUSSION QUESTIONS

1. Conduct a VUCA Analysis for Boeing.
2. Conduct Porter's Five Forces analysis for Boeing.
3. Examine the PEST analysis of the macroenvironment, which is favorable toward Boeing.

CHAPTER NOTES

1 https://hbr.org/2014/01/what-vuca-really-means-for-you.
2 https://hbr.org/2014/01/what-vuca-really-means-for-you.
3 https://hbr.org/2014/01/what-vuca-really-means-for-you.
4 https://cmr.berkeley.edu/2018/11/61-1-management-innovation-in-a-vuca-world-challenges-and-recommendations/#:~:text=Management%20Innovation%20in%20a%20VUCA,Innovation.
5 https://cmr.berkeley.edu/2018/11/61-1-management-innovation-in-a-vuca-world-challenges-and-recommendations/#:~:text=Management%20Innovation%20in%20a%20VUCA,Innovation.
6 https://cmr.berkeley.edu/2018/11/61-1-management-innovation-in-a-vuca-world-challenges-and-recommendations/#:~:text=Management%20Innovation%20in%20a%20VUCA,Innovation.
7 https://oxfordre.com/economics/display/10.1093/acrefore/9780190625979.001.0001/acrefore-9780190625979-e-715?d=%2F10.1093%2Facrefore%2F9780190625979.001.0001%2Facrefore-9780190625979-e-715&p=emailA4Y88kTMFqmiM#:~:text=In%20addition%2C%20the%20ending%20of,the%20Trade%20and%20Cooperation%20Agreement.
8 https://www.forbes.com/sites/committeeof200/2025/06/24/how-smart-leaders-thrive-in-volatile-uncertain-complex-and-ambiguous-vuca-times/.
9 https://www.forbes.com/sites/committeeof200/2025/06/24/how-smart-leaders-thrive-in-volatile-uncertain-complex-and-ambiguous-vuca-times/.
10 https://www.ecb.europa.eu/press/economic-bulletin/focus/2022/html/ecb.ebbox202108_01~e8ceebe51f.en.html.
11 https://hbr.org/2014/01/what-vuca-really-means-for-you.
12 https://thesystemsthinking.com/navigating-vuca-environments-as-a-systems-thinking-practitioner/#:~:text=Navigating%20VUCA%20environments%20is%20one,succeed%20in%20a%20VUCA%20world.
13 https://hbr.org/2014/09/a-framework-for-understanding-vuca.
14 https://hbr.org/2014/09/a-framework-for-understanding-vuca.
15 https://hbr.org/2022/01/can-big-tech-be-disrupted.
16 https://qz.com/1773368/how-amazon-created-a-retail-revolution.
17 https://een.ec.europa.eu/blog/7-steps-foster-culture-innovation-inside-your-business#:~:text=Innovation%20requires%20learning%20and%20experimentation,elevate%20equity%2C%20and%20lead%20inclusively.
18 https://www.thehersheycompany.com/en_us/home/newsroom/blog/consumers-are-focusing-more-on-health-and-hershey-is-here-for-it.html#:~:text=With%20more%20consumers%20focused%20on,incorporate%20wellness%20into%20their%20snacking.
19 https://drinkolipop.com/pages/our-story#:~:text=Our%20Foundational%20Ingredients,your%20microbiome%20and%20digestive%20health.
20 https://s22.q4cdn.com/959853165/files/doc_financials/2024/ar/Netflix-10-K-01272025.pdf.
21 https://www.mckinsey.com/features/mckinsey-center-for-future-mobility/our-insights/new-twists-in-the-electric-vehicle-transition-a-consumer-perspective.
22 Knecht, M. (2014). *Diversification, industry dynamism, and economic performance: The impact of dynamic-related diversification on the multi-business firm* (1st ed.). Springer Gabler. https://doi.org/10.1007/978-3-658-02677-6
23 Knecht, M. (2013). Industry dynamism. In *Diversification, industry dynamism, and economic performance: The impact of dynamic-related diversification on the multi-business firm* (pp. 90–128). Wiesbaden: Springer Fachmedien Wiesbaden.
24 Farjoun, M., & Levin, M. (2011). A fractal approach to industry dynamism. *Organization Studies*, *32* (6), 825–851.
25 https://calebandbrown.com/blog/crypto-volatility/#:~:text=Regulation%20is%20an%20important%20factor,a%20presidential%20election%20policy%20platform.
26 Chowdhury, S. K., & Endres, M. L. (2021). The influence of regional economy-and industry-level environmental munificence on young firm growth. *Journal of Business Research*, *134*, 29–36.
27 https://onlinelibrary.wiley.com/doi/abs/10.1002/bse.1902#:~:text=Munificence%20refers%20to%20the%20availability,the%20measurement%20of%20industrial%20munificence.
28 https://onlinelibrary.wiley.com/doi/abs/10.1002/bse.1902#:~:text=Munificence%20refers%20to%20the%20availability,the%20measurement%20of%20industrial%20munificence.

29 https://www.sciencedirect.com/science/article/pii/S0377221725003583#:~:text=Broadly%2C%20the%20pharmaceutical%20supply%20chain,McKinsey%20Global%20Institute%2C%202020).
30 Hamilton, L., & Webster, P. (2018). *The international business environment* (4th ed.). Oxford: Oxford University Press.
31 Hamilton, L., & Webster, P. (2018). *The international business environment* (4th ed.). Oxford: Oxford University Press.
32 https://www.bbc.com/news/articles/cn93e12rypgo.
33 https://taxfoundation.org/research/federal-tax/trump-administration-tax-proposals/#:~:text=President%20Trump%20has%20proposed%20a,analysis%20our%20Budget%20Reconciliation%20Tracker.&text=Your%20browser%20can't%20play%20this%20video.&text=An%20error%20occurred.,is%20disabled%20in%20your%20browser.
34 https://www.brookings.edu/articles/quantitative-easing-and-housing-inflation-post-covid/.
35 https://www.worldbank.org/en/publication/wdr2022/brief/chapter-1-introduction-the-economic-impacts-of-the-covid-19-crisis#3.
36 https://bevi.co/blog/history-of-poppi-soda-olipop/.
37 Porter, M. E. (2008). The five competitive forces that shape strategy. *Harvard Business Review*, *86* (1), 78.
38 Porter, M. E. (2008). The five competitive forces that shape strategy. *Harvard Business Review*, *86* (1), 78.
39 Porter, M. E. (2008). The five competitive forces that shape strategy. *Harvard Business Review*, *86* (1), 78.
40 https://www.appeconomyinsights.com/p/online-travel-industry-showdown.
41 https://www.appeconomyinsights.com/p/online-travel-industry-showdown.
42 https://panmore.com/microsoft-corporation-five-forces-analysis-porters-recommendations.
43 Porter, M. E. (2008). The five competitive forces that shape strategy. *Harvard Business Review*, *86* (1), 78.
44 Porter, M. E. (2008). The five competitive forces that shape strategy. *Harvard Business Review*, *86* (1), 78.
45 Porter, M. E. (2008). The five competitive forces that shape strategy. *Harvard Business Review*, *86* (1), 78.
46 https://www.insightflyer.com/as-a-pilots-point-of-view-differentiating-boeing-and-airbus/.
47 https://hbr.org/2016/06/why-sourcing-local-food-is-so-hard-for-restaurants.
48 https://www.washingtontechnology.com/opinion/2018/05/how-to-differentiate-in-a-commoditized-market/347972/#:~:text=Don't%20try%20to%20address,not%2C%20give%20it%20the%20boot.
49 https://www.businessofbusiness.com/articles/a-brief-history-of-video-streaming-by-the-numbers/#:~:text=Netflix%20introduced%20streaming%20services%20in,into%20free%20and%20paid%20subscriptions.
50 Fainshmidt, S., Smith, A., & Judge, W. Q. (2016). National competitiveness and Porter's diamond model: The role of MNE penetration and governance quality. *Global Strategy Journal*, *6* (2), 81–104.
51 Wu, Y., Xiao, X., & Song, Z. (2017). Competitiveness analysis of coal industry in China: A diamond model study. *Resources Policy*, *52*, 39–53.
52 https://www.sciencedirect.com/science/article/abs/pii/S0301420722003129.
53 https://www.cnbc.com/2024/05/03/the-top-countries-where-companies-are-scooping-up-american-tech-workers.html.
54 https://www.bostonbrandmedia.com/news/why-germany-is-seen-as-the-car-center-of-the-world#:~:text=Germany%20is%20renowned%20for%20its,that%20push%20the%20industry%20forward.
55 https://onlinelibrary.wiley.com/doi/full/10.1002/bse.3538.
56 https://www.lexserviceauto.com/what-makes-japanese-made-vehicles-so-special#:~:text=Innovation%20is%20at%20the%20heart,service%20your%20car%2C%20call%20LexService.
57 https://www.sciencedirect.com/science/article/abs/pii/S0048733313000139.
58 https://bluebonnet.coop/brief-history-electric-appliances.
59 Audretsch, D. B., & Feldman, M. P. (1996). Innovative clusters and the industry life cycle. *Review of Industrial Organization*, *11* (2), 253–273.
60 https://www.wired.com/gallery/best-meal-kit-services-1/.
61 https://www.foxbusiness.com/lifestyle/how-kodak-went-from-film-giant-financial-peril#:~:text=Riddled%20with%20debt%2C%20it%20filed,to%20commercial%20printing%20and%20tech.

FURTHER READING

Anand, J., & Singh, H. (1997). Asset redeployment, acquisitions and corporate strategy in declining industries. *Strategic Management Journal, 18*(S1), 99–118.

Faster Capital. (June 28, 2024). How does the investment rating affect the cost of capital for companies. Fastercapital.com. Retrieved from https://fastercapital.com/topics/how-does-the-investment-rating-affect-the-cost-of-capital-for-companies.html

Golembieski, M. (May 10, 2024). *6 Ways to improve working capital.* J. P. Morgan. Retrieved from https://www.jpmorgan.com/insights/credit-and-financing/working-capital/6-ways-to-increase-working-capital

Porter, M. E. (2008). The five competitive forces that shape strategy. *Harvard Business Review, 86*(1), 78–93. Retrieved from https://hbr.org/2008/01/the-five-competitive-forces-that-shape-strategy

CASE REFERENCES

Agnihotri, A., & Bhattacharya, S. (2026). *Boeing: Struggling and sustaining with crisis.* Thousand Oaks, CA: SAGE Publications. https://doi.org/10.4135/9798348853594

Alpha Street. (July 2, 2024). Can Boeing's (BA) recovery plan help the company regain altitude? Alphastreet.com. Retrieved from https://news.alphastreet.com/can-boeings-ba-recovery-plan-help-the-company-regain-altitude/

Bauer, P. (2024). Boeing 707: Jetliner. *Britannica.* Retrieved from https://www.britannica.com/technology/Boeing-707

BlackJet. (December 25, 2024). Private jet manufacturers. Blackjet.com. Retrieved from https://www.blackjet.com/post/private-jet-manufacturers

Boeing. (March 30, 2015). Tours of Boeing facilities. Boeing.com. Retrieved from https://www.boeing.com/company#tours

Boeing. (May 14, 2021). International space station. Boeing.com. Retrieved from https://www.boeing.com/space/international-space-station

Boeing. (December 31, 2023). The Boeing Company: Form-10K: For the fiscal year ended December 31, 2023. Investors.boeing.com. Retrieved from https://s2.q4cdn.com/661678649/files/doc_financials/2023/q4/BOEING-10Q-Q42023-013124.pdf

Boeing. (2024). The Boeing Company: 2023 annual report. Investors.boeing.com. Retrieved from https://s2.q4cdn.com/661678649/files/doc_financials/2023/ar/Boeing-2023-Annual-Report.pdf

Bowen, S. (2024). Boeing: Global equity, diversity & inclusion 2023 report. Boeing.com. Retrieved from https://www.boeing.com/sustainability/diversity-and-inclusion/annual-report#letter-from-leadership

Cabral, A. R. (October 23, 2024). Boeing boss unveils four-point turnaround strategy as third-quarter losses nearly quadruple to $6bn. *The National.* Retrieved from https://www.thenationalnews.com/business/aviation/2024/10/23/boeing-boss-unveils-four-point-turnaround-strategy-as-third-quarter-losses-nearly-quadruple-to-6bn/

Catchpole, D. (May 21, 2025). Boeing increases 737 production pace as quality, safety culture improves. *Reuters.* Retrieved from https://www.reuters.com/business/autos-transportation/boeing-increases-737-production-pace-quality-safety-culture-improves-2025-05-21/

Evans, B. (November 20, 2024). The past, present, and future of Boeing in space. *Astronomy.* Retrieved from https://www.astronomy.com/space-exploration/the-past-present-and-future-of-boeing-in-space/

Fernholz, T. (October 24, 2024). Boeing's new CEO doesn't sound bullish on space. *Payload*. Retrieved from https://payloadspace.com/boeings-new-ceo-doesnt-sound-bullish-on-space/

German, K. (June 19, 2024). 2 Years after being grounded, the Boeing 737 Max is flying again. *CNET*. Retrieved from https://www.cnet.com/tech/tech-industry/boeing-737-max-8-all-about-the-aircraft-flight-ban-and-investigations/

Gil, B. (October 25, 2024). Boeing is looking for an escape hatch from the space business. *Quartz*. Retrieved from https://qz.com/boeing-nasa-space-business-1851681727

Insinna V. (September 20, 2024). Boeing defense chief Ted Colbert pushed out. *Breaking Defense*. Retrieved from https://breakingdefense.com/2024/09/boeing-defense-chief-ted-colbert-pushed-out/

Isidore, C. (May 3, 2024). Boeing has lost $32 billion since 2019, with no end in sight. How long can it keep losing money? *CNN*. Retrieved from https://edition.cnn.com/2024/05/03/business/boeing-losses-outlook/index.html

Johnsson, J., & Joshua, J. (October 15, 2024). Boeing to raise as much as $25 billion to avert cash crunch. *Bloomberg*. Retrieved from https://www.bloomberg.com/news/articles/2024-10-15/boeing-reaches-10-billion-credit-pact-to-shore-up-balance-sheet

Josephs, L. (May 23, 2024). Boeing expects a 2024 cash burn, slow recovery of airplane deliveries amid crisis, CFO says. *CNBC*. Retrieved from https://www.cnbc.com/2024/05/23/boeing-cfo-deliveries-cash-flow-max-crisis.html

Laidley, C. (October 24, 2024). Boeing turnaround will require 'Hurculean' effort—Here's why analysts are pptimistic. *Investopedia*. Retrieved from https://www.investopedia.com/boeing-turnaround-effort-what-analysts-are-optimistic-earnings-labor-strike-8732740

Market.us. (July 2025). Global aircraft manufacturing market size, share analysis report by aircraft type (fixed-wing aircrafts, rotary-wing aircrafts, helicopters, unmanned aerial vehicles (UAVs), other aircraft types), by end-user (commercial aviation, military and defense, government & public services, other end-users), region and companies – industry segment outlook, market assessment, competition scenario, trends and forecast 2025–2034. Retrieved from https://market.us/report/aircraft-manufacturing-market/

Mazein, E., & AFP. (October 15, 2024). Boeing's strategy of cost-cutting in face of major strike and talent shortage confuses experts. *Fortune*. Retrieved from https://fortune.com/2024/10/15/boeing-strategy-cost-cutting-major-strike-talent-shortage-confuses-experts/

O'Connell, B. (February 28, 2020). History of Boeing: Timeline and facts. *The Street*. Retrieved from https://www.thestreet.com/investing/history-of-boeing

Reed, T. (July 5, 2024). Boeing/Airbus duopoly is aging and impeded. Boom Supersonic wants a spot. *Forbes*. Retrieved from https://www.forbes.com/sites/tedreed/2024/07/05/the-boeingairbus-duopoly-is-aging-and-impeded-boom-supersonic-wants-a-spot/

Reuters. (October 25, 2024). Boeing exploring sale of its space business, WSJ reports. Reuters.com. Retrieved from https://www.reuters.com/business/aerospace-defense/boeing-explores-sale-its-space-business-wsj-reports-2024-10-25/

Roth, E. (October 25, 2024). Boeing reportedly considers selling off its space business. *The Verge*. Retrieved from https://www.theverge.com/2024/10/25/24279693/boeing-considers-selling-space-business-starliner

Sodhi, M. S. (January 12, 2024). Boeing needs to get real: The 737 Max should probably be scrapped. *The Conversation*. Retrieved from https://theconversation.com/boeing-needs-to-get-real-the-737-max-should-probably-be-scrapped-221023

Stobierski, T. (April 21, 2020). Cash flow vs. profit: What's the difference? Hbs.edu. Retrieved from https://online.hbs.edu/blog/post/cash-flow-vs-profit

Supply Chain 247. (August 12, 2024). Two-thirds of Boeing's $6billion cost cutting will come from its supply chain. Supplychain247.com. Retrieved from https://www.supplychain247.com/article/two-thirds_of_boeings_6billion_cost_cutting_will_come_from_its_supply_chain/supply_chain_council

Supply Chain Brain. (March 21, 2024). Boeing sees massive cash drain as 737 Max episode takes toll. Supplychainbrain.com. Retrieved from https://www.supplychainbrain.com/articles/39315-boeing-sees-massive-cash-drain-as-737-max-episode-takes-toll

Thomas, G. (October 16, 2024). Boeing moves to shore up cash reserves. Airlineratings.com. Retrieved from https://www.airlineratings.com/articles/boeing-moves-to-shore-up-cash-reserves

TipRanks. (October 14, 2024). Boeing's strategic reset poised for financial recovery by 2027: Buy rating affirmed. *Business Insider*. Retrieved from https://markets.businessinsider.com/news/stocks/boeing-s-strategic-reset-poised-for-financial-recovery-by-2027-buy-rating-affirmed-1033842851

TOI Business Desk. (April 15, 2025). China orders halt to Boeing jet deliveries as trade war with US intensifies. *Times of India*. Retrieved from https://timesofindia.indiatimes.com/business/infrastructure/china-orders-halt-to-boeing-jet-deliveries-from-as-trade-war-with-us-intensifies/articleshow/120305185.cms

CHAPTER 2

Competitive Dynamics

Learning Objectives

After completing this chapter, students should be able to:

- Distinguish between competitive and hypercompetitive industries;
- Identify direct vs indirect competitors;
- Examine competitive intensity in the industry;
- Evaluate the role of antitrust authorities in identifying cartels.

HYPERCOMPETITIVE INDUSTRIES

Firms need to adapt their competitive strategies based on the industry's competitive landscape, or they risk becoming obsolete. Managers not only need to anticipate competitor moves, identify industry trends, and leverage these trends advantageously, but also defend their competitive position against peers in the industry. However, industries vary in the intensity of competition. While some industries experience normal competition, others are characterized by hypercompetition.

Competition vs. Hypercompetition

The way companies such as Uber and Lyft, or Amazon and eBay, or Apple and Microsoft compete differs from the way firms like Nucor and US Steel compete with each other in the steel industry.[1] Overall, the steel industry is much more stable than the ride-hailing, online retail, or software industry.[2]

In recent years, businesses have struggled to maintain their market positions, and industry dynamics have become increasingly volatile.[3] One of the significant environmental factors contributing to this volatility is the increasing competition in the industry, as existing players adjust their strategies, and new rivals enter the market. However, hypercompetition is also relevant in duopoly markets, such as those between Coke and Pepsi, Uber and Lyft, and Boeing and Airbus.[4]

DOI: 10.4324/9781003568100-2

New rivals, for instance, enter the market with new technologies that drive already existing firms to retaliate by launching innovative products or other customer acquisition and retention tactics. Thus, their prior technology, which was otherwise a source of competitive advantage, becomes nullified, and incumbent firms do not possess any sustainable competitive advantage. On the contrary, they also face the risk of disruption. For instance, with the introduction of online movie streaming services, such as Netflix, not only did DVD players like Blockbuster lose their competitive advantage but also became extinct from the market, as they failed to take appropriate competitive actions in response to the new rival.[5] On the contrary, the energy drink segment became hypercompetitive in response to BodyArmor's launch. Incumbent players, such as Coca-Cola and Pepsi, retaliated by launching their own new flavor versions of energy drinks, e.g., Powerade and Gatorade. In fact, Coca-Cola became so aggressive that it eventually acquired BodyArmor.[6]

Reasons for Hypercompetition

An industry becomes hypercompetitive due to exogenous factors such as technological innovations, the globalization of companies, changes in government policy, and increasing market openness. For instance, technological innovations could be introduced by both entrepreneurial firms, as discussed above, which could either disrupt incumbent players or result in hypercompetition if the incumbent player retaliates.[7] An incumbent firm can also launch innovation. When Apple launches a new iPhone model, Samsung retaliates with its own updated smartphone.[8]

Hypercompetition could also result from identity domain clashes between two firms. *Identity domain* is the "top management team (TMT) members' consensual understanding of the competitive arena that best demonstrates and reinforces organizational identity in the marketplace."[9] Thus, the identity domain reflects top managers' views about how they see themselves in the competitive marketplace. For example, Volvo's identity is more in terms of safety, and Maruti Suzuki (a leading car manufacturer in India) identifies its vehicles as the most fuel-efficient cars in India. These identities hold the highest psychological and cognitive values for Volvo's and Maruti Suzuki's managers, respectively. The psychological and cognitive values are formed over a long period of time, following the companies' significant investments in developing core competencies, which also contributed to their success.[10]

Additionally, when a clash in identity domains between two firms occurs, managers are emotionally motivated to defend their turf and preserve the competitive arena, leading to hypercompetition. Additionally, when a clash in identity domains between two firms occurs, managers are emotionally motivated to defend their turf and preserve the competitive arena, leading to hypercompetition. When Pizza Hut identifies itself with quality pizza, while Papa John's identity is also associated with better-quality ingredients and hence better-quality pizza, and Domino's Pizza associates itself with timely and quick delivery of hot pizza,[11] a severe advertising war ensued between Pizza Hut and Papa John's. Pizza Hut claimed that its pizzas were of the highest quality. In response, Papa John's asserted that their sauce and dough were superior to those of Pizza Hut, and they used fresh tomatoes and filtered water. The two companies engaged in comparative advertising, making the competition between them hypercompetitive, as the identity domains of Pizza Hut and Papa John's were closely associated with the quality of pizza.[12] In contrast, for Domino's, the timely delivery of hot pizza was of greater psychological significance.

Test of Hypercompetition

If an industry is competitive or hypercompetitive, it can be identified through three key aspects of the industry dynamics: market stability versus instability, the frequency and speed of competitive attacks and counterattacks, and the absence of a sustainable competitive advantage.

Market stability versus instability.[13] Companies such as Trulia versus Zillow or Microsoft versus Apple compete more aggressively to acquire and retain customers; consequently, a market leadership position is not sustained by a given competitor for a very long period.[14] In some industries, product differentiation is reduced significantly, and products essentially become commodities. For example, the energy drink market or the probiotic drink market, where several competitors compete on the same aspects, including price, new flavor variants, and low sugar content. Overall, the less sustainable the market leadership or differentiation position, the more hypercompetitive the industry is.[15]

Frequency and speed of competitive attacks and counter attacks.[16] One of the most essential criteria is that industry structure may become unstable simply by virtue of competitors' attacks and counterattacks in the industry. Competitors may attack each other through various strategic and tactical actions, such as launching new products, frequently changing prices, or employing aggressive marketing tactics.[17] For example, in the fast-food chain industry, players such as McDonald's and Wendy's constantly adjust prices, launch innovative menu items, and invest in aggressive advertising and promotions.[18] The same practices are seen in the automobile and soft beverage industries. Overall, in a hypercompetitive environment, the competitive action of one firm triggers a series of responses among rival firms across various value chain activities, ranging from innovation to marketing to production.

Absence of a sustainable competitive advantage.[19] Sustainable competitive advantage implies a unique position that a company holds due to the resources it possesses, which other firms do not have and cannot imitate. In the pharmaceutical industry, patents provide a temporary competitive advantage.[20] However, innovation can erode the value of patents—for instance, several COVID vaccines, drugs, etc. In a hypercompetitive environment, firms' superior performance, i.e., returns above the industry average, is not sustained for a very long time. Instead, hypercompetition makes the notion of sustainable competitive advantage unrealistic.

TYPES OF COMPETITORS: DIRECT VS. INDIRECT COMPETITORS

Direct Vs. Indirect Competitors can be differentiated through strategic groups. A strategic group refers to a group of firms in a given industry that follow a similar competitive strategy.[21] Firms in an industry pursuing low cost, differentiation, or focused differentiation will form three different strategic groups, respectively. Porter defined a *strategic group* as a set of firms within an industry that are similar to one another and different from firms outside the group on one or more key dimensions of their strategy.[22]

A strategic group can be visually understood using a strategic group map. For drawing a strategic group map, a firm needs to select two competitive dimensions across two axes. These dimensions can include any competition-oriented attributes. In the food industry, the axes can be price and quality, or geographic scope of business and quality, or menu variety and price. Table 2.1 presents a strategic group in the US fast food restaurant industry, categorized by menu variety and price. Price and menu variety can vary from low to high. Domino's and Burger King fall under the same strategic group as they both have low menu variety and low prices. Pizza Hut and KFC form another strategic group, characterized by moderate prices and a limited menu. Red Lobster and Olive Garden, on the other hand, offer a moderate menu with higher prices.[23]

Firms may also create a strategic group at a broader industry level. In the US food industry, based on the level of food preparation (ready-to-cook, ready-to-eat, and raw) and the level of convenience (high vs. low), food products can be categorized into four strategic groups, as shown in Table 2.2. Table 2.2 reveals that online grocery delivery companies, such as Instacart

TABLE 2.1 Restaurant Positioning Map: Price vs. Menu Variety

		Menu Variety		
		Low	**Limited**	**Moderate**
Price level	Low	Dominos, Burger King	Little Caesars, Popeyes	Denny's, IHOP
	Moderate	Five Guys, Shake Shack	Pizza Hut, KFC	Applebee's, Chili's
	High	Ruth's Chris Steak House	The Capital Grille	Red Lobster, Olive Garden

Source: Developed by the Authors.

TABLE 2.2 Competitive Landscape of Food Preparation and Convenience

		Food Preparation Level		
		Prepared	**Semi Prepared**	**Unprepared**
Consumer convenience level	More	Meal delivery companies like Uber Eats and Grubhub	Meal kit delivery companies like Hello Fresh and Blue Apron	Online grocery delivery companies like Instacart and FreshDirect
	Moderate	Fast-casual restaurants like Panera Bread and Chipotle	Ready-to-cook/ ready-to-heat meals from stores like Trader Joe's and Whole Foods	Online grocery pickup services like Walmart Pickup and Target Drive Up
	Less	Dine out restaurants like The Cheesecake Factory and BJ's Restaurant & Brewhouse	Take-and-bake/ in-store prepared meal counters like Costco Meal Kits and Whole Foods Prepared Foods	Grocery stores like Walmart and Costco

Source: Developed by the Authors.

or Amazon Fresh, fall under the "unprepared food and more convenient" category, as subscribers of these companies save on the cost and energy invested in traveling to a grocery store. Similarly, grocery retailers such as Walmart and Giant fall under unprepared food and less convenient category as visiting grocery stores to buy grocery is more inconvenient than home delivery.

COMPETITIVE PROFILING MATRIX

Competitive profiling matrix refers to a strategic tool used to compare competitors in terms of assessing their strengths and weaknesses.[24] It is carried out by first identifying critical success factors (CSFs) in an industry and then rating the performance of competitors across those factors. There are four components of the competitive profiling matrix: CSFs, their weights, scores of companies across each factor, and the total score of companies.

Critical success factors, also known as Key Success Factors (KSFs), refer to key attributes that determine performance within a given industry. CSFs vary across industries and can encompass both internal and external factors.[25] The more CSFs a firm identifies, the more reliable the competitive analysis becomes. Some of the most common CFSs include workplace culture, innovation, product quality, customer service, product range, and customer loyalty, among others.

Each CSF needs to be *weighted* between 0.1 and 1.0. The lower the weight, the less critical the CSF, and the higher the weight, the more important the CSF in a given industry. For example, for a business hotel, location is much more CSF than price competitiveness. Moreover, the sum of all weights should be equal to 1.0.[26]

Next, each competitor should be assigned a *score* based on their performance in a specific parameter. The score can range from 1 to 5, where a rating of 5 implies excellent performance or a significant strength of the competitor, and 1 represents the least performance, suggesting a major weakness.[27]

Scoring competitors based on their performance is a subjective process. Once competitors have been scored, for every CSF, the weight of each attribute should be multiplied by the score received by each competitor. This process gives a weighted score for each competitor. In the hotel industry, CSFs are location, brand reputation, customer service, pricing, and technology savviness, among others. To compare the focal hotel against its closest competitor, a hotel can rate itself and its competitor on various CSF parameters. Table 2.3 presents a comparison of hotels A and B on various CSFs. In Table 2.3, Hotel B is performing better than Hotel A as a competitor.

Table 2.4 presents a similar analysis for mobile phone operating systems that differ by company. For example, Apple's operating system is iOS, Samsung offers Android, and Huawei offers Harmony OS. Table 2.4 displays that Android is the most potent competitor in the industry. Its rating is particularly high in market share, distribution channels, customization, openness, and cloud integration. HarmonyOS is the weakest player and does not score high relative to its competitors across any parameter. Huawei thus needs to develop strategies for enhancing its performance across key CSFs, particularly those that carry significant weight, and improve its rating against competitors to emerge as a prominent player in the industry.

TABLE 2.3 Competitive Profile Matrix (Hotel A Vs. Hotel B)

Strategic Dimension	Key Competitive Factor	Weight	Hotel A Rating	Hotel A Weighted Score	Hotel B Rating	Hotel B Weighted Score
Location strategy	Location attractiveness	0.13	2	0.26	3	0.39
	Geographic coverage	0.08	4	0.32	3	0.24
Service offering	Variety of room types	0.05	3	0.15	1	0.05
	Capability in launching new services	0.04	3	0.12	3	0.12
Market position	Market share	0.14	2	0.28	4	0.56
	Brand reputation	0.07	4	0.28	2	0.14
	Customer retention	0.02	2	0.04	4	0.08
Operational efficiency	Revenue per employee	0.08	1	0.08	2	0.16
	Cost efficiency	0.05	1	0.05	3	0.15
Digital and technology capability	Technology integration	0.11	3	0.33	4	0.44
	Digital visibility and online presence	0.15	3	0.45	3	0.45
Marketing capability	Marketing effectiveness	0.08	1	0.08	2	0.16
Total		1		2.44		2.94

Source: Author's analysis based on competitive profile matrix methodology.

COMPETITOR INTELLIGENCE

Competitor intelligence refers to the process by which firms gather, analyze, and apply information they have collected about their competitors to gain a competitive advantage over them.[28] To access competitor information, firms generally rely on publicly available resources such as announcements made by competitors, their annual reports, or market research reports. Competitor intelligence involves first segregating direct competitors from indirect competitors. Tools such as strategic group analysis can help in this regard.

Then the competitor's strengths, weaknesses, and strategies are analyzed. A competitive profiling matrix can help understand competitors' strengths and weaknesses in relation to a given firm on critical success factors. For analyzing strategies, firms generally focus on market-based strategies, such as the nature of the products offered, customer perception of them, their pricing, and so on.

TABLE 2.4 Competitive Profile Matrix (Android Vs. iOS Vs. HarmonyOS)

Strategic Dimension	Key Competitive Factor	Weight	Android Rating	Android Weighted Score	iOS Rating	iOS Weighted Score	HarmonyOS Rating	HarmonyOS Weighted Score
Market position	Market share	0.13	4	0.52	2	0.26	2	0.26
	Number of applications available	0.1	4	0.4	4	0.4	2	0.2
Product development	Frequency of software updates	0.06	3	0.18	4	0.24	2	0.12
	Interface and design quality	0.07	3	0.21	3	0.21	3	0.21
Brand strength	Product brand reputation	0.05	3	0.15	3	0.15	2	0.1
	Corporate brand reputation	0.1	4	0.4	4	0.4	3	0.3
Distribution and market access	Distribution channels	0.11	4	0.44	2	0.22	3	0.33
User experience	Ease of use and usability	0.11	3	0.33	3	0.33	3	0.33
	System reliability (crash frequency)	0.08	1	0.08	4	0.32	3	0.24
System flexibility	Customization capabilities	0.04	4	0.16	2	0.08	2	0.08
	Platform openness	0.02	4	0.08	2	0.04	2	0.04
Digital ecosystem	Cloud service integration	0.12	4	0.48	2	0.24	2	0.24
Marketing capability	Marketing effectiveness	0.04	2	0.08	4	0.16	2	0.08
Total score		1		3.51		3.05		2.53

Note: Ratings range from 1 (major weakness) to 4 (major strength). Weighted scores are calculated by multiplying the relative importance weight of each factor by the rating assigned to each operating system.

Source: Author's calculation based on the Competitive Profile Matrix (CPM) framework.

Obtaining information on competitors' undisclosed strategies, such as upcoming new products they have not yet announced, is a challenging task. Trying to access such information is also an ethically challenging endeavor. Yet, firms sometimes indulge in poaching to access competitors' information.[29] They hire key employees from competitors to gain insider information, as well as expertise, of key personnel of the competitor firm.[30] To avoid sensitive information leakage, firms these days require executives to sign non-disclosure agreements (NDAs), under which they are not allowed to share sensitive information with any key competitors after leaving the job. Such agreements nullify the competitor's interest in poaching an employee from a rival firm. Sometimes firms also engage in espionage. For instance, in the competitive rivalry between GM and Volkswagen, GM's executives leaked sensitive papers related to GM's competitive strategy to Volkswagen, resulting in a USD 100 million lawsuit in which Volkswagen ultimately paid GM.[31]

LEVEL OF COMPETITION: HERFINDAHL INDEX

The *Herfindahl Index* (HHI) measures the concentration of firms in an industry, and an analyst, a firm, or antitrust authorities calculates it by adding the squares of the market shares of all firms in that industry.[32] Higher scores imply that competition is less in the industry. Antitrust authorities use this measure to determine whether they should allow mergers and acquisitions in a given industry. When HHI is above 2,500, it indicates a highly concentrated industry,[33] meaning that a very small number of players dominate the entire industry. A smaller concentration of players creates a risk of cartel formation and price regulation by a few players in the industry. Consequently, consumer welfare suffers. An HHI index below 1,000 indicates a highly competitive market, characterized by the absence of a dominant player.[34] Thus, if an industry has four firms and their market shares are 40%, 30%, 15%, and 15%, then HHI can be calculated as $40^2 + 30^2 + 15^2 + 15^2 = 2{,}950$. Since this HHI score is above the threshold of 2,500, the industry is highly concentrated. Antitrust authorities are less likely to permit any merger or acquisition in this industry. Furthermore, players are likely to be more scrutinized for their competitive versus anticompetitive actions, given the high likelihood of cartel formation.

Cartel Formation

Cartel formation refers to an anticompetitive strategy in which competing firms tacitly collude with each other, with the intention of manipulating the market.[35] Instead of competing against each other, they cooperate, but with the intention of exploiting the customers or suppliers and increasing their profits. For instance, they can opt for price fixing, where all competitors artificially hike the prices of the product, leaving customers with no choice but to pay an inflated price.[36] Competitors may also allocate markets among themselves, with one competitor selling in a particular territory while another sells in another territory, thus restricting customer choice. Similarly, companies may choose to control the output of the product, creating artificial scarcity, which automatically leads to a price hike due to a demand-supply gap.[37]

Apart from cartel formation, mergers and acquisitions are also an issue. In 2022, when Spirit and Frontier, the two ultra-low-cost airlines in the US, were considering a merger, it was not approved by antitrust authorities.[38] Analysts expected the merger to create the fifth-largest airline in the US, next to the Big 4, namely United Airlines, Delta Airlines, American Airlines, and Southwest Airlines. While Spirit and Frontier believed that the merger would increase consumer welfare and enable them to better compete against the Big 4, antitrust authorities believed the merger would lead to a price hike and harm consumer welfare.[39] Figure 2.1, presents the airline industry market share (%) for 2024. Based on Figure 2.1, Table 2.5 presents the HHI score of 1,570, indicating a value below the threshold of 2,500. Based on this, the antitrust authorities should have allowed a merger of Spirit and Frontier, as they are minority players. If they had merged, then, in 2021 market share percentage terms, the HHI would have been 1,594, still comparatively below the threshold of 2,500. Therefore, the HHI index calculation for the US airline industry suggests that the merger was less likely to result in the merged airline becoming a dominant player in the industry, with its market power not increasing significantly. However, if we examine the strategic group of ultra-low-cost airlines and recalculate HHI and market share only for this group, which consists of JetBlue, Spirit, Frontier, and Southwest, then even before the merger, market power is concentrated, and post-merger, it is likely to become even higher. Thus, antitrust authorities did not allow the merger of Spirit and Frontier.

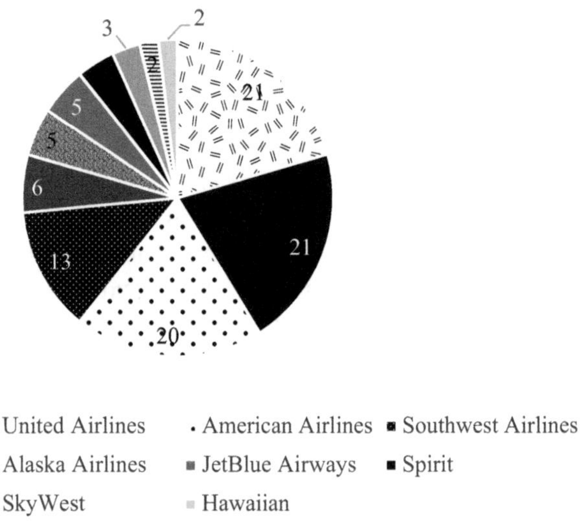

FIGURE 2.1 Market Share of Airlines in the US (%) in 2024

Source: Developed by the Authors Based on Information Available at: Statista Research Department. (2025, November 19). *Domestic market share of leading U.S. airlines in 2024*. Retrieved from https://www.statista.com/statistics/250577/domestic-market-share-of-leading-us-airlines/

TABLE 2.5 Market Concentration in the US Airline Industry

Airline	Market Share[2]
Delta Air Lines	441
United Airlines	441
American Airlines	400
Southwest Airlines	169
Other	36
Alaska Airlines	25
JetBlue Airways	25
Spirit	16
Frontier	9
SkyWest	4
Hawaiian	4
Herfindahl Index	1,570

Note: The Herfindahl–Hirschman Index (HHI) is calculated by summing the squared market share of each firm in the industry. Higher values indicate greater market concentration.

Source: Developed by the authors based on information available in Figure 2.1.

ASSIGNMENT QUESTIONS

1. You are trying to enter the sports drink market. Would you anticipate hypercompetition in this industry? Draw a strategic plan about a series of competitive actions you will take and further actions you will take in response to anticipated responses from your competitors.
2. Conduct a strategic group analysis for the industry of your choice in your home country.
3. Consider an industry of your choice and identify the critical success factors that drive success in that industry. Further, do competitive profiling for players in that industry. Consider the top three players for the analysis.

CASE STUDY **2.1**

BrandYourself

Managing Online Reputation

> **Learning Outcomes**
>
> After analyzing this case study, students should be able to:
>
> 1. Analyze strategic group formation in emerging digital industries.
> 2. Apply strategic management analytical tools.
> 3. Evaluate industry competition and ethical implications.

INTRODUCTION

New York-based Brandyourself.com Inc (BrandYourself) "helps individuals to protect and improve their online reputation and online privacy, as well as features include social media clean up, negative search result protection, removal of private information from data brokers, and dark web scans".[40] The company provides online reputation management software and services to approximately 1 million people.[41] It even received one of the largest offers ever made, USD 2 million, on the ABC television show *Shark Tank*. On the show, Patrick Ambron, co-founder and CEO of BrandYourself, turned down the funding offer.[42] *Share Tank* is an American business reality television show.

As more than 75% of HR departments searched individuals' online presence during the recruiting and hiring process, the demand for reputation management companies has increased in recent years.[43] Traditional reputation management companies charged thousands of dollars, making it unfeasible for most individuals to afford to hire a company to manage their reputation online. BrandYourself's freemium service do it yourself (DIY) helped put relevant and positive information about a candidate on top of the Google search page ("BrandYourself Competitors, Revenue," n.d.). However, these efforts by reputation management companies present ethical dilemmas, as they buried negative reviews, news, and comments about companies and individuals behind positive articles, blogs, and comments, misleading those seeking to learn about individual's online presence.[44] Moreover, companies such as Guaranteed Removals were not only burying information, but even eliminating such links[45], a capability that BrandYourself did not have. How can Ambron resolve the ethical dilemma that confronts him? Should he invest research and development capabilities into the permanent removal of negative links for his clients?

BACKGROUND

BrandYourself was started in 2013 when co-founder Pete Kistler did not receive an internship in a college as the college admission officers mistook him for a drug dealer with the same name as determined from an online search.[46] At the time, Kistler did not have the skills to improve his search results. Traditional reputation management companies charged thousands of dollars each month to manage a person's online reputation (Dangremond, 2015). With help from his friends Ambron and Evan McGowan-Watson, who had a background in *search engine optimization* (SEO), Kistler was able to eliminate the erroneous connection of his name to drug dealing and clean up his online reputation (Dangremond, 2015). Kistler, Ambron, and McGowan-Watson realized that the problem of besmirched online reputation, as experienced by Kistler, is likely to be faced by millions of other people, many of whom would welcome assistance in developing a positive online presence (Dangremond, 2015). Given the expensive nature of traditional online reputation management companies, Kistler, Ambron, and McGowan-Watson decided to create a system, using SEO, to empower individuals to control their own online reputation management (Dangremond, 2015). Even low-tech savvy individuals can use the BrandYourself DIY reputation management software to improve their online presence ("BrandYourself Competitors, Revenue," n.d.). An SEO approach "involves achieving the highest position or ranking practical in the natural or organic listings as the main body of the search engine results pages across a range of specific combination of keywords (or keyphrases) entered by search engine users".[47]

In 2013, the co-founders launched concierge services for people who needed help using the company software. As a part of this service, clients received a dedicated Reputation Specialist who developed and implemented a customized strategy to establish or enhance a positive personal brand ("BrandYourself Competitors, Revenue," n.d.). In 2020, BrandYourself had annual revenue of USD 19.1 million. The company had 132 employees ("BrandYourself Competitors, Revenue," n.d.).

THE WORKING OF SEO

After entering a search query in a search engine such as Google, an individual receives a page called the *search engine results page* (SERP). The SERP presents both "organic results" and "pay-per-click ads" (or PPC). The organic results were influenced by SEO, whereas a company paid for the PPC ads.[48] Search engines use more than 200 different factors, such as responsive design of website, page speed of a website, etc., to generate search results ("What is SEO," 2018). A pay-per-click advertisement "is an online advertising model in which advertisers pay each time a user clicks on one of their online ads".[49] In contrast, an organic search is "also known as natural search, [and] refers to unpaid search results".[50]

Online reputation management, also known as known as *astroturfing*, worked by manipulating algorithms that Google used to present search results.[51] With this manipulation, positive results related to the searched entity were displayed at the top of results (Cellan-Jones, 2011). *According to Ambron, u*nlike other reputation management companies in which search engine scientists optimized page ranking for a client, BrandYourself demystified "the process"[52]. He added, "We try to make it as transparent as possible so you're not feeling like you're forced to pay 'Search Engine Scientists' as they call them" (Holmes, 2012). Ambron further mentioned, "It's just a different mentality. We want to empower you, not charge you" (Holmes, 2012). Rankings "refers to a website's position in the search engine results page" ("Ranking," n.d.). Although the SEO process of improving the search results was time-consuming, it was not complicated, and BrandYourself offered a DIY tool kit for free and charged only for advanced services (Holmes, 2012).

Search engine optimization specialists of traditional reputation companies offered reputation management services; BrandYourself automated this process through its software. Traditional reputation management companies also provided little explanation on how reputation management worked (Ambron, 2016)[53]. BrandYourself launched the "Ultimate Online Reputation Management Guide," which guided customers through the basics of how search engines work and also offered tips a subscriber could use to improve the Google search results. If a subscriber needed help after reading the guide, the BrandYourself team of experts would assist the subscriber with specific problems and could offer suggestions to the individual (Ambron, 2016).

SERVICES OF BRANDYOURSELF

A study conducted by Kaplan in 2013 reported that in the US, colleges rejected approximately 12% of college applicants due to questionable posts and images that the colleges found on candidates' social media[54]. In fact, 31% of college admission officers checked social media to find if candidates made a good fit with their educational institution[55]. In a survey conducted by CareerBuilder in 2017, 70% of 2,380 participating employers screened the candidate, and 54% of them made hiring decisions using objectionable social media feeds as one of the criteria.[56] Companies even outsourced the screening of candidates' online presence to firms such as Fama Technologies. Ben Mones, CEO of Fama Technologies, stated that they were not overly interested in uncovering recreational alcohol use. Rather they wanted to ensure that the firm is not hiring bullies or bigots. Mones said, "Employers are looking for folks who don't think that misogynistic comment is wrong" (Dishman, 2018). Concurring with Mones' view, Ambron said, "Candid posts that use vulgar or insensitive language are clear red flags. In addition, slang usage and unprofessional "funny" posts have been frequently flagged as troubling for hiring managers" (Dishman, 2018).

The artificial intelligence platform at BrandYourself also used a similar no-nonsense approach for uncovering inappropriate content (Dishman, 2018). For subscribers, the software explored content posted or tagged as long as ten years ago, and then provided recommendations for negative content removal. With an annual fee of USD 99,

BrandYourself's software continued to monitor social platforms and online presence and alerted candidates if anything new showed up that needed a candidate's attention (Dishman, 2018). BrandYourself software scanned for "provocative or inappropriate photographs, videos, or information, drinking or using drugs, posting discriminatory comments related to race, gender, religion, and bad-mouthing their previous company or fellow employee" (Dishman, 2018).

In 2017, BrandYourself had 30,000 users who were paid customers and an additional 500,000 people who used its free version.[57] In 2018, the number of users increased to approximately one million. At this time, the company began to aim its services at high school students before they started applying for colleges and universities ("BrandYourself Competitors, Revenue," n.d.).

Student Makeover Services

With students as the primary targets, BrandYourself offered "student makeover" services. Though the student candidates could manually explore past posts and delete the potentially problematical ones, with the student makeover service, an automated search was introduced that could explore even deeper for searches beyond social media.[58] The service found any online references that a student had made regarding sex, alcohol, drugs, and even politics and religion (Grant, 2017). It was priced at USD 99 annually, and BrandYourself needed access to students' profiles for the program to hunt the search. Based on search results, students and their parents could decide what post or content they wanted to delete (Grant, 2017).

Furthermore, student makeover services also provided an overall online reputation score, indicating how likely a students' reputation could negatively impact their college (and career) aspirations (Grant, 2017). Ambron said, "More and more colleges and employers are using this type of technology to screen applicants." He further added, "We are the first ones to give it back to the consumer" (Grant, 2017). Ambron believed that it was unfair on the part of colleges to hold students responsible for the content they might have posted years ago as a teenager (Grant, 2017). Few Harvard students got their admission revoked due to their social media posts; however, posts that related to sexual assault and jokes that child abuse was sexually arousing were deemed a problem (Grant, 2017).

Commenting on the ability to delete social media posts, Ambron mentioned that it depended on the kind of offending information. He said, "If it's simply a poorly judged social media post, you can hopefully delete it right away, which minimizes the chances of it being flagged during an employment screening" (Dishman, 2018). However, if employers had a legal subpoena or took a screenshot, then deleted posts could also become accessible (Dishman, 2018). For comments, posts, or blogs posted on Google, the only way to bury negative information was to bury it with more accurate, positive information, though it could take months for the same. Ambron explained, "The idea is that if there's negative information out there about you (like an ex bashing you online), you want to surround it with more accurate information that better represents your personality, professionalism, and overall brand" (Dishman, 2018). This required time and maintenance.

Enhancing Positive Reputation

The 2017 CareerBuilder survey also revealed that 44% of employers' decisions were influenced by positive social content that reflected experience and expertise of a candidate signaling his or her great communication and creativity skills (Dishman, 2018). With increasing competition and tightening job market, job seekers who could demonstrate a sterling online presence through positive aspects such as professional communication, showcasing their expertise, and interacting with various people on social media were expected to be preferred candidates (Dishman, 2018). BrandYourself, apart from identifying offending information, also highlighted positives that could boost the image. The software could recommend which social media profiles one should have to achieve their professional goals and to rank them high in Google search results (Dishman, 2018). For instance, when a high-level Disney, AOL, and AG Interactive executive who pioneered in the virtual world was Googled before using BrandYourself, multiple results for a singer-songwriter by the same name appeared before any of the executive's work showed up. Populating a website, a LinkedIn profile, and Twitter and Medium accounts with regular, quality content about the executive's expertise resulted in him appearing before the songwriter (Dishman, 2018).

Alert Services

BrandYourself artificial intelligence also alerted candidates when someone was searching for them on Google. For instance, when someone from Ogilvy searched an advertising student, BrandYourself's software could alert the candidate that "somebody from Ogilvy just Googled" your name and found your BrandYourself profile. Ambron said, "It's similar to LinkedIn's NASDAQLNKD feature that tells you when someone else searches you on LinkedIn but applied to the entire web".[59] Commenting on the unique selling proposition, the CEO added, "There is nobody on the web providing this level of specific intelligence for individuals and our traffic has exploded because of it." Ambron further mentioned, "We're building the most sophisticated software on the market to help people manage their online presence." "This is just one of many features in the works" (Bedigian, 2012).

Privacy Management Services

Ambron also provided online privacy security services in which its software found a subscriber's exposed private information, such as the address, age, and phone number, from more than 25 major data brokers and remove such exposed content ("Remove Personal Info," n.d.). Also, if a BrandYourself subscriber's password or account was exposed by hackers online, the software sent an alert to the subscriber. As a basic feature, it also offered a free privacy scan ("Remove Personal Info," n.d.). Data brokers are "companies that collect data themselves or buy it from other companies (like a credit card company), crawl the internet for useful information about users—legally or otherwise—and aggregate that information with data from other sources (e.g., offline)".[60]

COMPETITORS

Several online reputation management companies charge hefty prices and earn substantial revenues (see Table 2.3). Experts at Reputation.com charged USD 5,000 for reputation management (Holmes, 2012). Commenting on high prices charged by online reputation management firms, Ambron said, "Search Engine Optimization for reputation management isn't as complicated as it's made out to be" (Holmes, 2012).

Commenting on managing reputation online by individuals themselves, Ambron said, "It's terrible that this model doesn't work for average people" (Holmes, 2012). He further mentioned,

> It's too expensive. It's unsustainable. If Pete's thing pops up again, he's going to have to pay another $5,000 because he can't change it himself. So we kind of became obsessed with creating a product that made it easy, and even fun, for anybody to do themselves without having any price or technical barriers.
>
> (Holmes, 2012)

BrandYourself users submitted one to three flattering (or, not unflattering) links about themselves, such as a LinkedIn profile, a personal website, or other websites that features the customer. BrandYourself then evaluated each link's SEO and made recommendations to make these pages appear higher in search results through tactics such as customized URLs (uniform resource locator) or frequent content updates of these URLs. A URL "is the mechanism used by browsers to retrieve any published resource on the web".[61]

THE ROAD AHEAD

Ambron said, "We can't guarantee results," but adds that nobody else can either (Holmes, 2012). He further added, "That's not how search engines work. But we can guarantee that if you follow our steps, your positive content will be as optimized as humanly possible." According to media reports, BrandYourself was more reliable than some of its competitors and it did not ask for money for basic services. For personalized services, BrandYourself charges were minimal, and cheaper than other SEO service providers (Holmes, 2012). Of course, some of its competitors were likened to a snake-oil salesperson, who "is someone who knowingly sells fraudulent goods or who is a fraud, charlatan, and the like"[62]. However, new players such as Guaranteed Removals were emerging, who guaranteed to permanently delete online content related to blogs, articles or newspapers, reviews or complaints, or content on other public forums ("Guaranteed Removal. Online Reputation," n.d.). Guaranteed Removals did not charge unless the content was removed, which could be a two to four week process. Furthermore, unless they felt that the party asking for link removal was not a public threat, Guaranteed Removals removed harmful content about individuals and corporations when requested ("Guaranteed Removal: Frequently," n.d.). Their fee ranged from USD 3,000 to USD 15,000 ("Guaranteed Removal: Frequently," n.d.). Ambron said online reputation management companies would need to continuously innovate as the development of web consumers' needs also evolved (Ambron, 2016).

DISCUSSION QUESTIONS

1. Explain how BrandYourself created new strategic group.
2. Conduct a competitive profiling matrix for BrandYourself.
3. Comment if BrandYourself is operating in a competitive or hypercompetitive industry.

FURTHER READING

D'Aveni, R. A. (1994). *Hypercompetition*. New York: Free Press.

Labrecque, L. I., Markos, E., & Milne, G. R. (2011). Online personal branding: Processes, challenges, and implications. *Journal of Interactive Marketing, 25*(1), 37–50. https://doi.org/10.1016/j.intmar.2010.09.002.

Porter, M. E. (1979). The structure within industries and companies' performance. *The Review of Economics and Statistics, 61*(2), 214–227. https://doi.org/10.2307/1924589

CASE STUDY **2.2**

Mapping Competitive Strategies

A Cluster Analysis of the Banana Chips Industry

Learning Outcomes

After completing this case study, students will be able to:

1. Analyze competitive strategies within an industry.
2. Apply quantitative analytical techniques to strategic management problems.
3. Interpret cluster analysis results to support entrepreneurial decision-making.

In June 2025, Ronald Smith, an entrepreneur, decided to enter the rapidly growing UK banana chips industry. However, he struggled to determine how to position his product competitively. Should he pursue quality differentiation, marketing differentiation, low-cost leadership, or innovation differentiation? He wanted to avoid adopting a strategy already pursued by many competitors in order to prevent commoditization and sustain a unique competitive advantage.

Because the market was fragmented, with several established firms and startups operating in the banana chips category, Smith hired a strategy consulting firm to analyze the industry's competitive dynamics. After conducting qualitative research, the consultants informed Smith that competitors pursued different competitive strategies and used distinct tactics to create competitive advantage.

Firms that pursued quality differentiation emphasized quality across the entire value chain. They trained farmers to cultivate high-quality banana crops and encouraged them to use superior seeds and organic fertilizers to maximize yield. In manufacturing facilities, these firms implemented strict quality control measures, such as Six Sigma and benchmarking, to ensure premium output. During packaging and distribution, they used high-grade airtight packaging materials to preserve freshness.

Firms that pursued marketing differentiation also maintained high product quality but focused more heavily on promotion and brand visibility. They invested significantly in advertising and occasionally offered limited-time price promotions. These firms also collaborated with social media influencers to attract younger consumers and increase brand appeal at retail outlets.

A third group pursued innovation differentiation. These firms maintained acceptable quality and promotion levels but emphasized product innovation. For example, they introduced baked chips instead of fried ones and offered unique flavors such as tomato or mint.

When the consultants presented these findings, Smith felt perplexed. Although firms emphasized all three differentiation dimensions, each firm appeared to prioritize one dominant strategic orientation. Smith also questioned the absence of a distinct low-cost strategy. The consultants explained that cost consciousness represented a critical success factor across the industry and that all firms invested in cost control. However, Smith observed significant price variations across brands, which suggested that some firms actively pursued low-cost positioning. He therefore wanted to determine how many firms followed each strategy and identify the least crowded strategic space.

To answer this question, the consultants conducted an empirical analysis to group competitors by their dominant strategic orientations. They decided to apply cluster analysis. Before doing so, they designed and administered a survey to identify which competitive strategies firms emphasized and to explore whether additional strategic dimensions existed beyond those identified qualitatively. They therefore conducted exploratory factor analysis prior to cluster analysis.

The consultants developed a 16-item questionnaire. Sample items asked respondents to indicate the extent to which their firm had emphasized the following over the past five years: "Invest in new product development," "Invest in accessing reliable distribution networks," "Invest in strict product quality control," and "Invest in reducing manufacturing costs." They measured each item on a 7-point Likert scale ranging from 1 (no emphasis) to 7 (major and constant emphasis).

The consultant obtained a list of 450 global firms in the banana chips industry from the Global Business Directory. He contacted the human resources departments of these firms and asked them to forward the survey link to their CEOs. The consultants received 336 completed questionnaires.

The consultants used SPSS (Version 31.0) to conduct exploratory factor analysis with varimax rotation. Because the case focuses on cluster analysis, the report does not detail the factor analysis procedure. The factor analysis revealed a four-factor solution, which the consultants labeled as Quality Differentiation (QD), Marketing Differentiation (MD), Low-Cost Strategy (LC), and Innovation Differentiation (ID). While the initial qualitative assessment emphasized three differentiation strategies, the empirical results revealed the low-cost strategy as a distinct and measurable strategic orientation in the industry.

Next, the consultants calculated the average scores for each dimension to generate summated factor scores for every respondent (CEO). These scores appear in Data.xlsx file. Finally, the consultants performed K-means cluster analysis using the summated scores for QD, MD, LC, and ID. They conducted the analysis in SPSS. Data.xlsx present the data for K-mean Clustering (PI). The steps for performing cluster analysis are given below. Output.xlsx presents the results for both the two-cluster and three-cluster solutions. (Available in www.routledge.com/9781032938912). Through this analysis, the consultants grouped firms into strategic clusters based on similarities in their emphasis on quality, marketing, cost, and innovation, thereby enabling Smith to identify how the competitive space was structured within the industry.

STEPS FOR CLUSTER ANALYSIS (THREE-CLUSTER SOLUTION)

Go to SPSS → Open → Data → Select the Data.xlsx file → Choose Sheet "Data_for_KMeans" → Click Open → Go to Analyze → Select Classify → Click K-Means Cluster → Move LC_Score, QD_Score, ID_Score, and MD_Score into the "Variables" box → Enter 3 in the "Number of Clusters" field → Click Options → Select "Initial cluster centers" and "ANOVA table" → Click Continue → Click OK to run the analysis → In the Output window, double-click the "Final Cluster Centers" table → Select the table → Right-click → Choose "Create Graph" (or "Chart Builder") → Select Line Graph → Click OK to generate the graphical output.

Please see Data and Output support material files in www.routledge.com/9781032938912.

Repeat the same process to generate a two-Cluster Solution by opting: "Enter 2" in the "Number of Clusters" field

DISCUSSION QUESTIONS

1. What conclusions can Smith draw from the cluster analysis about the competitive strategies of existing firms?
2. What implications does the cluster analysis have for Smith's competitive strategy as an entrepreneur?
3. What could explain why qualitative analysis did not identify a low-cost strategy as a distinct competitive strategy, whereas empirical cluster analysis revealed it?
4. What conclusions can Smith draw from the cluster analysis regarding his choice of competitive positioning?

CHAPTER NOTES

1 https://www.careerchange.com/industry-update-big-tech-2024-02/.
2 https://www.copperberg.com/a-steel-manufacturer-has-gone-online-why-the-shift-to-e-commerce-and-what-is-ahead/.
3 https://dcomin.host.dartmouth.edu/files/Philippon.pdf.
4 https://quartr.com/insights/company-research/the-coca-cola-and-pepsi-duopoly-the-secret-ingredients.
5 https://www.foundernest.com/resources/blog-posts/netflix-vs-blockbuster-a-cautionary-tale-of-innovation-ignored.
6 https://www.thedrum.com/news/2021/04/29/with-coke-acquisition-the-balance-bodyarmor-attacks-with-25m-summer-campaign.
7 Christensen, C. M., Johnson, C. W., & Horn, M. B. (2008). *Disrupting class: How disruptive innovation will change the way the world learns*. New York, NY: McGraw-Hill.
8 https://www.ndtv.com/offbeat/samsung-takes-a-dig-at-apple-after-unveiling-of-iphone-17-series-icant-believe-9248335#:~:text=Read%20Time:%203%20mins,welcome%20to%20the%20party%20%23iCant%22.
9 Livengood, R. S., & Reger, R. K. (2010). That's our turf! Identity domains and competitive dynamics. *Academy of Management Review*, *35* (1), 48–66.
10 Burgelman, R. A., & Grove, A. S. (1996). Strategic dissonance. *California Management Review*, *38* (2), 8–28.

11 https://www.inc.com/andrea-olson/how-dominos-pizza-changed-marketing-game.html#:~:text=Domino's%20realized%20they%20weren't,with%20a%20warmer%20built%20inside.
12 https://via.library.depaul.edu/cgi/viewcontent.cgi?article=1300&context=jatip#:~:text=In%20February%201998%2C%20Papa%20John's,re%2Dmanufactured%20tomato%20paste.%22.
13 https://www.sciencedirect.com/science/article/pii/S0024630123000353#:~:text=A%20hypercompetitive%20market%20is%20characterized,Aveni%2C%201994%2C%201998).
14 https://hbr.org/1982/11/the-surprising-case-for-low-market-share.
15 https://warroom.armywarcollege.edu/articles/the-new-defense-normal-nine-fundamentals-of-hyper-competition/#:~:text=Dartmouth%20University's%20Richard%20D'Aveni%20first%20defined%20hypercompetition,recreating%20advantages%20at%20the%20expense%20of%20rivals.
16 https://oxfordre.com/business/display/10.1093/acrefore/9780190224851.001.0001/acrefore-9780190224851-e-16?p=emailASmEw4eRkyjPw&d=/10.1093/acrefore/9780190224851.001.0001/acrefore-9780190224851-e-16.
17 https://oxfordre.com/business/display/10.1093/acrefore/9780190224851.001.0001/acrefore-9780190224851-e-16?p=emailASmEw4eRkyjPw&d=/10.1093/acrefore/9780190224851.001.0001/acrefore-9780190224851-e-16.
18 https://www.modernretail.co/marketing/fast-food-chains-like-mcdonalds-wendys-are-locked-in-a-price-war/#:~:text=Major%20quick%2Dservice%20restaurant%20chains,%2D%20to%20mid%2Dincome%20customers.
19 https://www.tandfonline.com/doi/full/10.1080/0965254X.2022.2160485.
20 https://www.rstreet.org/commentary/the-economics-of-the-pharmaceutical-sector-innovation-competition-and-patent-policy/.
21 https://jsbs.scholasticahq.com/article/129664-strategic-groups-path-to-the-efficiency-frontier.
22 Dranove, D., Peteraf, M., & Shanley, M. (1998). Do strategic groups exist? An economic framework for analysis. *Strategic Management Journal*, *19* (11), 1029–1044.
23 https://nypost.com/2024/04/03/business/olive-garden-is-too-expensive-if-youre-making-less-than-75k/#:~:text=By,and%20Ruth's%20Chris%20Steak%20House.
24 https://strategicmanagementinsight.com/tools/competitive-profile-matrix-cpm/.
25 https://strategicmanagementinsight.com/tools/competitive-profile-matrix-cpm/.
26 https://strategicmanagementinsight.com/tools/competitive-profile-matrix-cpm/.
27 https://strategicmanagementinsight.com/tools/competitive-profile-matrix-cpm/.
28 Cavallo, A., Sanasi, S., Ghezzi, A., & Rangone, A. (2021). Competitive intelligence and strategy formulation: Connecting the dots. *Competitiveness Review: An International Business Journal*, *31* (2), 250–275.
29 Treviño, L. H., & Weaver, G. R. (1997). Ethical issues in competitive intelligence practice: Consensus, conflicts, and challenges. *Competitive Intelligence Review*, *8* (1), 61–72.
30 Crane, A. (2005). In the company of spies: When competitive intelligence gathering becomes industrial espionage. *Business Horizons*, *48* (3), 233–240.
31 https://www.latimes.com/archives/la-xpm-2000-may-23-fi-32945-story.html#:~:text=DETROIT%20%E2%80%94%20A%20federal%20grand%20jury,memory%20loss%20and%20brain%20damage.
32 Kwoka Jr, J. E. (1985). The Herfindahl index in theory and practice. *The Antitrust Bulletin*, *30* (4), 915–947.
33 Pavic, I., Galetic, F., & Piplica, D. (2016). Similarities and differences between the CR and HHI as an indicator of market concentration and market power. *British Journal of Economics, Management & Trade*, *13* (1), 1–8.
34 Pavic, I., Galetic, F., & Piplica, D. (2016). Similarities and differences between the CR and HHI as an indicator of market concentration and market power. *British Journal of Economics, Management & Trade*, *13* (1), 1–8.
35 https://www.sciencedirect.com/science/article/pii/S0167268124001562.
36 https://www.sciencedirect.com/science/article/pii/S0167268124001562.
37 https://www.sciencedirect.com/science/article/pii/S0167268124001562.
38 https://www.travelweekly.com/Travel-News/Airline-News/Spirit-Frontier-merger-agreement-canceled.
39 https://www.justice.gov/archives/opa/pr/justice-department-statements-jetblue-terminating-acquisition-spirit-airlines#:~:text=In%20March%202023%2C%20the%20Justice%20Department%2C%20California%2C,under%20Section%207%20of%20the%20Clayton%20Act.
40 *Brandyourself.com inc.* (n.d.). Bloomberg. https://www.bloomberg.com/profile/company/0206668D:US.
41 *Improve your online reputation. Protect your online piracy.* (n.d.). BrandYourself. https://brandyourself.com/.
42 *BrandYourself competitors, revenue, alternatives and pricing.* (n.d.). Growjo.com. https://growjo.com/company/BrandYourself.

43 Hall, J. (2017, March 12). *The case for online reputation management: By the numbers*. Forbes. https://www.forbes.com/sites/johnhall/2017/03/12/the-case-for-online-reputation-management-by-the-numbers/?sh=2da6fba03f6f.
44 *Is reputation management ethical?* (2018, January 21). Reputationx.com. https://www.reputationx.com/orm/ethics.
45 *Bury your negative search results*. (n.d.). Guaranteed Removals. https://www.guaranteedremovals.com/push-down-complaints/.
46 Dangremond, S. (2015, May 19). *These guys say they can bury your negative Google results*. Town & Country. https://www.townandcountrymag.com/society/a3182/brand-yourself/.
47 *Search engine optimisation (SEO)*. (2011, December 8). Smart Insights. https://www.smartinsights.com/search-engine-optimisation-seo/.
48 *What is SEO and how does SEO work?* (2018, August 1). WebFX. https://www.webfx.com/internet-marketing/how-SEO-works.html.
49 *Pay-Per-Click advertising: What is PPC & how does it work?* (2014, October 10). WordStream. https://www.wordstream.com/pay-per-click-advertising.
50 *Organic search: What is organic search?* (2014, December 25). WordStream. https://www.wordstream.com/organic-search.
51 Cellan-Jones, R. (2011, December 6). *Bell Pottinger, Google and Wikipedia*. BBC. https://www.bbc.co.uk/news/technology-16049359.
52 Holmes, D. (2012, March 8). *Brandyourself and the billion-dollar SEO and reputation management industry*. Fast Company. https://www.fastcompany.com/1823003/brandyourself-and-billion-dollar-seo-and-reputation-management-industry.
53 Ambron, P. (August 4, 2016). *Why the online reputation management industry is changing—and where it needs to go*. Medium. https://medium.com/@patrickambron/why-the-online-reputation-management-industry-is-changing-and-where-it-needs-to-go-9cf536183c82.
54 Shaffer, S. (2014, December 19). *How social media can affect college admissions*. Teenlife.com. https://www.teenlife.com/blogs/social-media-can-affect-college-admissions.
55 Dennner, W. (n.d.). *How social media can help (and harm!) your university application*. Waynedenner.com. https://www.waynedenner.com/blog/how-social-media-can-help-and-harm-your-university-application/.
56 Dishman, L. (2018, March 15). *This AI platform helps jobseekers fix their social media reputation*. Fast Company. https://www.fastcompany.com/40541793/this-ai-platform-helps-jobseekers-fix-their-social-media-reputation.
57 Kessler, S. (2017, May 31). *The perfect graduation gift: A $100 widget to scrub social media accounts of embarrassing posts*. Quartz. https://qz.com/994406/the-perfect-graduation-gift-a-100-widget-to-scrub-social-media-accounts-of-embarrassing-posts/.
58 Grant, M. (2017, June 14). *How high schoolers can clean up their social media for admissions*. Bustle. https://www.bustle.com/p/this-student-makeover-tool-goes-through-your-online-history-to-prepare-for-college-admissions-64452.
59 Bedigian, L. (May 3, 2012). *Is this the next Instagram?* Benzinga. https://www.benzinga.com/general/entrepreneurship/12/05/2556875/is-this-the-next-instagram.
60 Wlosik, M. (2020, November 25). *What is a data broker and how does it work?* Clearcode. https://clearcode.cc/blog/what-is-data-broker/.
61 *What is a URL?* (2021, January 13). MDN Web Docs. https://developer.mozilla.org/en-US/docs/Learn/Common_questions/What_is_a_URL.
62 *Snake Oil—The new cure to all your marketing needs in just 5 easy steps!* (2019, August 16). Fireworx. https://www.fwx.co.uk/snake-oil-the-new-cure-to-all-your-marketing-needs-in-just-5-easy-steps/.

FURTHER READING

Hair, J. F., Black, W. C., Babin, B. J., & Anderson, R. E. (2019). *Multivariate data analysis* (8th ed.). Hampshire: Cengage Learning, EMEA.

Murray, A. I. (1988). A contingency view of Porter's "generic strategies". *Academy of Management Review*, *13*(3), 390–400.

CHAPTER 3

Generic Competitive Strategies

> **Learning Objectives**
>
> After reading this chapter, students will be able to:
>
> - Examine different competitive strategies that firms may pursue;
> - Comprehend the value chain activities of a firm;
> - Evaluate the implications of competitive strategies on the value chain activities of firms;
> - Explore how firms can achieve sustainable competitive advantage.

COST LEADERSHIP STRATEGY

Michael E. Porter suggested three generic *competitive strategies* that firms can use as a foundational framework for positioning themselves within an industry and achieving a sustainable competitive advantage. Firms can achieve competitive strategies through cost leadership, differentiation, or market focus.[1]

- A *low-cost strategy* implies a firm taking strategic actions to become the lowest-cost producer in its industry.[2] A firm passes the cost savings it achieves compared to its competitors to customers in the form of comparatively low prices within the industry. Walmart is the lowest-cost retailer in the US retail sector.[3] Its low-cost strategy results in the lowest price in the industry.

  The sources of low-cost advantage can range from economies of scale (both in production and purchasing, i.e., bulk raw material purchasing) to proprietary technology or preferential access to raw materials, among others.[4] Operational efficiency is critical for pursuing a low-cost strategy. Walmart, for instance, has preferred supplier relationships that help it negotiate low bulk purchases from its suppliers and offer "everyday low prices."[5]

  Typically, a firm works to lower costs across all value chain activities. A low-cost producer, as part of its human resource management, will not pay employees above the

DOI: 10.4324/9781003568100-3

industry average salary, but rather the average salary.[6] A firm's R&D would be focused more on process technology than product technology.[7] Thus, rather than introducing new products, a low-cost producer would be focused on process innovation that can help it invent technologies for more effective and efficient production and operations management.[8] Similarly, marketing activities would be more focused on word of mouth rather than aggressive advertising, as advertising is likely to increase the product's cost.[9] A firm may also give up e-commerce sales as online retailing may increase the cost of distribution. Primark, a low-cost retailer, for instance, does not allow online sales as it believes that the cost of delivery plus return services would overall increase its cost of sales.[10]

Differentiation Strategy

Differentiation strategy can be pursued in the following ways as explained below.

- *Product differentiation* implies a firm investing in superior quality of a product, which results in superior product performance, high durability and reliability, or consistent product performance, among other parameters.[11] Godiva Chocolate, for instance, uses premium quality ingredients that make its chocolates high-quality.[12] Owing to distinctiveness, a firm is also able to charge a premium price for its differentiation strategy. Firms can also create differentiation based on marketing activities and innovation, in addition to a focus on quality, which is referred to as quality-based differentiation.

  In a differentiation strategy, which commands a premium price, superior quality could be real or perceived. A firm achieves a perceived high level of superior quality through investment in a brand name or image,[13] also referred to as *differentiation based on marketing*. For example, L'Oreal is a licensed manufacturer of Prada perfumes, and L'Oreal's mass manufacturing facility manufactures Prada perfumes.[14] Marketing differentiators create an image in the minds of customers that their company's products are superior to those of competitors and convey a perceived uniqueness.[15] Firms convey messages through advertisements and promotions. However, the marketing campaign can also be drawn on unique product attributes, relevant brand stories, or customer service norms to create a positive brand image in the minds of consumers.

  Firms create *innovation differentiation* through innovation. Innovators with innovation differentiation develop products that are distinctive, novel, and have superior design and performance.[16] Innovation differentiation requires engagement in research and new product development activities. For example, Apple invests in innovation differentiation, launching categories such as the Mac, iPhone, iPad, and Apple TV.[17] Once again, Apple's innovation strategy is achieved not just through investment in R&D, but by tailoring all value chain activities for innovation. As part of its human resource management, Apple designs its organizational structure and culture to promote employee creativity and innovation, as well as interdepartmental communication for effective product development based on customer feedback.[18] Apple's marketing strategy focuses on seamless user experience; i.e., how its products integrate into customers' everyday lives. Apple focuses on creating an emotional connection with customers, rather than just highlighting unique product features.[19] Apple products are also premium-priced, owing to the recouping of R&D investment costs, as well as commanding a premium price for their unique differentiation.

Overall, a low-cost strategy has a lower gross profit margin, whereas differentiation has a relatively higher gross profit margin due to differences in the prices charged to customers.[20] For instance, where Walmart has a gross profit margin of approximately 20%, Apple has a gross profit margin of 40%.[21]

Focused differentiation implies focusing on a relatively narrow target market, characterized by either extremely low costs or extremely high product quality differentiation.[22] Ultra-low-cost retailers, such as Dollar Tree or Family Dollar, and premium-quality fashion clothing retailers, such as Armani or Gucci, focus on very low-income and extremely wealthy customer segments, respectively. Where ultra-low-cost retailers such as Dollar Tree focus on more local brands and ultra-small packages from branded retailers,[23] focused differentiation retailers like Capri focus on premium product quality.

Price Justification for Premium Quality Products

Firms price premium quality products extremely highly, not just to signal to consumers the high quality of their products, but also to convey the actual nature of the superior quality ingredients and manufacturing techniques used. For instance, "Cashmere," considered the finest quality wool, is taken from goats living in conditions lower than −40 degrees Fahrenheit.[24] The short hair from cashmere goats is around 14 microns thick, compared to widely available merino wool, which is 15–25 microns thick, compared to human hair, which is 100 microns thick.[25] Experts consider cashmere to be finer, stronger, lighter, and softer than wool, and three times more insulating than merino wool. Because cashmere wool is thin and short, it is challenging to weave and requires high-end engineering capabilities that mass-market textile companies often lack. Even if these mass-market textile companies receive supplies of cashmere, the finest raw wool material, they will likely produce inferior fabrics without the right technical equipment and expertise. Luxury-grade textile companies can afford to purchase this equipment, invest in technological expertise, and then recoup the cost through high prices.[26]

Cashmere is derived from the undercoat of goats, while sheep fleece, or wool, is the wool coating that covers the outer body of a sheep and has a coarser feel than cashmere.[27] Moreover, much more manual labor is involved in procuring enough material to make one garment from cashmere. Four to eight cashmere goats are needed for one sweater, while producers use one sheep's fleece to create three sweaters. This increased labor and goat production costs also add to the high price point. If one sweater requires one pound of cashmere, then, given cashmere's average market price of USD 150/kg, one sweater utilizing half a kilogram of cashmere will likely have a material cost of USD 75.[28] On average, luxury brands like Loro Piana sell cashmere sweaters for USD 1,700.[29] For cashmere, transportation costs, import duties, design, manufacturing, and labor costs were around USD 250. With a price tag of USD 1,700, the gross profit margin is around 85%. However, luxury consumers were willing to pay this high price owing to the warmth of the material, highlighting the significance of quality in purchase decisions.[30]

VALUE CHAIN ANALYSIS

Porter introduced the concept of *value chain analysis* and defined it as a system of internal processes or activities performed by a firm "to design, produce, market, deliver and support its product."[31] A firm's competitive strategy has implications for how it manages its value chain activities. For instance, as discussed in Section "Generic Competitive Strategies," a low-cost competitive strategy will prompt the firm to invest in a more efficient procurement system, as exemplified by Walmart. In contrast, a product differentiation strategy will drive the firm to invest in procuring high-quality raw materials, such as cashmere woolen fabric. Figure 3.1 presents a diagram of value chain activities.

- Porter distinguishes value chain activities into two categories, namely primary and secondary.[32] *Primary value chain activities* are revenue-generating activities that directly involve converting inputs into outputs, as well as delivering and providing after-sales support.[33] These activities are *inbound logistics* (the act of bringing raw materials to facilities), *operations* (generally manufacturing activities that convert raw materials into finished products), and *outbound logistics* (the act of delivering finished products) to the customer, which could be a wholesaler, retailer, or customer, depending on the delivery model chosen. For example, where multinational companies make deliveries directly to retailers such as Walmart, ready-to-cook category firms, such as HelloFresh, make

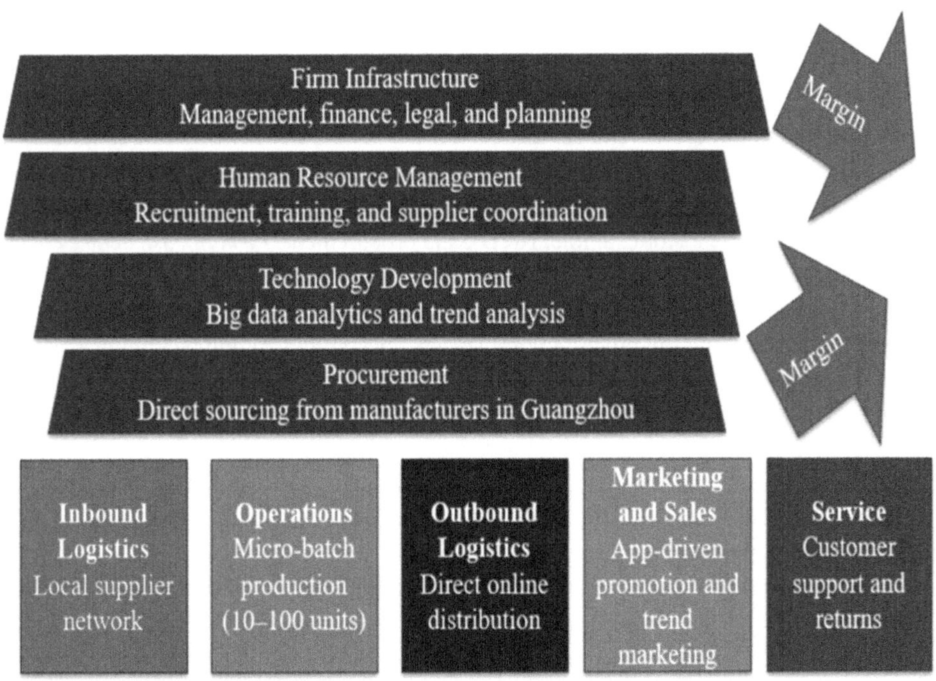

FIGURE 3.1 Porter's Value Chain Model in the Context of Shein

Source: Developed by the Authors

deliveries directly to customers.[34] Again, in the computing industry, where incumbent firms like HP made deliveries to retailers like Target, a startup like Dell computers, as a direct competitor, made deliveries directly to end customers, thereby ensuring low prices by saving the commission costs paid to retailers.[35] Marketing and sales encompass various activities, including pricing, advertising, and channel management. Service refers to after-sales services, including repair, installation, and other related activities.

Inbound logistics refer to the processes that involve receiving and managing the flow of raw materials from suppliers into a firm's facilities. A firm's wide range of activities, including inventory ordering, transportation, receiving, and warehousing, are a part of inbound logistics.[36] Efficient inbound logistics can help organizations gain a competitive advantage by reducing lead times and diminishing the need for expedited shipping, which could be expensive.[37] It also helps to sustain quality, as careful inspection of goods upon receipt and the use of appropriate storage facilities help retain the quality of raw materials.

Operations focus on optimizing the internal processes responsible for transforming inputs into outputs. Operations managers generally rely on operations management tools, such as business process reengineering, Six Sigma, and lean management, for reducing costs and maximizing revenues.[38]

Outbound logistics encompasses activities related to collecting, storing, and delivering final products to customers. Finished goods warehousing and order processing are part of outbound logistics.[39]

Marketing and sales refer to activities associated with effectively marketing a firm's products to customers. Thus, advertising and promotional campaigns, as well as other sales force activities, form part of sales and marketing.[40] *After-sales service* refers to activities associated with providing support to customers after the sale, such as product installation, training, and replacements.

- *Secondary value chain activities* do not directly add to revenues but help in realizing them. These activities encompass firm infrastructure, human resource management, technology development (for example, R&D), and procurement. *Firm infrastructure* consists of functions such as management, finance, legal, and planning. Every function performed in an organization is associated with *technology*. These technologies can be related to both the product and the process. For instance, telecommunication technology, accounting automation software, and product design research all fall under technology development. *Procurement* refers to the activities associated with purchasing raw materials that a firm uses in its value chain. Where inbound logistics refers to the act of managing procured raw materials, such as warehouse management, procurement is more associated with activities of finding suppliers, managing relationships with them, or determining the quantity of raw materials a firm needs to procure.[41]

A firm's competitive strategy has implications for how it manages value chain activities. Shein, for instance, followed an ultra-fast fashion model, launching new designs weekly.[42] In fact, between July and December 2021, Shein added 2,000 and 10,000 individual styles to its app every day.[43] Young consumers were overwhelmed by the numerous choices, so they intended to try them all and were okay with discarding the clothes after short-term wear. To align its value chain activities, such as R&D, with the ultra-fast fashion model, Shien invested in big data analytics for insights into customer needs.[44] Shein developed a tracking system that captures products of all kinds on clothing retail websites. The tracking system analyzed popular colors, price changes, and usage patterns. Shein also utilized Google Trends Finder to analyze trending words in various countries across different categories, including color, fabric, and style.[45] For example, using Google Trends, Shein accurately predicted the trend of lace and Indian cotton in the US in the summer of 2018.[46] This data helped Shein conduct an appropriate R&D level for fashion designs to differentiate itself from other competitors. Due to data analytics, Shein had almost real-time access to customer data, allowing them to explore new designs within seven days.[47]

Shein also invested in a low-cost strategy. Accordingly, Shein followed a micro-batch production or on-demand business model where the e-retailer first ordered 10–100 copies of any given garment and sold them on their website.[48] Because of the micro-batch, Shein reduced wastage and stock-out risk, as the e-retailer only sent those designs for mass production that sold quickly under the small-batch model. As a local player with a presence in China, Shein was able to convince contract manufacturers to adopt small-batch manufacturing more easily.[49] Shein was co-located with its vendor base in Guangzhou, China, allowing it to work directly with manufacturers, thereby eliminating the need for agents, traders, or intermediaries. Eliminating intermediaries also reduced overall product costs and offered direct and immediate access to any innovation throughout their supply chain, with quick decision-making. However, margins were thin, and manufacturers had to complete orders by very short deadlines, which resulted in long working hours for workers in these manufacturing units. Shein paid its suppliers on time, which helped manufacturers to maintain their cash flow.[50]

SUSTAINABLE COMPETITIVE ADVANTAGE

Sustainable competitive advantage implies an advantage a firm has over competitors that helps it to either lower costs or increase revenues in the long run.[51] The long run generally means a time frame of 10–15 years. Whether a resource or capability can provide a sustainable competitive advantage is determined by four factors: valuable, rare, inimitable, and non-substitutable.[52]

- *Valuable* implies any resource that increases efficiency or effectiveness for customers. *Efficiency* means the firm can manage any of the value chain activities in a more efficient manner.[53] Walmart's relationships with its suppliers enable it to negotiate better terms with suppliers and purchase extensive inventories at discounted prices.[54] This way, Walmart can save costs and pass benefits to customers through low prices, contributing to its strategy of everyday low prices. Thus, the relationship with suppliers offers a competitive advantage. However, whether it is sustainable or not depends on whether the relationship resource is rare, inimitable, or non-substitutable as well.

Effectiveness implies adding value for customers or creating better value for customers, such as enhancing customer experience through loyalty points or rewards.[55] However, whether loyalty points can be a source of sustainable competitive advantage depends on their imitability, rarity, and non-substitutability. Starbucks offers customers stars in return for the purchase of products.[56] After accumulation of a certain number of stars, they can get a free drink of their choice or a souvenir.[57]

- *Rarity* implies that only a few competitors can possess a particular resource. IKEA, for instance, to reduce customers' waiting time at the checkout counter (and hence increasing their effectiveness), became the first company to launch self-service checkouts. However, over the years, not only its competitors but also firms in other industries have introduced the practice of self-checkouts, where customers can scan goods on their own and pay for them. Thus, although self-checkout counters are a valuable resource, they are not rare as every retailer offers them. Therefore, now it has become a critical success factor for any large retailer to succeed.
- *Inimitable* implies that a competitor cannot copy a resource or capability. If a competitor cannot copy or imitate a resource or capability, it becomes an inimitable resource. Inimitability is one of the key criteria for creating sustainable competitive advantage. Rare resources generally contribute to inimitability because, if a resource is rare, competitors may not be able to obtain it, and thus it creates a sustained competitive advantage. Moreover, a resource becomes inimitable when competitors face substantial costs or are otherwise unable to imitate the resource. This inability to imitate is usually possible if a resource is generated due to historical conditions or complex social relationships, as the same history or the same kind of intangible relationships are challenging to imitate. For instance, in B2B businesses, every business has strong ties with its clients. However, such resources often arise from unique historical conditions, complex social interactions, ambiguous causes, or intangible assets, such as corporate culture and reputation, making them inimitable.
- *Non-substitutable* implies that there are no substitutes or strategic equivalents available for a given resource or capability.[58] In other words, competitors may not be able to achieve the same competitive advantage that the focal firm has, owing to a lack of other equivalent resources that the firm possesses. A firm's unique, specific knowledge, for instance, will have no other strategic equivalent substitute, and so competitors will not be able to achieve that competitive advantage. Such resources or capabilities are usually tied to the unique history or organizational processes of a firm. Such historical paths and processes are difficult to replicate, making them non-substitutable. When Xiaomi launched its electric vehicles (EVs) in 2024, specifically the SU7 model, it was able to leverage its prior manufacturing knowledge from smartphone systems.[59] Unlike other competitors, it could invest in automation facilities and utilize smartphone manufacturing knowledge that most of its competitors lacked, thereby venturing into the EV category.[60] Xiaomi's unique knowledge set became non-substitutable, as competitors could not leverage historical knowledge from related product categories, giving Xiaomi EV a competitive edge and helping it outpace even Tesla in sales in China just after the launch of its SU7 EV.

ASSIGNMENT QUESTIONS

1. Select three companies of your choice and explain how they are pursuing and implementing low-cost, quality differentiation, and focused differentiation strategies. What would you suggest further to improve their strategies for a better competitive advantage?
2. For the three companies you have selected in Assignment Question 1, explain the value chain implications for different generic strategies. To what extent are firms appropriately implementing their competitive strategy from the value chain perspective.
3. Critically analyze the statement that sustainable competitive advantage may not exist. From your home country, pick up a couple of companies that have shown sustainable superior performance over the past ten years. What do you think is their source of competitive advantage?

CASE STUDY **3.1**

Analyzing US Hotel Industry Dynamics through Factor Analysis

Learning Outcomes

After completing this case study, students will be able to:

1. Apply factor analysis to identify industry drivers;
2. Interpret industry dynamics using strategic frameworks;
3. Develop strategic responses for new market entrants.

Ronald Smith intended to establish a small hotel chain in the US, as his friends and relatives suggested that the hotel industry had good profit margins and was growing. However, he recalled from his business classes as an MBA student that the hotel industry was being disrupted by Airbnb on one end and by digital technologies such as Zoom, Teams, etc., on the other. He decided to delve deeper into the industry and ordered market research reports from various publishing houses and consultancy groups. Reports suggested that hotel industry dynamics were influenced by several factors.

Newer business models such as Airbnb were becoming successful, with Airbnb even reporting a 100% growth rate from 2017 to 2018 and by 2022. This growth was not a result of market expansion, but market share distribution, where hoteliers reported a 1.3% decline in room bookings and a 1.5% drop in hotel revenue (Shortterm Sage, 2022). Airbnb was approximately 33% less expensive than hotels, especially for large groups traveling together (French, 2024). As per surveys, 60% of customers preferred Airbnb over hotels (JadeCaps, 2024; Temblador, 2019).

Then, several websites, such as Trivago and Kayak, also made hotel price comparison easier for customers, and online travel agents offered discounts that hotels did not, except for loyalty points. (Seemann, 2024). Moreover, hotel loyalty programs were not perceived as value-adding by 61% of guests, according to survey reports (Connolly, 2022).

Travel websites such as Agoda, Expedia, or Hotels.com offered options such as "book now, pay later" or free cancellations to a specific date (Joanne, 2002). But customers exploited these features, making multiple bookings only to cancel most of them at the last minute. This also adversely impacted on the hotels, as they ended up with large unsold room inventory at the last moment (River Landing, 2024).

While revenue drivers were struggling, hotels had to incur significant expenses to deliver a seamless guest experience. They needed high-quality furniture, especially beds. Hoteliers purchase furniture from both national and international manufacturers based on factors such as price, product quality, and delivery time. Though hotels had several options for furniture suppliers, on average, the furnishings for one room cost approximately USD 1,200 (Furniture Roots, 2021). Constructing a hotel is a capital-intensive task, with costs ranging between USD 212 and USD 550 per square foot for a three-star hotel.

Smith was convinced the hotel industry was unattractive, but before reaching any conclusion, he wanted to better understand industry dynamics and explore whether he could change any aspect of them. So, he hired a strategy consultant to provide him with some data and guidance on the attractiveness of the hotel industry. The consultant informed Smith that he could help Smith identify different factors affecting industry profitability, and then Smith could decide which factor he would like to twist to change industry dynamics. The consultant developed a 23-question survey questionnaire. Each item was measured on a 7-point Likert scale ranging from 1 (*strongly disagree*) to 7 (*strongly agree*).

Next, the consultant selected a random sample of 258 hotels from the US hospitality industry in the Global Business Directory. The consultant obtained 220 completed questionnaires from hotel CEOs, who were approached through the respective hotels' HR departments. Refer to Data.xlsx for the collected data and survey questions.

The following were the steps for factor analysis (Figure 3.2).

The consultant shared the analysis with Smith. Refer to the Output.xlsx file. The consultant needed to discuss the results and explain how they were arrived at, as well as the statistical meaning and significance of each step used in the analysis. The consultant also had to highlight the relative importance of each factor and explain the same to the hotel manager. How well the consultant presented and explained the analysis was to be seen.

Go to Analyze→ Dimension reduction → Factor (click it) → Input all the 23 items or questions in the Variable list box → Click on Descriptives and select KMO and Bartlett's test sphericity → Click Continue → Click Extraction → Select principal component as the extraction method and keep the Eigen value as 1 → Click Continue → Click Rotation → Select Varimax → Click Continue → Select Options → Click Sorted by size and cick suppress small coefficients and keep the absolute value below 0.40 → Click Continue → Click Ok.

FIGURE 3.2 Steps for Conducting Factor Analysis in SPSS.

Source: Developed by the Authors

DISCUSSION QUESTIONS

1. Apply factor analysis to identify the key structural forces shaping hotel industry dynamics, and interpret the resulting factors within an appropriate theoretical framework.
2. Explain how each identified factor shapes the profitability conditions of the hotel industry.
3. Recommend strategic actions Smith can take to influence or reshape industry dynamics.

FURTHER READING

Grundy, T. (2006). Rethinking and reinventing Michael Porter's five forces model. *Strategic Change*, *15*(5), 213–229.

Malhotra, N., Nunan, D., & Birks, D. (2017). *Marketing research: An applied approach* (5th ed.). Harlow: Pearson Education Limited.

REFERENCES

Connolly, E. (March 28, 2022). What today's guests really want when it comes to hotel loyalty programs might surprise you. *LinkedIn*. Retrieved from https://www.linkedin.com/pulse/what-todays-guests-really-want-when-comes-hotel-loyalty-connolly/

French, S. (August 12, 2024). Are Airbnbs more cost-effective than hotels? *Nerdwallet*. Retrieved from https://www.nerdwallet.com/article/travel/are-airbnbs-more-cost-effective-than-hotels

Furniture Roots. (April 4, 2021). Where exactly do hotels get their furniture & fixtures from? Furnitureroots.com. https://furnitureroots.com/where-do-hotels-get-their-furniture/

JadeCaps. (March 8, 2024). Airbnb replacing hotels? The shifting landscape of travel accommodation. *LinkedIn*. Retrieved from https://www.linkedin.com/pulse/airbnb-replacing-hotels-shifting-landscape-xmbuc/

Joanne. (February 21, 2002). Do you make multiple reservations for the same trip? Fodors.com. https://www.fodors.com/community/united-states/do-you-make-multiple-reservations-for-the-same-trip-163619/

River Landing. (February 12, 2024). Are hotels cheaper last minute? A comprehensive guide. Riverlanding.com. https://riverlanding.com/blog/hotels-cheaper-last-minute/

Seemann, K. (August 19, 2024). The 17 best websites for booking hotels at the cheapest prices [2024]. Upgradepoints.com. https://upgradedpoints.com/travel/hotels/best-websites-for-booking-cheap-hotels/

Shortterm Sage. (July 7, 2022). Hotels vs. Airbnb: How the hotel industry tried but can never destroy short-term rentals. Shorttermsage.com. https://shorttermsage.com/hotels-vs-airbnb-how-hotel-industry-can-never-destroy-short-term-rentals

Temblador, A. (May 14, 2019). Airbnb vs. Hotels: New data shows travelers' preferences. *Travel Pulse*. Retrieved from https://www.travelpulse.com/news/hotels-and-resorts/airbnb-vs-hotels-new-data-shows-travelers-preferences

CASE STUDY

3.2

Identify competitive strategies in the Watch industry based on following information and comment to what extent strategy is being implemented effectively across value chain activities.

TABLE 3.1 Value chain Activities and Competitive Strategy Implications

Characteristic	Category 1	Category 2	Category 3
Production technique	Automation manufacturing	Hand-made craft	Hand-made
Employee skill	Unskilled, toolmakers	High	High
Distribution channel	retail stores	Exclusive: jewelers	Exclusive: jewelers
Marketing	TV commercials,	Point of sale demonstrations; Exclusive/ Print magazines,	Jewelers' recommendations;
Product technology	Pin-lever (older)	Jewels (current)	Jewels (cutting edge technology)
Target market	Middle class	Middle class	Upper class
Need fulfilled	Functional, everyday	Special occasions, jewelry	Special occasions, status symbol
Price	*Low* (USD 7–13)	Medium (USD 40–100)	Very high (>USD 1,000)

Source: Developed by the Authors.

CASE STUDY **3.3**

MasterClass-Exploring Growth

Learning Outcomes

After completing this study, students will be able to:

- Identify and evaluate the competitive strategy of a digital platform;
- Analyze value chain activities that support strategic positioning;
- Assess sources of competitive advantage in digital platforms;
- Evaluate strategic growth options for digital businesses.

Agnihotri, A., & Bhattacharya, S. (2022). *MasterClass: Exploring growth.* Thousand Oaks, CA: SAGE Publications. https://doi.org/10.4135/9781529779974

INTRODUCTION

Yanka Industries Inc., doing business as MasterClass, is a San Francisco-based online education solution provider where students could access tutorials and lectures pre-recorded by experts in their respective fields (Loizos, 2018). For example, political messaging was taught by Karl Rove and David Axelrod; Will Wright instructed game design; economics with Nobel laureate Paul Krugman; and, also space exploration with Chris Hadfield (Rudin, 2019). MasterClass was co-founded by David Rogier (CEO) and Aaron Rasmussen in 2012 (Loizos, 2016). In May 2020, the MasterClass app won Webby Awards in two categories- Media Streaming and Apps, Mobile & Voice (Education Reference) (Kastrenakes & Peters, 2020). The Webby Awards is a "leading international award honoring excellence on the Internet" (About the Webby Awards, n.d.).

The startup had two types of access passes- an all-access pass, which cost USD 180 per annum, and a single class pass, which cost USD 90 per annum (Duffy, 2020). Its library of courses grew from 34 to 51 between 2013 and 2018 and further to 85 in September 2020 (Chocano, 2020; Rudin, 2019). MasterClass also completed a USD 100 million funding round in May 2020 at a market valuation of USD 800 million. The funding aimed to assist its continued growth in course offerings and to grow internationally (Adams, 2020). Between 2015 and 2020, MasterClass raised USD 240 million through different funding rounds (Adams, 2020). However, the risk of piracy also increased with online streaming of videos (Stokel-Wlaker, 2019). Rogier had challenges of further growing the MasterClass business. What growth options could he opt for? Should Rogier focus on individual subscribers or corporate subscribers for faster growth? How can he resolve the potential piracy issue?

BACKGROUND

The MasterClass platform and app were launched in 2015 when *universities offered online lectures using their star professors* (Rudin, 2019). *During the same time*, startups such as Coursera and CreativeLive were also offering online course learning material to students. MasterClass integrated these attributes of online courses, with the addition of celebrities as instructors (Rudin, 2019). MasterClass was launched with just three courses: Dustin Hoffman teaching acting, Serena Williams teaching Tennis, and James Patterson teaching writing.

MasterClass claimed that they transformed online education by enabling anyone in the world to learn from the best professionals in their respective fields (Careers at MasterClass, n.d.). Their website mentioned, "We are deconstructing what makes an actor able to cry on demand, how an athlete defies gravity, and what it takes to write a bestseller" (Careers at MasterClass, n.d.). The online learning content was available to students anywhere anytime, which supported MasterClass's mission "to ignite the greatness in others" (Careers at MasterClass, n.d.). Some of the famous professionals teaching at MasterClass included Gordon Ramsay, Martin Scorsese, Helen Mirren, Margaret Atwood, Annie Leibovitz, Steph Curry, Carlos Santana, and Timbaland (Careers at MasterClass, n.d.).

Master class was headquartered in San Francisco, with additional offices in Los Angeles. In September 2020, the startup's estimated revenue was USD 120 million and employed 378 people (MasterClass's Competitors, Revenue..., 2020). After the COVID-19 pandemic hit in early 2020, MasterClass subscribers spent twice as much time on the platform as they did earlier (Chocano, 2020).

OPERATIONS

MasterClass realized that if celebrity instructors taught an advanced level curriculum of their professions on its platform, subscribers' cohorts were likely to be very small (Chocano, 2020) (as in any field, not many professionals would have joined a particular course). With the potential of limited subscribers and hence limited growth, MasterClass would not have achieved hundreds of millions of dollars of investments. Therefore, most courses were targeted at general audiences (Chocano, 2020). Commenting on the target market Atwood, the author of *The Handmaid's Tale*, said, "if you're doing something online, it could be anybody. It's more like publishing a book. It's out there. It's accessible. You don't know who may be accessing it" (Chocano, 2020).

MasterClass produced the courses directly with the celebrity instructors so that professionals could exactly cover what they wanted to learn (MasterClass Support, 2020). Class components included pre-recorded video content, class workbooks, interactive assignments, and community activities (MasterClass Support, 2020). Students could view videos any time, with the facility to pause, fast-forward, and re-watch as many times as they wanted. Students could also share their thoughts, upload performances, and comment on others' work (MasterClass Support, 2020). Each course had 2–5+ hours of video content split into individual lesson videos by the instructor. Professionals also provided a downloadable PDF (Portable Document Format) workbook that students could use to supplement the videos (MasterClass Support, 2020). Number of weeks that a student required to complete the course varied with his or her own pace. Each class's duration ranged from 5 to 25 minutes in length—though some classes had longer lessons (MasterClass Support, 2020).

Instructors could also choose to provide feedback to selected students on their assignments. MasterClass also had a provision where instructors from time to time could host special live Question & Answer sessions and opportunities for student participation (MasterClass Support, 2020). Apart from this, there were certain unique opportunities for students. For instance, MasterClass hosted a competition, and the winner student got a chance to co-author a book with the best-selling author James Patterson (MasterClass Support, 2020).

In 2019, Neil Gaiman, Jodie Foster, Natalie Portman, and David Lynch joined MasterClass. The startup believed that having multiple stars from the same field was not a problem rather an added advantage as each celebrity instructor had their own way of teaching. Rogier said, "If you look at the classes on filmmaking with Ron Howard and Martin Scorsese, they are different kinds of classes" (Rudin, 2019) (see Table 3.1). MasterClass's trailers on celebrities teaching subjects became so popular that they spawned their own Saturday Night Live parodies, "MasterClass: Quarantine Edition" (Chocano, 2020). Saturday Night Live is a late-night comedy showcase on the NBC channel.

MasterClass offered single class and all-access passes. A single class pass was for a single course, and with an all-access pass, a student could access multiple courses each year. Students could also gift all-access passes to others for which the access period started only after pass activation (MasterClass Support, 2020). The all-access pass provided access to all existing and up to be added courses in the future. However, if a subscriber of MasterClass did not find it worthy, they could cancel the subscription in 30 days with a full refund (MasterClass Support, 2020).

COPYRIGHT ISSUES

Subscribers were allowed to download most of the class materials from MasterClass's website, not video lessons. Some videos were downloadable on the iOS app (iPhone and iPad) for offline viewership (Can I Download a Class, 2020). In 2018, illegal piracy websites had 190 billion visits (Stokel-Wlaker, 2019). Commenting on the piracy risk of streaming services, Dan Rayburn, a streaming media expert, mentioned, "That the battle with piracy was equal for all streaming services including Netflix, Amazon or Apple." It was believed that keeping 100% of the content safe was challenging (Stokel-Wlaker, 2019). Streaming service providers such as Netflix were also facing piracy issues for any hit series. For instance, in 2015, its "House of cards" season three was downloaded illegally approximately 682,000 times within the first 24 hours of the series being made available on torrent services. This download was more than a 100% increase in piracy compared to season two. Season two's illegal download on the first day of it being made available on torrent services was approximately 321,000 times. The show was pirated mostly in China—60,000 downloads, followed by the US (50,008), and then India (47,106), and Australia (40,557) (Trefis Team, 2015).

COMPETITION

Although leveraging celebrities as instructors was a unique concept, MasterClass had several competitors (see Table 3.2). Since its launch, MasterClass differentiated itself from other start-ups in the online course sector by specializing in high-production-quality video series with the biggest names instead of focusing on the quantity of content that most competitors did (Peckham, 2018). Much of its USD 1.9 million in seed funding was utilized by MasterClass to recruit the initial talent (Dustin Hoffman) and produce only one class, their first class (on acting) (Peckham, 2018). The online course sector was also known as MOOCs, or massively open online courses.

Some media sources portrayed MasterClass as "doubling down on celebrity glitz" instead of offering courses that teach any content (Table 3.3). According to a *Vox* covered story,

TABLE 3.2 Celebrity Instructors on MasterClass (September 2020)

Film & TV	Sports & Games
Martin Scorsese Teaches Filmmaking	Serena Williams Teaches Tennis
Jodie Foster Teaches Filmmaking	Stephen Curry Teaches Shooting Ball Handling and Scoring
Natalie Portman Teaches Acting	Phil Ivey Teaches Poker Strategy
Music & Entertainment	Simone Biles Teaches Gymnastics Fundamentals
Usher Teaches the Art of Performance	**Design, Photography & Fashion**
Timbaland Teaches Producing and Beatmaking	Frank Gehry Teaches Design and Architecture
Danny Elfman Teaches Music for Film	Diane Von Furstenberg Teaches Building a Fashion Brand
Judd Apatow Teaches Comedy	Marc Jacobs Teaches Fashion Design
Writing	**Lifestyle**
James Patterson Teaches Writing	Bobbi Brown Teaches Makeup and Beauty
Dan Brown Teaches Writing Thrillers	**Science & Technology**
Judy Blume Teaches Writing	Dr. Jane Goodall Teaches Conservation
Culinary Arts	**Business, Politics & Society**
Gordon Ramsay Teaches Cooking	Bob Woodward Teaches Investigate Journalism
Alice Waters Teaches Home Cooking	Paul Krugman Teaches Economics and Society
Massimo Bottura Teaches Modern Italian Cooking	Howard Schultz Teaches Business Leadership

Source: What type of classes does MasterClass offer? (2020). *MasterClass*. Retrieved from https://masterclasshelp.zendesk.com/hc/en-us/articles/205575237-What-type-of-classes-does-MasterClass-offer-.

TABLE 3.3 MasterClass Competitors (September 2020)

Items	MasterClass	Udacity	Udemy
Founded	2012	2011	2012
Tags	Education; technology; edtech; e-learning platform;	Education; technology; adult education; edtech; e-learning; tech learning	Education; technology adult education edtech; higher education platform;
Employees	378	1,942	3,986
Valuation (USD billion)	0.8	1.1	3.3
Twitter followers ('000)	63	232	236
Latest funding round (USD million)	100	115	100
Total funding (USD million)	240	174	323

Source: MasterClass's Competitors, Revenue (2020)[61].

Serena William's tennis class was "just technical enough to be useless to a novice and inane to anyone who has taken a tennis lesson" (Adams, 2020). MasterClass treated celebrities as partners. The celebrity instructors received a USD 100,000 payment upfront and a share of at least 30% of revenue. However, Rogier mentioned that he held the bargaining power after initial challenging days of recruiting instructors, and was turning away nine out of ten celebrities who wanted to offer courses on MasterClass's platform (Adams, 2020).

THE ROAD AHEAD

Students took a combination of different classes with the MasterClass all-access pass, such as writing classes with sports classes, which happened due to overlap of interest (Rudin, 2019). According to media reports, MasterClass subscribers were not only interested in being taught by world-class professionals but also something more abstract that was beyond a particular profession: a vision of success (Rudin, 2019). According to competitors, Masterclass subscribers were likely to dwindle as most people may not sign up for courses from different instructors. However, Rogier mentioned that most subscribers watched at least three classes in a particular year (Adams, 2020). In 2020, Rogier wanted to expand the course offerings and grow internationally. In the same month, one-third of its sales were from members outside the USA (Adams, 2020); and Rogier believed that if MasterClass courses could be offered in regional languages and not only in English, the customer base could be further enhanced (Adams, 2020).

DISCUSSION QUESTIONS

1. What generic competitive strategy is Masterclass pursuing?
2. How Masterclass's value chain activities support its strategy.
3. Explain the nature of the competitive advantage that Masterclass has.

CHAPTER NOTES

1 Ormanidhi, O., & Stringa, O. (2008). Porter's model of generic competitive strategies: An insightful and convenient approach to firms' analysis. *Business Economics*, *43* (3), 55–64.
2 Ormanidhi, O., & Stringa, O. (2008). Porter's model of generic competitive strategies: An insightful and convenient approach to firms' analysis. *Business Economics*, *43* (3), 55–64.
3 https://www.analysisgroup.com/globalassets/insights/publishing/2024_understanding_walmarts_impact_on_the_us_economy_and_communities.pdf.
4 https://www.analysisgroup.com/globalassets/insights/publishing/2024_understanding_walmarts_impact_on_the_us_economy_and_communities.pdf.
5 https://www.analysisgroup.com/globalassets/insights/publishing/2024_understanding_walmarts_impact_on_the_us_economy_and_communities.pdf.
6 Walters, D., & Lancaster, G. (2000). Implementing value strategy through the value chain. *Management Decision*, *38* (3), 160–178.
7 Walters, D., & Lancaster, G. (2000). Implementing value strategy through the value chain. *Management Decision*, *38* (3), 160–178.
8 Walters, D., & Lancaster, G. (2000). Implementing value strategy through the value chain. *Management Decision*, *38* (3), 160–178.
9 Walters, D., & Lancaster, G. (2000). Implementing value strategy through the value chain. *Management Decision*, *38* (3), 160–178.
10 https://www.wsj.com/video/series/the-economics-of/how-primark-built-a-thriving-fashion-business-without-selling-online/F503AB11-8963-400B-A6F0–1BE47CA7C006#:~:text=support%20HTML5%20video.-,How%20Primark%20Built%20a%20Thriving%20Fashion%20Business%20Without%20Selling%20Online,Read%20More.
11 Ormanidhi, O., & Stringa, O. (2008). Porter's model of generic competitive strategies: An insightful and convenient approach to firms' analysis. *Business Economics*, *43* (3), 55–64.
12 https://www.godiva.com/#:~:text=Unparalleled%20Belgian%20heritage%20since%201926,and%20the%20world's%20finest%20ingredients.
13 https://brandingstrategyinsider.com/perceived-quality-critical-asset-for-brands/#:~:text=David%20Aaker%204%20min,Perceived%20Quality%20Drives%20Financial%20Performance.
14 https://www.pradagroup.com/en/news-media/news-section/prada-and-loreal.html.
15 https://hbr.org/1980/01/marketing-success-through-differentiation-of-anything.
16 Hull, C. E., & Rothenberg, S. (2008). Firm performance: The interactions of corporate social performance with innovation and industry differentiation. *Strategic Management Journal*, *29* (7), 781–789.
17 https://hbr.org/2020/11/how-apple-is-organized-for-innovation#:~:text=Why%20a%20Functional%20Organization?,a%20few%20of%20the%20improvements.
18 https://www.cypris.ai/insights/learn-from-the-best-how-apple-is-organized-for-innovation.
19 https://cda.academy/hidden-genius-behind-apples-marketing-strategies/.
20 https://www.cnbc.com/2025/01/30/apples-gross-margin-hits-record-as-services-business-keeps-growing.html#:~:text=Cook's%20emphasis%20on%20services%20has,has%20climbed%20to%20$3.6%20trillion.
21 https://www.cnbc.com/2025/01/30/apples-gross-margin-hits-record-as-services-business-keeps-growing.html#:~:text=Cook's%20emphasis%20on%20services%20has,has%20climbed%20to%20$3.6%20trillion.
22 Sharp, B. (1991). Competitive marketing strategy: Porter revisited. *Marketing Intelligence & Planning*, *9* (1), 4–10.
23 https://finance.yahoo.com/news/dollar-tree-vs-walmart-money-120027599.html?guce_referrer=aHR0cHM6Ly93d3cuZ29vZ2xlLmNvbS8&guce_referrer_sig=AQAAAGdjRK8rPsHBBAJx5KdVsG9cKNVTFUwGHCrVqsKxjPbIBPyJFwmFDuiq6QITpO34J-U9T2IlRfzLP_gJW6znjnL7XfsifYkpUMF045cFE0kd2F83NM80WsRx9pKlnpFsGZg2UQcMwChX2yUsFjBhSQVvK3Z9oTtmJETpwq9cRM_h.
24 https://recurvecap.com/insights/brunello-cucinelli-a-study-of-the-cashmere-supply-chain.
25 https://recurvecap.com/insights/brunello-cucinelli-a-study-of-the-cashmere-supply-chain.
26 https://recurvecap.com/insights/brunello-cucinelli-a-study-of-the-cashmere-supply-chain.

27 https://www.pashwrap.com/blogs/news/fleece-vs-cashmere-which-one-reigns-supreme-in-the-world-of-warmth-and-comfort#:~:text=Warmth%20and%20Insulation:%20Both%20fleece,on%20personal%20preference%20and%20budget.
28 Recurve Capital. (June 6, 2023). Brunello Cucinelli – A study of the cashmere supply chain. Recurvecap.com. Retrieved from https://recurvecap.com/insights/brunello-cucinelli-a-study-of-the-cashmere-supply-chain.
29 Recurve Capital. (June 6, 2023). Brunello Cucinelli – A study of the cashmere supply chain. Recurvecap.com. Retrieved from https://recurvecap.com/insights/brunello-cucinelli-a-study-of-the-cashmere-supply-chain.
30 Recurve Capital. (June 6, 2023). Brunello Cucinelli – A study of the cashmere supply chain. Recurvecap.com. Retrieved from https://recurvecap.com/insights/brunello-cucinelli-a-study-of-the-cashmere-supply-chain.
31 https://www.thestrategyinstitute.org/insights/value-chain-analysis-explained-boost-efficiency-cut-costs-and-gain-competitive-advantage.
32 Porter, M. E. (1980). *Value chain analysis*. London: Oxford Press Ltd.
33 Porter, M. E. (1980). *Value chain analysis*. London: Oxford Press Ltd.
34 https://www.hellofresh.com/eat/meal-kits-for-singles.
35 https://hbr.org/1998/03/the-power-of-virtual-integration-an-interview-with-dell-computers-michael-dell.
36 Porter, M. E. (1980). *Value chain analysis*. London: Oxford Press Ltd.
37 Porter, M. E. (1980). *Value chain analysis*. London: Oxford Press Ltd.
38 Porter, M. E. (1980). *Value chain analysis*. London: Oxford Press Ltd.
39 Porter, M. E. (1980). *Value chain analysis*. London: Oxford Press Ltd.
40 Porter, M. E. (1980). *Value chain analysis*. London: Oxford Press Ltd.
41 Porter, M. E. (1980). *Value chain analysis*. London: Oxford Press Ltd.
42 https://norna.ai/index.php/2023/12/04/how-shein-revolutionised-retail-for-the-21st-century/#:~:text=How%20does%20it%20work?,difficult%20to%20even%20compare%20them.%E2%80%9D.
43 https://time.com/6247732/shein-climate-change-labor-fashion/.
44 https://www.steadypace.sa/en/post/the-role-of-artificial-intelligence-in-developing-shein-strategies-1#:~:text=Big%20data%20analysis%20to%20identify,the%20needs%20of%20young%20consumers?
45 https://www.wired.com/story/shein-is-officially-the-biggest-polluter-in-fast-fashion-ai-is-making-things-worse/#:~:text=At%20every%20step%2C%20data%20was,an%20ultra%2Dfast%20supply%20chain.
46 https://www.imd.org/ibyimd/innovation/shein-shows-that-you-can-be-disruptive-without-disruption/.
47 https://www.library.hbs.edu/working-knowledge/how-shein-and-temu-conquered-fast-fashion-and-forged-a-new-business-model.
48 https://www.sheingroup.com/our-business/our-business-model/.
49 https://www.reuters.com/business/retail-consumer/how-chinas-shein-became-fast-fashion-giant-2023-11-28/.
50 https://www.bbc.com/news/articles/cdrylgvr77jo.
51 Huang, K. F., Dyerson, R., Wu, L. Y., & Harindranath, G. (2015). From temporary competitive advantage to sustainable competitive advantage. *British Journal of Management*, *26* (4), 617–636.
52 Barney, J. (1991). Firm resources and sustained competitive advantage. *Journal of Management*, *17* (1), 99–120.
53 Barney, J. (1991). Firm resources and sustained competitive advantage. *Journal of Management*, *17* (1), 99–120.
54 https://www.extensiv.com/blog/supply-chain-management/walmart.
55 Michael E. Porter. (1996). *What is strategy? Harvard Business Review, 74* (6), 61–78. https://hbr.org/1996/11/what-is-strategy.
56 https://easy-feedback.com/blog/customer-experience-explained/customer-experience-examples/.
57 https://easy-feedback.com/blog/customer-experience-explained/customer-experience-examples/.
58 Barney, J. (1991). Firm resources and sustained competitive advantage. *Journal of Management*, *17* (1), 99–120.
59 https://teqnoverse.medium.com/su7-ev-why-did-xiaomi-succeed-where-apple-failed-b469589d6f36.
60 https://teqnoverse.medium.com/su7-ev-why-did-xiaomi-succeed-where-apple-failed-b469589d6f36.
61 MasterClass's competitors, revenue, number of employees, funding, acquisitions & news. (September, 2020). *Owler*. Retrieved from https://www.owler.com/company/masterclass3.

FURTHER READINGS

CFI. (September 5, 2018). Ansoff Matrix: The product/market expansion grid. Corporatefinancein-stitute.com. Retrieved from https://corporatefinanceinstitute.com/resources/knowledge/strategy/ansoff-matrix/

Osterwalder, A., Pigneur, Y., Bernarda, G., Smith, A., & Papadakos, T. (2014). Value proposition design: How to create products and services customers want. *Strategyzer*. Retrieved from https://www.strat-egyzer.com/canvas/business-model-canvas

CASE REFERENCES

Agnihotri, A., & Bhattacharya, S. (2022). *MasterClass: Exploring growth*. Thousand Oaks, CA: SAGE Publications. https://doi.org/10.4135/9781529779974

About the Webby Awards. (n.d.). *Webby Awards*. Retrieved from https://www.webbyawards.com/about/

Adams, S. (May 20, 2020). MasterClass just raised $100 million to produce more celebrity edutainment. *Forbes*. Retrieved from https://www.forbes.com/sites/susanadams/2020/05/20/masterclass-just-raised-100-million-to-produce-more-celebrity-edutainment/?sh=342837253428

Can I Download a Class? (2020). *MasterClass*. Retrieved from https://masterclasshelp.zendesk.com/hc/en-us/articles/204896668-Can-I-download-a-class-

Careers at MasterClass: How Do We Make the World's Best Classes? (n.d.). Careers.masterclass.com. Retrieved from https://careers.masterclass.com/index.html

Chocano, C. (September, 2020). What is MasterClass actually selling? *The Atlantic*. Retrieved from https://www.theatlantic.com/magazine/archive/2020/09/what-is-masterclass-actually-selling/614200/

Duffy, J. (May 12, 2020). MasterClass. PC Mag. Retrieved from https://uk.pcmag.com/education-reference/125738/masterclass

Kastrenakes, J., & Peters, J. (May 20, 2020). Here are all the winners of the 2020 Webby Awards. *The Verge*. Retrieved from https://www.theverge.com/2020/5/20/21263445/2020-webby-awards-winners-lil-nas-x-nasa-jon-krasinski

Loizos, C. (February 23, 2016). MasterClass raises $15 million for online classes taught by celebrities. *TechCrunch*. Retrieved from https://techcrunch.com/2016/02/23/masterclass-raises-15-million-for-online-classes-taught-by-celebrities/

Loizos, C. (October 3, 2018). MasterClass, the education platform featuring all-star instructors, will soon teach you how to run for office, too. *TechCrunch*. Retrieved from https://techcrunch.com/2018/10/03/masterclass-new-offerings/

MasterClass Support. (2020). MasterClass: Frequently asked questions. MasterClass.com. Retrieved from https://masterclasshelp.zendesk.com/hc/en-us/articles/221036408-Frequently-Asked-Questions

MasterClass's Competitors, Revenue, Number of Employees, Funding, Acquisitions & News. (September, 2020). *Owler*. Retrieved from https://www.owler.com/company/masterclass3

Peckham, E. (September 12, 2018). MasterClass is mastering scale as a media business. *TechCrunch*. Retrieved from https://techcrunch.com/2018/09/11/masterclass-is-mastering-scale-as-a-media-business/

Rudin, D. S. (January 16, 2019). The idea that successful people can teach their secrets isn't new. Now MasterClass is selling it for $180. *Vox*. Retrieved from https://www.vox.com/the-goods/2019/1/16/18177077/masterclass-subscription-video-serena-williams-how-to-famous

Stokel-Wlaker, C. (March 26, 2019). To compete with Netflix, online piracy is upping its game. *Wired*. Retrieved from https://www.wired.co.uk/article/online-video-piracy-is-on-the-rise

Trefis Team. (March 17, 2015). Is Piracy a serious threat to Netflix? Forbes. Retrieved from https://www.forbes.com/sites/greatspeculations/2015/03/17/is-piracy-a-serious-threat-to-netflix/#430d19d47856

CHAPTER 4

Corporate-Level Strategy

Learning Objectives

After completing this chapter, students should be able to:

- Comprehend the concept of diversification and the motives for diversification;
- Examine different types of diversification;
- Examine how industry-relatedness varies across different conceptualizations;
- Conduct resource allocation decisions across different business units based on their performance.

DIVERSIFICATION

Large firms typically operate across various business segments through their business divisions or subsidiaries. Unilever has five business divisions, namely Beauty & Wellbeing, Personal Care, Home Care, Nutrition, and Ice Cream.[1] It is the top management team that decides on resource allocation across different business segments and makes decisions on which industries to compete in, which businesses to exit, and which businesses to expand through diversification. Firms diversify for several reasons, including reducing risk, driving revenue growth, earning a competitive advantage, stabilizing the business during an industry decline, facilitating cross-selling, and leveraging a corporate reputation.

- *Reducing the Risk.* Firms that diversify their business across different product lines can spread risk across various businesses, making them less vulnerable to losses in case one of the businesses performs poorly. Instead of relying only on media, Disney diversified its revenue streams by venturing into other entertainment businesses such as theme parks and the sports segment.[2]
- *Revenue Growth.* Diversification also helps businesses expand their revenue base, apart from reducing the risk associated with a single line of business. As firms enter new markets, they are able to draw on a new customer base, which helps them enhance their

DOI: 10.4324/9781003568100-4

revenue stream. Amazon began as an e-commerce business focused on books and later expanded into various product categories, enabling it to earn revenues from multiple product lines that it could sell on its online platform.[3]

- *Earning a Competitive Edge.* Sometimes, businesses can leverage knowledge from one segment into another, giving them a competitive advantage over other players in the field, while also helping to diversify their revenue streams. Xiaomi could leverage its smartphone manufacturing expertise to manufacture electric vehicles that became an instant success in the Chinese market.[4]
- *Stabilizing the Business When the Industry Is in the Decline Phase.* Sometimes, as part of the industry life cycle, when a business reaches the decline phase, diversifying into another stream of business helps to streamline and stabilize revenue flow. When the film photography business was in decline, Fuji diversified into other industries, such as medical equipment and cosmetics, to reduce its reliance on the photography industry.[5]
- *Cross Selling.* Cross-selling implies introducing new products to an existing market or launching older products to a newer market. When a financial institution, selling a retirement plan, begins to offer life insurance and other investment products, it has the potential to cross-sell these products. Financial institutions can leverage their existing customer base to introduce them to related products and services across different categories, thereby cross-selling various products and diversifying their revenue streams.
- *Leveraging Corporate Reputation.* Sometimes, when a firm earns a reputation in a given market, it diversifies into different businesses under the same brand name to leverage its reputation and expand its customer base into new product categories launched by the firm. Instead of buying products from an unknown firm, customers may prefer to purchase products and services from a reputable company, even if the firm has an established reputation in a different business segment. Leveraging reputation is more common in emerging markets, where business groups, owing to their established reputation, expand across different lines of business. For instance, the Tata Group of India operates in the food, automobile, and software sectors.[6]

TYPES OF DIVERSIFICATION

Firms may pursue different types of diversification, including horizontal, vertical, conglomerate, Concentric, and geographic.

- *Horizontal Diversification.* In this type of diversification, a company adds new, but related product or service categories to its product portfolio that appeal to its already existing customer base. Beverage companies like Coca-Cola or PepsiCo introducing new lines of drinks, such as energy drinks like BodyArmor or Gatorade, for their existing customers, is an example of horizontal diversification.[7]
- *Vertical Diversification.* This type of diversification refers to the forward or backward integration of company operations, where the company either takes a step back in its value chain and sets up its own raw material sourcing facilities (backward integration) or moves a step forward and acquires distribution channels to reach customers directly

(forward integration). Both forward and backward integration help with greater control over quality and costs. As vertical diversification eliminates suppliers and third-party retailers, profit margins also potentially increase. Apple, for instance, designs and manufactures its own chips[8] (backward integration), controls software development, and sells products through its own retail stores (forward integration). Apple thus follows a vertically integrated model with both backward and forward integration, which enables it to manage quality and costs better, as well as the entire customer experience, while also achieving significant profit margins.

- *Conglomerate Diversification.* A firm leveraging conglomerate diversification moves into a completely unrelated set of businesses. General Electric expanded into several business sectors, including aviation, healthcare, energy, and financial services, primarily through acquisitions.[9] All these businesses had no technological or commercial similarities with each other, thus making it case of conglomerate diversification.
- *Concentric Diversification.* In concentric diversification, a firm expands to product or service lines that are technologically related to its existing product lines. Concentric diversification results in technological or operational synergy, as a firm may utilize the same manufacturing or technological facilities to expand product lines for both existing and new customer bases. A desktop manufacturer also produces laptops, or a beverage company introduces different flavors of juice. When Apple diversifies from its hardware into services like iCloud and Apple Music, which are related to its core consumer technology products, it pursues concentric diversification.[10]
- *Geographical Diversification.* When a firm enters a new geographical market, typically a new country or continent, this expansion is considered geographical diversification. All multinational companies, i.e., companies that have their operations established across different countries and capture a customer base across multiple countries, make a case for geographic diversification. For example, Amazon and Spotify pursue geographic diversification.[11]

RELATED VS. UNRELATED DIVERSIFICATION

Measuring the relatedness and unrelatedness of an industry can happen in three ways, i.e., SIC (Standard industrial classification) code approach, core competence approach, and synergy approach.

- *SIC Code Approach.* According to this approach, firms exhibit related diversification, depending on similarity at the two-digit, three-digit, and four-digit SIC codes. A SIC code (Standard Industrial Classification code) refers to a four-digit number that classifies a company's primary business activity. SIC codes are also used in the Division of Corporation Finance, where staff members are assigned to review company financials based on the SIC code of the company. For example, a firm operating in the Metal Mining sector (SIC 1,000) would have officials from the Office of Energy & Transportation review the company's financials. Figure 4.1 presents a sample list of SIC codes of companies

Regulatory Offices

- **Office of Energy & Transportation**
  - Metal Mining (1000, 1040, 1090)
  - Coal Mining (1220, 1221)
  - Oil & Gas Extraction (1311)
  - Oil & Gas Services (1381)
- **Office of Real Estate & Construction**
  - Residential Construction (1520, 1531)
  - Non-Residential Construction (1540)
- **Office of Manufacturing**
  - Meat Processing (2011, 2013)
  - Poultry Processing (2015)
  - Dairy Products (2020, 2024)
  - Fruit & Vegetable Processing (2030, 2033)
  - Bakery Products (2050, 2052)
  - Beverage Manufacturing (2080, 2082, 2086)

FIGURE 4.1 Classification of SIC Codes by Regulatory Compliance Offices

Source: Developed by the Authors Based on Information Available at USS&EC. (2021, June 3). Standard Industrial Classification (SIC) code list. Retrieved from https://www.sec.gov/search-filings/standard-industrial-classification-sic-code-list

and their compliance departments. For each SIC, the first digit corresponds to a broad industry sector, the first two digits reflect a major industry group, the third digit defines the industry subgroup, and the fourth digit specifies the precise product category.[12] Thus, under Food and Kindred industry "2," 20 reflects different industry major groups like meat packaging and dairy products, further industry subgroups canned fruits and jams and jellies "203," and specific product subgroups like malt drinks and canned soft drinks "2,082" and "2,086." An industry is considered related if there is a match to a two-digit code, where a four-digit match implies 100% relatedness, a three-digit match reflects 75% relatedness, and a two-digit match indicates moderate relatedness at 50%. Figure 4.2 presents the broad industry sectors as per SIC classification.

Competency refers to skill sets that a firm can leverage across different businesses by integrating multiple streams of technology.[13] Honda Motor's core competence lies in its ability to develop small, reliable, and efficient engines.[14] Honda Motor first leveraged this core technical strength to develop two-wheelers and later diversified into four-wheeler automobiles, lawn mowers, all-terrain vehicles, and boat motors. Honda also applied its unique engine technology and manufacturing expertise across aircraft engines.[15] Thus, although aircraft, lawn mowers, and four-wheelers apparently belong to different product categories, they are all related diversification for Honda, owing to similarity in engine-related technology. Similarly, Casio's specialization in miniaturization and precision mechanics drove it to diversify across various electronics product categories, including calculators, watches, and electronic musical instruments.[16] For musical instruments, Casio leveraged its expertise in precision electronics and miniaturization, developed through calculators and watches, to develop reliable digital keyboards and pianos.[17]

- *Synergy Approach.* The third approach to related diversification is based on synergy. Businesses are considered related when they can create synergy, which occurs when two

Industry Sectors (Code Classification)

- **0100–0999 Agriculture, Forestry, and Fishing**
  Crop production, livestock farming, forestry operations, and fishing activities related to natural resource harvesting.
- **1000–1499 Mining**
  Extraction of natural resources including metals, coal, crude petroleum, and natural gas.
- **1500–1799 Construction**
  Residential and non-residential building construction, infrastructure development, and related contracting services.
- **2000–3999 Manufacturing**
  Transformation of raw materials into finished or intermediate goods through mechanical, chemical, or industrial processes.
- **4000–4999 Transportation, Communications, and Utilities**
  Transportation services, communication networks, and utilities providing electricity, gas, and water.
- **5000–5199 Wholesale Trade**
  Bulk distribution of goods to retailers, businesses, and institutional buyers.
- **5200–5999 Retail Trade**
  Direct sale of goods and merchandise to final consumers through physical or online outlets.
- **6000–6799 Finance, Insurance, and Real Estate**
  Financial services including banking, insurance, credit institutions, and real estate activities.
- **7000–8999 Services**
  Professional, personal, educational, healthcare, hospitality, and other service-based industries.

FIGURE 4.2 Industry Sector Classification by Standard Industry Code Ranges

Source: Developed by the Authors Based on Information Available at Infobel Pro. (2023, September 29). What is a SIC code? Retrieved from https://www.infobelpro.com/en/blog/sic-codes

or more businesses develop benefits together.[18] Different types of synergies can be realized across businesses, including cost synergy, revenue synergy, and financial synergy.

Cost synergy implies a reduction in operating costs resulting from the sharing of resources, which typically arises from economies of scope.[19] Thus, when a company shares manufacturing, distribution, or sales facilities across business units, resources are utilized more efficiently, resulting in cost savings and creating cost synergy. Pharmaceuticals and cosmetics manufacturing may occur in the same facilities, as both require a sterile, highly controlled environment. Their mixing, processing, and packaging equipment is also similar. Accordingly, to achieve cost synergy, Johnson & Johnson not only manufactures a wide range of pharmaceutical products across several key therapeutic areas, including immunology, oncology, neuroscience, infectious diseases, cardiovascular, metabolism, and pulmonary hypertension,[20] but also manufactures personal care products under brands like Neutrogena and Clean & Clear, among others.[21]

Revenue synergy arises when two businesses complement each other in a way where the joint revenues earned by a diversified company from two businesses are potentially higher when two different lines of business operate. This higher revenue usually occurs because of complementary products, cross-selling, or gaining access to new markets because of revenue synergy. Disney's diversification into theme parks, television, and merchandise created an interconnected intellectual property (IP) ecosystem, where content was cross promoted across different businesses, including film, television, streaming, theme parks, and merchandise. Furthermore, a successful Marvel movie led to the development of a new Marvel-related attraction at a theme park, a related Disney+ series, and associated merchandise.[22] Thus, Disney leveraged a single hit from one business to result in multiple income streams. This "synergy" minimized the risk and maximized the value through cross-selling.

A business can appear to be a case of unrelated diversification according to the SIC approach, but it may display relatedness according to other approaches. When Philip Morris decided to venture into the pharmaceutical business, particularly in lung inhalers,[23] according to the SIC code approach, as a tobacco company, this appeared to be a case of unrelated diversification. The SIC code for pharmaceuticals is 2,834. The four-digit SIC code for tobacco and related products is 2,131. The two businesses had just one-digit code similarity, i.e., "2," implying unrelated businesses. However, Philip Morris acknowledged its expertise in inhalation and aerosolization, which could be helpful in drug delivery. Anthony Hickey, an inhaled drug delivery expert at RTI International, a nonprofit research institute, also mentioned that Philip Morris's expertise on the behavior of aerosols in the lungs could be of immense help in developing treatments for chronic obstructive pulmonary disease (COPD) and other lung diseases.[24] Thus, from a core competency approach, Philip Morris's diversification into the pharma sector was related. Similarly, according to the SIC code approach, insurance and tobacco businesses are also unrelated (manufacturing vs. service, completely different SIC codes, with no match even at the one-digit level). By venturing into life insurance and offering discounts on premiums to those switching from tobacco to nicotine, Philip Morris could expand its customer base for both smoke-free products and insurance products.[25]

PERFORMANCE DIFFERENCES IN RELATED VS. UNRELATED DIVERSIFICATION

Research studies suggest that as the unrelatedness of businesses increases during diversification, the overall performance of the corporate parent tends to decrease.[26] The entropy approach determines the extent to which a corporate parent is relatedly or unrelatedly diversified. *Entropy is a measure of a firm's diversification and is calculated*[27] as follows:

$$E_T = \sum_{i=1}^{N} P_i \ln\left(\frac{1}{P_i}\right)$$

where:

E_T = Entropy measure of total diversification.

P_i = Proportion of business activity (sales) in SIC and "*i*," for a corporation with "*N*" difference four-digit SIC businesses.

ln = natural logarithm

Example of E_T Calculation for a Four-Digit SIC Businesses

A firm operates in film photography, X-ray apparatus, and cosmetics business, and the revenues from each division are USD (273 + 116 + 472) million = USD 760 million. Next, the proportions of sales by the given four-digit SIC codes can be calculated as follows: USD 273 million/USD 760 million, USD 116 million/USD 760 million, and USD 372 million/USD 760 million, which are 0.36, 0.15, and 0.49, respectively.

According to the formula for E_T, we divide "1" by proportion of sales = 1/0.35, 1/0.15, and 1/0.48 = 2.85; 6.66; 1.61. We further take ln (natural log) of these values = ln(2.85); ln(6.66); ln(2.32) = 1.04; 1.89; 0.47. Next, we multiply ln values with proportion of sales = 0.35 × 1.04; 0.15 × 1.89; 0.62 × 0.47 = 0.3640; 0.2835; 0.2914. Finally, we add all values = 0.3640 + 0.2835 + 0.2914 = 0.9389. This is the total diversification index (entropy) for a firm.

Example of E_T Calculation for a Two-Digit SIC Businesses

We use the same example and a similar procedure as used to calculate the entropy for *four-digit SIC Businesses*. The firm's total revenue from film photography, X-ray apparatus, and cosmetics businesses was USD (273 + 116 + 472) million, equaling USD 760 million.

The firm's proportions of sales by given two-digit SIC codes are as follows: Film photography and X-ray businesses share the same two-digit SIC, i.e., "38." Thus, we combine the sales using two-digit SIC codes before dividing them by total sales. Accordingly, the new proportion at two-digit SIC business of photography and X-ray is USD (273 + 116) million/USD 760 million = 0.51, and for cosmetics, the proportion is USD 472 million/USD 760 million = 0.62.

Next, dividing "1" by proportion of sales = 1/0.51; 1/0.62 = 1.96; 1.61 and taking ln (natural log) of the proportions = ln(1.96); ln(1.61) = 0.67; 0.47. Then, multiplying ln values with proportion of sales = 0.51 × 0.67; 0.62 × 0.47 = 0.3417; 0.2914. Summing all values = 0.3417 + 0.2914 = 0.6331. This is the entropy of unrelated diversification, as firms with different two-digit SIC codes are unrelated.

Finally, we can calculate the *related diversification index* by subtracting the unrelated diversification index from the total diversification index, i.e., 0.9389 – 0.6331 = 0.3058. As the entropy value of unrelated diversification is higher than that of related diversification, this implies that the firm is more unrelatedly diversified than related.

CORPORATE PORTFOLIO MANAGEMENT THROUGH BCG MATRIX

This BCG matrix guides corporate parent for resource allocation decisions.[28] This matrix encourages CEOs to invest in high-potential businesses that achieve high-growth rates in high-growth industries, i.e., Stars and Question Marks. The matrix also encourages CEOs to harvest their top-performing businesses in stable or declining industries, i.e., Cash Cows. The stable profits can be used to fund stars, question marks, or other new ventures. Finally, the BCG matrix advises CEOs to divest or reposition underperforming Dogs, i.e., businesses that are performing poorly in a declining industry.[29]

In the BCG matrix, corporate business portfolios are plotted in a four-square matrix. The Y-axis stands for the rate of market growth, and the X-axis represents the market share of the corporate division in a given industry. The matrix has four quadrants, namely: Stars, Question Marks, Cash Cows, and Dogs. Stars represent a corporate division that operates in a high-growth industry and holds a significant market share in its respective industry. Investment is necessary to maintain market leadership. Cash cows represent business units that operate in a low-growth industry but possess a high market share, resulting in steady cash flow. Corporate parents are encouraged not to divest such businesses but to utilize earnings to support other parts of the business. Question marks operate in high-growth markets but have low market share, requiring close analysis to determine their future potential. Dogs refer to business units that are low performers in a given industry, and the industry is also in a stage of decline.

BCG Analysis for Coca-Cola

Table 4.1 presents a BCG matrix.

TABLE 4.1 BCG Matrix

		Market Share	
		High	Low
Industry growth rate	High	Stars	Question mark
	Low	Cash cow	Dogs

Source: Developed by the authors.

- *Core Competence Approach.* Core *Star (Diet Coke and Coke Zero):* Given the increasing awareness of the adverse effects of sugar and growing health consciousness among consumers, the market for sugar-free drinks is booming. Capitalizing on this trend, Coca-Cola launched Diet Coke and Coke Zero, achieving a high market share and making them star performers.[30]
- *Cash Cow (Coca-Cola Classic).* As consumer preferences shift toward healthy beverages, the market for sugar-based beverages, such as soft drinks, has been in decline. However, Coca-Cola Classic remains the top performer in this category, making it a cash cow for Coca-Cola.[31]
- *Question Mark (Dasani).* The bottled water market is a high-growth market. However, unlike the beverage category, Coca-Cola is struggling to maintain a dominant market position in the bottled water category, facing competition from other players, such as Nestlé, whose brand is a better performer. Coca-Cola's bottled water brand, Dasani, held a rank of 12 in terms of market leadership, making it a distant player from the top position.[32] Dasani is thus a question mark for Coca-Cola. Coca-Cola has the opportunity to increase Dasani's market share, given the market growth and demand, and needs to refine the competitive strategy for Dasani.
- *Dogs (Coca-Cola BlāK).* Coca-Cola tried new products in slow-growth markets such as sugar beverages. It accordingly launched Coca-Cola BlāK (coffee-flavored Coke). However, it was not well-received by consumers, and finally, Cola discontinued this category.[33]

CORPORATE STRATEGY IN EMERGING MARKETS THROUGH BUSINESS GROUPS

Business groups present a special case of a conglomerate firm, where business units are unrelatedly diversified across different industries and the businesses link with each other via common ownership, but in a more complex manner than a typical conglomerate.[34] A business group has a *network of interconnected firms* through equity holdings of family members, and it acts as a quasi-internal market for financial and human resources.[35] Business groups can be of different types, such as family-owned groups that are more prevalent in emerging markets like India, where various family members hold equity across multiple businesses and pass them down across different generations.[36] The Reliance group of Ambani's and the Tata group, led by the late Ratan Tata, are prominent examples.

Then, business groups can also be led by the government, as seen in China, where state-owned enterprises are more prevalent, such as PetroChina.[37] In Japan, business groups are referred to as Keiretsu, and common ownership across businesses is held by major banks.[38] Mitsubishi Group and Toyota Group are prime examples. They are also referred to as financially linked groups. Business groups in these markets rely on politicians for protection against global competitors, as well as assistance with loans from public banks offering low-interest rates or subsidies, and public sector contracts.[39] Politicians, on the other hand, expected business groups to contribute toward state-led initiatives and enhance job opportunities.[40]

ASSIGNMENT QUESTIONS

1. What are the different reasons for a firm's diversification? Give one example from your home country for each reason you explore.
2. What are the different types of diversification? Give one example of each type from your home country as you explain different types of diversification.
3. Explain three different approaches of related and unrelated diversification. Give two examples where a firm may be relatedly diversified from one perspective but unrelated diversification from another perspective.
4. Conduct BCG matrix analysis for one of the multi-divisional companies in your home country.

CASE STUDY

4.1

Strategic Diversification in a Declining Industry

An SPSS-Based MANCOVA Analysis for FickClick

In April 2025, Charles Smith, CEO of FickClick (a hypothetical US-based startup), sought to expand his business. He operated in the digital photography industry, providing still and video portrait photography services to the general public, but he was experiencing revenue losses. As the photography industry was in decline (Cooke, 2025), Smith faced a dilemma: should he pursue growth opportunities in related photography sectors or look to unrelated industries for new revenue streams, seeking a path to sustainable competitive advantage?

Smith wanted to assess his chances of success if he pursued unrelated diversification. To inform his decision, he hired a strategy consultancy firm to analyze the dynamics of related and unrelated diversification and their impact on financial performance. The consultancy firm collected annual reports from 100 US firms in 19 service sectors that diversified in 2024, noting each firm's ROA, ROCE, and whether diversification was related (1) or unrelated (0). Relatedness was determined using two-digit SIC codes; a move was deemed related if the new unit matched the primary industry's code. Firm size, measured as the log number of employees, was included as a control variable. The consultancy firm provides the collected data in *Data.xlsx*.

See Data file in Online Support Material in www.routledge.com/9781032938912.

Using SPSS (Statistical Package for the Social Sciences) Version 31.0, the consultancy firm conducted a Multivariate Analysis of Covariance (MANCOVA) on the dataset. See Figure 4.3, for steps of **SPSS Steps of MANCOVA.**

The consultancy firm provides the dataset in *Data.xlsx* and reports the statistical results in *Output.xlsx*. In the analysis, the consultants treated ROA and ROCE as dependent (outcome) variables, diversification type ("1" = related; "0" = unrelated) as the independent (predictor) variable, and firm size as the covariate. The consultancy firm then presented the MANCOVA results to Smith.

Please see online Support Material: Output data file in www.routledge.com/9781032938912.

Go to Analyze→ General Linear Model → Multivariate (click it)→ Input ROCE and ROA variables in the Dependent Variables list box; Input the Diversification variable in the Fixed Factor(s) list box [Diversification coded as "1"= related diversification and "0"= unrelated diversification]; Input the Firm Size variable in the Covariate(s) list box → Click on Model and select Full Factorial→ Click Continue →Click on EM (Estimated Marginal) Means→ Input Diversification Variable in Display Means for list box; Select Compare main effects and select Sidak as the Confidence interval adjustment method→ Click Continue→ Click on Options→ Select Descriptive Statistics, Homogeneity Tests, and Estimates of effect size→ Click Continue→ Click Ok.

FIGURE 4.3 SPSS Steps of Multivariate Analysis of Covariance (MANCOVA)

Source: Developed by the Authors

DISCUSSION QUESTIONS

1. Why did the consultant choose MANCOVA instead of ANOVA for the analysis?
2. Based on the MANCOVA results, how does diversification type influence firm financial performance (ROA and ROCE) after controlling for firm size, and what strategic implications should Smith draw from these findings?
3. How should Smith interpret the empirical evidence on diversification performance, and how should he integrate SIC classification, core competencies, and strategic fit frameworks when deciding his diversification strategy?

FURTHER READING

Field, A. (2024). *Discovering statistics using IBM SPSS statistics* (6th ed., Chapter 17, pp. 785–810). Thousand Oaks, CA: SAGE Publications.

REFERENCE

Cooke, A. (February 4, 2025). Why photography is struggling and what that means for you. *Fstoppers.* Retrieved from https://fstoppers.com/business/why-photography-struggling-and-what-means-692029

CASE STUDY **4.2**

Growth Strategic Options of Kraft Heinz

Agnihotri, A., & Bhattacharya, S. (2021). *Growth strategic options of Kraft Heinz*. Sage Business Cases. https://doi.org/10.4135/9781529754216

INTRODUCTION

In February 2019, Pittsburg, USA-based Kraft Heinz Co (hereafter *Kraft Heinz*), which produces a wide variety of food products, made three announcements. Kraft Heinz stated that it had written down brand goodwill by USD 15.4 billion, implying that expected future earnings could be reduced by USD 25 relative to previous estimates (Tully, 2019). It also informed shareholders that the US Securities and Exchange Commission was probing into some accounting policies of the company. Finally, in the fourth quarter of 2018, the company incurred USD 12.6 billion in losses (Kraft-Heinz Is in Trouble, 2019). According to Bernardo Hees, then CEO of Kraft Heinz, brands were written down due to supply chain and operation problems (Kraft-Heinz Is in Trouble, 2019).

Industry experts had differing opinions about the perils of Kraft Hein, which they primarily attributed to zero-based budgeting (ZBB). (ZBB involves the creation of budgets from the scratch rather than by extrapolation from previous year's expenditures.) Kraft Heinz adopted ZBB from 3G Capital Inc to enhance efficiency. 3G Capital Inc is a New York-based global investment company and a substantial shareholder in Kraft Heinz. Commenting on ZBB, Eddy Hargreaves, an analyst at Investec Ltd, an international investment group, stated that other consumer product companies, such as Unilever, Mondelez International, Diageo, and Kellogg, also used ZBB but that these companies did not experience consequences similar to those of Kraft Heinz. Hargreaves further explained,

> I think it's a black eye for Kraft Heinz management for not implementing it in as a sophisticated way as might be necessary, or maybe they just implemented it too hard, too fast, I don't think ZBB per se is the problem.
>
> (Geller & Naidu, 2019)

Also, the head of investment at a European consulting firm stated, "To catch up with the shift of consumer demand for better-for-you and sustainable food, you have to innovate. And to innovate you simply can't use ZBB" (Geller & Naidu, 2019).

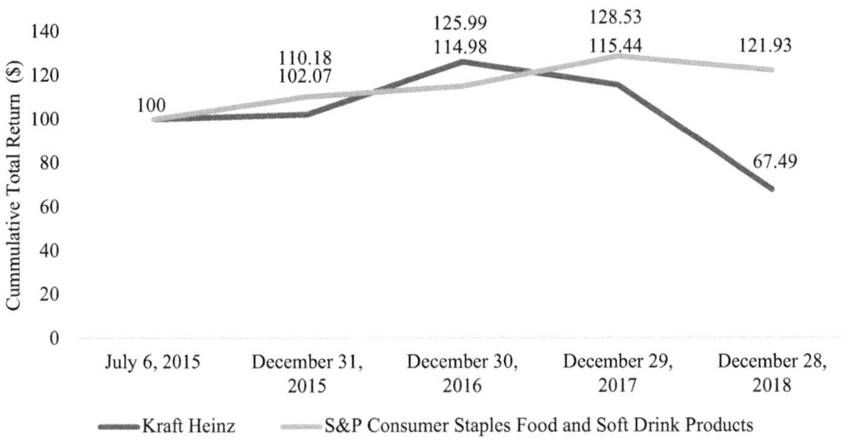

FIGURE 4.4 Cumulative Total Return on Kraft Heinz Common Stock Versus S&P Consumer Staples Food and Soft Drink Products (USD)

Source: Form 10-K: The Kraft Heinz Company. (June 7, 2019). *The Kraft Heinz Company: Investor relations*. Retrieved from http://ir.kraftheinzcompany.com/static-files/e0ec203b-d7c4-4025-b263-52cfe321960f

Furthermore, Kraft Heinz became the worst performing S&P 500 Consumer Staples Food and Soft Drink Products stock (see Figure 4.3). In February 2019, Kraft Heinz had leverage that was 4.4 times the company's 2018 adjusted earnings. The company stated that its goal has been to slash the leverage ratio to just three times earnings (Egan, 2019). According to analysts, high leverage could leave less cash for investment in Kraft Heinz's faltering brands (Egan, 2019). In July 2019, the company appointed a new CEO, Miguel Patricio, who as a marketing head had previously turned around Anheuser-Busch InBev SA/NV (AB InBev), a Leuven, Belgium based manufacturer of alcoholic beverages (Egan, 2019). Patricio expressed his intent to focus on rebuilding Kraft Heinz brands such as *Osar Mayer* and *Velveeta*. He further stated, "I think the obsession for efficiency has to be much bigger than the obsession for cutting costs" (Naidu, 2019). Analysts considered Patricio's appointment an encouraging sign of Kraft's focus on growth than efficiency (Sanchez, 2019).

What strategic options should Patricio pursue for the growth of Kraft Heinz? Should he discontinue the implementation of ZBB and invest more in innovation? Is a high debt earnings ratio likely to impact Patricio's decision? How should he manage the brand portfolio of Kraft Heinz?

BACKGROUND

Kraft Heinz was (in 2015) the third-largest food and beverage company in North America and the fifth-largest food company in the world. Eight of its brands were worth more than USD 1 billion. Some of the iconic brands included *Kraft, Heinz, Weight Watchers' Smart Ones, Capri Sun, Oscar Mayer*, and *Philadelphia*. A merger of Kraft Foods and H. J. Heinz Co in March 2015 gave birth to Kraft Heinz. In 2013, Warren Buffet, CEO of Berkshire Hathaway Inc, partnered with 3G Capital to acquire Heinz for USD 28 billion. In 2015, Buffett and 3G

TABLE 4.2 Kraft Heinz Financials (2016–2018)

	2016	2017	2018
Net sales (USD billion)	26.30	26.08	26.27
Cost of products sold (USD billion)	17.15	17.04	17.35
Gross profit (USD billion)	9.15	9.03	8.92
Selling, general and administrative expenses (USD billion)	3.55	2.98	19.14
Operating income (USD billion)	5.60	6.06	−10.22
Interest expense (USD billion)	1.28	1.23	1.28
Net income (USD Billion)	3.61	10.93	−10.25
Basic earnings per share (USD)	2.81	8.98	−8.36

Source: Form 10-K: The Kraft Heinz Company. (June 7, 2019). *The Kraft Heinz Company: Investor relations*. Retrieved from http://ir.kraftheinzcompany.com/static-files/e0ec203b-d7c4-4025-b263-52cfe321960f.

Capital again teamed up to acquire Kraft Foods for USD 40 billion (Rosenbaum, 2019). In 2018, Kraft Heinz had 38,000 employees. For the financial year 2018, the company had net sales of USD 26.27 billion and earnings before interest, taxes, depreciation, and amortization of USD 7 billion (Kraft Heinz: Key Metrics, 2019) (see Table 4.2).

Need for Merger

3G Capital estimated savings of USD 1.7 billion from the merger of Kraft Foods and H. J. Heinz Co (Hirsch, 2019a). One of the driving forces for the merger was the anticipation of better bargaining power with retailers and specialty stores. The company expected more shelf space, resulting in a higher operating margin (Trefis Team, 2015). Kraft Heinz also pressured retailers for in-store promotions and shelf space, based on its status of being the third-largest food company in the USA, which made them believe they would have a better bargaining power over retailers. Consequently, in 2017, they lost the contract for Planters peanuts with Walmart's Sam's Club. Later, after several rounds of negotiations, Walmart restored the contract. However, this temporary loss of this contract resulted in a 28% decline in sales in the salted snacks category of Kraft Heinz (Hirsch, 2019b). Buffet stated "We may have made a mistake in terms of trying to push hard against certain… retailers and finding out that we weren't as strong as we thought" (Hirsch, 2019b).

Furthermore, in 2019, Kraft Heinz's Research and Development (R&D) investment was 0.4% of sales and was less than half the amount spent by competitors, such as Mondelez International or Nestle SA (Barker, 2019). According to media reports, Kraft-Heinz's marketing spend was also less than peers. In 2018, Kraft Heinz's marketing spend was 3.2% of its sales, where for AB InBev, marketing expense was 20% of its sales (Sonenshine, 2019). Consequently, for fiscal 2018, Kraft Heinz reported losses (see Table 4.2). This occurred when in the USA the consumer packaged goods industry was already experiencing a rapid transition of power, from big household-name brands to venture capital funded-startups who offered more healthy offerings to customers (Duberstein, 2018c). Furthermore, large retailers, with their private label brands such as **Costco's** *Kirkland* brand or **Kroger's** *Simple Truth* brand, were of reasonable quality and low-priced (Duberstein, 2018b). According to research conducted by Nielsen in 2019, in the USA, private label brands experienced sales growth of 33.2% between 2012 and 2017, while national brands gained 1% (Private Label Growth Outshines, 2019).

POST-MERGER GROWTH STRATEGY

Zero-Based Budgeting

Kraft Heinz was burdened with a heavy debt of USD 30 billion when the company turned to ZBB in 2017 (Gasparro & Monga, 2019). 3G Capital, the owner of Kraft Heinz, was considered a standard-bearer for ZBB. ZBB is an accounting practice that the company had perfected and popularized, on a global stage (Gasparro & Monga, 2019). 3G Capital used a similar approach to turn around the poor performance of AB InBev and Burger King (Dowd, 2019).

Using ZBB, Kraft Heinz made deep cuts to expenditure in all aspects ranging from corporate overhead to R&D. Within four months of the merger, the company terminated 10% of the employees (Sanchez, 2019). In a single day, the company asked 11 out of 12 senior executives to leave (Colvin, 2017). Between 2016 and 2017, Kraft Heinz first reduced its cost of goods sold by 4.4%. Next, Selling, General and Administrative Expense was also reduced by 15% during this period. R&D expenditure was reduced from USD 120 million in 2016 to USD 93 million in 2017, which, according to analysts, implied muscle was being eliminated with the fat (Tully, 2019).

Data-Driven Marketing

As a part of data-driven marketing efforts, Kraft Heinz largely relied on social media interaction data to drive sales. For example, based on social media data, the company identified three consumer segments who were consuming cheese products of the Philadelphia brand. These were Quick & Easy, Kid Friendly, and Entertaining. Next, Kraft Heinz catered to these consumer segments with the most appropriate advertisement (Post-Integration Business Update ..., 2018). This helped the company cut the cost of media impression by 40% between 2015 and 2017 while raising the quality of impression at the same time (Post-Integration Business Update ..., 2018).

Growth in Emerging Markets

In emerging markets such as Brazil, China, India, Argentina, and Malaysia, an increase in disposable income has led to an increase in demand for convenience and processed foods (Demand for Ready-to-Eat ...," 2019). In the global ranking of the market potential index of the food processing industry, China and India stood at first and fourth positions, respectively, among all countries in the world (Food Processing: Market Potential Index, 2017) (see Table 4.3). Kraft Heinz also reported growth in these markets. Its net sales for the second quarter of 2018 increased by 0.7%, largely due to growth in emerging markets (Kraft Heinz Benefits ..., 2018). To fasten its entry in emerging markets, in 2017, Kraft Heinz unsuccessfully

TABLE 4.3 2017 Food Processing Market Potential Index (Emerging Economies)

	Rank	Market Growth Rate Index	Market Capacity Index	Market Size Index
China	1	53	100	100
India	4	45	80	38
Malaysia	25	58	9	9
Brazil	37	25	50	21
Argentina	70	42	19	11

Source: Food Processing: Market Potential Index. (2017). *International Business Center Michigan State University*. Retrieved from https://ibc-static.broad.msu.edu/sites/globaledge/medc/industry-mpi/pdfs/food-processing-MPI-Insights-and-Rankings-2017.pdf.

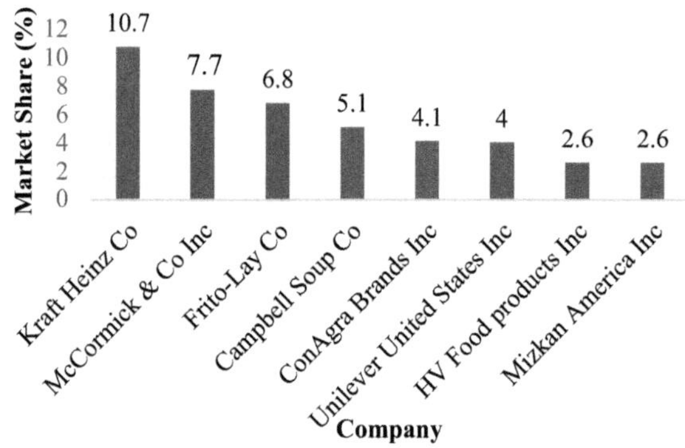

FIGURE 4.5 Company Shares of Sauces, Dressings, and Condiments in the USA (%) (2018)

Source: Sauces, Dressings and Condiments in the US. (November 2019). Passport. Retrieved from https://www.portal.euromonitor.com/portal/magazine/homemain

tried to acquire Unilever for USD 143 billion, as it had a strong presence in emerging markets (Kraft Heinz Pivots ..., 2017). Kraft Heinz reinvested its foreign subsidiary earnings to support growth in international markets (Form 10-K ..., 2016). In January 2016, Kraft Heinz had USD 1.6 billion of cash and short-term investments in possession from international subsidiaries. Internationally, Kraft Heinz was present in 30 countries (Form 10-K ..., 2016). As a part of its restructuring effort, 3G Capital closed some of the international plants, such as one in Spain (Colvin, 2017).

Brand Portfolio

For managing its brand portfolio, Kraft Heinz used different approaches for different brands. For example, in the sauces, dressings, and condiments category, Kraft Heinz's brand was the market leader in the USA (see Figure 4.5). Furthermore, this product category contributed most to the revenue stream of Kraft Heinz (see Table 4.4). In the USA, the sauces and condiments market was expected to grow annually by 1.3% between 2019 and 2023 (Consumer

TABLE 4.4 Net Sales by Product Category (USD Billion) (2017–2018)

Product Category	2016	2017	2018
Condiment and sauces	6.30	6.43	6.75
Cheese and dairy	5.54	5.41	5.29
Ambient foods	2.49	2.56	2.58
Frozen and chilled foods	2.55	2.58	2.55
Meats and seafood	2.66	2.57	2.51
Refreshment beverages	1.52	1.51	1.51
Coffee	1.49	1.42	1.44
Instant and nutrition	0.76	0.76	0.76
Deserts, toppings, and baking	1.05	1.03	1.04
Nuts and salted snacks	1.07	0.97	0.97
Other	0.85	0.84	0.89

Source: Form 10-K: The Kraft Heinz Company. (June 7, 2019). *The Kraft Heinz Company: Investor relations*. Retrieved from http://ir.kraftheinz company.com/static-files/e0ec203b-d7c4-4025-b263-52cfe321960f.

Market Outlook: Sauces ..., 2019). In response to this forecast, Kraft Heinz strengthened its offering in the Ketchup category by launching *Heinz Organic* and *Heinz Sriracha* ketchup versions to suit the taste of different sets of consumers (Post-Integration Business Update ..., 2018). Kraft Heinz's competence in the ketchup category was further exploited to launch mustard and barbecue sauce versions in 2018. In the packaged meal category, which was the third-most important category for Kraft Heinz, the company launched macaroni and cheese, which were free from any artificial flavors (Post-Integration Business Update ..., 2018).

For the *Oscar Mayer* brand, Kraft Heinz eliminated traditional hot dogs and lunch meats and launched in 2017 a new version that had no added nitrates and no artificial preservatives in their meats; making it the first national-level manufacturer in the USA to do so. Kraft Heinz did this without any changes in prices. Greg Guidotti, Head of Marketing of the Oscar Mayer brand, stated, "*Oscar Mayer* is America's most iconic hot dog brand, and, as the equity leader, we felt it was time to take a stand for the love of a better hot dog." He further added, "We heard from hot dog fans across the country that they wanted a hot dog without artificial preservatives in meat or added nitrates and nitrites—all without compromising on the great *Oscar Mayer* taste they know and love" (The Oscar Mayer Brand's ..., 2017).

Similarly, in the frozen food category, in 2016 Kraft Heinz launched a new brand, *Devour*, which the company considered the single biggest innovation launch in the frozen meals category (Post-Integration Business Update ..., 2018). Kraft Heinz also re-invented the nutritional offerings of the existing *Smart Ones* brand and launched *SmartMade*, through which the company offered a healthy diet frozen option to customers. In 2017, these two brands, Devour and SmartMade, generated USD 100 million in retail sales in the USA (Post-Integration Business Update ..., 2018). This was considered a strong growth in revenues after years of decline in the frozen food category (Ballard, 2017) (see Figure 4.6 for the market share of leading brands

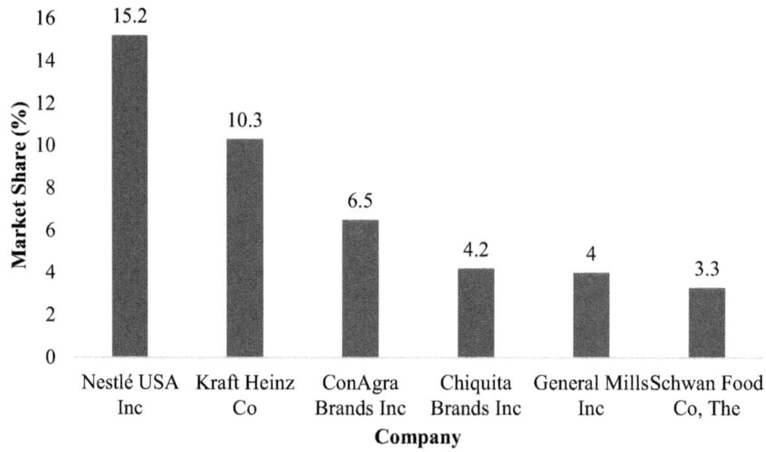

FIGURE 4.6 Company Shares of Ready Meals in the USA (%) (2018)

Source: Ready Meals in the US. (November 2019). Passport. Retrieved from https://www.portal.euromonitor.com/portal/magazine/homemain

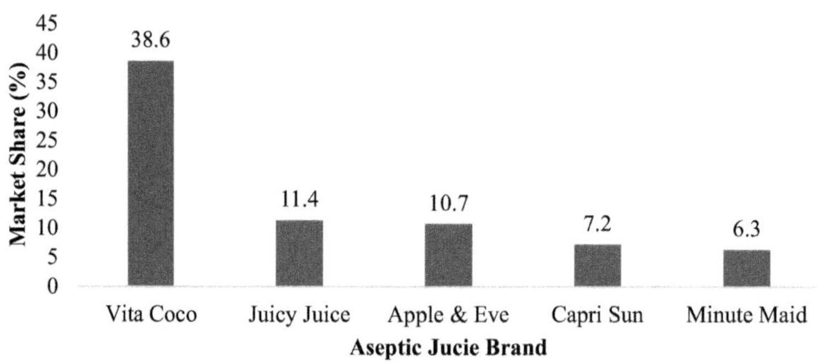

FIGURE 4.7 Aseptic Juice Brand Share in the USA (%) (2018–2019)

Source: 2019 State of the Beverage Industry: Juice Category Challenged to Maintain Market Share. (July 15, 2019). *Beverage Industry.* Retrieved from https://www.bevindustry.com/articles/92243-2019-state-of-the-beverage-industry-juice-category-challenged-to-maintain-market-share

in the Ready Meals segment, of which the frozen food category is a critical sub-component). According to The NPD Group, a market intelligence company headquartered in the UK, with an increasing millennial population, the frozen meal category was bound to grow (U.S. Consumers Return ...," 2019). Even in the beverage category where Kraft Heinz's market share was relatively low, in 2017 the company launched four new variants of Capri Sun (a juice brand), made with all-natural ingredients and with no added preservatives. Nevertheless, the sale of Capri Sun decreased during 2018 and 2019 (Haddon, 2019) (see Figure 4.7 for Capri Sun's market share in the US market in 2018–2019). This was despite the juice segment growing in the USA at only a 1% compound annual growth rate with a 55% contribution from bars and restaurants (Consumer Market Outlook: Juices: USA, 2019).

Kraft Heinz also innovated its marketing strategy by hiring new employees as salespeople for working in supermarkets, rather than relying on third-party merchandizers. These salespeople were given 60,000 hours of custom-made training on industry trends, the latest innovation, R&D, and marketing trends. Hees, the former CEO of Kraft Heinz, stated, "We started doing this in 2017. I can guarantee you that it's paying off and we're actually doubling down on this" (Duberstein, 2018b).

According to analysts, the innovation efforts of Kraft Heinz were not complete. For instance, in the cheese and dairy segment, which was the second-most selling product category for the company (see Table 4.4), Kraft Heinz did not invest in trends such as artisanal cheese (Hirsch, 2019b). In 2018, the artisanal cheese market in the US was expected to increase to USD 19 billion, with smaller cheesemakers making half of the total market (Siegner, 2018).

GROWTH OF COMPETITORS

In 2018, global merger and acquisition activities among the world's top 50 consumer goods companies, including Procter & Gamble, L'Oréal, Nestle SA, and Unilever, increased by 45%—in comparison to 60 such deals in 2017—at a value of USD 145 billion (Cheng, 2018). Most food companies were acquiring smaller and more innovative brands that reported high-growth rates, such as Kellogg's acquisition of Kashi, General Mills acquisition of Annie's Organics, or Danone acquisition of WhiteWave Foods (Kraft Heinz Pivots ..., 2017). Conagra Foods agreed to buy Pinnacle Foods for nearly USD 11 billion, and General Mills acquired natural pet foods label Blue Buffalo for USD 8 billion. Many of these acquisitions occurred in emerging markets (Cheng, 2018). Nestlé, for example, acquired Egyptian instant coffee company Caravan and L'Oréal bought a Mexican cosmetics company. Several competitors invested in startups as well. Unilever, for example, invested in the meal-kit startup Sun Basket and digital advertising startup Celtra (Cheng, 2018).

The Kraft Heinz strategy resonated with these trends. In 2018, the company acquired Ethical Bean, a Canadian coffee brand, which was Canada's first "B Corporations" (i.e., a company that met certain high standards of environmental and social stewardship). For example, scanning the QR code on Ethical Bean's coffee package informed consumers about the source (i.e., the farm) of coffee beans (Duberstein, 2018c). In March 2018, Kraft Heinz also launched Springboard, a platform dedicated to accelerating the growth of food and beverage startups, especially those startups that had Natural & Organic, Specialty & Craft, Health & Performance, or experiential brands. Sergio Eleuterio, General Manager of Springboard Brands, stated, "We are committed to support and partner with teams that will impact the future of our industry." "We are actively searching for emergent, authentic brands that can expand into new categories, and are looking to build a network of founders to help shape the future of foods and beverages" (Kraft Heinz Launches New Platform ..., 2018). Selected teams had a chance to not only receive funding from Kraft Heinz but also receive support for additional funding (Kraft Heinz Launches New Platform ..., 2018). By March 2019, Kraft Heinz supported five selected brands, namely Blake's Seed—makers of allergen-free snacks, Brami—manufacturer of shelf-stable, marinated lupini beans, Ka-Pop!—the maker of ancient grain-based chips,

Origin Almond—manufacturer of liquid essence of almonds based on cold-press technology, and Tiny Giants—maker of plant-based yogurts (Scully, 2019).

Kraft Heinz competitors attempted to adopt the ZBB strategy. 3G Capital insiders mentioned that acquiescing to investors' pressure, several food companies also implemented ZBB, which made them less lucrative acquisition targets (Gasparro & Monga, 2019). For instance, Campbell restructured its organization to eliminate management layers, Kellogg slashed 2,000 jobs, and the Mondelez ex-CEO stopped flying first class. Mondelez also held fire-drills to rehearse how executives would tackle phone calls from 3G Capital with an acquisition offer (Gasparro & Monga, 2019). In terms of product performance, some competitors, such as Conagra Foods, were doing well in the frozen meal category (Hirsch, 2018), whereas other competitors, such as Campbell soup, were facing a crisis similar to that faced by Kraft Heinz. Analysts believed these companies were experiencing difficulty because of the increasing shift of consumers toward healthy alternatives (Hirsch, 2018).

FAILED DIVESTURE EFFORTS

In 2019, Kraft Heinz tried to sell four of its big brands that were not doing well. These included Breakstone's sour cream and cottage cheese, Plasmon baby food, Maxwell House (a leading brand in the ground coffee market of the USA, see Figure 4.8), and Ore-Ida frozen potato products. Kraft Heinz expected to sell Breakstone's for USD 400 million, Plasmons for USD 800 million, Ore-Ida for USD 2 billion, and Maxwell House for more than USD 3 billion. However, due to a lack of consumer demand for these products, potential buyers also lowered their interest and none of them could be sold (Sun, 2019). Kraft Heinz expected to use the proceeds from the divesture of these brands for debt payment (Hirsch, 2019c). In 2019, Kraft Heinz reduced dividend payments to shareholders by 36% to service its debt (Egan, 2019).

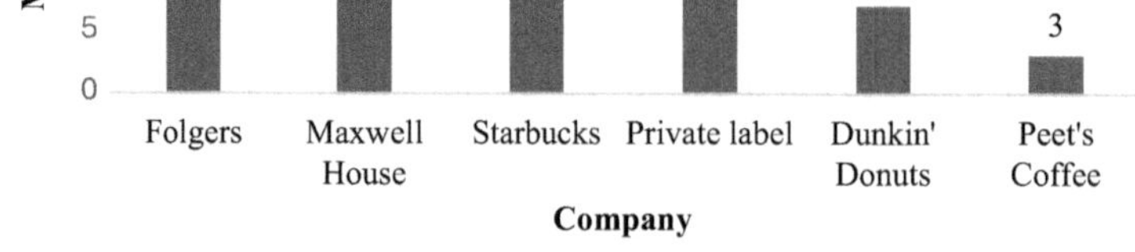

FIGURE 4.8 Market Share of Leading Ground Coffee Brands (%) (2017)

Source: Market Share of the Leading Ground Coffee Brands in the US in 2017. (April 2017). *Statista*. Retrieved from https://www.statista.com/statistics/586537/market-share-ground-coffee-brands-united-states/

THE ROAD AHEAD

Patricio was planning to upscale some of the Kraft Heinz brands. He stated, "There is a big premiumization going on," which, according to him, presented "an opportunity in the food industry" (Barker, 2019). Experts did not agree with this strategy. Tim Calkins, a former Kraft Foods executive and present marketing Professor at Kellogg School of Management stated, "It's hard to see a hot dog brand like Oscar Mayer will command a premium price. Oscar Mayer is an incredibly well-known brand. But most people wouldn't call it a premium brand" (Barker, 2019). Moreover, other experts believed that consumers were more driven by fresh foods than packaged food, offered by upstart brands (Perspectives on Retail and Consumer Goods, 2019). For packaged food, retailers offered private-label products at a lower price, Consequently, those consumers who were not health-conscious, preferred to shift to these low-price tags (Whiteman, 2019). Lemann expressed his surprise to how consumer product companies got disrupted. He stated, "I've been living in this cozy world of old brands and big volumes… We bought brands that we thought could last forever… You could just focus on being very efficient… All of a sudden we are being disrupted" (Duberstein, 2018b). However, David Gardner and Tom Gardner, popular investors, believed that Kraft Heinz stock was one of the ten stocks worth buying as they believed that focus on innovation and marketing, in the long run, would pay off (Duberstein, 2018a).

Commenting on the turnaround of the Kraft Heinz brand, Patricio stated, "My profile will bring a much more consumer-centric [vision]." Patricio also emphasized that his focus would be on improving Kraft Heinz's speed, sales growth, and brand building (Hirsch, 2019b). According to David Kass, professor at the University of Maryland, in the Kraft Heinz merger, the problem was Kraft Foods, not H. J. Heinz Co, required innovation. He stated, "the problem resides within the Kraft side of Kraft Heinz — the Heinz side is perfectly fine" (Reibstein & Kass, 2019). For example, between 2010 and 2014, Kraft Foods' share in the US market for packaged macaroni and cheese, declined to 78% from 82% of March 2010, as consumers shifted to Annie's Inc that was considered more natural and organic (Baertlein, 2014).

Robert Moscow, a research analyst, on the contrary, believed that Kraft Heinz needed an entire reorganization around a completely new mission, where it should capitalize on the creative forces of its workforce, rather than tightening the reign through cost-cutting measures (Georgescu, 2019). In 2019, the company had a debt of USD 10.3 billion, which was likely to mature by 2024, and analysts expected that this could constrain turnaround initiatives that Patricio was intending to take (Sun, 2019). Moreover, 3G Capital and Buffet wanted to reduce the debt and bring debt to equity ratio to order of three, so that they could fund further acquisitions of competitors such as General Mills or Kellogg (Gara, 2015).

DISCUSSION QUESTIONS

1. Map Kraft Heinz's growth moves onto the Ansoff Matrix.
2. Considering the product life cycle stage of Kraft Heinz, evaluate if ZBB was needed.
3. How can Kraft Heinz manage its product portfolio?
4. Using Porter's three tests of diversification, evaluate Kraft Heinz's bet on organic and startups.

CHAPTER NOTES

1 https://www.unilever.com/news/news-search/2022/our-compass-organisation-introducing-unilevers-five-new-business-groups/.
2 https://www.investopedia.com/how-disney-makes-money-4799164#:~:text=4-,Disney's%20Business%20Segments,7%25%20YOY%20to%20$1.2%20billion.
3 https://quartr.com/insights/company-research/amazon-from-books-to-everything.
4 https://techbuzzchina.substack.com/p/platform-or-price-war-xiaomis-double.
5 https://d3.harvard.edu/platform-rctom/submission/fujifilm-transformation-from-a-photographic-film-maker/.
6 https://www.ebsco.com/research-starters/business-and-management/tata-group.
7 https://www.cnn.com/2025/04/17/food/bodyarmor-rebrand#:~:text=1.-,Coca%2DCola%20is%20giving%20BodyArmor%20a%20major%20makeover%20in%20hopes,weekend%20during%20the%20NHL%20playoffs.
8 https://www.cnbc.com/2023/12/01/how-apple-makes-its-own-chips-for-iphone-and-mac-edging-out-intel.html#:~:text=Apple%20first%20debuted%20homegrown%20semiconductors,course%2C%20is%20our%20silicon.%22.
9 https://www.cnbc.com/2021/11/09/ge-to-break-up-into-3-companies-focusing-on-aviation-healthcare-and-energy.html.
10 https://medium.com/the-vultures/apple-the-future-of-this-tech-giant-1218708f0f30.
11 https://www.goodwatercap.com/insights/thesis/understanding-spotify/.
12 https://teams.live.com/meet/9316708446025?p=IfnZwCgZTSGpYh5DbQ.
13 Prahalad, C. K. (1993). The role of core competencies in the corporation. *Research-Technology Management*, *36* (6), 40–47.
14 https://thinkinsights.net/strategy/core-competency.
15 https://global.honda/en/sustainability/integratedreport/automobile-business-strategy/.
16 https://world.casio.com/content/dam/casio/global/corporate/en/ir/library/annual/2022/integrated_2022_4_en.pdf.
17 https://www.casio-intl.com/asia/en/emi/products/cdp235r/#:~:text=These%20pianos%20are%20equipped%20with%20an%20effect%20function.
18 Zhou, Y. M. (2011). Synergy, coordination costs, and diversification choices. *Strategic Management Journal*, *32* (6), 624–639.
19 Liu, Z., & Nagurney, A. (2011). Risk reduction and cost synergy in mergers and acquisitions via supply chain network integration. *Journal of Financial Decision Making*, *7* (2), 1–18.
20 https://www.thomasnet.com/insights/johnson-and-johnson-brands/.
21 https://www.prophecymarketinsights.com/blogs/Top-10-Companies-in-Skin-Care-Market.
22 https://www.cnbc.com/2025/07/17/disney-ip-anchors-theme-parks.html.
23 https://www.pmi.com/media-center/news/pmi-progresses-on-acquisition-of-three-pioneering-pharmaceutical-companies-to-accelerate-beyond-nicotine-vision#:~:text=On%20September%2016th%2C%202021%2C%20Philip,and%20inhaled%20and%20oral%20therapeutics.
24 https://www.pmiscience.com/en/news-events/scientific-update-magazine/a-smoke-free-future-and-beyond/#:~:text=For%20example%2C%20PMI%20scientists%20developed,nonanimal%20approaches%20for%20further%20investigations.
25 https://sustainablebrands.com/read/philip-morris-international-is-now-in-the-life-insurance-business#:~:text=Philip%20Morris%20International%20Is%20Now,with%20plans%20to%20expand%20internationally.
26 Pandya, A. M., & Rao, N. V. (1998). Diversification and firm performance: An empirical evaluation. *Journal of Financial and Strategic Decisions*, *11* (2), 67–81.
27 Bettis, R. A. (1981). Performance differences in related and unrelated diversified firms. *Strategic Management Journal*, *2* (4), 379–393.
28 https://www.bcg.com/about/overview/our-history/growth-share-matrix.
29 https://www.bcg.com/about/overview/our-history/growth-share-matrix.
30 https://uk.news.yahoo.com/coca-cola-results-beat-higher-122935508.html.
31 https://edrawmax.wondershare.com/business-tips/coca-cola-bcg-matrix-analysis.html.
32 https://www.statista.com/chart/31772/leading-bottled-water-brands-by-global-market-share/.
33 https://www.historyoasis.com/post/coca-cola-blak.

34 Cuervo-Cazurra, A. (2006). Business groups and their types. *Asia Pacific Journal of Management, 23* (4), 419–437.
35 Cuervo-Cazurra, A. (2006). Business groups and their types. *Asia Pacific Journal of Management, 23* (4), 419–437.
36 Lodh, S., Nandy, M., & Chen, J. (2014). Innovation and family ownership: Empirical evidence from I ndia. *Corporate Governance: An International Review*, *22* (1), 4–23.
37 https://thediplomat.com/2013/06/reforming-chinas-state-owned-enterprises/.
38 Gilson, R. J., & Roe, M. J. (1993). Understanding the Japanese keiretsu: Overlaps between corporate governance and industrial organization. *The Yale Law Journal, 102* (4), 871–906. https://doi.org/10.2307/796835
39 https://www.promarket.org/2023/07/17/do-business-groups-in-asia-really-spur-innovation/.
40 https://www.promarket.org/2023/07/17/do-business-groups-in-asia-really-spur-innovation/.

FURTHER READINGS

15 Companies That Completely Reinvented Themselves and Made Big Money. (January 10, 2014). Lmc123.com. Retrieved from https://lmc123.com/en/news-room/315-15-companies-that-completely-reinvented-themselves-and-made-big-money

Cardello, H. (March 29, 2019). Why big food companies like Kraft Heinz aren't cutting the mustard. *Forbes*. Retrieved from https://www.forbes.com/sites/hankcardello/2019/03/29/why-big-food-companies-like-kraft-heinz-arent-cutting-the-mustard/#5caf588e710e

Jurevicius, O. (May 1, 2013). BCG growth-share matrix. *Strategic Management Insight*. Retrieved from https://strategicmanagementinsight.com/tools/bcg-matrix-growth-share.html

Levitt, T. (1965). Exploit the product life cycle. *Harvard Business Review, 43*(6), 81–94. https://corporatefinanceinstitute.com/resources/management/ansoff-matrix/

Zero-Based Budgeting (ZBB). (January 23, 2020). *Investopedia.* Retrieved from https://www.investopedia.com/terms/z/zbb.asp

CASE REFERENCES

Agnihotri, A., & Bhattacharya, S. (2021). *Growth strategic options of Kraft Heinz*. Sage Business Cases. https://doi.org/10.4135/9781529754216

Baertlein, L. (March 30, 2014). Kraft challenged by "healthier" macaroni and cheese brands. *Reuters*. Retrieved from https://www.reuters.com/article/us-kraft-macandcheese/kraft-challenged-by-healthier-macaroni-and-cheese-brands-idUSBREA2T09C20140330

Ballard, J. (October 1, 2017). Kraft Heinz has the right recipe for growth. *The Motley Fool*. Retrieved from https://www.fool.com/investing/2017/10/01/kraft-heinz-has-the-right-recipe-for-growth.aspx

Barker, D. (August 23, 2019). Here's the problem with 'premiumization' at Kraft Heinz. *Crain's Chicago Business.* Retrieved from https://www.chicagobusiness.com/consumer-products/heres-problem-premiumization-kraft-heinz

Cheng, A. (July 10, 2018). CPG giants, desperate for growth, seek out once-unthinkable tie-ups and push M&A to 15-year high. *Forbes.* Retrieved from https://www.forbes.com/sites/andriacheng/2018/07/10/changing-consumer-behavior-has-pushed-cpg-giants-buying-binge-to-a-15-year-high/#15007d34944f

Colvin, G. (January 19, 2017). How Kraft Heinz plans to build a new global food giant. *Fortune.* Retrieved from https://fortune.com/longform/kraft-heinz-merger-3g-capital/

Consumer Market Outlook: Juices: USA. (2019). Statista.com. Retrieved from https://www.statista.com/outlook/20030000/109/juices/united-states#market-ontradeRevenueShare

Consumer Market Outlook: Sauces & Condiments: USA. (2019). Statista.com. Retrieved from https://www.statista.com/outlook/40070000/109/sauces-condiments/united-states

Demand for Ready-to-Eat Processed Foods Leads to Growth in Food Processing Equipment. (January 4, 2019). *Refrigerated & Frozen Food.* Retrieved from https://www.refrigeratedfrozenfood.com/articles/96231-demand-for-ready-to-eat-processed-foods-leads-to-growth-in-food-processing-equipment

Dowd, K. (May 23, 2019). How 3G capital and a $50B buyout turned Kraft Heinz upside down. *PitchBook.* Retrieved from https://pitchbook.com/news/articles/how-3g-capital-and-a-50b-buyout-turned-kraft-heinz-upside-down

Duberstein, B. (March 2, 2018a). 3 positives inside Kraft Heinz' "disappointing" earnings. *The Motley Fool.* Retrieved from https://www.fool.com/investing/2018/03/02/3-positives-inside-kraft-heinz-disappointing-earni.aspx

Duberstein, B. (May 16, 2018b). 3 Reasons to buy Kraft Heinz stock, 1 reason to sell. *The Motley Fool.* Retrieved from https://www.fool.com/investing/2018/05/16/3-reasons-to-buy-kraft-heinz-stock-1-reason-to-sel.aspx

Duberstein, B. (October 3, 2018c). Kraft Heinz's latest acquisition shows its strategy is changing. *The Motley Fool.* Retrieved from https://www.fool.com/investing/2018/10/03/kraft-heinzs-latest-acquisition-shows-its-strategy.aspx

Egan, M. (February 25, 2019). Kraft Heinz exposes Corporate America's debt problem. *CNN.* Retrieved from https://www.cnn.com/2019/02/25/investing/kraft-heinz-stock-debt/index.html

Food Processing: Market Potential Index. (2017). *International Business Center Michigan State University.* Retrieved from https://ibc-static.broad.msu.edu/sites/globaledge/medc/industry-mpi/pdfs/food-processing-MPI-Insights-and-Rankings-2017.pdf

Form 10-K, 2016: Kraft Heinz. (March 3, 2016). *Securities and Exchange Commission.* Retrieved from https://ir.kraftheinzcompany.com/static-files/3f28b8a3-cc22-4e19-a6c7-5b649d0b5ea9

Gara, A. (July 6, 2015). Kraft Heinz will prove the power of Warren Buffett's dealmaking partnership with 3G Capital. *Forbes.* Retrieved from https://www.forbes.com/sites/antoinegara/2015/07/06/kraft-heinz-will-prove-the-power-of-warren-buffetts-dealmaking-partnership-with-3g-capital/#30fc4e961a4c

Gasparro, A., & Monga, V. (February 22, 2019). It shook the food business by snagging Burger King, Kraft and Heinz. Now 3G is reeling. *The Wall Street Journal.* Retrieved from https://www.wsj.com/articles/it-shook-the-food-business-by-snagging-burger-king-kraft-and-heinz-now-3g-is-reeling-11550875206

Geller, M., & Naidu, R. (February 22, 2019). Kraft Heinz' problems shine light on controversial budget tool. *Reuters.* Retrieved from https://www.reuters.com/article/us-consumer-kraft-heinz/kraft-heinz-problems-shine-light-on-controversial-budget-tool-idUSKCN1QB2CF

Georgescu, P. (March 6, 2019). Kraft Heinz needs to get creative. *Forbes.* Retrieved from https://www.forbes.com/sites/petergeorgescu/2019/03/06/kraft-heinz-needs-to-get-creative/#7a6f61e92aba

Haddon, H. (February 26, 2019). Supermarkets soured on Kraft Heinz and its pricing tactics. *The Wall Street Journal.* Retrieved from https://www.wsj.com/articles/kraft-heinzs-tough-approach-on-costs-hurt-grocery-relationships-11551182402

Hirsch, L. (July 28, 2018). Why 149-year-old Campbell Soup is at a crossroads. Retrieved from https://www.cnbc.com/2018/07/28/campbell-soup-at-149-years-old-is-facing-a-crossroads.html

Hirsch, L. (April 22, 2019a). CNBC'S Lauren Hirsch: Kraft Heinz CEO Bernado Hees to step down, will be replaced by Ab Inbev's Miguel Patricio. *CNBC.* Retrieved from https://www.cnbc.com/2019/04/22/cnbcs-lauren-hirsch-kraft-heinz-ceo-bernardo-hees-to-step-down-will-be-replaced-by-ab-inbevs-miguel-patricio.html

Hirsch, L. (April 23, 2019b). Kraft Heinz's new CEO inherits challenges left behind by cost-cutting. *CNBC.* Retrieved from https://www.cnbc.com/2019/04/23/kraft-heinzs-new-ceo-inherits-challenges-left-behind-by-cost-cutting.html

Hirsch, L. (April 23, 2019c). Kraft Heinz weighs sale of Ore-Ida frozen potato business. *CNBC.* Retrieved from https://www.cnbc.com/2019/04/23/kraft-heinz-weighs-sale-of-ore-ida-frozen-potato-business.html

Kraft Heinz Benefits from Sales Growth in Asia and Latin America. (August 3, 2018). *Food Bev Media.* Retrieved from https://www.foodbev.com/news/kraft-heinz-relies-on-emerging-markets-to-offset-poor-us-sales/

Kraft Heinz: Key Metrics. (November, 2019). *Kraft Heinz*. Retrieved from https://ir.kraftheinzcompany.com/overview

Kraft Heinz Launches New Platform to Shape Next Generation of Food. (March 7, 2018). *Kraft Heinz*. Retrieved from https://ir.kraftheinzcompany.com/index.php/news-releases/news-release-details/kraft-heinz-launches-new-platform-shape-next-generation-food

Kraft Heinz Pivots to Emerging Markets. (February 28, 2017). *Gro intelligence*. Retrieved from https://gro-intelligence.com/insights/articles/kraft-heinz-unilever-merger-emerging-markets

Kraft-Heinz Is in Trouble. (February 22, 2019). *The Economist*. Retrieved from https://www.economist.com/business/2019/02/22/kraft-heinz-is-in-trouble

Naidu, R. (April 23, 2019). Kraft Heinz's new CEO looks beyond cost-cutting, big M&A. *Reuters*. Retrieved from https://www.reuters.com/article/us-kraft-heinz-ceo-strategy/kraft-heinzs-new-ceo-looks-beyond-cost-cutting-big-ma-idUSKCN1RZ007

Perspectives on Retail and Consumer Goods. (January 2019). *McKinsey & Company*. Retrieved from https://www.mckinsey.com/~/media/McKinsey/Industries/Retail/Our%20Insights/Perspectives%20on%20retail%20and%20consumer%20goods%20Number%207/Perspectives-on-Retail-and-Consumer-Goods_Issue-7.ashx

Post-Integration Business Update: The Kraft Heinz Company. (February 15, 2018). *Kraft Heinz*. Retrieved from https://ir.kraftheinzcompany.com/static-files/67db0f7b-755c-44a4-8f9e-7455d2781aa6

PrivateLabelGrowthOutshinesNationalBrands.(April23,2019). *Winsightgrocerybusiness*.Retrievedfrom https://www.winsightgrocerybusiness.com/retailers/private-label-growth-outshines-national-brands

Reibstein, D., & Kass, D. (March 12 2019). Can Kraft Heinz catch up with its changing market? Knowledge@Wharton. Retrieved from https://knowledge.wharton.upenn.edu/article/how-kraft-heinz-can-make-a-comeback/

Rosenbaum, E. (February 22, 2019). Warren Buffett's Kraft Heinz deal was unlike any Berkshire has done. He may not want to repeat it. *CNBC*. Retrieved from https://www.cnbc.com/2019/02/22/buffett-kraft-heinz-deal-was-new-approach-for-berkshire-and-a-warning.html

Sanchez, L. (April 29, 2019). Can a new CEO turn thing around for Kraft Heinz? *The Motley Fool*. Retrieved from https://www.fool.com/investing/2019/04/29/can-a-new-ceo-turn-things-around-for-kraft-heinz.aspx

Scully, J. (March 6, 2019). Kraft Heinz enlists five start-ups to join second Springboard class. *Foodbev Media*. Retrieved from https://www.foodbev.com/news/kraft-heinz-adds-five-start-ups-to-springboard-incubator-initiative/

Siegner, C. (January 4, 2018). Report: Specialty cheeses are gaining popularity through in-store delis. *Grocery Dive*. Retrieved from https://www.grocerydive.com/news/grocery--report-specialty-cheeses-are-gaining-popularity-through-in-store-delis/534367/

Sonenshine, J. (September 4, 2019). Kraft-Heinz: Things might get worse before they get better, analysts say. *The Street*. Retrieved from https://www.thestreet.com/markets/kraft-heinz-what-analysts-are-saying-15077312

Sun, L. (July 25, 2019). No one wants to buy Kraft Heinz's dying brands. *The Motley Fool*. Retrieved from https://www.fool.com/investing/2019/07/25/no-one-wants-to-buy-kraft-heinzs-dying-brands.aspx

The Oscar Mayer Brand's Most Iconic Product Undergoes Major Quality Improvements for the Love of Hot Dogs. (May 1, 2017). *BusinessWire*. Retrieved from https://www.businesswire.com/news/home/20170501005499/en/Oscar-Mayer-Brand%E2%80%99s-Iconic-Product-Undergoes-Major

Trefis Team. (March 30, 2015) Analysis of the Kraft-Heinz Merger. *Forbes*. https://www.forbes.com/sites/greatspeculations/2015/03/30/analysis-of-the-kraft-heinz-merger/#677b9000c9a8

Tully, S. (February 22, 2019). Kraft Heinz disaster shows that brutal cost-cutting won't save packaged foods. *Fortune*. Retrieved from https://fortune.com/2019/02/22/kraft-heinz-disaster-cost-cutting/

U.S. Consumers Return to the Convenience of Frozen Foods. (May 1, 2019). *NPD*. Retrieved from https://www.npd.com/wps/portal/npd/us/news/press-releases/2019/u-s--consumers-return-to-the-convenience-of-frozen-foods/

Whiteman, L. (May 28, 2019). Why shares of Kraft Heinz are falling on Tuesday. *Fox Business*. Retrieved from https://www.foxbusiness.com/markets/why-shares-of-kraft-heinz-are-falling-on-tuesday

CHAPTER 5

Corporate Governance

Learning Objectives

After completing this chapter, students will be able to:

- Evaluate the role of the Board of Directors in conducting corporate governance of firms;
- Critically analyze how CEOs can influence board power and compensation paid to themselves;
- Evaluate how the CEO and shareholders' activism affects firms;
- Examine issues faced by women executives through the lens of gender intelligence and the glass ceiling.

ROLE OF BOARD OF DIRECTORS

The Board of Directors represents the supra top management team (TMT) that exists to protect shareholder interests, i.e., they are representative of shareholders. However, depending on voting rights, the Board of Directors may ultimately be selected by the CEO. Mark Zuckerberg, CEO of Meta, primarily selects Meta's Board of Directors due to the voting rights he holds at Meta (formerly Facebook).[1] Zuckerberg created a special dual-class stock structure that gave him control over majority voting rights despite owning only a minority of the shares. Meta has established a two-tiered stock system, comprising Class A and Class B stocks. Shareholders possessing Class A stock have one vote per share. Shareholders possessing Class B stock have ten votes per share.[2] Zuckerberg owned 99.8% of the Class B stock and offered only Class A stock to external investors.[3]

The board's role is to protect shareholders' interests and ensure that the TMT conducts the firm's operations appropriately and ethically, ultimately leading to an increase in shareholder value. The board achieves this objective by providing strategic oversight and guidance to top management, who are responsible for managing the day-to-day operations of a business. The Board of Directors is of two types: executive and non-executive. Executive directors are part of

DOI: 10.4324/9781003568100-5

the TMT, alongside the CEO and the CFO. Non-executive directors are independent directors who are primarily responsible for maintaining objectivity in a firm's strategies and protecting shareholders' interests. A Chairman typically leads a board and oversees various subcommittees, such as a compensation committee, audit committee, or investment committee.[4]

With increasing sustainability concerns, boards have recently faced pressure from shareholders to drive top management to incorporate ESG (Environmental, Social, and Governance) policies into their business strategies. ESG is explained as follows:

- *Environmental.* The environmental aspect refers to how a company reduces or mitigates the adverse impact of its activities on the natural environment, such as wastewater treatment or using natural gas-based power rather than coal-based power, or ways to reduce greenhouse gas emissions.[5]
- *Social.* The social aspect refers to how the company considers the human impact of its operations. The social element encompasses not only employees but also the community members impacted by the firm's operations, including customers and community residents.[6] Diamond mining companies, such as De Beers, lead to the displacement of rural or indigenous communities as they mine the land.[7]

  Companies then need to provide an alternate shelter as part of their ESG responsibilities. Other aspects of social responsibility include adhering to labor and human rights standards, ensuring employee well-being, promoting diversity, and fostering inclusion. From the customer perspective, this implies ensuring product quality and safety with minimal product recall crisis and ensuring customer satisfaction.
- *Governance.* The governance aspect of ESG is more traditional, encompassing the fiduciary duty of the Board of Directors, which includes ensuring the appropriate composition of the top management team, CEO compensation, transparency, and regulatory compliance.

Boards have responded to ESG pressures by establishing subcommittees to oversee ESG functions. In 2023, the Starbucks board created the Environmental, Partner, and Community Impact (EPCI) committee.[8] Beth Ford, CEO of Land O'Lakes, headed the new committee as the independent chair. The committee was responsible for monitoring Starbucks' management's progress in implementing and achieving ESG goals. Nestlé's board took a step further, tying senior executives' pay to the company's ESG performance since 2021.[9]

CEO COMPENSATION

A Board generally offers three components as part of CEO compensation. One is the base salary, followed by short-term incentives such as bonuses based on the CEO's annual performance, and finally long-term incentives, including ESOPs (i.e., stock options). The stock market performance of publicly listed firms determines the value of the stock options. Stock options ensure that the CEO's values and interests are in alignment with those of shareholders, and they devise strategies that lead to an overall increase in the firm's shareholder value, thereby increasing the value of their stock options.

Depending on the extent of the CEO's influence over the board, they can ultimately informally determine their own compensation. However, as a formality, the Board of Directors make a formal announcement about CEO compensation. In 2024, the Delaware court ruled against Elon Musk's compensation of USD 56 billion.[10] The court declared that Tesla board members lacked independence in deciding Musk's compensation and that, as a controlling stockholder with 72% holding, Musk significantly influenced the board in his compensation payout.

Another way a CEO can influence board decisions is by holding the position of board chairman. When the CEO serves in a dual role as both board chairman and CEO, conflicts of interest arise, as the chairman CEO evaluates their own performance and decides on compensation. Companies that have a CEO as chairman include multinationals such as Cisco Systems or The Coca-Cola Company. Given governance and board independence issues, the dual role structure of CEOs has been in decline.[11] According to a CNBC observation, in 2005, only 30% of S&P 500 companies had a split CEO and board chair role, whereas by 2019, this had increased to 53%.[12]

BOARD'S SUCCESSION PLANNING OF THE CEO

CEO selection is a board decision. However, incumbent CEOs play a critical role in succession planning, as well as in influencing the board's decision about a new CEO. The Crown Heir, Horse Race, and Coup d'Etat are different succession processes. In the *Crown Heir* succession process, the CEO's choice dominates the Crown Heir succession process, and the board is aware of its preferences in advance. The primary decision-maker is the incumbent CEO, though their choice may unfold over time.[13] Steve Jobs followed the Crown Heir approach, where he identified and groomed Tim Cook for the CEO role. Before becoming the CEO, Cook worked as the Chief Operating Officer at Apple.[14]

Horse racing is another category of succession process. In the Horse Race succession process, several critical insiders compete against each other, and based on objective performance evaluations, a new CEO is selected.[15] In this process, the incumbent CEO has a crucial influence on decision-making. However, the criteria used to evaluate candidates are evolving and unclear. Several sources, such as peer references, are consulted to provide performance evaluations of candidates. Candidates may also try to influence decision-makers through lobbying efforts. In the Horse Race succession process, the organization may not select an internal candidate. If this is the case, the process restarts, and the company may focus on external CEO candidates.[16] General Electric's (GE) 1999–2000 succession process was a horse race, where CEO Jack Welch set up an explicit, time-bound competition among three internal candidates for the CEO position: Jeff Immelt, Bob Nardelli, and Jim McNerney. The candidates underwent a series of assessments and were trained for several strategic activities to gauge their suitability for the CEO role.[17]

In a *Coup d'Etat*, the selection process typically happens when the current leadership is in crisis. In this process, a non-CEO entity, like the Board of Directors, dominates the CEO selection process. The process unfolds in a relatively short period. A non-CEO entity may sow the seeds of revolution well in advance, but overthrowing the incumbent CEO succeeds only when conditions change enough to empower a non-incumbent coalition.[18] Knowledge of an insurgency is kept from the incumbent because if the plan becomes public, the incumbent CEO may destroy it or launch a viable counterattack. A coup begins with a minority faction asserting that the current leader is no longer adequate. Members of this insurgent coalition typically include a subset of top management in concert with the Board of Directors or some subset of the board.[19]

Insider vs. Outsider CEO

Research studies suggest that insider CEOs (i.e., CEOs who work within the same organization and advance through the ranks to the CEO position) are generally more successful than outsider CEOs. However, choice largely depends on the company's specific situation, especially if the firm is performing well or is in crisis.[20] Insider CEOs outperform outsider CEOs when firms are in a healthy state at the time of the CEO transition.[21] If a firm is facing financial, reputational, legal, or any other challenge, such as disruptive forces, then external CEOs performed better.[22] It was for this reason that when Ferrari decided to venture into the electric vehicle (EV) category, instead of promoting a CEO from within who had more automobile engineering expertise, they hired an external CEO from the electronics and semiconductor industry, given that the technology of EVs resembled that of the semiconductor industry than the traditional gasoline-based automobile industry.[23]

When a firm is not seeking any strategic change and is in good financial health, surveys have shown that 51% of insider CEOs perform better than outsider CEOs.[24] This difference in performance occurs because firms generally have a strong succession planning process in place, where strong internal candidates are groomed for the role of CEO for several years before they are ready to take on the role. Healthy companies have more resources available for the development of senior executives. However, if a company is in crisis, then outsider CEOs may outperform insider CEOs. After Chipotle faced criticism related to food safety issues, Brian Nicoll, an outsider CEO, was able to rescue the company from a reputation crisis.[25] Niccol had work experience at Taco Bell, and after being hired by Chipotle following a significant food safety crisis in 2018, he modernized the business through digital innovation, improved operations, and invested in employee culture, focusing first on food safety.[26]

CEO ACTIVISM

CEO activism refers to the practice of CEOs taking a public stance on environmental, social, and political issues. These issues are generally not directly related to their business, yet CEOs share their opinions on these topics via various channels, such as social media and news outlets. CEOs share their perspective on social issues, as the majority of stakeholders, such as consumers and employees, expect CEOs to express their opinions; however, this practice can be controversial and spark debate. The proportion of S&P 500 companies with CEO activism increased from approximately 1% in 2011 to over 37% in 2019, indicating a significant rise in CEO activism. Surveys suggest that 65%–86% of people believe that CEOs should engage in activism on current issues, as it can drive meaningful change in society.[27] CEO activism also impacts their firm's performance. It can increase consumers' intentions to purchase the company's products if the CEO's views align with the majority of its customers' policy preferences; otherwise, it can backfire.

Perceived corporate hypocrisy also influences consumer behavior in response to CEO activism.[28] In 2020, Goya Foods CEO, Robert Unanue, upon invitation from the White House during President Trump's first regime, where he signed an executive order for the Hispanic community, commented,

> We are all truly blessed, at the same time, to have a leader like President Trump who is a builder, and that's what my grandfather did. He came to this country to build, to grow, to prosper. And so, we have an incredible builder and we pray—we pray for our leadership, our president, and we pray for our country, that we will continue to prosper and to grow.[29]

Soon after Unanue made this comment, Goya's consumers began to call for a boycott of the brand. The issue also started to trend on X (formerly Twitter) under the hashtags "#Goyaway" and "#BoycottGoya."[30] Politicians and members of the public reacted strongly to the CEO's statements. Facebook also experienced a boycott when marketers expressed unease about how it handled misinformation and hate speech, including its permissive approach to certain posts by President Trump that were considered inappropriate by the marketers.[31]

Furthermore, in July 2020, companies such as Starbucks Corporation (Starbucks) and Diageo Plc (Diageo) announced that they would pause their advertising on Facebook. These companies were among the biggest spenders on Facebook advertisements, with Starbucks spending USD 95 million and Diageo spending USD 23 million on the platform in 2018. American Honda Motor Co., Ltd., Levi Strauss & Co., and Patagonia, Inc., also boycotted Facebook.[32] The social network's stock price was adversely affected, as these and other big customers boycotted and withdrew their advertisements from Facebook. In response, Facebook adopted policies against both hate speech and problematic political posts.[33]

As US consumers became more interested in the political leanings of their favorite brands,[34] several startups emerged those shared details about their CEOs, executives, and employees, as well as their political contributions to various parties. Startups such as Goods Unite Us, Inc. and Zippia offered applications that captured and communicated the political leanings of their executives.[35] Yet another startup, BuyCott, offered an application that allowed consumers to filter the brands that supported the causes they favored.[36] Overall, adopting a political stance can help a company solidify its bond with consumers, although it can also alienate specific customers when a value mismatch occurs.[37]

GENDER INTELLIGENCE

Gender intelligence refers to understanding and accepting naturally occurring differences between different genders.[38] Gender intelligence extends beyond biological and cultural differences, encompassing attitudinal and behavioral differences across genders.[39] Individuals who are high on gender intelligence are better able to comprehend and appreciate how differences in behavior could influence workplace dynamics.[40] They also leverage these differences to improve workplace processes, such as collaboration and decision-making.

Organizations generally operate on the fundamental belief that balanced gender representation is essential.[41] This is a more tangible belief, where organizations assume that closing the gender ratio gap in the workplace would lead to greater equity. However, women's representation or closing the gender gap does not necessarily mean that women are accepted in the workplace.[42] It could be more lip service, where, to external stakeholders, it may appear that organizations do not discriminate based on gender, but that may not be the case.[43] Overall, filling women's quota may not enhance workplace diversity.[44]

Executives need to develop gender intelligence. Executives, instead of expecting women to behave like men or creating a workplace climate that makes women perceive they cannot enter the masculine group unless their behavior is more masculine, should accept and appreciate gender differences.[45] Both men and women bring different talents to the workplace that need to be respected and nurtured. Executives should respect and appreciate women's caring, compassionate, and empathetic attitudes as much as the competitive and aggressive attitudes that males generally exhibit.[46] During the COVID-19 pandemic or similar threats posed by the macro environment, organizations must accept and acknowledge the natural abilities of empathy and compassion that women bring to the workplace. Thus, instead of ignoring or adopting an attitude where corporate executives behave as if they must tolerate the gender difference, executives need to celebrate it.[47] An appreciated feminine leadership style is essential for organizations and women executives,[48] as individuals who behave outside their actual personality tend to lose productivity and are perceived as less competent by others.

With gender intelligence, organizations can undoubtedly increase workplace diversity, much like accepting and acknowledging cultural differences between different ethnicities, such as those between Asian and American cultures. Similarly, organizations should accept gender differences instead of merely tolerating them.[49] Men must understand the cultural aspects that women value and offer a more inclusive work environment where such gender differences are accepted.

Moreover, by developing gender intelligence, organizations can also gain economic benefits.[50] Similar to the cultural diversity that enhances organizations' creativity, innovation, and financial performance, gender diversity (beyond lip service with gender intelligence) could further enhance a firm's global competitiveness. For instance, at Microsoft Africa, Lillian Barnard, the CEO, has raised the brand value of Microsoft through her women-centric policies, elevating its best place to work employer brand identity from third position to first position.[51] In fact, male subordinates took pride in reporting to Barnard and appreciated her leadership.[52] This appreciation would not have been possible had male subordinates not accepted and acknowledged the gender differences and their value. Barnard's emphasis on women employees during meetings could have demotivated male employees, or they could have felt reverse biasness. However, given Barnard's emphasis on gender intelligence, male subordinates likely understood that women in the workplace needed encouragement to overcome their hesitation and be listened to carefully and respectfully, so that they could freely present their opinions.

Glass Ceiling and Gender CEO

Although women make up a substantial part of the workforce, comprising 46.9% in the US as of 2025, their representation in top positions, such as CEO, is significantly smaller, at 8.2% for Fortune 500 firms. *Glass ceiling* refers to an invisible barrier that prevents women from advancing into senior leadership roles or results in pay discrepancies between genders. In the US, women earn approximately 20 cents less than what men earn for the same job. Although women generally start their careers at the same wage as men, the wage gap persists and continues to increase as their careers progress.[53] One of the factors responsible for this is parenthood. Women aged between 25 and 44 generally take a career break due to pregnancy, family care, or reduced work hours. These aspects reduce their wages.[54] Similarly, when women seek career progression, owing to stereotypes of caregivers, who would potentially take a career break for family reasons, an unconscious bias arises in recruitment and promotion decisions.[55] Consequently, their promotion to senior positions suffers, as these roles demand more commitment and overtime work, leading to a work-life imbalance.[56]

In a related issue known as the *glass cliff*, companies tend to prefer women CEOs when an organization is experiencing a crisis. Instead of appointing turnaround specialists, they hire women CEOs. This appointment happens as either the board believes that non-traditional candidates can bring in a fresh perspective, or they believe that the given organization ought to decline, they can hand over the ship to a female sailor to see if they can surpass the storm.[57] If a woman CEO can save the sinking ship, then after this savior effect, board members replace the female CEO with a male CEO.[58]

Women also take the captain's role of a sinking ship, as they believe that this is probably their only chance to prove their mettle.[59] Robert Nakasone turned around Toys' R Us in 1998. However, after its performance stabilized, she was replaced by former CEO Michael Goldstein.[60] Patricia Russo, former CEO of Lucent Technologies, also faced a similar fate, as after stabilizing the company, Ben Verwaayen replaced her for three consecutive years of negative shareholder returns.[61] However, if a woman CEO fails to save the failing organization, then it further perpetuates negative stereotypes regarding women as incapable leaders.[62] The "queen bee" label is given to women who pursue individual success in male-dominated work settings (organizations in which men hold most executive positions) by adjusting to the masculine culture and by distancing themselves from other women.

SHAREHOLDER ACTIVISM

Shareholder activism refers to a form of corporate governance in which shareholders with significant equity stakes in a company use their influence to guide the firm's strategy, particularly when they believe the firm is failing to deliver consistent shareholder value. These activists are not individual retail investors, but rather large institutional investors, such as Elliott Investment Management. In 2025, Elliott Investment Management acquired USD 4 billion stake in PepsiCo. As the company's performance fell below that of Dr. Pepper, the group began pressuring CEO Ramon Laguarta for an overhaul of operations. These activists typically demand CEO changes when CEOs fail to deliver the expected shareholder returns.

Activists also chart out strategic changes they want to see in the organization. Elliott Investment Management at PepsiCo clearly outlined that PepsiCo should spin off its bottling operations and focus on branding and marketing, the traditional competencies of the company.[63] They also demanded that PepsiCo divest underperforming units, such as the Frito-Lay division, which has been reporting declining sales for several years.[64] Elliott Investment Management made the demands in the wake of the consistent decline in PepsiCo's market valuation, which peaked in 2023 but deteriorated by 25% by 2025, reaching a value of approximately USD 200 billion.[65]

Although activists generally increase the market value of firms by an average of about 4.75%, the effectiveness depends on the type of demand activists are making. However, sometimes CEOs find demand to be irrational and do not comply with it. In 2017, Nelson Peltz, a billionaire activist investor, in the wake of enhancing P&G's shareholder value, demanded that P&G should split all its business units[66] and referred to its centralized R&D center as "a hobby," which, according to CEO Taylor, implied killing innovation at P&G with separate business units each having independent decision-making authority.[67] Some activists, such as Hedge fund investors, are more interested in short-term returns, and their activism can result in the long-term deterioration of firm performance, even if short-term performance improves.[68]

FOUNDER CEOs

Founder CEOs are better risk-takers than traditional CEOs, given their entrepreneurial spirit and fondness for innovation.[69] Professional CEOs generally take a more risk-averse approach to managing the business, ensuring sustained growth. Although risk-takers to some extent, compared to entrepreneurial and founder CEOs, they are more conservative. Founder CEOs also have more emotional attachment to their firms and consider their firms as their "babies or legacies."[70] Accordingly, they also draw higher levels of "psychic income" from their founded firms. However, as an organization moves through its life cycle and reaches the maturity stage, risk conservativeness becomes increasingly important, and founder CEOs hire or the board replaces them with professional CEOs.[71] Given that founder CEOs are unable to relinquish their psychological attachment to the firm they founded, they often retain control over firm operations even after stepping down from the CEO position, by taking a board position and maintaining a significant stake in the company. Jeff Bezos from Amazon, Bill Gates of Microsoft, and Larry Page and Sergey Brin, as the founders of Google (now Alphabet), followed this approach.

Sometimes, professional CEOs are unable to drive the organization through periods of financial turmoil, and a turnaround is required. At that time, organizations hire back founder CEOs. Given their better ability to understand firm operations and changing market dynamics, founder CEOs also turn out to be expert turnaround specialists for their firms. Steve Jobs, Howard Schultz, Michael Dell, Jack Dorsey, and Kevin Plank all returned as CEOs, leading to the effective turnarounds of Apple, Starbucks, Dell computers, X (formerly Twitter), and Under Armour, respectively. Steve Jobs was ousted from Apple by its board in 1985. However, in the mid-1990s, as Apple was on the verge of bankruptcy, Jobs was rehired, who, through strategic innovation and the launch of new product lines such as iPhones and iPads, gave new life to Apple.[72] Schultz also stepped down as CEO of Starbucks in 2000. However, after the 2008 financial crisis, as consumer discretionary spending decreased amid rising inflation, he was rehired and successfully turned around Starbucks.[73]

ASSIGNMENT QUESTIONS

1. Provide one example of a company where the CEO used voting rights to their advantage, thereby taking away informal power from Board members.
2. Give one example of a company that is fulfilling ESG initiatives and one company that is lagging in ESG initiatives. What are the reasons for the same?
3. There are four ways to conduct a CEO search during succession planning. What are those four ways? Give an example of each, preferably from your home country.
4. Give one example of CEO activism from your home country. How did stakeholders respond to it? Mainly covers employees' and customers' reactions. Especially explore if activism led to any controversy.
5. Critically analyze the concept of gender intelligence.

CASE STUDY 5.1

Disney

Restructuring for Success with Video Streaming Service Disney+

Agnihotri, A., & Bhattacharya, S. (2022). *Disney: Restructuring for success with video streaming service Disney+*. Sage Business Cases. https://doi.org/10.4135/9781529795110

INTRODUCTION

Robert A. Chapek, CEO of The Walt Disney Company (Disney), in October 2020, restructured Disney's Media and Entertainment division to focus more on streaming video services and be valued like Netflix Inc. (Netflix) (Donnelly & Lang, 2020). By implementing a direct-to-consumer strategy (Whitten, 2020b), Disney was aiming at centralizing its media businesses "into a single organization that will be responsible for content distribution, ad sales and Disney+ [Disney's online video streaming service]" (Whitten, 2020b). Chapek said, "We are tilting the scale pretty dramatically [toward streaming]." Shareholders cheered at this news as Disney's share price increased by 5% on the restructuring announcement (Whitten, 2020b). Disney was also planning to redirect dividend payments toward streaming after Dan Loeb, shareholder activist investor, recommended Chapek to divert a USD 3 billion dividend payout toward Disney+ content (Whitten, 2020b). Such requests from activists were considered unusual as they generally pressurized companies for more dividends (Sherman, 2020a). Industry analysts, however, expressed concerns. Some of Disney's media and entertainment division's senior executives did not figure in the unit heads' list as Disney was restructuring the division (Donnelly & Lang, 2020).

Moreover, when shareholder activist Loeb advised Chapek to completely give up movie theaters as a distribution channel and focus on video streaming, cinema players expressed disappointment. They mentioned it might be difficult for Disney to return to cinemas if, in the future, they decide to do so (Pulver, 2020). In January 2021, as Netflix was planning to offer a movie every week of 2021 (Faughnder, 2021), will the restructuring of Disney's Media and Entertainment division help Chapek grow Disney+? To what extent should Chapek follow the advice of Loeb? Should he switch Disney media completely toward streaming?

BACKGROUND

Disney is an American diversified multinational mass media and entertainment conglomerate with headquarters in Burbank, California. After Comcast, it was the world's second-largest media conglomerate in terms of revenue (Walt Disney Company, 2012). Brothers Walt Disney and Roy O. Disney founded Disney on October 16, 1923, as the Disney Brothers Cartoon Studio (Walt Disney Company, 2012). The company first established itself as a leader in the American animation industry and then diversified into live-action film production, television, and theme parks. Later, Disney also diversified in theater, radio, music, publishing, and online media (Walt Disney Company, 2012). Disney's divisions included Walt Disney Parks and Resorts, Disney Media Networks, Disney Direct-to-consumer, and Disney Consumer Products and Interactive Media. In 2020, Disney generated USD 65.40 billion in revenue, a 6% decline from 2019 (see Table 5.1). In the same year, Disney had 223,000 employees (Ziady, 2020). Also in 2020, Disney's Media Networks generated the most revenue and profits. Yet the COVID-19 pandemic adversely hit its Parks, Experiences, and Products segment (see Table 5.1).

TABLE 5.1 Disney Segments' Financials (USD Billion) (2016–2020)

Revenues	**2016**	**2017**	**2018**	**Revenues**	**2019**	**2020**
Media Networks	23.7	23.5	24.5	Media Networks	24.8	28.4
Parks and Resorts	17.0	18.4	20.3	Parks, Experiences, and Products	26.2	16.5
Studio Entertainment	9.4	8.4	10.0	Studio Entertainment	11.1	9.6
Consumer Products & Interactive Media	5.5	4.8	4.7	Direct-to-Consumer & International	9.4	17.0
				Eliminations	−2.0	−6.1
Total	55.6	55.1	59.4	**Total**	69.6	65.4
Segment Operating Income				**Segment Operating Income**		
Media Networks	7.8	6.9	6.6	Media Networks	7.5	9.0
Parks and Resorts	3.3	3.8	4.5	Parks, Experiences, and Products	6.8	−0.1
Studio Entertainment	2.7	2.4	3.0	Studio Entertainment	2.7	2.5
Consumer Products & Interactive Media	2.0	1.7	1.6	Direct-to-Consumer & International	−1.8	−2.8
				Eliminations	−0.2	−0.5
Total	15.7	14.8	15.7	**Total**	14.8	8.1

Source: The Walt Disney Company: Form 10-K (2020). (October 3, 2020). *Securities and Exchange Commission*. Retrieved from https://otp.tools.investis.com/clients/us/the_walt_disney_company/SEC/sec-show.aspx?FilingId=14530203&Cik=0001744489&Type=PDF&hasPdf=1, p. 41; The Walt Disney Company: Form 10-K (September 29, 2018). *Securities and Exchange Commission*. Retrieved from https://www.annualreports.com/HostedData/AnnualReportArchive/w/NYSE_DIS_2018.pdf, p. 32.

LAUNCH OF DISNEY+

The following subsections present a brief overview of the launch of Disney+, its subscriber base, and issues with the platform.

Launch and Subscribers

Disney+ was launched in the US on November 12, 2019 (Spangler, 2019) when Robert A. Iger was the CEO of Disney. Iger quit Disney's CEO position in February 2020, after which the role was assumed by Chapek (Bob Chapek Named ..., 2020). Before becoming the Disney CEO, Chapek held leadership positions across Disney's Parks, Consumer Products, and Studio businesses (Bob Chapek Named ..., 2020).

Disney's direct-to-consumer decision implementation speed was partly influenced by the global COVID-19 pandemic that resulted in losses for theatrical business and drove customers toward streaming options (Whitten, 2020b). Chapek said, "I would not characterize it as a response to Covid" (Whitten, 2020b). He further added, "I would say Covid accelerated the rate at which we made this transition, but this transition was going to happen anyway." Despite the prominent presence of Netflix and Amazon in streaming services, since the launch of Disney+, Disney added more than 60 million subscribers by August 2020 (Stoll, 2021a). In 2019, Disney predicted that it would have more than 60–100 million subscribers of Disney+ by 2024 (Sherman, 2020a). The rapid subscriber accumulation of Disney+ made Loeb confident that investing capital in it then paying a dividend was a justified option. It could help Disney+ be valued more like Netflix (Sherman, 2020a). Loeb's *Third Point Capital* was one of the largest shareholders in Disney (Whitten, 2020b). Loeb wrote to Chapak: "By reallocating a dividend of a few dollars per share, Disney could more than double its Disney+ original content budget" (Sherman, 2020a). He further added,

> The ability to drive subscriber growth, reduce churn, and increase pricing present the opportunity to create tens of billions of dollars in incremental value for Disney shareholders in short order, and hundreds of billions once the platform reaches larger scale.

The subscription base of Disney+ was primarily due to its large catalog of movies, "Star Wars," and Marvel content, though Disney had not invested much in original programming (Sherman, 2020a). By August 2020, Disney had 100 million paid subscribers across its streaming offerings, with the majority being subscribers to Disney+ (Whitten, 2020b). Other legacy media companies, such as Comcast's NBCUniversal, AT&T's Warner Media, and Viacom CBS, were also transitioning away from box office movies and cable TV and investing in subscription streaming services (Sherman, 2020a).

Issues with the Disney+ Platform

In 2019 Michael Paull, Disney's streaming services president, commenting on the user interface of Disney+, said, "As a principle, we wanted a simple, elegant experience."

He further added, "We want to make this easy. We don't want the product to get in the way of the content" (The Disney+ Interface ..., 2019). However, when Disney+ was launched, users encountered several problems while opening the app due to site overload (as 10 million subscribers signed on the first few days). There were also design issues, such as the absence of "Recently Watched" or "Continue watching" features on the platform, though Disney rectified these problems later (Waniata & Marshall, 2020). Still, movie searches on Disney's platform remained a problem. For instance, searching 101 Dalmatians, as "101" in the search pane generated a list of live-action films or an animated sequel, but not the original movie because Disney+ had designated the original movie as "One hundred and one" in the library (Waniata & Marshall, 2020). The Disney+ search system was not smart enough to list it under 101 (Waniata & Marshall, 2020).

DISNEY'S RESTRUCTURING

The following presents the restructuring efforts of Disney:

Separating Content Creation and Distribution

Chapek separated content creation units from content distribution (The Walt Disney Company Announces ..., 2020). According to the CEO, he expected the strategy to increase Disney's effectiveness in creating new content and getting it delivered in the way consumers preferred to consume it. He said, "Managing content creation distinct from distribution will allow us to be more effective and nimble in making the content consumers want most, delivered in the way they prefer to consume it" (The Walt Disney Company Announces ..., 2020). He further added,

> Our creative teams will concentrate on what they do best—making world-class, franchise-based content—while our newly centralized global distribution team will focus on delivering and monetizing that content in the most optimal way across all platforms, including Disney+, Hulu, ESPN+, and the coming Star international streaming service.

At Disney, three distinct groups managed content creation—Studios, General Entertainment, and Sports—headed by Alan F. Horn and Alan Bergman, Peter Rice, and James Pitaro. Disney expected all leaders to report directly to Chapek. Disney's parks, experiences, and consumer products businesses had no changes in structure (The Walt Disney Company Announces ..., 2020).

Content Creation Subdivisions

Studio. Horn and Bergman were designated to lead Disney's Studio division. The studio content division was responsible for creating branded theatrical and episodic content for theaters and streaming services. This division included The Walt Disney Studios' content engines, including Disney live-action, and Walt Disney Animation Studios, Pixar Animation Studios, Marvel Studios, Lucasfilm, 20th Century Studios, and Searchlight Pictures (The Walt Disney Company Announces …, 2020).

General Entertainment. Rice led Disney's General Entertainment content and was responsible for creating general entertainment episodic and original long-form content for its streaming platforms and cable and broadcast networks (The Walt Disney Company Announces …, 2020). This division included 20th Television, ABC Signature, Touchstone Television; ABC News; Disney Channels; Freeform; FX; and National Geographic.

Sports. Disney appointed Pitaro the Chairman of the Sports division. He was responsible for the sports content, including ESPN's live sports programming, sports news, and original and non-scripted sports-related content, for the cable channels, ESPN+, and ABC (The Walt Disney Company Announces …, 2020).

Distribution

In the reorganization, Disney promoted Kareem Daniel, the former president of Disney's consumer products, games, and publishing division, to oversee the Media and Entertainment Distribution group (Whitten, 2020c). Daniel had profit and loss responsibility of Disney+, and his profile included content distribution, sales, and advertising (Whitten, 2020b). He intended to use analytics to discover the best ways of reaching Disney's audience, i.e., releasing content through traditional windows before it was made available through streaming (Muscaro, 2020). Generally, movies released on video streaming platforms were low-budget films. For example, "The Love Birds," an R-rated comedy released by Netflix in 2020, had an estimated production budget of USD 16 million, where mainstream movies had a production budget of more than USD 100 million and usually recouped costs and profits through cinema halls (Whitten, 2020a).

Disney's reorganization segregated the Direct-to-Consumer and International business operations with Rebecca Campbell leading International Operations (The Walt Disney Company Announces …, 2020). Chapek said that the new structure "gives us maximum flexibility when on which platform content will be available," including determining if the movie be released in theaters or on Disney+ (Muscaro, 2020). With the emphasis on streaming and refocusing the company's orientation on content creation, industry analysts expressed their surprise at the lack of mention of distinguished creative executives in Disney that did not get any leadership roles. These included Dana Walden, ex-chair of Disney Television Studios and ABC Entertainment, and Ricky Strauss, ex-president of content and marketing for Disney+ (Donnelly & Lang, 2020). Similarly, in 2019, Disney poached Netflix's director of original film Matt Brodie for Disney+. Disney expected Brodie to monitor Disney+'s international content development for the non-US markets (Easton, 2019).

Chapek also mentioned that restructuring the Media and Entertainment division could result in layoffs. It was likely to be on a lesser scale than layoffs in theme parks, owing to the COVID-19 pandemic (Whitten, 2020b). In September 2020, Disney terminated the services of 28,000 people from its theme parks (Whitten, 2020b).

CONSUMER BEHAVIOR IN THE VIDEO STREAMING INDUSTRY

Cable TV subscription locked customers into their contracts for at least a year, while streaming services offered free trials and easy cancellation of the subscription. Dull content for one month was enough to trigger consumers to end a subscription and switch to a competing service (Hersko, 2019). In 2020, consumers were subscribing to multiple streaming platforms primarily due to new content (Share of Subscription Video ..., 2021; Westcott, 2020) (see Figure 5.1 & Table 5.2). Disney, ViacomCBS, and NBCUniversal all were charging less than

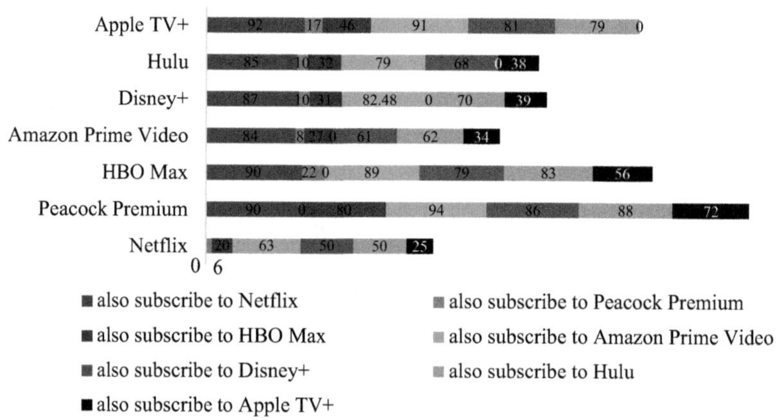

FIGURE 5.1 Share of Subscription Video on Demand Subscribers Who Also Subscribe to Other Services in the US (December, 2020) (Percentage)

Source: Share of Subscription Video on Demand (SVoD) Subscribers Who also Subscribe to Other Services in the US as of December 2020, by Service. (January 27, 2021). *Statista.* Retrieved from https://www.statista.com/statistics/778912/video-streaming-service-multiple-subscriptions/

TABLE 5.2 Reasons for Subscribing and Canceling Streaming Services (US) (%) (2019–2020)

Reasons for Subscribing to a Streaming Service	%	Reasons for Canceling a Streaming Service	%
Broad range of shows and movies	51	Too expensive	36
New, original content not available elsewhere	45	Free trial or discount ended	35
Previously released content not available elsewhere	27	Finished watching the content that led me to subscribe	24
Free trial or discount rate	24	Content I liked disappeared from the platform	17
Ad-free viewing experience	17	Replaced with a new paid subscription service	17
Shows and movies appropriate for children	16	Access content via a free, ad-supported streaming service	14
Bundled with other services	15	No live sports to watch	13
		Lack of new content I am interested in	11

Source: Adapted from: Westcott, K., Loucks, J., Downs, K., Arkenberg, C., & Jarvis, D. (2020). Digital media trends survey (14th ed.). *Deloitte.* Retrieved from https://www2.deloitte.com/us/en/insights/industry/technology/digital-media-trends-consumption-habits-survey/summary.html.

USD 10 a month for streaming services. Disney+ was charging USD 6.99 per month, while Viacom CBS kept the price at USD 5.99 per month with ads. A limited version of NBCUniversal's *Peacock* streaming service was free, and a more robust package was available for USD 4.99 (Sherman, 2020b). Analysts considered low prices as the reason for consumers' continuation with multiple subscriptions (see Table 5.2). However, consumers were also frustrated with having to subscribe to multiple platforms. Commenting on consumer frustration, Kevin Westcott, vice chairman of Deloitte, said, "There are over 300 streaming services in the United States right now, and the average household only subscribes to three or four, so there could be too many choices" (Hersko, 2019). He further added, "Consumers are frustrated they have to subscribe to so many services to get what they want. I don't think we'll see the continuous launching of more streaming services in the years ahead."

DISNEY VERSUS NETFLIX

Founded in 1998 as an online DVD rental platform, Netflix has been a leader in streaming video service (Moskowitz, 2021). In the third quarter of 2020, Netflix generated USD 6.5 billion in revenue and had 195 million subscribers globally (Stoll, 2021e, 2021f). Between 2013 and 2019, Netflix's original content titles increased from 16 to 371 (Stoll, 2021b). In 2019, the company had approximately 8,600 full-time employees (Stoll, 2021c).

Netflix was expected to spend more than USD 17 billion on content creation by December 2020 and surpass USD 28 billion by 2028 (Sherman, 2020a). In contrast, Disney had a budget of spending approximately USD 1 billion on Disney+ original content in its fiscal year 2020 and USD 2.5 billion by 2024, though the COVID-19 pandemic delayed Disney's investment (Sherman, 2020a).

Disney+ also mainly offered content for kids, unlike Netflix that primarily catered to adult content (Britt, 2019). However, Netflix was actively investing in kids' content as well (Lee, 2021). Kids had the potential to watch the same movie or show tirelessly hundreds of times (Tom, 2017).

Disney's original content streaming in the top 10 series list was less than Netflix's, though it had some edge over Netflix in streaming movies (see Table 5.3). In 2019, Disney+ had 7,500 TV episodes and 500 movies compared to Netflix's 47,000 TV episodes and 4,000 movies (Stoll, 2021d). Disney also had a licensing deal with Netflix. According to the agreement, every Disney film released between January 2016 and December 2018 would be added to the Netflix library in 2026. The list included *Black Panther, Beauty and the Beast, Incredibles II, Coco, Avengers: Infinity War, Star Wars: The Last Jedi,* and *Solo: A Star Wars Story* (Travers, 2019). Moreover, once added to Netflix, Disney could not stream these movies on its platform (Travers, 2019). Bloomberg reported that Netflix has some of Disney's "most-popular shows locked up for years" (Bui, 2019).

Netflix's focus was on volume, and it promised a "new movie every week" in 2021 and had a slate of 70 movies lined up for release in 2021 (Faughnder, 2021). For shows and series, while Netflix followed the binging model, i.e., "to watch a large number of televisions program (especially all the shows from one series) in succession" (Binge-Watch Is Collins' …, 2015),

TABLE 5.3 Top-10 Streaming Content of 2020: Original Series and Movies (Billion Minutes) by Streaming Service

Top 10 Streaming Content of 2020-Original Series (Streaming Service)	Steaming Minutes (Billion)	Top 10 Streaming Content of 2020—Movies (Streaming Service)	Steaming Minutes (Billion)
Ozark (Netflix)	30	Frozen II (Disney+)	15
Lucifer (Netflix)	19	Moana (Disney+)	11
The Crown (Netflix)	16	Secret Life of Pets 2 (Netflix)	9
Tiger King (Netflix)	16	Onward (Disney+)	8
The Mandalorian (Disney+)	15	Dr Seuss' the Grinch (Netflix)	6
The Umbrella Academy (Netflix)	13	Hamilton (Disney+)	6
Great British Baking Show (Netflix)	13	Spenser Confidential (Netflix)	5
Boss Baby: Back in Business (Netflix)	13	Aladdin (2019) (Disney+)	5
Longmire (Netflix)	11	Toy Story 4 (Disney+)	4
You (Netflix)	11	Zootopia (Disney+)	4

Source: Adapted from: Tops of 2020: Nielsen Streaming Unwrapped. (January 12, 2021). Nielsen.com. Retrieved from https://www.nielsen.com/us/en/insights/article/2021/tops-of-2020-nielsen-streaming-unwrapped/

Disney+ opted to release only one new episode of its shows per week. Typically, a series had eight episodes. This made subscribers pay for at least two months of service to watch all the episodes (Alexander, 2019) as they couldn't binge-watch. Strauss, head of content division prior to restructuring, said,

> We're just getting started so it made sense to build our fan base with episodic content coming out once a week in a more tradition model, because we felt that if we put everything out at once it would be harder for us to build the audience, rather than having people tuning in. To be honest, also some stuff won't be ready to binge, it's coming in as the months go by.
>
> (Rawden, 2019)

In January 2021, Strauss, a key executive involved in the launch of Disney+, resigned from Disney (Andreeva, 2021).

STREAMING VERSUS CINEMA

During the COVID-19 pandemic, Disney decided to launch two of its movies, Mulan and Soul, that the company initially scheduled for release on movie screens on Disney+ (Pulver, 2020). Comcast's NBCUniversal executives also reached an agreement with movie theater companies like AMC, Cinemark, and Cineplex to shorten the time for which movies were exclusively featured in theaters, i.e., from three months to 17 days (D'Alessandro, 2020). Disney-owned Marvel Studios produced *Black Widow* at a cost of USD 150 million to USD 200 million, with the potential of USD 750 million to more than USD 1 billion revenues at the global box office

(Whitten, 2020a). Disney would then generate a second round of revenues once *Black Widow* was made available on home videos and on-demand. Pushing these big-budget movies straight to home video of Disney+ implied less money for Disney (Whitten, 2020a).

Loeb also stated that subscription-based streaming had more revenue potential than one-time ticket sales in cinema theaters (Donnelly & Lang, 2020). He said, "I don't think they appreciate the tiger they have by the tail, which is to say the value they can drive by moving into a subscription model, which has been adopted by everyone from Microsoft to Amazon" (Donnelly & Lang, 2020). Despite Disney having control of brands like Marvel, Pixar, and Lucasfilm, in October 2020, Netflix surpassed Disney in terms of market capitalization with USD 244 billion, where Disney was valued at USD 233 billion (Donnelly & Lang, 2020). According to sources, this happened due to Netflix's subscription-based business model (Donnelly & Lang, 2020). Subscription-based models, in general, experienced 100% growth between 2011 and 2016, to the extent that the term "subscription economy" was coined (Luna, 2018). Peter Csathy, chairman of CREATV Media, said, "The Street [referring to The Wall Street] loves subscription business models and recurring revenue models" (Donnelly & Lang, 2020). He further added, "Locking consumers into some kind of monthly payment plan is the holy grail for investors."

According to experts, a focus on streaming could divert hundreds of millions of dollars in ticket sales to cinema theaters and other ancillary businesses, though COVID-19 enabled Disney to take these risks (Donnelly & Lang, 2020). Jason Squire, a professor at USC's School of Cinematic Arts, said, "As far as a theatrical release being shifted to streaming — these are very tough decisions" (Donnelly & Lang, 2020). He further added, "They involve sacrificing grosses. But the reality is there are no domestic grosses during coronavirus." Phil Clapp, chief executive of UK Cinema Association, cautioned that Hollywood's decisions to launch movies directly on streaming videos could "risk causing irreparable damage to key markets" and that when the studios want to rerelease their blockbusters, "it may be too late for many European cinemas" (Pulver, 2020).

THE ROAD AHEAD

Disney's focus on streaming services implied, similar to Netflix, that it wanted to be valued more for subscriber growth and less for traditionally used financial metrics of a conglomerate such as profit margin (Donnelly & Lang, 2020). Commenting on Disney+'s ability to grow and create shareholder value the way Disney wants, Chapek said, "Given the incredible success of Disney+ and our plans to accelerate our direct-to-consumer business, we are strategically positioning our company to more effectively support our growth strategy and increase shareholder value" (Sperling, 2021). Loeb also wrote to Chapek that "A more aggressive content roadmap will distinguish Disney as the only traditional US media company able to thrive in a world beyond the box office and the cable TV ecosystem, alongside digital-first businesses like Netflix and Amazon" (Sherman, 2020a). However, concerns remained regarding the effectiveness of Disney's restructuring and focusing more on streaming than movies. Can Chapek benefit shareholders from this restructuring? To what extent should he incorporate activist shareholder's suggestions in his strategic decisions?

DISCUSSION QUESTIONS

1. How shareholder activism shaped Disney's strategy?
2. How did the restructuring affect Disney's board oversight and management accountability?
3. Do you think any agency problems could arise from legacy influence versus current management?
4. Critically evaluate how restructuring affected the "S" and "G" dimensions of Disney's ESG performance.

CHAPTER NOTES

1 https://observer.com/2023/06/mark-zuckerberg-2023-shareholder-meeting/.
2 https://observer.com/2023/06/mark-zuckerberg-2023-shareholder-meeting/.
3 https://observer.com/2023/06/mark-zuckerberg-2023-shareholder-meeting/.
4 Carson, E. (2002). Factors associated with the development of board sub–committees. *Corporate Governance: An International Review*, *10* (1), 4–18.
5 Câmara, P., & Morais, F. (Eds.). (2022). *The Palgrave handbook of ESG and corporate governance*. Cham: Palgrave Macmillan.
6 Câmara, P., & Morais, F. (Eds.). (2022). *The Palgrave handbook of ESG and corporate governance*. Cham: Palgrave Macmillan.
7 https://www.aljazeera.com/features/2012/2/11/canada-mining-boom-leaves-natives-in-the-cold#:~:text=Environmental%20concerns,have%20nowhere%20else%20to%20go.%E2%80%9D.
8 https://about.starbucks.com/press/2023/starbucks-announces-intention-to-establish-a-new-environmental-partner-and-community-impact-board-committee-focused-on-oversight-of-stakeholder-promises/.
9 https://www.nestle.com/investors/corporate-governance.
10 https://www.npr.org/2024/12/03/nx-s1-5214484/elon-musk-tesla-compensation#:~:text=A%20CEO's%20superstar%20status%20can,enough%20to%20change%20McCormick's%20mind.
11 https://www.cnbc.com/2019/11/05/its-not-just-boeing-more-companies-are-splitting-ceo-and-chairman-roles.html.
12 https://www.cnbc.com/2019/11/05/its-not-just-boeing-more-companies-are-splitting-ceo-and-chairman-roles.html.
13 (1995). Four ways to choose a CEO: Crown heir, horse race, coup d'Etat, and comprehensive search. *Human Resource Management*, *34* (1pring), 141–164. https://doi.org/10.1002/hrm.3930340109.
14 http://apple.com/in/leadership/tim-cook/
15 Friedman, S. D. (Spring 1995). Four ways to choose a CEO: Crown Heir, horse race, Coup d'Etat, and comprehensive search. *Human Resource Management*, *34* (1), 141–164. https://doi.org/10.1002/hrm.3930340109.
16 Friedman, S. D. (Spring 1995). Four ways to choose a CEO: Crown Heir, horse race, Coup d'Etat, and comprehensive search. *Human Resource Management,* 34(1), 141–164. https://doi.org/10.1002/hrm.3930340109.
17 https://hbr.org/2012/03/a-ceo-succession-horse-race-is.
18 Friedman, S. D. (Spring1995). Four ways to choose a CEO: Crown Heir, horse race, Coup d'Etat, and comprehensive Search. *Human Resource Management, 34* (1), 141–164. https://doi.org/10.1002/hrm.3930340109.
19 Friedman, S. D. (Spring1995). Four ways to choose a CEO: Crown Heir, horse race, Coup d'Etat, and comprehensive search. *Human Resource Management, 34* (1), 141–164. https://doi.org/10.1002/hrm.3930340109.
20 https://journals.aom.org/doi/10.5465/AME.1987.4275652#:~:text=Exhibit%201%20shows%20the%20net,the%20difference%20was%20statistically%20insignificant.
21 https://www.spencerstuart.com/~/media/pdf%20files/research%20and%20insight%20pdfs/ceo-succession-making-the-right-choices_04jul2011.pdf.

22 https://www.spencerstuart.com/~/media/pdf%20files/research%20and%20insight%20pdfs/ceo-succession-making-the-right-choices_04jul2011.pdf.
23 https://www.reuters.com/business/autos-transportation/ferrari-appoints-stm-exec-benedetto-vigna-new-ceo-2021–06–09/#:~:text=Summary,a%20pure%20luxury%20goods%20company.
24 https://www.spencerstuart.com/~/media/pdf%20files/research%20and%20insight%20pdfs/ceo-succession-making-the-right-choices_04jul2011.pdf.
25 https://www.businessinsider.com/how-ex-taco-bell-ceo-brian-niccol-turned-around-chipotle-2019-12#:~:text=Brian%20Niccol%20has%20managed%20to,Chipotle%20locations%20in%20the%20US.
26 https://www.businessinsider.com/how-ex-taco-bell-ceo-brian-niccol-turned-around-chipotle-2019-12#:~:text=Brian%20Niccol%20has%20managed%20to,Chipotle%20locations%20in%20the%20US.
27 https://www.catalyst.org/en-us/insights/2024/ceo-activism-trend-brief.
28 https://corpgov.law.harvard.edu/2018/11/27/the-double-edged-sword-of-ceo-activism/.
29 Chiu, A. (2020). Goya's CEO said the U.S. is 'truly blessed' with President Trump. Latinos are now boycotting. *Washington Post,* July 10, 2020, accessed July 24, 2025. www.washingtonpost.com/nation/2020/07/10/goya-boycott-trump/.
30 Bremner, J. (2020, July 10). *Who owns Goya Foods? Calls for #BoycottGoya mount after CEO praises Trump. Newsweek.* https://www.newsweek.com/who-owns-goya-foods-calls-boycottgoya-mount-after-ceo-praises-trump-1516873
31 All the companies quitting Facebook. *New York Times,* July 7, 2020, accessed July 24, 2020. Retrieved from www.nytimes.com/2020/06/29/business/dealbook/facebook-boycott-ads.html.
32 All the companies quitting Facebook. *New York Times,* July 7, 2020, accessed July 24, 2020. Retrieved from www.nytimes.com/2020/06/29/business/dealbook/facebook-boycott-ads.html.
33 All the companies quitting Facebook. *New York Times,* July 7, 2020, accessed July 24, 2020. Retrieved from www.nytimes.com/2020/06/29/business/dealbook/facebook-boycott-ads.html.
34 Kosloff, S., Greenberg, J., Schmader, T., Dechesne, M., & Weise, D. (2010). Smearing the opposition: Implicit and explicit stigmatization of the 2008 US Presidential candidates and the current US President. *Journal of Experimental Psychology: General, 139*(3), 383–398.
35 Friedmann, S. (2019). Here's how you can find out which companies are backing Trump's 2020 campaign. *Bustle,* August 7, 2019, accessed July 24, 2020. Retrieved from www.bustle.com/p/how-to-find-out-which-companies-support-trump-so-you-know-where-your-moneys-going-18556393.
36 Friedmann, S. (2019). Here's how you can find out which companies are backing Trump's 2020 campaign. *Bustle,* August 7, 2019, accessed July 24, 2020. Retrieved from www.bustle.com/p/how-to-find-out-which-companies-support-trump-so-you-know-where-your-moneys-going-18556393.
37 Bailey, J. R., & Phillips, H. (2020). How do consumers feel when companies get political? *Harvard Business Review,* February 17, 2020, accessed July 31, 2020. Retrieved from https://hbr.org/2020/02/how-do-consumers-feel-when-companies-get-political.
38 https://www.credera.com/en-us/insights/importance-gender-intelligence.
39 https://www.credera.com/en-us/insights/importance-gender-intelligence.
40 https://www.credera.com/en-us/insights/importance-gender-intelligence.
41 Gender Intelligence Group. (January 26, 2015). What Is Gender Intelligence®? Genderintelligence.com. Retrieved from https://www.genderintelligence.com/what-is-gender-intelligence/
42 Walker, B. (March 1, 2023). Leading lady. *Dialogue.* Retrieved from https://dialoguereview.com/leading-lady/
43 Walker, B. (March 1, 2023). Leading lady. *Dialogue.* Retrieved from https://dialoguereview.com/leading-lady/
44 Gender Intelligence Group. (January 26, 2015). What Is Gender Intelligence®? Genderintelligence.com. Retrieved from https://www.genderintelligence.com/what-is-gender-intelligence/
45 Gender Intelligence Group. (January 26, 2015). What Is Gender Intelligence®? Genderintelligence.com. Retrieved from https://www.genderintelligence.com/what-is-gender-intelligence/
46 Africa Tech Perspectives. (August 9, 2022). Women in Tech: Spotlight on inclusivity with Digital Council Africa's Juanita Clark. *Connecting Africa.* https://www.connectingafrica.com/author.asp?section_id=768&doc_id=779538
47 Gender Intelligence Group. (January 26, 2015). What Is Gender Intelligence®? Genderintelligence.com. Retrieved from https://www.genderintelligence.com/what-is-gender-intelligence/
48 Africa Tech Perspectives. (August 9, 2022). Women in Tech: Spotlight on inclusivity with Digital Council Africa's Juanita Clark. *Connecting Africa.* https://www.connectingafrica.com/author.asp?section_id=768&doc_id=779538

49 Gender Intelligence Group. (January 26, 2015). What Is Gender Intelligence®? Genderintelligence.com. Retrieved from https://www.genderintelligence.com/what-is-gender-intelligence/
50 Gender Intelligence Group. (January 26, 2015). What Is Gender Intelligence®? Genderintelligence.com. Retrieved from https://www.genderintelligence.com/what-is-gender-intelligence/
51 CHRO South Africa. (November 25, 2019). Microsoft South Africa named as the top company to work for in 2020. Chro.co.za. Retrieved from https://chro.co.za/articles/microsoft-south-africa-named-as-the-top-company-to-work-for-in-2020/
52 Barnard, L. (2022). Lillian Barnard's post. *LinkedIn*. Retrieved from https://na.linkedin.com/posts/lillian-barnard-986b86144_startup-ato-microsoftstartupssummit-activity-7000416158138929152-ddCi
53 https://www.pewresearch.org/social-trends/2023/03/01/the-enduring-grip-of-the-gender-pay-gap/.
54 https://www.pewresearch.org/social-trends/2023/03/01/the-enduring-grip-of-the-gender-pay-gap/.
55 https://www.imd.org/blog/leadership/glass-ceiling/.
56 https://www.imd.org/blog/leadership/glass-ceiling/.
57 https://www.theguardian.com/sustainable-business/2014/aug/05/fortune-500-companies-crisis-woman-ceo-yahoo-xerox-jc-penny-economy#:~:text=Marissa%20Mayer%20poses%20at%20Google's,more%20diverse%20path%20for%20long.
58 https://www.theguardian.com/sustainable-business/2014/aug/05/fortune-500-companies-crisis-woman-ceo-yahoo-xerox-jc-penny-economy#:~:text=Marissa%20Mayer%20poses%20at%20Google's,more%20diverse%20path%20for%20long.
59 https://www.theguardian.com/sustainable-business/2014/aug/05/fortune-500-companies-crisis-woman-ceo-yahoo-xerox-jc-penny-economy#:~:text=Marissa%20Mayer%20poses%20at%20Google's,more%20diverse%20path%20for%20long.
60 https://www.theguardian.com/sustainable-business/2014/aug/05/fortune-500-companies-crisis-woman-ceo-yahoo-xerox-jc-penny-economy#:~:text=Marissa%20Mayer%20poses%20at%20Google's,more%20diverse%20path%20for%20long.
61 https://www.theguardian.com/sustainable-business/2014/aug/05/fortune-500-companies-crisis-woman-ceo-yahoo-xerox-jc-penny-economy#:~:text=Marissa%20Mayer%20poses%20at%20Google's,more%20diverse%20path%20for%20long.
62 https://www.theguardian.com/sustainable-business/2014/aug/05/fortune-500-companies-crisis-woman-ceo-yahoo-xerox-jc-penny-economy#:~:text=Marissa%20Mayer%20poses%20at%20Google's,more%20diverse%20path%20for%20long.
63 https://www.wsj.com/finance/pepsi-activist-elliott-investment-management-9a46654e.
64 https://www.wsj.com/finance/pepsi-activist-elliott-investment-management-9a46654e.
65 https://www.wsj.com/finance/pepsi-activist-elliott-investment-management-9a46654e.
66 https://www.cincinnati.com/story/money/2017/08/31/ceo-david-taylor-hedge-fund-head-nelson-peltz-wants-p-g-units-out-cincinnati/620122001/.
67 https://www.cincinnati.com/story/money/2017/08/31/ceo-david-taylor-hedge-fund-head-nelson-peltz-wants-p-g-units-out-cincinnati/620122001/.
68 https://www.hec.edu/en/activist-hedge-funds-good-some-bad-others.
69 Lee, M. M., Kim, J. J., & Bae, J. (2016). Are founder CEOs better innovators? Evidence from S&P 500 firms. *Academy of Management Proceedings, 2016* (1), 13311. https://doi.org/10.5465/AMBPP.2016.13311abstract
70 Lee, M. M., Kim, J. J., & Bae, J. (2016). Are founder CEOs better innovators? Evidence from S&P 500 firms. *Academy of Management Proceedings, 2016* (1), 13311. https://doi.org/10.5465/AMBPP.2016.13311abstract
71 Lee, M. M., Kim, J. J., & Bae, J. (2016). Are founder CEOs better innovators? Evidence from S&P 500 firms. *Academy of Management Proceedings, 2016* (1), 13311. https://doi.org/10.5465/AMBPP.2016.13311abstract
72 https://medium.com/@26shruti.kaushik/how-apple-revived-itself-through-innovation-a-story-of-reviving-the-brand-the-company-apple-inc-ea3194ea5b1d.
73 https://www.businessinsider.com/howard-schultz-creators-2016-6#running-starbucks-came-with-setbacks-too-when-schultz-returned-as-the-companys-ceo-in-2008-he-stepped-back-to-serve-as-chairman-during-an-8-year-hiatus-he-spent-a-few-years-leading-starbucks-massive-turnaround-tripling-profits-from-315-million-to-945-million-by-2010-14.

FURTHER READING

Girod, S. G. J., & Karim, S. (March–April, 2017). Restructure or reconfigure? *Harvard Business Review*. Retrieved from https://hbsp.harvard.edu/product/R1702K-PDF-ENG

Greenwood, R., & Schor, M. (January 2008). When (not) to listen to activist investors. *Harvard Business Review*. Retrieved from https://hbr.org/2008/01/when-not-to-listen-to-activist-investors

Hill, L. A. (January, 2007). Becoming the boss. *Harvard Business Review*. Retrieved from https://hbr.org/2007/01/becoming-the-boss

Hinkel, J., Poppe, H., Tonner, M., & Witten, C. (June 4, 2015). Agitators and reformers: How to respond to activist investors. *BoardSpan*. Retrieved from https://boardspan.com/users/0/library/agitators-and-reformers-how-to-respond-to-activist-investors

Leinwand, P., & Gilcreast, A. (November 30, 2016). Why top management should listen to activist investors. *Harvard Business Review*. Retrieved from https://hbr.org/2016/11/why-top-management-should-listen-to-activist-investors

Toma, A., Roghé, F., Noakes, B., Strack, R., Kilmann, J., & Dicke, R. (April 25, 2012). Flipping the odds for successful reorganization. *BCG*. Retrieved from https://www.bcg.com/publications/2012/people-organization-design-flipping-odds-successful-reorganization

Vadana, I. I., Torkkeli, L., Kuivalainen, O., & Saarenketo, S. (2019). The internationalization of born-digital companies. In A. Chidlow, P. N. Ghauri, T. Buckley, E. C. Gardner, & A. Qamar (Eds.). *The changing strategies of international business* (pp. 199–220). The Academy of International Business. Cham: Palgrave Macmillan. https://doi.org/10.1007/978-3-030-03931-8_10

CASE REFERENCES

Agnihotri, A., & Bhattacharya, S. (2022). *Disney: Restructuring for success with video streaming service Disney+*. Sage Business Cases. https://doi.org/10.4135/9781529795110

Alexander, J. (August 29, 2019). Disney is leading the charge against Netflix by returning to weekly episode releases. *The Verge*. Retrieved from https://www.theverge.com/2019/8/29/20831410/disney-plus-apple-hulu-netflix-binge-episodes-full-season-drop-vs-weekly-release-streaming-model

Andreeva, N. (January 6, 2021). Ricky Strauss departs Disney after 9 years; served as Disney+'s president of Content & Marketing at launch. Deadline.com. Retrieved from https://deadline.com/2021/01/ricky-strauss-departs-disney-president-of-content-marketing-at-launch-1234665922/

Binge-Watch Is Collins' Dictionary's Word of the Year. (November 5, 2015). *BBC*. Retrieved from https://www.bbc.com/news/entertainment-arts-34723515

Bob Chapek Named Chief Executive Officer of the Walt Disney Company. (February 25, 2020). Thewaltdisneycompany.com. Retrieved from https://thewaltdisneycompany.com/bob-chapek-named-chief-executive-officer-of-the-walt-disney-company/

Britt, R. (October 15, 2019). Disney+ mega movie list is good for kids, bad for parents. Fatherly.com. Retrieved from https://www.fatherly.com/news/disney-plus-movies-kids-parents/

Bui, H. T. (June 3, 2019). Disney movies won't be leaving Netflix as immediately—Or as permanently—As you think. Slashfilm.com. Retrieved from https://www.slashfilm.com/warnermedia-disney-movies-leaving-netflix-deals/

D'Alessandro, A. (July 28, 2020). Universal & AMC Theatres make peace, will crunch theatrical window to 17 days with option for PVOD after. Deadline.com. Retrieved from https://deadline.com/2020/07/universal-amc-theatres-theatrical-window-crush-pvod-agreement-1202997573/

Donnelly, M., & Lang, B. (October 13, 2020). Disney's streaming reorganization cheers investors but confuses insiders. *Variety*. Retrieved from https://variety.com/2020/film/news/disney-streaming-netflix-coronavirus-1234803258/

Easton, J. (June 26, 2019). Netflix film exec joins Disney+. *Television Business Journal*. Retrieved from https://tbivision.com/2019/06/26/netflix-film-exec-joins-disney/

Faughnder, R. (January 12, 2021). The wide shot: Five big questions for Hollywood in 2021. *Los Angeles, Times.* Retrieved from https://www.latimes.com/entertainment-arts/business/newsletter/2021-01-12/wide-shot-five-burning-questions-for-hollywood-the-wide-shot

Hersko, T. (June 13, 2019). Nearly half of U.S. consumers are frustrated with a bloated streaming market. *IndieWire*. Retrieved from https://www.indiewire.com/2019/06/too-many-streaming-services-television-decentralization-1202149596/

Lee, W. (January 12, 2021). In streaming wars, Disney+ bests Netflix in most popular movies in 2020. *Los Angeles Times.* Retrieved from https://www.latimes.com/entertainment-arts/business/story/2021-01-12/disney-netflix-ces-streaming-most-popular-movies

Luna, J. (August 17, 2018). Why every business will soon be a subscription business. *Sandford Business.* Retrieved from https://www.gsb.stanford.edu/insights/why-every-business-will-soon-be-subscription-business

Moskowitz, D. (May 16, 2021). Who are Netflix's main competitors? *Investopedia*. Retrieved from https://www.investopedia.com/articles/markets/051215/who-are-netflixs-main-competitors-nflx.asp

Muscaro, T. J. (December 11, 2020). Theaters vs. Disney+: Disney clarifies 2021 movie releases. Insidethemagic.net. Retrieved from https://insidethemagic.net/2020/12/disney-2021-movie-distribution-tm1/

Pulver, A. (October 12, 2020). Cinemas 'shocked and dismayed' by Disney decision to launch Soul on streaming. *The Guardian.* Retrieved from https://www.theguardian.com/film/2020/oct/12/cinemas-shocked-and-dismayed-by-disney-decision-to-launch-soul-on-streaming-pixar

Rawden, J. (October 22, 2019). Is Disney+ making the right choice by not using the Binge model?" *Cinema Blend*, October 22, 2019, accessed February 8, 2021. Retrieved from https://www.cinemablend.com/television/2482856/is-disney-making-the-right-choice-by-not-using-the-binge-model

Share of Subscription Video on Demand (SVoD) Subscribers Who also Subscribe to Other Services in the United States as of December 2020, by Service. (January 27, 2021). *Statista.* Retrieved from https://www.statista.com/statistics/778912/video-streaming-service-multiple-subscriptions/

Sherman, A. (October 7, 2020a). Activist investor Dan Loeb calls on Disney to end its $3 billion annual dividend and use the funds for Disney+ content. *CNBC.* Retrieved from https://www.cnbc.com/2020/10/07/dan-loeb-calls-on-disney-to-suspend-dividend-invest-it-in-disney-plus.html

Sherman, A. (December 10, 2020b). WarnerMedia won't cause an industry shake-up: Other studios unlikely to end theatrical window in 2021. *CNBC.* Retrieved from https://www.cnbc.com/2020/12/10/disney-nbcuniversal-viacomcbs-unlikely-to-follow-warnermedias-2021-movie-plan.html

Spangler, T. (April 11, 2019). Disney+ to launch in November, priced at $6.99 monthly. *Variety*. Retrieved from https://variety.com/2019/digital/news/disney-plus-streaming-launch-date-pricing-1203187007/

Sperling, N. (October 12, 2021). Disney reorganization puts a sharper focus on streaming. *The New York Times.* Retrieved from https://www.nytimes.com/2020/10/12/business/media/disney-streaming-reorganization.html

Stoll, J. (January 13, 2021a). Disney+'s number of subscribers worldwide from 1st quarter 2020 to 4th quarter 2020. *Statista.* Retrieved from https://www.statista.com/statistics/1095372/disney-plus-number-of-subscribers-us/

Stoll, J. (January 13, 2021b). Number of original content titles produced by Netflix worldwide from 2012 to 2019. *Statista.* Retrieved from https://www.statista.com/statistics/883491/netflix-original-content-titles/

Stoll, J. (January 13, 2021c). Number of Netflix employees from 2015 to 2019, by type. *Statista.* Retrieved from https://www.statista.com/statistics/587671/netflix-employees/

Stoll, J. (January 13, 2021d). Content available on Disney's new streaming service's (Disney+) compared to Netflix in the United States as of April 2019. *Statista.* Retrieved from https://www.statista.com/statistics/1041104/disney-catalog-netflix-comparison-us/

Stoll, J. (February 3, 2021e). Revenue generated by Netflix from 1st quarter 2013 to 4th quarter 2020. *Statista.* Retrieved from https://www.statista.com/statistics/273883/netflixs-quarterly-revenue/;

Stoll, J. (February 3, 2021f). Number of Netflix paid subscribers worldwide from 1st quarter 2013 to 4th quarter 2020. *Statista*. Retrieved from https://www.statista.com/statistics/250934/quarterly-number-of-netflix-streaming-subscribers-worldwide/

The Disney+ Interface Feels Empty But Elegant Compared to Netflix. (August 26, 2019). *The Verge*. Retrieved from https://www.theverge.com/2019/8/26/20830219/disney-plus-hands-on-first-look-demo-design-d23-wars-pixar-marvel

The Walt Disney Company: Form 10-K (September 29, 2018). *Securities and Exchange Commission*. Retrieved from https://www.annualreports.com/HostedData/AnnualReportArchive/w/NYSE_DIS_2018.pdf, p. 32.

The Walt Disney Company Announces Strategic Reorganization of Its Media and Entertainment Businesses. (October 12, 2020). Thewaltdisneycompany.com. Retrieved from https://thewaltdisneycompany.com/the-walt-disney-company-announces-strategic-reorganization-of-its-media-and-entertainment-businesses/

Tom. (August 22, 2017). Why can children watch the same movie or show 100 times in a week and not get tired of them? Tvovermind.com. Retrieved from https://www.tvovermind.com/can-children-watch-movie-show-100-times-week-not-get-tired/

Travers, B. (June 2, 2019). Netflix deals mean that Disney movies could come back in 2026. *IndieWire*. Retrieved from https://www.indiewire.com/2019/06/netflix-movies-leaving-for-disney-could-return-1202146618/

Walt Disney Company. (2012). *Library of Congress*. Retrieved from https://www.loc.gov/item/lcwaN0015612/

Waniata, R., & Marshall, R. (June 8, 2020). Disney+ review update: Streamer finds its footing. Digitaltrends.com. Retrieved from https://www.digitaltrends.com/media-streamer-reviews/disney-plus-review/

Westcott, K., Loucks, J., Downs, K., Arkenberg, C., & Jarvis, D. (2020). Digital media trends survey (14th ed.). *Deloitte*. Retrieved from https://www2.deloitte.com/us/en/insights/industry/technology/digital-media-trends-consumption-habits-survey/summary.html

Whitten, S. (April 23, 2020a). Why Hollywood is sticking with movie theaters and only a few films are heading to streaming. *CNBC*. Retrieved from https://www.cnbc.com/2020/04/23/why-hollywood-is-sticking-with-movie-theaters-and-not-streaming.html

Whitten, S. (October 12, 2020b). Disney says its 'primary focus' for entertainment is streaming—Announces a major reorg. *CNBC*. Retrieved from https://www.cnbc.com/2020/10/12/disney-reorganizes-to-focus-on-streaming-direct-to-consumer.html

Whitten, S. (October 13, 2020c). Meet Kareem Daniel, the head of Disney's new distribution unit. *CNBC*. Retrieved from https://www.cnbc.com/2020/10/13/meet-kareem-daniel-the-head-of-disneys-new-distribution-unit.html

Ziady, H. (November 26, 2020). Disney increases number of planned layoffs to 32,000 employees. *CNN Business*. Retrieved from https://edition.cnn.com/2020/11/26/media/disney-layoffs/index.html

CHAPTER 6

Corporate Innovation

Learning Objectives

After completing this chapter, students will be able to:

- Examine how co-creation takes place;
- Explore how firms can leverage a blue ocean strategy for innovation;
- Evaluate the significance of the corporate venture capital arm for innovation;
- Critically analyze challenges for corporate innovation due to patent trolls.

USER INNOVATION

Research suggests that users of products actually generated 20%–80% of critical inventions across different industries. Businesses were too late to innovate in the mountain bike category, as users themselves had already begun to modify their existing bikes with bicycle wheels to ride down mountains. Sometimes, these users themselves become entrepreneurs, such as the founder of Dropbox, who launched his business after realizing how often he forgot his flash drive; this could have been the case with others as well. Even a sweat-wicking shirt was not a typical corporate innovation. Kevin Plank, a former college football player, invented it.[1] Exhausted with his cotton shirts getting soaked with sweat during practice, Plank was motivated to invest in a sweat-wicking shirt.

Firms need to incorporate users and their perspectives into corporate innovation, which can benefit them in several ways. First, as users have firsthand experience with the product, they are better equipped to identify its shortcomings and unmet needs. These unmet needs, when discussed with businesses, can result in better, user-friendly innovations.[2] Then, some users are experts in their field and can act as influencers to promote innovation conducted by the firm based on users' ideas. Finally, when multiple users are engaged in product development, as is often the case with open innovation, users are more motivated to use the products, as they have been part of the product development journey.[3]

DOI: 10.4324/9781003568100-6

BLUE OCEAN STRATEGY

In the competition chapter, we studied how firms struggle to find a sustainable competitive advantage over their competitors as they compete against them. W. Chan Kim and Renée Mauborgne suggested that successful firms, instead of trying to beat the competition, search for uncontested market space, where competition does not exist. Thus, firms pursuing a *Blue Ocean* operate in product categories where there is no competitor. All industries in existence today were once blue oceans, including automobiles and electronics. Radical innovations were the driving forces behind the creation of these industries. However, firms may create a blue ocean out of existing industries and product categories. Kim and Maourbogne have suggested tools, such as the Eliminate-Reduce-Raise-Create (ERRC) grid, that firms can use to extend product boundaries in search of new markets and thereby create a blue ocean. *Eliminate* implies eradicating the taken-for-granted assumptions in the industry. *Reduce* implies diminishing the taken-for-granted assumptions in the industry. *Raise* implies increasing those factors in the industry that are generally not offered and *create* implies adding new factors in the industry that were never offered before.

In the circus industry, for instance, whenever an individual thinks of circus traits, that come to mind are animal shows and slapstick comedy. These are taken for granted assumptions, implying that when visiting a circus, one is most likely to see animal shows and comedy. With the Blue Ocean Strategy's ERRC curve, the first step, i.e., eliminate, would imply eliminating the taken-for-granted assumption in the circus industry, such as offering a circus without animal shows or reducing slapstick comedy in the circus being created from a Blue Ocean perspective.

Circuses typically lacked artistic elements such as music, dance, and storytelling. These aspects were more common in live theater. However, circus companies may add these elements, which they would otherwise offer at a lesser level. Then, certain aspects, such as unified thematic narratives and immersive multi-sensory atmospheres, were completely absent from the circus industry and can be added from scratch, implying the creation of these factors in the circus industry.

Cirque du Soleil revolutionized the circus industry by expanding its boundaries with the addition of more acrobats, dance, and music themes, while eliminating animal shows and reducing slapstick comedy. Cirque du Soleil became an instant hit among viewers. Moreover, when the industry boundary is extended, it generally caters to a new segment of customers. Circus, for instance, was more appealing to kids due to its animal shows; however, dance-based performances in Cirque du Soleil became more attractive to the young and middle-aged sections of the audience. Cirque du Soleil thus created a blue ocean for itself.

Similarly, in the wine industry, some of the taken-for-granted assumptions are bitter taste and the nature of the vineyard. Sweet and fruity flavor traditionally are generally absent in wine as a product category. Yellow Tail, a new wine, was introduced by Australian entrepreneurs with the intent of creating a blue ocean, as the wine industry was already saturated with multiple competitors. Thus, instead of focusing on wine drinkers (typical customers of the wine industry), Yellow Tail focused on non-wine drinkers and made wine more relevant for them. They thus eliminated the complexities of the vineyard and the bitter taste of wine, creating fruity wine flavors, reducing the variety of wine characteristics, and focusing on simpler, easy-to-drink wine styles. Yellow Tail raised the accessibility and appeal of wine to non-wine drinkers by making wine consumption easier and less intimidating.

CORPORATE VENTURE CAPITAL ARM

Corporate venture capital (CVC) refers to a division of a large corporation that invests corporate funds into innovative startups. This way, without directly investing in R&D in-house, large corporations can keep track of emerging innovative technologies. Startups share technologies with CVCs, given the equity investment of CVCs in startups. Startups also benefit as they gain access to the parent company's networks, market expertise, and distribution channel resources, where innovative products can be pilot tested. Google (Alphabet), Microsoft, and Unilever all have their CVCs named as Google Ventures, M12, and Unilever Ventures, respectively. Google Ventures invested in NEST, a smart home technology company, and later acquired it for USD 3.2 billion. This acquisition, facilitated by a CVC arm investment, helped Google strengthen its position in the Internet of Things (IoT) market.[4] Google also invested in Uber. Uber benefited from Google's technology, including its mapping services, which not only contributed to Uber's growth but also generated substantial financial returns for Google.[5]

CVC arms offer several benefits to both startups and their corporate parents. Corporate parents can offer more innovative products without direct investment in R&D. Firms can leverage their established distribution channels and customer networks to rapidly test new products launched by startups, while also opening up their network and distribution resources to startups. For instance, Kraft Heinz, through its venture capital arm, Evolv Ventures, invested USD 3.5 million in a vegan cheese startup, New Culture, which is developing dairy-free mozzarella.[6] The new culture was likely to benefit from Kraft Heinz's distribution channels to pilot test dairy-free mozzarella.[7]

As incumbent firms invest in multiple startups across different sectors, they can gain a buffer against uncertainties affecting their core business operations. If a startup investment fails, the risk is limited due to the limited investment in the startup, compared to in-house expansion of the business in new markets with intensive R&D. Johnson & Johnson's CVC allows the company to partner with several startups in the healthcare sector, thereby accelerating its speed to enter new therapeutic areas while minimizing risk.[8]

INCUMBENT FIRMS COMBATTING DISRUPTIVE TECHNOLOGIES THROUGH INNOVATION

Typically, startups have displaced large incumbent firms in the past from their business. For instance, digital photography displaced Kodak, Netflix displaced DVD players like Blockbuster, Uber disrupted the yellow taxi market, and Amazon disrupted specialty retailers like Toys "R" Us with its e-commerce model. With CVCs now in place, incumbent firms keep a better track of newer technologies and innovation, and instead of being displaced by startups, they gradually acquire disruptive startups after making an initial equity investment in them.[9] BodyArmor threatened the dominant position of Coca-Cola's sports drink Powerade, owing to its "healthier" image. Coca-Cola not only made an initial investment in BodyArmor, but as the brand became successful, it also later acquired it.[10]

Some incumbent firms, such as Microsoft, have been able to combat disruptive technologies by diversifying into innovative fields rather than adhering to a myopic vision and restricting their investment to their core business only. Microsoft countered the disruptive force of cloud computing by transitioning from a "Windows-First" philosophy to a "Cloud-First" strategy. Bearing the risk of cannibalization, Satya Nadella, CEO of Microsoft, opted for cloud computing instead of trying to defend Windows, which was a desktop-centric operating system, compared to central storage like a cloud-integrated platform. Retaining user-friendly features of Windows for consumers, Microsoft launched Windows 365, which retained the Windows experience for users, including its apps and settings, with the added benefit of the Microsoft Cloud, where users can store information on any device. Thus, Microsoft transitioned from an operating system experience tied to specific hardware, i.e., a laptop or desktop computer, to a portable, cloud-based storage solution.

When new trends emerge, companies these days adapt to those trends rather than trying to defend their existing products. Even leading beverage companies like Coca-Cola and PepsiCo launched new drinks, such as energy drinks or zero-calorie versions like Coke Zero or Diet Pepsi. The launch of these new drinks was related to the increasing health consciousness among consumers, and rather than trying to defend traditional colas like Coca-Cola Classic and Pepsi, which were essentially sugary beverages, they were trying to offer something new. These new launches, although they lowered sales of traditional products, helped these incumbent firms expand their overall markets.

INCREASING SCOPE OF THE FIRM WITH TECHNOLOGICAL INNOVATION

A key challenge for firms is how to exploit their technological innovation to enhance revenue-earning opportunities.[11] Expanding the scope of the firm based on current technology and its iterations helps to enhance revenue-earning streams for firms while also reducing reliance on a single line of business. For example, before the launch of the iPod in 2001, Apple was primarily a personal computer company operating in both hardware and software markets. However, a completely unrelated industry, namely the music industry, was facing a critical challenge: illegal downloads through peer-to-peer services such as Napster, which were adversely affecting traditional album sales. Apple devised a solution, challenging the album-based sales model with an individual song-based sales model through iTunes. Listeners could download individual songs for USD 0.99. Furthermore, by leveraging its hardware capabilities, Apple invented the iPod, a portable device capable of storing up to 1,000 songs, which was significantly more than a traditional MP3 player. By integrating its iPod with iTunes, Apple expanded the scope of its business and ventured into the service market, establishing a new revenue stream.

Tesla also leveraged its technology to enter an unfamiliar market. For instance, Tesla used its EV battery technology to expand into the energy storage market. Before Tesla's energy storage device, Powerwall, in 2015, home battery storage was a geeky task for consumers. Tesla's Powerwall was easy to install. By using Powerwall, homeowners can store excess solar energy and use it during peak-rate periods, especially at night, resulting in even lower utility bills and a more economical and environmentally friendly lifestyle. Musk further leveraged technology to serve B2B markets by developing large-scale Powerpack and Megapack systems, which helped stabilize electricity grids and increase their reliance on renewable energy, particularly during power failures, thereby preventing blackouts.

Sometimes, firms innovated to solve their internal problems, which resulted in an increased overall scope of the firm. For instance, as Amazon expanded its e-retailing business, it faced challenges with storing customer data that required a massive IT infrastructure.[12] Before cloud computing, managing such infrastructure was expensive for Amazon, which drove Amazon to innovate and develop solutions internally. Although designed to solve its own customer data storage problem, Amazon realized that it could easily expand the scope of its firm and enter the B2B sector with a scalable cloud computing service, which eventually led to the creation of the Amazon Web Services division.

ROLE OF HUMAN RESOURCE MANAGEMENT MECHANISMS IN PROMOTING INNOVATION

In high-tech industries, firms often use governance mechanisms, such as technology committees established by the board of directors, to monitor technology development and innovation initiatives by top management. Cray Inc., Hewlett Packard, and Chiquita Brands in the food sector formed "Strategic Technology Assessment Committee," "Technology Committee"[13] and "Food Innovation, Safety & Technology Committee" respectively to oversee innovation directives.[14] For socially impactful innovations, a board of directors with a political background can be especially useful, given the public policy knowledge they possess.[15] Moreover, as corporate innovation is inherently risky, having a politically connected board member on the technology committee can also facilitate preferential access to bank loans, often at lower interest rates.[16]

Although the role of organizational culture in promoting creativity and innovation is well established, specific values that promote innovation and teamwork can be at odds with each other. CEOs who promote an individualistic culture in the workplace can foster better innovation, particularly radical innovation. This promotion of radical innovation occurs because breakthrough innovation requires challenging taken-for-granted assumptions and overhauling systems, in contrast to incremental innovation that involves several rounds of product iterations to improve product performance incrementally.[17] In companies that promote individualistic thinking, employees tend to disagree with the opinions of their peers, which may be detrimental to team spirit but beneficial for innovation. CEOs need to strike a balance between team culture and individualistic culture in the workplace.[18]

One of the less explored issues in innovation is how employee well-being influences their innovative capability, while researchers have emphasized the role of factors such as job satisfaction, stress levels, and leadership support. However, contemporary research suggests that employees' sleep levels can significantly influence innovation. Those who sleep for five to six hours are generally less productive employees compared to those who sleep for seven to eight hours.[19] Employees with insufficient sleep may struggle to generate novel ideas, which is a fundamental basis for innovation.[20] Thus, organizations' human resources must promote the well-being of employees.

STRATEGIC CHALLENGES FOR INNOVATION: PATENT TROLLS

Although corporate innovation is vital, challenges such as patent trolls can adversely affect a firm's innovation productivity. Patent troll firms, or non-practicing entities (NPEs), tend to be small (e.g., VirnetX has just 20 employees).[21] Although they hold patent portfolios, these patents are rarely used to develop products or commercialize them.[22] Patent troll firms merely aggregate as many patents as possible, then target cash-rich firms and sue them for intellectual property infringement.[23] Large companies such as Apple, the International Business Machines Corporation (IBM), Samsung, or the Microsoft Corporation (Microsoft) file for patents because they intend to use the patented products or processes. Thus, patents filed by larger corporations are genuine and aimed at protecting the exclusivity of products, given they have invented or developed them after "spending huge sums on research and development, meant to capture a better market share through innovative products."[24]

NPEs believe that the likelihood of a positive legal outcome after suing a cash-rich firm for IPR violation is high (for example, as VirnetX did in Marshall, East Texas), and then they file the lawsuit, in the hope that cash-rich firms will be able to make immediate payments. Sometimes, NPE patent infringement litigation targets divisions of conglomerates that do not contribute to overall cash flow.[25] For instance, an NPE might sue a firm for alleged information technology infringement, even if the firm earned all its revenue from its unrelated lumber division and its information technology division was unprofitable.[26] In 2019, 59.2% of patent infringement cases filed by NPEs were in the high-tech sector.[27]

According to research, when NPEs sue cash-rich firms for IPR violations or patent litigation, it results in a 25% reduction in R&D expenditures by large corporations.[28] For instance, in one case, sales of medical imaging software firms that were sued by a patent troll declined compared to those that were not. This happened as the focal firm stopped investing in incremental innovations. The firm believed that any further innovation would only further increase the likelihood of being sued unconstitutionally. Firms are also demotivated to innovate, as they lose more money paying patent trolls than they could earn from commercializing their innovations.[29]

ASSIGNMENT QUESTIONS

1. What are the benefits of user innovation? Provide one example of user-based innovation that was highly successful in your home country. Explore the different steps the company took to pursue user innovation.
2. Develop a blue ocean strategy for an entrepreneur in your chosen industry, utilizing the ERRC model.
3. What is CVC? Provide one example from your home country where an investment by a corporate venture arm failed. Explore reasons for the same.
4. Can a firm leverage technology to expand the scope of its business? Give one example from your home country.

CASE STUDY **6.1**

Vimeo

Developing Blue Ocean for B2B Customers

Agnihotri, A., & Bhattacharya, S. (2023). *Vimeo: Developing Blue Ocean for B2B customers*. Sage Business Cases. https://doi.org/10.4135/9781529622652

INTRODUCTION

Vimeo.com Inc (Vimeo) is a New York-based video hosting, sharing, and services platform provider. Led by Anjali Sud (CEO), Vimeo focused on delivering high-definition videos to B2B (Business to Business) clients across a range of devices. Experts considered Vimeo as a competitor to YouTube by serving as a viewing platform (Patel, 2021). Since 2014, after Sud joined Vimeo, it began to operate like a software company helping businesses and creators edit and publish high-quality videos (Sanchez, 2021). Several entrepreneurs, such as flower shop owners and mom-and-pop restaurants needed to drive traffic to their website or the store (Patel, 2021). They did this by posting video ads on social media sites, such as Instagram and Facebook (Patel, 2021). But video shooting implied hiring a crew, writing a script, shooting the actual video, and finally editing it using professional software. This process was a lot to get a 20-second video that had a shelf life of just a day (Patel, 2021). For cash-crunched entrepreneurs, this was even more challenging. Through its OTT (Over the Top) platform, Vimeo offered an app that did all this for companies (Patel, 2021). The app offered templates, stocked licensed footage, music, and everything required for video production. Sud said, "We take it all and boil it down for you so you can create video for social media to drive your customers to your site or your store, in a matter of minutes" (Patel, 2021). Sud added, "Our goal is to help any business or professional or organization, use video the same way that they use text or image as a powerful way to communicate" (Patel, 2021). The video medium of communicating and advertising further strengthened during the COVID-19 pandemic, which helped Vimeo grow in this valuable niche of the video communication ecosystem (Patel, 2021).

However, in July 2022, Vimeo laid off 6% of its workforce due to an economic downturn that amounted to around 70 employees in total, consisting of ten employees from video hosting, sharing, and services, where it established its R&D center. The laying off happened after, in June 2021, Vimeo announced it would double its headcount by 2022 (Orbach, 2022). Moreover, although Vimeo reported profits for a quarter, it remained undervalued at the launch of its IPO (US SEC, 2021a; Weil, 2021). On the first day of its stock trading, i.e., on May 25, 2021, Vimeo traded at USD 42.31, down 18.8% from the expected value (Weil, 2021). Moreover, experts believed that Vimeo faced the risk of increasing competition in the video-making competitive space (Spangler, 2021). Dan Salmon, BMO Capital Market analyst, said, "We think Vimeo's biggest challenge will be a myriad of competitors from a variety of angles as the shift to video streaming comes in many forms" (Spangler, 2021). Competitors were expected to range from YouTube to smaller video-hosting providers like Brightcove and Kaltura (Spangler, 2021). How could Sud defeat the competitive threat in the newly captured B2B market space? How can she make the business grow? What can she do to improve the stock market performance of Vimeo?

BACKGROUND

Vimeo was founded in 2004 by Zach Klein and Jake Lodwick as an American video hosting, sharing, and services platform. The company's name is a blend of "video" and "me" (Taulli, 2021). Lodwick and Klein were programmers who also created several other websites, including CollegeHumor, part of Connected Ventures (Taulli, 2021). In 2006, InterActiveCorp (IAC) acquired the company, with CollegeHumor being the primary driver, though later Vimeo turned out to be a real gem (Taulli, 2021). IAC was a leading media and Internet company (Taulli, 2021). IAC followed the strategy of spinning off entrepreneurial firms after they had achieved sizeable scale and maturity. Some of its spinoffs were Expedia, LendingTree, and Ticketmaster, and in May 2021, Vimeo also joined the league (Taulli, 2021).

At the time of acquisition, Vimeo was a money-losing business with less than USD 40 million annual revenue (Bertoni & Gara, 2021). Vimeo was targeting the booming streaming business, for which it also hired executives from Paramount and Hulu (Bertoni & Gara, 2021). It signed contractual distribution agreements with firms like Lionsgate, CBS Interactive, and Spike Lee for content to effectively compete against Netflix, Amazon Prime, and HBO by offering Hollywood movies on its platform (Bertoni & Gara, 2021).

In 2014, Sud, who had business degrees from Wharton and Harvard Business School and worked at Amazon, joined Vimeo (Bertoni & Gara, 2021). In July 2017, Vimeo appointed Sud as the CEO, where she previously worked as General Manager and head of marketing. Sud changed the focus of Vimeo from a video streaming site to video creation and other video-related solution companies. Sud was also designated Young Global Leader of the World Economic Forum and was listed as one of Fortune's *40 Under 40* rising business leaders in 2018 (Fortune's 2018 40 Under 40, 2018).

Vimeo delivered high-definition video across several devices, leveraging on the Software-as-a-Service (SaaS) model (Deter, 2021). Vimeo designed its cloud platform to offer a single video solution for every business: from local Small and Medium Businesses (SMBs) to global enterprises, where SMBs could create engaging videos, collaborate with colleagues, and securely broadcast live events to audiences globally (Vimeo Raises $150 Million of Equity, 2020). From August 2019 to October 2020, Vimeo expanded its product portfolio based on customer segments with the launch of Vimeo Enterprise (targeted at larger organizations and offering internal broadcast and collaboration tools, Vimeo Create (a quick, easy video making tool for Small and Medium Businesses) and Vimeo Record (Ha, 2020) (a free video messaging tool for teams) (Vimeo Raises $150 Million of Equity, 2020). Sud said,

> Our goal is to radically simplify how businesses create and share video, with tools that are far more intuitive and cost effective than they've been historically. We're energized to access additional capital to pursue this enormous opportunity with the full focus and scale of the Vimeo platform.
>
> (Vimeo Raises $150 Million of Equity, 2020)

Since the COVID-19 pandemic, the Vimeo platform scaled to more than 200 million users globally (Patel, 2021). The company saw solid traction with its enterprise and collaboration products, with more than 3,500 enterprise customers, including Amazon, Starbucks, Deloitte, Zendesk, Rite Aid, and Siemens, and 1.6 million paying subscribers (see Figure 6.1). Vimeo became profitable in the third quarter of 2020, and its overall revenue grew 44% year-over-year (Vimeo Raises $150 Million of Equity, 2020). In November 2020, Vimeo was valued at USD 2.8 billion and raised USD 150 million from Thrive Capital and GIC, Singapore's sovereign wealth fund (Bertoni & Gara, 2021). By January 2021, its valuation reached USD 6 billion, and it received further funding of USD 300 million from T. Rowe Price and Oberndorf Enterprises (Bertoni & Gara, 2021).

In the first Quarter of 2021, Vimeo increased research and development expenses by USD 6.2 million, or 40%, compared to Quarter 1 of 2020, which included USD 5 million in compensation expense due to increased headcount and an increase of USD 1.3 million in stock-based compensation expense (US SEC, 2021a). Similarly, in the First Quarter of 2021, Vimeo's sales and marketing expenses also increased by USD 6.9 million, or 28%, with an almost 50% increase of USD 3.6 million attributed to compensation expense owing to growth

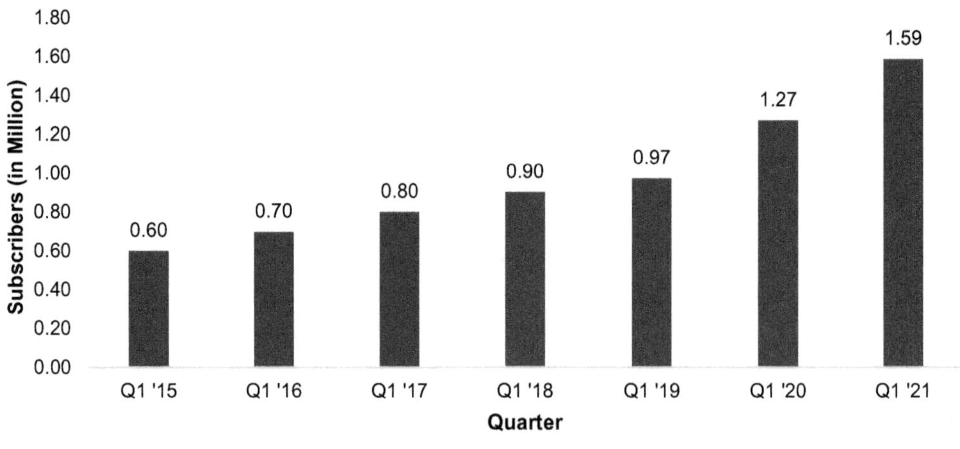

FIGURE 6.1 Number of Vimeo Subscribers Worldwide (Quarter 1, 2015–Quarter 1, 2021)

Source: Statista Research Department. (August 9, 2021). Number of Vimeo subscribers worldwide from 1st quarter 2015 to 1st quarter 2021. *Statista*. Retrieved from https://www.statista.com/statistics/705598/vimeo-subscribers-worldwide/

TABLE 6.1 Vimeo Financials (2020–2021) (USD Million)

	Three Months Ended March 31,	
	2020	**2021**
Revenue	56.97	89.42
Gross profit	18.36	64.47
Research and development expenses	15.29	21.48
Sales and marketing expenses	25.13	32.07
General and administrative expense	12.20	14.52
Total operating expense	55.80	70.06
Operating loss	–17.19	–5.60
Earnings (loss) before income taxes	–19.71	3.70

Source: US SEC. (May 21, 2021). Vimeo: Form 10Q (March 31, 2021). Vimeo.com. Retrieved from https://investors.vimeo.com/static-files/fcb36611-1c2c-44a2-af24-7adee05d070c.

in salesforce and USD 2.9 million in advertising costs (US SEC, 2021a) (see Table 6.1). In April 2021, Vimeo had more than 700 employees, about half in R&D and the rest spread across sales, marketing, and customer support (Bertoni & Gara, 2021). Vimeo's intellectual property included 15 registered patents in the "Information Storage" category (Vimeo, 2021).

THE PROBLEM WITH B2B CUSTOMERS & VIMEO'S SOLUTION

In 2014, when Sud joined Vimeo as its marketing director, she observed an emerging trend: SMBs were posting short advertising clips and product demos. Sud said, "It was everything from mom-and-pops to tech startups to the marketing department of large corporations" (Bertoni & Gara, 2021). She added, "They were so diverse, it had to be a trend." She also noticed that this segment of B2B customers was not being served amply. Sud added, "There was a huge group of users that no one was serving." With emerging opportunity in B2B advertising tools, Sud also realized that if Vimeo continues to operate in the streaming business, it would be very challenging to compete against deep-pocketed giants like Amazon Prime Video and Netflix (Bertoni & Gara, 2021). Sud in 2014 believed that Vimeo's future was not producing Hollywood hits but helping B2B customers in Silicon Valley (Bertoni & Gara, 2021). She wanted to shift Vimeo's focus from entertainment to entrepreneurs (Bertoni & Gara, 2021). Sud said, "Vimeo had long been a software company for filmmakers, but the market was too small" (Bertoni & Gara, 2021). She added, "There was another, much bigger market—businesses. What Squarespace and GoDaddy did for websites, we could do with video." She pitched her idea to Joey Levin, IAC CEO. To Levin, Sud said, "This is a real business that's relevant to a much larger audience than anyone thinks" (Bertoni & Gara, 2021). Levin gave Sud consent to test the idea (Bertoni & Gara, 2021). Levin said, "We like to find smart, talented, ambitious people, throw them into the deep end and see if they can swim" (Bertoni & Gara, 2021).

The IAC board gave Sud a team of 50 people and a year to develop some tools. Sud created an incubator within Vimeo and launched the Vimeo Business product (Sud & Roth, 2020). According to Sud, the product gained incredible traction from users (Sud & Roth, 2020). At the end of 2014, according to Sud, everyone at Vimeo said, "This is a huge market. It leans into our strengths, it's something no one else is doing, and it could be huge" (Sud & Roth, 2020). After the product launch, Sud dove into the data. She asked herself, "Who was using our tools? What were they using the most? What did they like, and what did they not like? When our subscribers left us, where did they go?" (Sud & Roth, 2020). That data indicated that the fastest-growing customer segment was small businesses. These businesses did not have the budgets to spend on external video production and were trying to reach their customers online (Sud & Roth, 2020).

Next, Sud's team developed tools for businesses to upload logos, insert buy-now buttons and add email capture to their videos (Bertoni & Gara, 2021). Vimeo's most significant asset was "Vimeo Create," a platform offering video creation tools that entrepreneurs and marketers used to develop their video-based assets (Alaupovic, 2020). Vimeo called its products Vimeo OTT products (Patel, 2021). The video-making facility offered by Vimeo had options to add attractive features such as brand fonts, colors, graphics, music, text captions, and access to a stock footage library (Alaupovic, 2020). Creators could use various custom templates from Vimeo, including seasonal announcements, promotional use, and several other categories (Alaupovic, 2020). Publishers were also able to develop videos from scratch using their footage or media (Alaupovic, 2020). Creators worked seamlessly with media from any device, including phone or Google Photos, Dropbox, Facebook, and even CRM workflows (Alaupovic, 2020). Vimeo offered video editing services through AI smart editor that included a feature-rich toolset without complex video editing (Alaupovic, 2020). Vimeo also provided tools to help businesses upload video content on Facebook and YouTube, company portal, website, or blog (Patel, 2021). To help small businesses, Vimeo acquired Magisto, an artificial intelligence startup founded in Israel that developed editing and production tools for short-form videos (La Monica, 2019). Sud commenting on the need for acquisition, stated, "People are building their own online video networks," "They are creating thriving businesses online to go direct to their audience and customers. You don't have to be a Hollywood studio or Netflix or Hulu or Amazon to have your own channel" (La Monica, 2019).

Vimeo offered a free Basic account and four subscription-based services. The free Basic account allowed 500 megabytes (MB) per week and 5 gigabytes (GB) per year of content space for file uploads and was available only to individuals (Choose a Plan, 2021). Vimeo Plus was the lowest-level subscription that cost USD 84 per year, allowing up to 5 GB per week and 250 GB per year to be uploaded (Choose a Plan, 2021), again available to individuals only. Vimeo Pro was the second level of subscription. It was designed for professionals and businesses, costing USD 240 per year and allowing 20 GB per week and one terabyte (TB) per year of content to be uploaded (Choose a Plan, 2021). Vimeo Premium was the third level of subscription that allowed 7 TB of storage per year. Vimeo Enterprise was the highest level of subscription wherein Vimeo customized the services according to the clients' requirements. Both Vimeo Premium and Vimeo Enterprise offered unlimited live streaming and several additional features like viewer-level analytics, graphics, polls, etc. (Choose a Plan, 2021).

Each of these tiers offered escalating levels of customer service and personalization (Choose a Plan, 2021). Sud believed Vimeo's pricing was a low-price proposition, which was possible because of economies of scale. She said, "If we were only serving 100 customers, we would never be able to justify that, but we have 200 million users on our site" (Patel, 2021). Vimeo acquired subscribers primarily through four strategies. The first involved the conversion of free users to subscribers through in-product messaging or word of mouth. The second strategy was acquiring subscribers through digital marketing channels. The third strategy involved actively leveraging the salesforce, usually for enterprise customers. Vimeo's fourth strategy was acquiring subscribers through third-party partnerships and integrations (US SEC, 2021b). Vimeo also deployed the "land and expand" strategy to maximize revenues from existing customers, where it inspired existing subscribers to upgrade to higher-priced plans over time (US SEC, 2021b). Vimeo further focused on increasing the number of employees, teams, and departments that could use Vimeo's platform and increase organization-wide contract value for enterprise customers (US SEC, 2021b).

Within a few years, Sud had transformed Vimeo into a one-stop shop to shoot, edit, store, and distribute video for enterprises (Bertoni & Gara, 2021). In the summer of 2017, Vimeo announced Sud as the CEO. She said, "It never occurred to me that they would offer me the position" (Bertoni & Gara, 2021). According to Sud, IAC investors said, "Anjali, you have been championing this, we will let you run it" (Sud & Roth, 2020). Vimeo reported revenues of USD 89 million during the first quarter of 2021, representing a 57% increase from the same period in 2020 (see Table 6.1). A 25% increase in average subscribers consisting of self-serve and enterprise customers and individuals, businesses, and organizations drove Vimeo's revenue growth (US SEC, 2021a). Vimeo further attributed the growth to average revenue per user growth in enterprise customers, whose average annual contract values were significantly more than other individual customers (US SEC, 2021a). Before the COVID-19 pandemic, Vimeo's growth was around 27%, but during the pandemic, growth blossomed even more. Sud said, "Overnight, video went from nice-to-have to need-to-have" (Bertoni & Gara, 2021).

VIMEO'S IMPACT ON CUSTOMERS AND FUTURE GROWTH POTENTIAL

Businesses were enhancing usage of video marketing techniques for a better online presence (Top 5 Trends in Video Production, 2016). A video on a website landing webpage increased the conversion rate of consumers by 80%. Including video in an email led to a 200%–300% increase in click-through rate (Top 5 Trends in Video Production, 2016). YouTube reports also suggested that the mobile video consumption base was increasing by 100% every year (Top 5 Trends in Video Production, 2016). Firms using Vimeo could also live stream videos, for instance, a yoga instructor or a dance studio live streaming their classes. CEOs of large Fortune 500 companies, such as Rite Aid, Amazon, or Starbucks, could securely broadcast CEO town halls or HR training to their employees globally in high-quality videos (Top 5 Trends in Video Production, 2016). Vimeo, in a way, offered TV studio-type capability in the hands of communication teams and HR professionals, demand for which since the COVID-19 pandemic rose drastically (Top 5 Trends in Video Production, 2016).

Though Vimeo could not create its streaming channel, several smaller enterprises launched their subscription channels on different platforms such as YouTube by leveraging on video production tools of Vimeo (Bertoni & Gara, 2021). Companies like Deloitte, Pottery Barn, and Forbes used Vimeo to deliver training and onboarding videos apart from live streaming corporate events to employees spread globally (Bertoni & Gara, 2021). Among SMBs, Vimeo clients ranged from indie filmmakers to Pilate instructors. Sud said, "We're both a 16-year-old video platform and a three-year-old software startup" (Bertoni & Gara, 2021). Before Vimeo, if someone wanted to develop a Netflix-like service, they were required to hire a set of engineers and designers for creating a template (Patel, 2021). Not only did it cost more resources but also more time (Patel, 2021). However, by offering video production tools to masses and economies of scale, Vimeo lowered the cost of video production (Patel, 2021).

Vimeo benefited video creators as they could, in a way, to create their channels on their apps, or Amazon, Roku, iOS, or websites and charge whatever they wanted from customers (Patel, 2021) (see Figure 6.2). Emphasizing customer benefit through Vimeo video production, Sud said,

> Wow, I can make way more money if I get a subset of my followers on YouTube to actually come and subscribe to my own channel and pay me directly, I can make more money than just purely on an ad model basis.
>
> (Patel, 2021)

In general, several developments were taking place in video production techniques, such as that in virtual reality and 4K video production and aerial and drone video shooting (Top 5 Trends in Video Production, 2016). Some of the trends in video marketing tools were:

Virtual Reality. Prominent players such as Samsung and Google were developing virtual reality technology, and hardware developers were implementing radical virtual reality changes for mass consumption (Top 5 Trends in Video Production, 2016). Big companies,

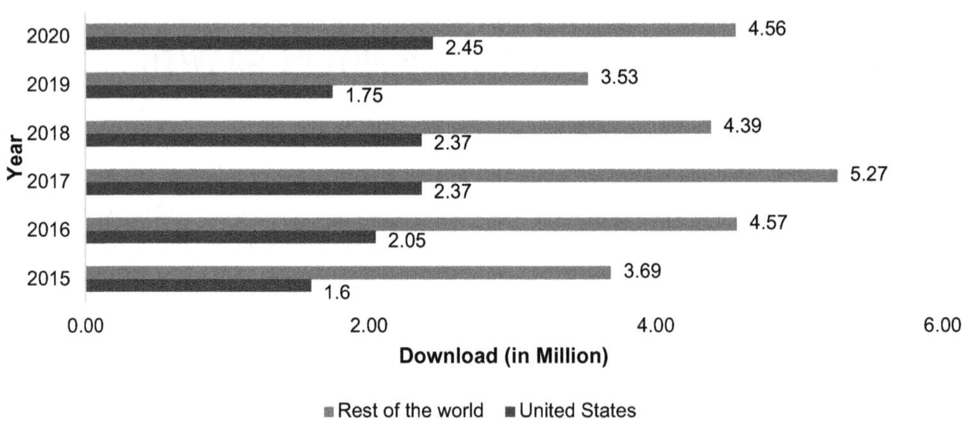

FIGURE 6.2 Number of Vimeo Mobile App Downloads Globally (in Million) (2015–2020)

Source: Statista Research Department. (July 26, 2021). Number of Vimeo mobile app downloads worldwide and in the US from 2015 to 2020. *Statista*. Retrieved from https://www.statista.com/statistics/1251969/vimeo-app-downloads-us-and-global/Vimeo Appoints Anjali Sud as CEO. (July 20, 2017). Vimeo.com. Retrieved from https://variety.com/2017/digital/news/vimeo-ceo-anjali-sud-ceo-1202501236/

such as Volvo, had already leveraged this technology for campaigns such as the #VolvoReality campaign (Top 5 Trends in Video Production, 2016).

4K or UHD (Ultra High Definition). This was yet another trend in video production that delivered the best picture quality in video. 4k had a standard resolution of 4,000 pixels compared to HD, which had 1,920 × 1,080 pixels. 4K technology was also available on mobile phones (Top 5 Trends in Video Production, 2016). Since 4K technology allowed for greater pixel density, it attracted users to shoot and capture the most delicate details while simultaneously offering better color depth when compared to standard HD technology (Top 5 Trends in Video Production, 2016). AI models were also able to generate a high-resolution image from a low-resolution image by gathering data from several images (Matcha, 2020).

Demand for Video Resumes. During the COVID-19 pandemic, as online hiring increased, demand for video resumes also increased (TNN, 2021). Video resumes could indicate the candidates' communication skills, confidence, exposure, and experience and helped companies eliminate candidates for interview rounds saving significant coordination, efforts, and cost (TNN, 2021). Video resumes also did away with limitations of text resumes that could be easily copied and pasted, defeating the very purpose of resumes (TNN, 2021).

VIMEO COMPETITORS AND ITS IPS UNDERPRICING

Vimeo positioned itself as a one-stop shop for all video needs (Perez, 2020). However, it was increasingly facing competition from several competitors on different fronts of the value chain of video solution provision. For instance, Brightcove offered a video content management system, video hosting, and live stream similar to Vimeo, though it was more expensive (Top 10 Vimeo Alternatives & Competitors, 2021). CloudApp was simpler to use compared to Vimeo. However, Vimeo did not offer live streaming services. Similarly, Vidyard, although it was easier to do business with, provided only video hosting services (Top 10 Vimeo Alternatives & Competitors, 2021) (see Table 6.2). Commenting on Vimeo's competitive advantage, Sud said,

> Video deployment at scale is really complex. While there are a couple of small, niche enterprise video companies in the market, none offer anything close to the scale we have. Our security features and support services are more sophisticated and advanced to support large teams.
>
> (Fischer, 2019)

Vimeo Versus YouTube

Although Vimeo shifted its focus on video production, it was often compared to YouTube as its competitor. YouTube was focused on entertainment, and its business model leveraged mainly on advertising. YouTube intended to attract creators and content to their platform (Patel, 2021). Vimeo, on the contrary, never made money from advertising. It was always more of a subscription product provider (Patel, 2021). Vimeo monetized through offering its tools for video creation. It helped businesses and professionals create video content for their customers or their employees (Patel, 2021). Differentiating Vimeo from YouTube, Sud

TABLE 6.2 Featurewise Comparison: Vimeo Versus Competitors

Company	Features	Comparison with Vimeo
Uscreen.tv	Video CMS, live stream but no hosting	Better at support; more expensive than Vimeo;
Adilo	Video hosting	Better at support than Vimeo;
Loom	Video CMS and video hosting, but not streaming	Easier to set up than Vimeo;
Brigthcove	Video CMS, video hosting, and live stream	More expensive than Vimeo;
CloudAapp	Video CMS and video hosting	Easier to do business with;
Wistia	Video hosting	Easier to administer, but more expensive than Vimeo;
Vidyard	Video hosting	More expensive;
Panopto	Video CMS and hosting, but no live streaming	More expensive than Vimeo, though better at support;

Source: Top 10 Vimeo Alternatives & Competitors. (2021). G2.com. Retrieved from https://www.g2.com/products/vimeo/competitors/alternatives.

said, "Today we do not view YouTube as a competitor. We really think of ourselves as a software-as-a-services company like a Slack, like a Dropbox, like a Zoom" (La Monica, 2019). Slack, Dropbox, and Zoom were three publicly traded software companies that offered storage and collaboration tools for businesses (La Monica, 2019). Sud acknowledged that given Vimeo's history as a "viewing destination" like YouTube, stakeholders continued to compare Vimeo with YouTube. Sud said, "We were sort of the more indie, higher end, more artistic version of YouTube," "That's probably how most people think of Vimeo" (La Monica, 2019).

As a video communication software company, Vimeo, unlike YouTube, did not make money from advertising, nor was much impacted by the traffic, viewing hours, and other metrics that were of concern to social media marketers (La Monica, 2019). But Vimeo helped several B2B businesses launch their advertisements and count their traffic or viewing hours on social media sites, including Twitter, Facebook, or Instagram. Sud said, "What we offer to creators is the ability to have a successful video strategy" (La Monica, 2019). She added, "We now view YouTube as a partner, not a competitor."

IPO Underpricing

On May 25, 2021, IAC completed the spinoff IPO of Vimeo (Deter, 2021). At the time of the IPO, Sud said,

> This is a proud moment for Vimeo, but just the beginning. Looking ahead, as an independent public company, we are well-positioned to keep innovating with urgency to expand our software suite and put the full power of video in the hands of every business and team in the world.
>
> (Deter, 2021)

Levin said,

> Vimeo has been part of IAC for 14 years, growing into a strong industry leader ready to stand on its own. Hard to believe that what started as a small team inside College Humor is now positioned to become a big public company with a world-class board of directors.
>
> (Deter, 2021)

However, Vimeo's shares fell on their first day of trading on the Nasdaq. Its closing price was USD 42.31, a decline of 18.8% from the launch price (Weil, 2021). According to analysts, it would further require Vimeo to report more growth in revenues (Weil, 2021). In early 2021, Vimeo had 1.6 million subscribers. Globally, there were over 300 million SMBs and more than 1 million enterprises, though Vimeo earned most revenues from SMBs (Taulli, 2021). Although the potential of growth of streamers was massive, according to analysts, investors were not sure how Vimeo was truly differentiating from others, especially YouTube (Ramstein, 2021). Sud admitted it might take more time for investors to acknowledge that Vimeo was a place to go to watch online videos. She said, "Most startups have a brand awareness challenge. Nobody knows who they are. For Vimeo, we actually have to change awareness" (La Monica, 2019).

THE ROAD AHEAD

Sud believed that the video creation industry would go through a similar kind of disruption to e-commerce and wanted to explore and exploit this opportunity to the fullest (Sud & Roth, 2020). Sud commenting on critical success factors of the video business, said,

> The way I would think of it is like, if you want to have a successful video business, there's three things you have to do. You have to have the content, you have to have the marketing, and you have to have the technology.
>
> (Patel, 2021)

Vimeo intended to keep the technology aspect of video production simple at an accessible price point so that several B2B customers could focus on creating great content and then marketing it (Patel, 2021).

Sud expected that following the COVID-19 pandemic, a hybrid work world would develop where video dominance would only accelerate (Patel, 2021). Vimeo was also testing the usefulness of artificial intelligence to edit raw footage into slick marketing content for restaurants and real estate industries (Patel, 2021). Sud mentioned that Vimeo's goal was to continue to simplify the user experience to the maximum extent possible (Patel, 2021). However, as companies shifted from email marketing to video marketing to attract clients, the competition was also expected to increase in the video-making tool industry. How could Sud lead the blue ocean she created? How could she make Vimeo grow in the future?

DISCUSSION QUESTIONS

1. Explain how Vimeo pursued a Blue Ocean strategy? Is it sustainable?
2. What organizational factors support Vimeo's innovation?
3. In what ways does Vimeo's B2B model reflect user innovation and co-creation. How could Vimeo leverage user communities to drive further product innovation and growth in the B2B segment?

CHAPTER NOTES

1 https://quartr.com/insights/business-philosophy/kevin-plank-and-the-rise-of-under-armour.
2 Using users: When does external knowledge enhance corporate product innovation? – Chatterji – 2014 – *Strategic Management Journal* – Wiley Online Library.
3 Using users: When does external knowledge enhance corporate product innovation? – Chatterji – 2014 – *Strategic Management Journal* – Wiley Online Library.
4 https://www.hubspot.com/startups/venture-capital-arms.
5 https://www.hubspot.com/startups/venture-capital-arms.
6 https://www.livekindly.com/kraft-heinz-invested-3-5-million-vegan-mozzarella-cheese/.
7 https://www.livekindly.com/kraft-heinz-invested-3-5-million-vegan-mozzarella-cheese/.
8 https://www.score.org/utah/resource/eguide/how-corporate-venture-capital-driving-innovation-and-growth#:~:text=1.,extend%20beyond%20mere%20financial%20transactions.
9 https://www.cnbc.com/2021/11/01/coca-cola-buys-full-control-of-bodyarmor-for-5point6-billion-.html#:~:text=Coca%2DCola%20announced%20Monday%20it,becoming%20its%20second%2Dlargest%20shareholder.
10 https://www.cnbc.com/2021/11/01/coca-cola-buys-full-control-of-bodyarmor-for-5point6-billion-.html#:~:text=Coca%2DCola%20announced%20Monday%20it,becoming%20its%20second%2Dlargest%20shareholder.
11 Technology and Corporate Scope: Firm and Rival Innovation as Antecedents of Corporate Transactions – Kaul – 2012 –*Strategic Management Journal* – Wiley Online Library.
12 https://www.techaheadcorp.com/knowledge-center/history-of-aws/#:~:text=2.,a%20service%2Doriented%20tech%20giant.
13 https://investors.hpe.com/governance/committees/technology-committee#:~:text=The%20Technology%20Committee%20assesses%20HPE's,mergers%20and%20acquisitions%20approval%20policies.
14 Aligning the Stars: How Technology Committees and Relevant Resources Drive Firm Innovation.
15 The role of political ties and political uncertainty in corporate innovation – ScienceDirect.
16 The role of political ties and political uncertainty in corporate innovation – ScienceDirect.
17 Individualistic CEO and corporate innovation: Evidence from U.S. frontier culture – ScienceDirect.
18 Individualistic CEO and corporate innovation: Evidence from U.S. frontier culture – ScienceDirect.
19 Workforce sleep and corporate innovation – ScienceDirect.
20 Workforce sleep and corporate innovation – ScienceDirect.
21 VirnetX's competitors, revenue, number of employees, funding and acquisitions. *Owler*, accessed March 17, 2020. Retrieved from www.owler.com/company/virnetx.
22 Nocera, J. (May 25, 2017). The town that trolls built. *Bloomberg*, accessed March 17, 2020. Retrieved from www.bloomberg.com/opinion/articles/2017-05-25/the-texas-town-that-patent-trolls-built-j34rlmjc.
23 Cohen, L., Gurun, U. G., & Kominers, S. D. (2019). Patent trolls: Evidence from targeted firms. *Management Science*, *65* (12), 5449–5956.
24 Bajpai, P. (February 11, 2016). The impact patent trolls have on innovation. *Nasdaq*, accessed April 15, 2025. Retrieved from www.nasdaq.com/articles/impact-patent-trolls-have-innovation-2016-02-11.
25 Cohen, L., Gurun, U. G., & Kominers, S. D. (2019). Patent trolls: Evidence from targeted firms. *Management Science*, *65* (12), 5449–5956.

26 Cohen, L., Gurun, U. G., & Kominers, S. D. (2019). Patent trolls: Evidence from targeted firms. *Management Science*, *65* (12), 5449–5956.
27 2019 Patent dispute report—Year in review. Unified Patent, January 1, 2020, accessed April 15, 2020. Retrieved from www.unifiedpatents.com/insights/2019/12/30/q4-2019-patent-dispute-report.
28 Shapiro, G. (July 13, 2016). Newegg's three-step solution to fighting patent trolls. *Medium | CTATech* (blog), accessed March 17, 2020. Retrieved from https://medium.com/ctatech/neweggs-three-step-solution-to-fighting-patent-trolls-2ac80ba9e744.
29 Bessen, J., & Meurer, M. J. (2014). The direct cost from NPE disputes. *Cornell Law Review*, *99* (2), 387–424.

FURTHER READINGS

Agnihotri, A., & Bhattacharya, S. (2023). *Vimeo: Developing Blue Ocean for B2B customers*. Sage Business Cases. https://doi.org/10.4135/9781529622652

CM Commerce Team. (March 19, 2020). How ecommerce shops cross-sell and upsell to increase customer lifetime value. Cm-commerce.com. Retrieved from https://cm-commerce.com/deep-dive/cross-sell-upsell-increase-customer-lifetime-value/

Corstjens, M., Carpenter, G., & Hasan, T. (May 3, 2021). When it comes to investing in product innovation, large CPG companies could learn a lot from their smaller competitors. *KelloggInsight*. Retrieved from https://insight.kellogg.northwestern.edu/article/cpg-product-innovation

Govindarajan, V., Rajgopal, S., & Srivastava, A. (February 26, 2018). Why financial statements don't work for digital companies. *Harvard Business Review*. Retrieved from https://hbr.org/2018/02/why-financial-statements-dont-work-for-digital-companies

Kim, W. C. (2005). Blue ocean strategy: From theory to practice. *California Management Review*, *47*(3), 105–121.

O'Connell, A. (July 9, 2014). Should marketing or R&D have more power? *Harvard Business Review*. Retrieved from https://hbr.org/2014/07/should-marketing-or-rd-have-more-power

Wong, D. (December 6, 2017). How SaaS companies can increase average account values & contract sizes. *Huffpost*. Retrieved https://www.huffpost.com/entry/how-saas-companies-can-in_b_12678548

York, J. (2013). SaaS growth strategy: A customer lifecycle approach. Chaotic-flow.com. Retrieved from https://chaotic-flow.com/media/saas-growth-strategy.pdf

CASE REFERENCES

Alaupovic, S. (April 14, 2020). 5 Things you need to know about Vimeo Create. Streamingmedia.com. Retrieved from https://www.streamingmedia.com/Articles/Editorial/Featured-Articles/5-Things-You-Need-to-Know-About-Vimeo-Create---140263.aspx?utm_source=related_articles&utm_medium=gutenberg&utm_campaign=editors_selection

Bertoni, S., & Gara, A. (May 31, 2021). How a young outsider turned failing Vimeo into a billion-dollar company. *Forbes*. Retrieved from https://www.forbes.com/sites/stevenbertoni/2021/04/14/how-young-outsider-turned-vimeo-into-billion-dollar-company/?sh=953b90b26880

Choose a Plan. (2021). Vimeo.com. Retrieved from https://vimeo.com/upgrade

Deter, A. (May 25, 2021). Vimeo stock hits Nasdaq after IAC spin-off IPO completed. *InvestmentU*. Retrieved from https://investmentu.com/vimeo-stock-ipo/

Fischer, S. (August 1, 2019). Vimeo launches enterprise tech business. Axios.com. Retrieved from https://www.axios.com/vimeo-launches-enterprise-tech-business-81a98128-ab82-4a30-9a45-16a6a69a7104.html

Fortune's 2018 40 Under 40. (2018). *Fortune*. Retrieved from https://fortune.com/40-under-40/2018/anjali-sud/

Ha, A. (October 27, 2020). Vimeo introduces free video messaging with Vimeo Record. *Tech Crunch*. Retrieved from https://techcrunch.com/2020/10/27/vimeo-record/

La Monica, P. R. (June 27, 2019). Vimeo is thriving as the anti-YouTube. Here's the CEO's plan for the future. *CNN*. Retrieved from https://www.cnn.com/2019/06/26/media/vimeo-anjali-sud/index.html

Matcha, A. C. N. (September 7, 2020). Latest technological advancements in video streaming with AI. Towardsdatascience.com. Retrieved from https://towardsdatascience.com/latest-technological-advancements-in-video-streaming-with-ai-293d3b8b2a7e

Orbach, M. (July 21, 2022). Vimeo slashes workforce by 6%, including in Israel R&D center. *CTech*. Retrieved from https://www.calcalistech.com/ctechnews/article/r1tzvk83c

Patel, N. (April 20, 2021). How Anajli Sud reinvented Vimeo. *The Verge*. Retrieved from https://www.theverge.com/2021/4/20/22392228/vimeo-ceo-interview-streaming-software-business-anjali-sud

Perez, S. (Fbruary 25, 2020). Vimeo's new app helps small businesses create professional social videos. *Tech Crunch*. Retrieved from https://techcrunch.com/2020/02/25/vimeos-new-app-helps-small-businesses-create-professional-social-videos/

Ramstein, W. (May 28, 2021). The reasons why the Vimeo IPO flopped. *FlowBank*. Retrieved from https://www.flowbank.com/en/research/lessons-learned-from-a-failed-vimeo-ipo

Sanchez, L. (August 7, 2021). What investors need to know about the Vimeo spin-off. *The Motley Fool*. Retrieved from https://www.fool.com/investing/2021/08/07/what-investors-need-to-know-about-the-vimeo-spin-o/

Spangler, T. (May 25, 2021). Vimeo stock slips 13% in debut as public company following IAC spinoff. *Variety*. Retrieved from https://variety.com/2021/digital/news/vimeo-stock-drops-iac-spinoff-1234981319/

Sud, A., & Roth, E. (December 15, 2020). The committed innovator: An interview with Anjali Sud, CEO of Vimeo. Mckinsey.com. Retrieved from https://www.mckinsey.com/business-functions/strategy-and-corporate-finance/our-insights/the-committed-innovator-an-interview-with-anjali-sud-ceo-of-vimeo

Taulli, T. (June 22, 2021). Vimeo stock: Can it stream profits for investors? Nasdaq.com. Retrieved from https://www.nasdaq.com/articles/vimeo-stock%3A-can-it-stream-profits-for-investors-2021-06-22

TNN. (January 7, 2021). Will video resume become a new trend. *Education Times*. Retrieved from https://www.educationtimes.com/article/editors-pick/80146933/will-video-resume-become-a-new-trend

Top 5 Trends in Video Production. (November 11, 2016). Flatworldsolutions.com. Retrieved from https://www.flatworldsolutions.com/creative-services/articles/top-5-trends-video-production.php

Top 10 Vimeo Alternatives & Competitors. (2021). G2.com. Retrieved from https://www.g2.com/products/vimeo/competitors/alternatives

US SEC. (May 21, 2021a). Vimeo: Form 10Q (March 31, 2021). Vimeo.com. Retrieved from https://investors.vimeo.com/static-files/fcb36611-1c2c-44a2-af24-7adee05d070c

US SEC. (May 26, 2021b). Vimeo, Inc.: Form-S1. Vimeo.com. Retrieved from https://investors.vimeo.com/static-files/3cc5c8b3-8e32-4832-b146-1f0a3b30fef3

Vimeo. (2021). Crunchbase. Retrieved from https://www.crunchbase.com/organization/vimeo/technology

Vimeo Raises $150 Million of Equity. (November 5, 2020). Vimeo.com. Retrieved from https://press.vimeo.com/115355-vimeo-raises-150-million-of-equity

Weil, D. (May 25, 2021). Vimeo sinks in first day of trading after spinning off from IAC. *The Street*. Retrieved from https://www.thestreet.com/investing/iac-sinks-in-first-day-of-trading-after-iac-spinoff

CHAPTER 7

Growth Strategies Leveraging Digitalization

Learning Objectives

After completing this chapter, students should be able to:

- Explore the role of servitization in transforming a firm's digitalization-based growth strategy;
- Evaluate how digital channels enhance firms' opportunities to expand revenue streams;
- Examine, using input and impact analysis, growth tactics and strategies that firms may pursue;
- Conduct a content analysis of customer feedback to inform the development or iteration of new products.

SERVITIZATION

Servitization involves selling products as integrated solutions, with a focus on services. Instead of a one-time sale of a physical product, firms sell the product as a service with a recurring subscription-based model. The client does not own the product, and at the end of its life, the manufacturer takes it back and replaces it with a newer model. For instance, a bulb-making company offers lighting-as-a-service and is growing through servitization.[1] In the servitization model, the customer does not own the product; instead, the service provider owns it, typically the product manufacturer. The customer pays for product usage through a fixed fee per unit of service consumed. Accordingly, the company remains responsible for the operation costs of the product, including its maintenance. Sometimes, a company launches newer versions of its product, making older versions obsolete, thus unethically forcing customers to upgrade to newer versions.[2] However, once the company bears the operating and maintenance costs, it can introduce updates to the product more responsibly, so that the cost of product manufacturing and development from previous versions is first recovered through

DOI: 10.4324/9781003568100-7

service revenues, thus making operations and product development more sustainable.[3] Firms may implement pricing in four ways to support servitization-based growth.

- *Usage-Based Pricing.* In usage-based pricing, the client is charged for actual product usage. Cloud computing firms, such as AWS or Microsoft Azure, implement a usage-based pricing model based on the amount of data stored on their servers.[4] Philips, as a growth strategy, introduced servitization through its "Pay per Lux" model, where customers paid for the amount of light (lux) used, and Philips eliminated the need to purchase lighting equipment itself. The model became especially popular in commercial settings, such as airports.[5] Once the light life ends, Philips would reintroduce the materials into the production process. This process also enhanced the sustainability aspect of Philips' business,[6] as customers might otherwise discard lights. However, with servitization, since they did not purchase the lighting, Philips took responsibility for replacing them, thereby increasing its opportunity to reuse the waste bulbs.[7]
- *Subscription-Based Pricing*: Here, firms charge a fixed fee to customers on a monthly or annual subscription basis, irrespective of the intensity or frequency of product usage. Firms can employ subscription in several ways:

  Flat Fee Subscriptions. In this type of subscription-based pricing, a service provider charges a single price for all services. Traditionally, streaming companies like Netflix have leveraged this model, offering unlimited streaming through monthly or yearly subscriptions. Similarly, Basecamp (a software service) charges a flat monthly fee for its project management tools. The user had no limitation on the usage of these tools.

  Tiered Pricing. In tiered pricing, service providers offer multiple tires of packages, each with its own incentives. For instance, Mobile service operators such as Tello or Lycamobile can provide a basic plan with limited data and calling minutes.[8] They also offer an advanced plan covering international calling and a higher GB plan for higher internet usage.[9]

  Tiered pricing offers advantages over fixed pricing, as cost-conscious customers can opt for a basic plan with limited services, rather than altogether opting out of the service due to high subscription prices. With tiered pricing, the firm can target a broader market and increase its revenues. Once a customer has subscribed to the basic subscription plan, they can be encouraged to opt for a higher-tiered plan in the future.

  In tiered pricing, a firm can also implement a decoy effect. In this technique, a firm may price different options in a way that entices customers to opt for a higher-priced subscription service. For example, a magazine company may offer three-tier plans: web-only (USD 75), print-only (USD 120), and Print+web (USD 125).[10] A customer might have otherwise opted for a lower-priced option, i.e., a single option. However, upon seeing that the print+web option is more economical than the print-only option (decoy effect), they may feel that by choosing the print+web option, they are making a more economical choice.[11]

  Freemium Subscription Model. In this model, the company offers the base model for free. However, as a base model, features are restricted.

  Lease Model. Here manufacturer gives product to customer on lease for a specified period. The manufacturer retains ownership, while also assuming responsibility for maintenance and operations. In this way, the manufacturer's objective shifts from selling the product to selling the service. A lease model increases the durability and sustainability of the product, as the manufacturer aims to extend the product's life cycle by virtue of owning it, rather than exploring ways to entice customers to buy newer versions, given that ownership remains with the manufacturer.

The lease model has become increasingly popular among manufacturers in recent years, driven by Industry 4.0 technologies such as the Internet of Things (IoT) and data analytics. Manufacturers leveraging Industry 4.0 technologies install IoT sensors in the leased product. These sensors collect real-time performance data on equipment. Then, based on predictive analytics—integrating product performance data with machine learning, AI, and statistical modeling—manufacturers can gauge when product maintenance is required, rather than waiting for customers to complain about equipment breakdown. Thus, predictive maintenance and live product performance monitoring help enhance asset performance, reduce maintenance costs, and improve the customer experience, given the low probability of equipment breakdown and low customer investment in the product (owing to the "as-a-service" model), making the lease model more popular among customers. Taking advantage of Industry 4.0 technologies, major equipment manufacturers such as Rolls-Royce for its aircraft engines, Xerox for its photocopiers, and Philips for its light bulbs, as well as commercial clients like airports, have shifted to a product-as-a-service model through leasing.

- *Product Business Model.* In this model, a firm sells a product to a customer with an add-on warranty for services. Nokian Tires Plc sells tires, and its service unit provides tire-related services to customers through direct contact with consumers. Thus, servitization is typically limited to after-sales service within a traditional manufacturing model.
- *Process-Oriented Business Model.* A process-oriented business model is an outsourcing-based business model, where a company is not only a manufacturer but also an outsourcing service provider. AWS offers its cloud computing platform to other players, including Netflix, for storing data. Since 2008, Netflix has been utilizing AWS's extensive data centers to deliver video content that requires minimal buffering and loads faster.[12] Developing cloud computing is a resource-intensive business decision, and to recoup costs and enhance growth prospects by generating additional income, firms share their resources with other participants in the industry. Similarly, L'Oréal utilizes its manufacturing facilities to produce Prada's perfumes, thereby driving growth through servitization, as L'Oréal provides manufacturing services to Prada.[13]

  However, a process-oriented servitization growth strategy requires the complete involvement of top management in attracting clients, as these clients may also be competitors. To avoid trust and opportunistic behavior issues, as well as business sensitivity, the lower-level sales team is generally not involved in creating the deal.[14]

Emerging digital technologies have made servitization more feasible, especially leasing, also known as a service agreement-based business model, where a company gives equipment or fleet on lease by leveraging digital technologies such as internet of things, artificial intelligence, and data analytics, which has given rise to a new generation of products, i.e., Smart products.[15] Smart products refer to manufactured items that have embedded features, such as sensors and software, which connect them with other devices that can collect, exchange, and process data through technologies like the IoT networks.

PRODUCT ITERATION-BASED GROWTH STRATEGIES

Firms can enhance product functionality and attract more customers by incorporating iteration into the product based on customer reviews. Amazon Basics improves its products based on online customer reviews. Over the years, it has become one of the most successful private-label brands. Online reviews can be easily analyzed using a content analysis or a sentiment analysis program. For very large datasets, firms may utilize machine learning algorithms. However, not all comments and reviews are equally effective in bringing meaningful product iterations. Managers can decide that based on the *Kano model*. The model differentiates between core features (i.e., features critical to product performance), performance enhancers (i.e., features that can enhance the product's functionality), and "delighters" (i.e., features that can create a wow factor among consumers).

Firms may collect customer reviews and feedback from multiple sources, including social media and review websites. These days, managers actively engage with customers on social networking sites such as X, Instagram, and Facebook. Corporations engage in social listening, implying that they monitor what customers are commenting about their brands on social media. This social listening helps firms identify trends, suggest new product ideas, and note any desired features listed by customers. It also allows managers to understand the pain points of customers, and sometimes managers even directly ask customers on social media platforms about changes they want to see in the product. Glossier, the beauty company, developed its growth strategy based on customer feedback.[16] Glossier created the popular Solution Exfoliating Skin Perfector in response to customer suggestions about using gentle chemicals. In 2015, Emily Weiss, the founder of Glossier, asked customers on her blog about what their dream cleanser would "look like?" "Smell like?" and "Feel like?" Three hundred seventy customers responded in comments.

Glossier then applied sentiment analysis on the comments that included keywords like mild, "glowy," and "moist."[17] The company sent the analysis to a chemist, who ensured that all three elements were present in the final product. The final product was "Milky Jelly Cleanser." This product received an average 4.3-star rating on Glossier's site and became a huge success, helping Glossier to grow as a company.[18] In fact, Glossier has built its entire growth strategy around product development based on customer feedback and insights gathered from social media. In 2010, Emily Weiss started a beauty blog called "Into The Gloss." At that time, she had no products to sell. By 2021, she had developed products based on customer insights, and her company had reached a valuation of USD 1.8 billion.[19]

Firms may use the following matrix (see Figure 7.1) to allocate resources for a growth strategy. For the *High-Impact Low-Effort (Quick Wins)* quadrant, a firm may require fewer efforts. Still, the outcome can be highly beneficial for the organization in terms of generating revenue or improving efficiency. For instance, after meeting with an important client, sending a follow-up email will require minimal effort yet impress the client about the work culture and ethics regarding customer centricity, which can potentially increase revenues. Alternatively, managers can automate a small, repetitive task, thus increasing efficiency. Similarly, updating

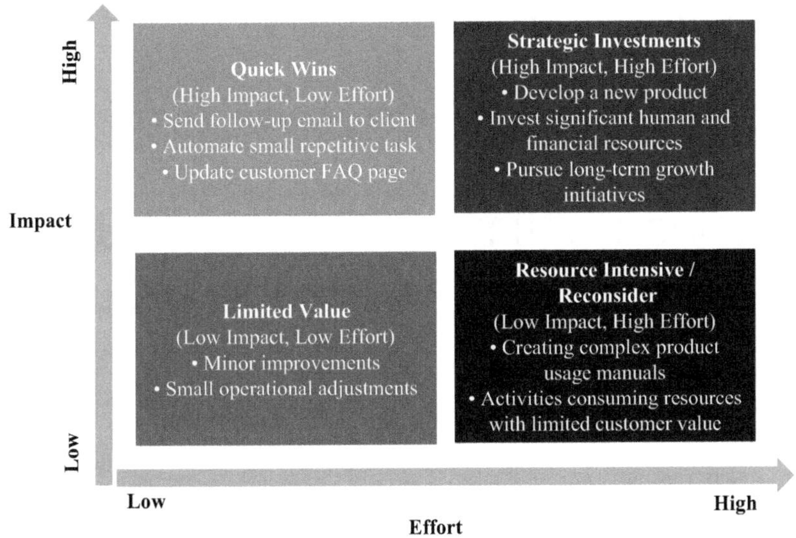

FIGURE 7.1 Effort Vs. Impact Matrix

Source: Developed by the Authors

the FAQs page for customers so that their queries are resolved without the need to contact a customer care representative could further enhance the firm's potential business.

A *High Impact High Effort* quadrant implies putting intensive resources into effort, which has the potential to create a huge impact on growth, such as developing a new product. Developing a new product requires substantial human and financial resources; however, it can offer a significant strategic advantage to the firm.

A *Low Impact High Effort* quadrant implies a firm investing considerable resources in pursuing growth, but these resources are not yielding sufficient impact. For instance, instead of creating a video demonstration, which can be brief, a firm invests resources in creating a product usage manual that is complex for consumers to decode. Consequently, customers may not buy the product.

ASSIGNMENT QUESTIONS

1. Explain how servitization can help firms to be more sustainable. Give examples from your home country.
2. Provide examples of various pricing tactics employed by firms from your home country in servitization.
3. Imagine you are the CEO of a coffee chain in your home country. Based on the impact and effort framework, devise four growth strategies for your coffee chain amidst increasing competition and the rising cost of raw ingredients, such as coffee beans.

CASE STUDY 7.1

Data-Driven Market Entry

Leveraging Sentiment Analysis to Guide ZapSmile's Expansion into the UK Electric Toothbrush Market

Liam Smith is the CEO of ZapSmile, a UK-based startup operating in the toothbrush industry. The company currently produces manual toothbrushes. However, Smith is planning to expand into the electric toothbrush segment, which in 2023 was valued at approximately USD 9.4 billion globally and is projected to grow to around USD 48.6 billion by 2042.

In the UK, the oral care market reached an estimated value of USD 2.8 billion in 2023, with the toothbrush category accounting for 31% of total sales. By 2022, nearly 72% of UK adults (approximately 37 million people) were using electric toothbrushes, indicating strong consumer adoption and growth potential.

Recognizing this opportunity, Smith intends to launch an innovative electric toothbrush in the UK market before expanding internationally. The UK electric toothbrush sector is highly competitive, with dominant brands such as Oral-B, Suri, Spotlight, and Philips Sonicare holding significant market shares.

In early 2025, ZapSmile's research and development team began working toward a planned UK launch by the end of the year. Alongside product development, Smith wanted to gain insight into consumer opinions about leading electric toothbrush products. Understanding customer sentiment would allow him to:

- Design an electric toothbrush incorporating features most valued by consumers.
- Shape the messaging and positioning of ZapSmile's promotional strategy.

To explore this further, Smith met with Atlas Efe Demir, a Behaviour Analyst at ZapSmile. During their discussion, Smith explained that he wanted to analyze UK consumers' opinions expressed in online product reviews of a leading electric toothbrush.

Demir outlined a structured plan to support these objectives:

1. Collect a sample of UK customer reviews from a major online retail platform for a leading electric toothbrush.

2. Conduct sentiment analysis to classify each review as positive or negative.
3. Perform attribute-based classification to identify which words, features, or tokens most strongly contribute to positive sentiment.

Demir visited Shopster.co.uk, a major UK e-commerce platform. He found that the electric toothbrush VoltClean Elite 3.0 was the highest-rated and most frequently reviewed product, with more than 20,500 customer reviews. Given the large volume of data, Demir questioned whether analyzing all reviews would be practical. Instead, he decided to begin with a smaller sample of approximately 60 product reviews.

Smith requested that Demir present the findings from this preliminary analysis. Based on the results, Smith would determine whether to conduct a larger-scale study involving thousands of reviews across multiple electric toothbrush brands.

Key considerations include determining the appropriate granularity level of sentiment analysis for classifying reviews as positive or negative, identifying actionable insights from the results, and evaluating whether the findings sufficiently support product design and marketing strategy decisions. Ultimately, Smith must decide whether expanding the analysis to a broader dataset would provide additional strategic value.

BACKGROUND PREPARATION

Before gathering data and carrying out the analysis, Demir reviewed academic sources and industry materials related to sentiment analysis to strengthen his understanding of the field. He revisited several fundamental concepts that would guide his work.

Sentiment refers to a person's feelings, opinions, or evaluations about a particular subject. It reflects how someone emotionally or cognitively reacts to something. For instance, a statement such as, "I am worried about my financial situation," communicates a negative sentiment. In general, sentiments are categorized as positive, negative, or neutral.

Sentiment analysis is the process of examining written text to determine the attitudes, emotions, or judgments expressed toward a product, service, or specific feature. Through this approach, analysts assess how individuals describe and evaluate particular attributes within their written comments, such as product reviews. The goal is to systematically identify whether the expressed opinion is favorable, unfavorable, or neutral.

Natural Language Processing (NLP) plays a central role in sentiment analysis. NLP is a branch of artificial intelligence that enables computers to interpret, analyze, and understand human language. It relies on machine learning techniques, where algorithms learn from data patterns and continuously improve their performance over time.

Levels of Sentiment Analysis Granularity can vary depending on the depth of analysis required. There are three main levels:

- **Document-level analysis**, where the entire text (for example, a full product review) is classified as positive, negative, or neutral.
- **Sentence-level analysis**, where each individual sentence within a text is evaluated separately for its sentiment.

- **Aspect-level analysis**, where the focus shifts to specific features or components mentioned in the text. At this level, the analyst identifies particular aspects (such as battery life, design, or performance) and determines the sentiment associated with each one.

For example, if someone writes, "The cleaning performance is excellent, but the battery life is disappointing," the overall review contains mixed sentiments. At the aspect level, "cleaning performance" would be labeled positive, while "battery life" would be labeled negative.

PRODUCT REVIEW DATASET

VoltClean Elite 3.0 ranked among the best-performing electric toothbrushes in the UK market. On Shopster's online retail platform, the product had accumulated more than 19,000 customer ratings and written reviews, reflecting its strong market presence and consumer engagement.

Following his earlier discussion with Smith, Demir recognized that analyzing the full dataset would be inefficient at the initial stage. Instead, he opted to work with a smaller subset of reviews to conduct a pilot analysis. The file *Sentiment_Data.xslx* includes 58 selected customer reviews that were used for this purpose (www.routledge.com/9781032938912).

Link file: Sentiment_Data.xslx.

PRODUCT REVIEW SENTIMENT ANALYSIS

Demir carried out sentiment analysis using the selected review sample. The dataset used for this analysis is available in the *Sentiment_Data.xslx* file (www.routledge.com/9781032938912).

For the analytical process, Demir utilized Orange Data Mining software (Version 3.37.0). Orange is an open-source platform designed for data analysis and visualization, created by researchers at the University of Ljubljana in Slovenia. Its drag-and-drop workflow interface simplifies complex analytical procedures, making it suitable for text mining tasks.

To perform sentiment analysis in Orange, the software must first be installed along with its "Text" add-on, which enables text preprocessing and classification functions. The workflow included preparing the textual data, running the sentiment classification model, and generating the results.

Once the analysis was completed, Demir was able to categorize each product review as either positive or negative. The results of the sentiment classification are presented in Figures 7.2 and 7.3.

PRODUCT REVIEW ATTRIBUTE CLASSIFICATION

After assigning sentiment labels to the reviews, Demir created an additional Excel dataset titled *Logistic_Data.xslx* (www.routledge.com/9781032938912). In this file, each review was marked as either positive or negative based on the earlier sentiment analysis results.

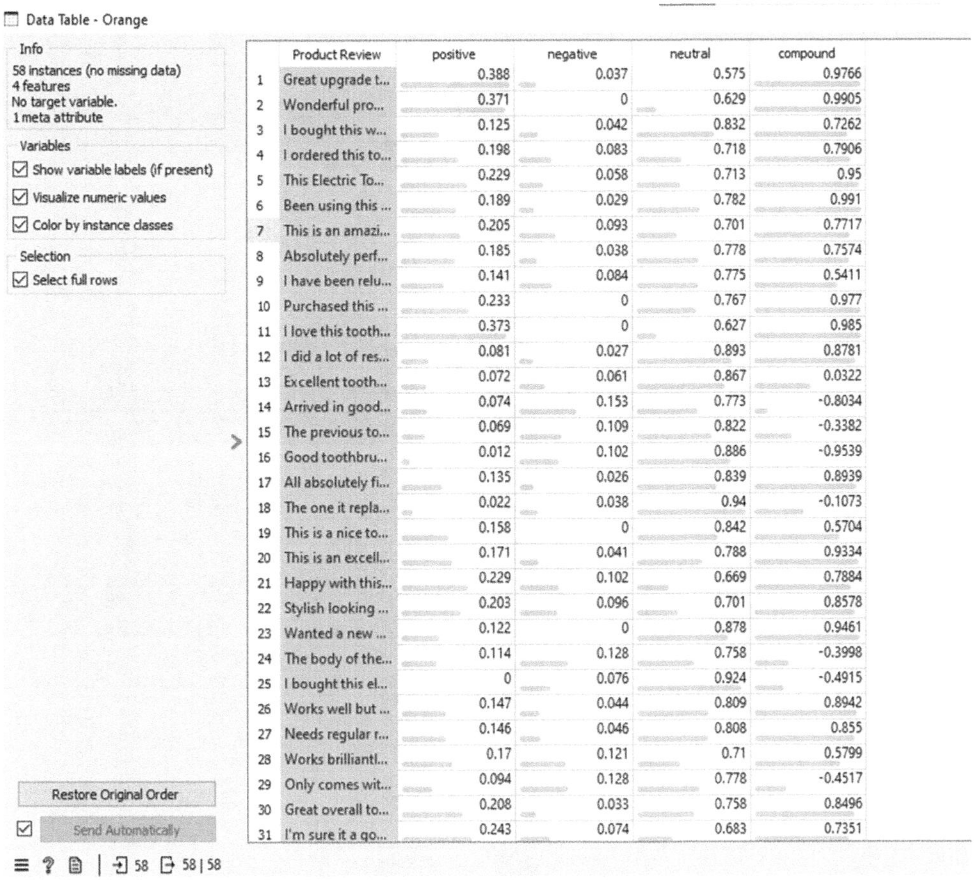

	Product Review	positive	negative	neutral	compound
1	Great upgrade t...	0.388	0.037	0.575	0.9766
2	Wonderful pro...	0.371	0	0.629	0.9905
3	I bought this w...	0.125	0.042	0.832	0.7262
4	I ordered this to...	0.198	0.083	0.718	0.7906
5	This Electric To...	0.229	0.058	0.713	0.95
6	Been using this ...	0.189	0.029	0.782	0.991
7	This is an amazi...	0.205	0.093	0.701	0.7717
8	Absolutely perf...	0.185	0.038	0.778	0.7574
9	I have been relu...	0.141	0.084	0.775	0.5411
10	Purchased this ...	0.233	0	0.767	0.977
11	I love this tooth...	0.373	0	0.627	0.985
12	I did a lot of res...	0.081	0.027	0.893	0.8781
13	Excellent tooth...	0.072	0.061	0.867	0.0322
14	Arrived in good...	0.074	0.153	0.773	-0.8034
15	The previous to...	0.069	0.109	0.822	-0.3382
16	Good toothbru...	0.012	0.102	0.886	-0.9539
17	All absolutely fi...	0.135	0.026	0.839	0.8939
18	The one it repla...	0.022	0.038	0.94	-0.1073
19	This is a nice to...	0.158	0	0.842	0.5704
20	This is an excell...	0.171	0.041	0.788	0.9334
21	Happy with this...	0.229	0.102	0.669	0.7884
22	Stylish looking ...	0.203	0.096	0.701	0.8578
23	Wanted a new ...	0.122	0	0.878	0.9461
24	The body of the...	0.114	0.128	0.758	-0.3998
25	I bought this el...	0	0.076	0.924	-0.4915
26	Works well but ...	0.147	0.044	0.809	0.8942
27	Needs regular r...	0.146	0.046	0.808	0.855
28	Works brilliantl...	0.17	0.121	0.71	0.5799
29	Only comes wit...	0.094	0.128	0.778	-0.4517
30	Great overall to...	0.208	0.033	0.758	0.8496
31	I'm sure it a go...	0.243	0.074	0.683	0.7351

FIGURE 7.2 Sentiment Analysis Results: Showing Positive, Negative, Neutral, and Compound Scores for Product Reviews

Source: Developed by the Authors

To further examine which textual elements influenced positive sentiment, Demir conducted a Logistic Regression analysis followed by a Nomogram visualization. Logistic regression is a statistical method used to estimate the likelihood of a particular outcome—in this case, whether a review is classified as positive or negative—based on predictor variables.

In this model:

- The dependent variable was the sentiment classification (positive or negative).
- The independent variable consisted of the textual features extracted from the product reviews.

The Nomogram provided a visual representation of the classification model, highlighting the top four words, features, or tokens that contributed most strongly to predicting positive sentiment. Orange (Version 3.37.0) was also used for this classification process.

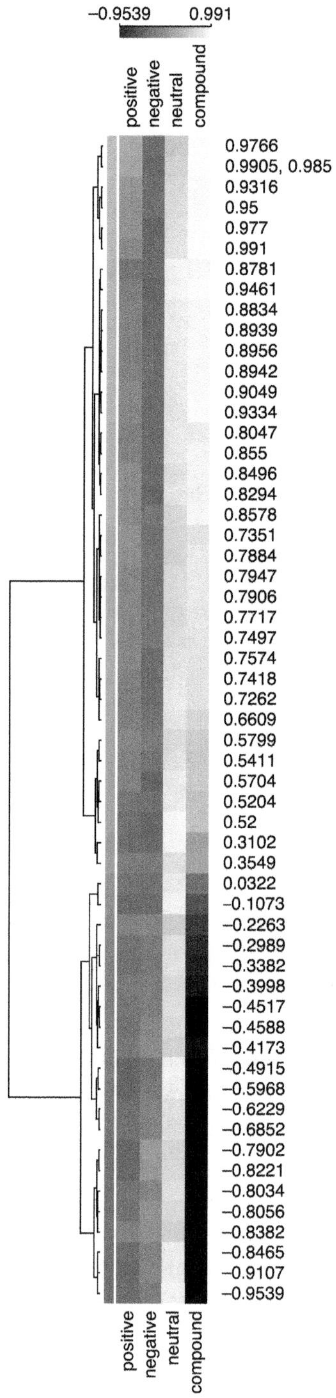

FIGURE 7.3 Heatmap Visualization of Sentiment Scores across Product Reviews with Hierarchical Clustering

Source: Developed by the Authors

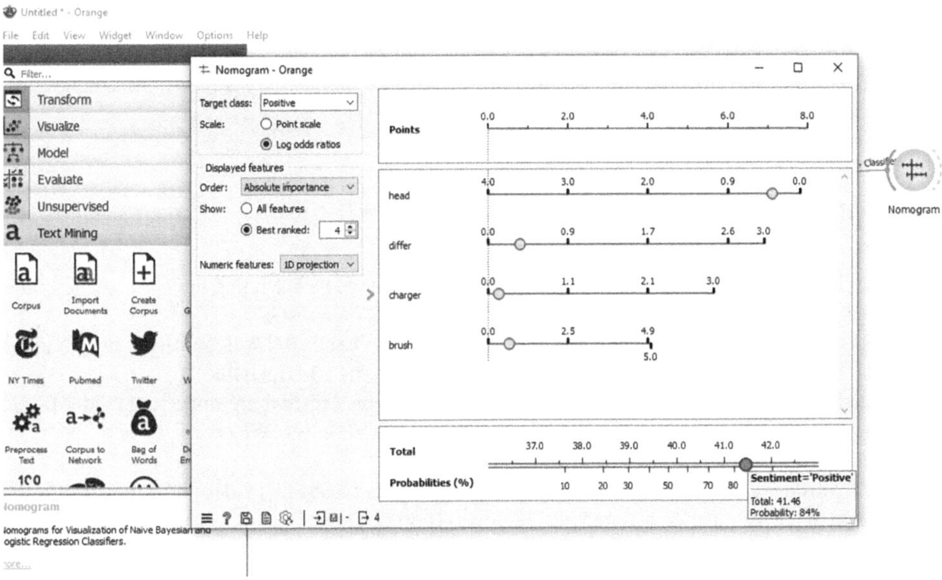

FIGURE 7.4 Nomogram Representation of Feature Contributions to Positive Sentiment Classification

Source: Developed by the Authors

Link file: Logistic_Data.xslx.

The findings from the attribute classification analysis are given in Figure 7.4.

REPORT TO THE CEO

Demir compiled his findings into a structured report and presented it to Smith. In the report, he explained the methodology applied, the reasoning behind each analytical stage, and the significance of the results obtained. He also interpreted the importance of the most influential words, tokens, and features that contributed to a review being classified as positive.

DISCUSSION QUESTIONS

1. At which level of sentiment analysis granularity did Demir classify each review as positive or negative? Conduct sentiment analysis on the Sentiment_Data.xslx dataset and review the results (www.routledge.com/9781032938912).
2. What steps did Karay apply on the Logistic_Data.xlsx dataset to perform attribute classification? Examine the output (www.routledge.com/9781032938912).
3. What strategic insights can Liam Smith derive from the analysis results?
4. What factors should Smith take into account when developing ZapSmile's promotional strategy for its electric toothbrush?

FURTHER READING

Liu, B. (2020). *Sentiment analysis: Mining opinions, sentiments, and emotions* (pp. 1–88). Cambridge: Cambridge University Press.

ADDITIONAL RESOURCES

TechonTea. (2019, March 23). How to download and install Orange Data Mining tool [Video]. *YouTube*. Retrieved from https://www.youtube.com/watch?v=_vgslAii7ho&t=23s

Orange Data Mining. (2015, December 21). Getting started with Orange 01: Welcome to Orange [Video]. *YouTube*. Retrieved from https://www.youtube.com/watch?v=HXjnDIgGDuI

Orange Data Mining. (2017, June 20). Getting started with Orange 16: Text preprocessing [Video]. *YouTube*. Retrieved from https://www.youtube.com/watch?v=V70UwJZWkZ8&list=PLmNPvQr9Tf-bxmjlFRg0AGjMzzd1y8_kB

Orange Data Mining. (2020, August 14). Text mining: Sentiment analysis [Video]. *YouTube*. Retrieved from https://www.youtube.com/watch?v=7Fnli0wc11g&t=2s

Orange Data Mining. (2017, June 28). Getting started with Orange 18: Text classification [Video]. *YouTube*. Retrieved from https://www.youtube.com/watch?v=zO_zwKZCULo&t=112s

CASE STUDY 7.2

General Motors Creating Shareholder Value through Diversification in Electric Vehicles

Can a Legacy Company Win?

Agnihotri, A., & Bhattacharya, S. (2023). *General motors creating shareholder value through diversification in electric vehicles: Can a legacy company win?* Sage Business Cases. https://doi.org/10.4135/9781529617221

INTRODUCTION

Mary T. Barra, CEO of General Motors Company (henceforth referred to as *GM*), was determined to be a significant player in the electric vehicles (EVs) market. In January 2021, Barra said, GM "was committed to fighting for EV market share until we are number one in North America" (Mason, 2021). In contrast, analysts believed a legacy company such as GM could not compete against aggressive and agile newcomers, specifically Tesla. By early 2021, Tesla was the market leader in EVs in the US (Mason, 2021) (see Figure 7.5 for the market share of electric cars in the US).

Barra had to experience several challenges while focusing on GM's diversification into EVs. First, GM faced labor strikes when Barra decided to lay off workers in an effort to increase investments in EVs. Next, GM's relation with LG Chem, its joint venture partner and a significant supplier of lithium-ion batteries, was also strained. Lithium-ion batteries provided the fuel (i.e., electricity) for EVs. Between December 2020 and August 2021, GM issued three recalls of its Chevrolet Bolt EVs due to fire issues with the LG Chem manufactured lithium-ion batteries. Barra decided to stop Chevrolet Bolt's production until reasons for the fire were known and rectified. Industry experts said, "To date, GM has failed at delivering" (DeBord, 2021).

Barra-led GM was also not following the same trajectory as other traditional automakers. Traditional automobile companies continued investing in conventional car research and

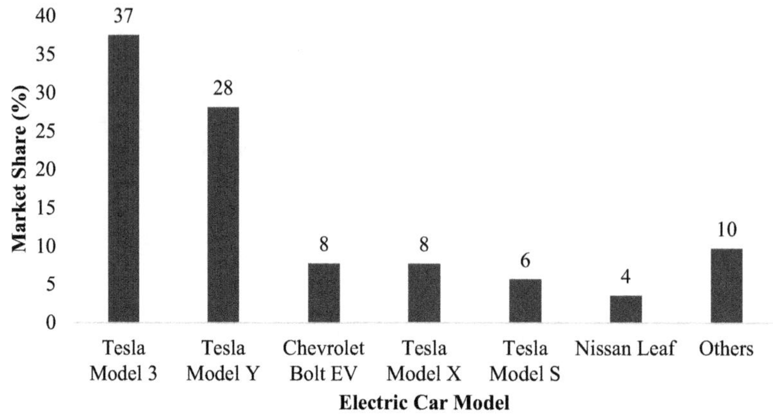

FIGURE 7.5 Market Share (%) of Electric Cars by Model in the US (2020)

Source: Developed by the Authors Based on Lambert, F. (February 16, 2021). Tesla owns 79% of the electric car market in the US, and that needs to change. *Electrek*. Retrieved from https://electrek.co/2021/02/16/tesla-owns-electric-car-market-us/

TABLE 7.1 Comparison of Big Three Automakers (GM, Ford, Fiat Chrysler Automobiles) and Tesla

Big Three vs. Tesla	No. of Cars Sold in 2020 (in Millions)	Market Valuation (USD Billion)		Profits (USD Billion)	
		December 2020	Jan-21	2020	2019
GM	6.83	59.89	69.08	6.43	6.73
Ford	1.93	35.09	45.83	−1.28	0.084
Fiat Chrysler Automobiles	3.08	22.07	47.1	0.029	2.9
Tesla	0.499	631.29	847.77	0.721	−0.862

Source: Developed by the authors based on YChart. (2021). Solutions. *Ycharts*. Retrieved from www.ycharts.com.[20]

development and not shifting entirely to electronic vehicles related innovation. Companies made such investments in recent decades because consumers in general were skeptical about buying EVs due to pricing and vehicle range (i.e., distance covered in a single charge). In contrast, in September 2021, Barra announced that GM would become a zero-emission vehicle producing company by 2035, focusing on EVs only (O'Kane, 2021).

Industry experts construed Barra's diversification into EVs as "overzealous" and "too ambitious" (DeBord, 2021). According to them, GM was aggressively venturing into EVs to please *The Wall Street* and get a "little of that Tesla magic and money" (Lienert, White, & Klayman, 2020). Tesla's market value was more than five times GM, Ford Motors, and Fiat Chrysler Automobiles combined. However, Tesla's sales were much smaller, and it also became profitable for the first time in 2020, since it began to produce automobiles in 2003 (see Table 7.1 for a comparison of the Big Three Automakers with Tesla). Barra, in her defense, said, "We think there's a huge opportunity to grow EV demand, and that's why we're accelerating our business" (Mishkin, 2020). Barra also reinforced that she would do everything "to drive shareholder value."

However, manufacturing EVs requires a set of competencies and capabilities different from those needed in the manufacturing of conventional gasoline engines. Market leader Tesla was also unable to find affordable EV solutions for the mass market. Was Barra becoming hypercompetitive while diversifying into EVs in an attempt to enhance shareholder value? What strategies can Barra deploy to compete against "new" modern automobile companies such as Tesla? How can she develop competency in developing affordable EVs for the mass segment?

COMPANY BACKGROUND

General Motors Company, founded in 1908, is an American automotive multinational corporation headquartered in Detroit, Michigan. William C. Durant founded it as a holding company. General Motors was the world's largest automaker from 1931 through 2007. In 2021, it ranked number 22 on the *Fortune 500* rankings of the largest USA corporations by total revenue (General Motors: Rank 22, 2021). General Motors manufactured vehicles in several countries. Its four core automobile brands were Chevrolet, Buick, GMC, and Cadillac. The company has had its share of financial problems. For example, in 2012, GM went bankrupt and survived only with the help of a federal bailout (Davies, 2016). Also, between 2018 and 2020, GM's net income declined (see Table 7.2). In 2020, GM had 155,000 employees globally (Carlier, 2021a).

TABLE 7.2 GM Financial Data (2018–2020)

		2018*	2019	2020
Net sales and revenue				
	Automotive	133.05	122.70	108.67
	GM Financial	14.00	14.54	13.81
	Total net sales and revenue	147.05	137.24	122.49
Costs and expenses				
	Automotive and other cost of sales**	120.66	110.65	97.54
	GM Financial interest, operating and other expenses	12.30	12.61	11.27
	Automotive and other selling, general and administrative expense	9.65	8.49	7.04
	Total costs and expense	142.60	131.76	115.85
	Operating income	4.45	5.48	6.63
	Automotive interest expense	0.66	0.78	1.10
Net income		8.01	6.67	6.32
	Net loss attributable to noncontrolling interests	0.01	0.07	0.11
Net income attributable to stockholders		8.01	6.73	6.43

* USD billion.

** GM reports Research and Development cost under automotive and other cost of sales.

Source: GM (2021). General Motors Company: Annual report. Investor.gm.com. Retrieved from https://investor.gm.com/static-files/f1b9d4ef-a7c1-4768-8789-c15985d72fab.[21]

BACKGROUND OF THE EV MARKET

Various components of the EV market macro-environment are discussed in the following sections.

Consumer Demand for EVs

UK-based IDTechEx, a market research firm, estimated that EVs would constitute 20% of the worldwide market by 2030 and around 80% by 2040. In 2020, 2% of all vehicles in the USA were electric, with Tesla selling the most EVs (Inside Factory Zero ..., 2021) (Table 7.3 lists a variety of advantages and disadvantages of EVs). A critical challenge for EV manufacturers was the readiness of consumers, once the pool of early adopters is depleted, to buy EVs. Not many consumers were willing to shift away from something they were familiar with and knew traditionally; i.e., gasoline-powered cars (Yergin, 2021). In 2021, only 10% of the UK customers were actively considering a battery-operated EV for their next purchase, owing to pricing and infrastructure concerns (Mahy, 2021). In 2021, a significant majority of US consumers were unwilling to pay any more than the median price of vehicles in the country, which is approximately USD 25,000, for an electric car, given that the median price of electric cars was USD 48,000 (Jenkins, 2021; Kane, 2021). Consumer skepticism toward EVs was also due to infrastructure issues such as the chances of the battery running out of charge before reaching a destination, too few charging stations, long charge times, among others (Blink, 2021). In a 2017 study by *Business Wire*, consumers expected full (that is, not hybrid electric-gasoline vehicles) EVs to travel approximately 644 km on a single charge. In 2021, the average range

TABLE 7.3 Advantage and Disadvantages of Electric Vehicles

Advantages	Disadvantages
Less noise pollution	Hight costs for new cars
No fumes	High depreciation in the first years
No direct greenhouse gas emissions	Battery may become weak over time
No air pollution	High costs for battery replacement
Works as well as gasoline-powered vehicles for short distances	Low range
Electric energy is less costly compared to fossil fuels	Charging may be an issue
Hedge against increasing gas prices in the future	Charging takes much longer
Larger average storage opportunities	Models will soon be outdated due to technological progress
Used electric cars can be quite inexpensive	Not eco-friendly if power derived from conventional energy sources
Less maintenance required	Limited selection of electric cars
Government subsidies	
In many cases, can be charged at home	

Source: Developed by the authors based on Electrical Car. (September 29, 2018). Advantages and disadvantages of Electric Cars. Electriccarlol.weebly.com. Retrieved from https://electriccarlol.weebly.com/pros-and-cons.html.

of the top-ten full-electric cars was approximately 480 km on a single charge (Business Wire, 2017; Carlier, 2021b).

Government Policies and Corporate Lobbying in the USA and Globally

Varying government policies exists in the US and other countries. The policies of several countries will be discussed below.

USA

The US government policies on vehicles changed with changes in administration. In the past, the Trump administration weakened auto emissions standards ostensibly to allow for cheaper cars for consumers, given that automobile companies had to invest in less research and development on controlling gas emissions (Rott & Ludden, 2020). In 2020, Barra also supported the Trump administration, trying to nullify California's 2018 rule of lowering fuel emissions (Davenport, 2021). However, shortly after the change in administration in early 2021, the Biden administration set the target to cut America's emissions 50% from 2005 levels by 2030, Barra changed her stance and announced that GM would, after 2035, sell only vehicles with zero emissions (Boudette & Davenport, 2021).

Globally

Globally, including the USA, governments were fueling consumers' EV purchases by offering generous tax incentives and subsidies and making emission standards more stringent. Britain, Ireland, and the Netherlands decided to ban new gasoline and diesel cars sales starting in 2030 (Boudette & Davenport, 2021). In 2020, China announced the requirement that vehicles sold there be electric by 2035. In Shanghai, China, the city offered free license plates for what Beijing called "new energy vehicles." Otherwise, consumers went through an auction to obtain a license plate for a car with a traditional engine (Yergin, 2021).

Infrastructure

The electronic vehicle charging infrastructure varied from country to country. In Japan, EV charging points have become more common than gas stations (Business Wire, 2015). In Europe, the Netherlands and the UK were working more aggressively to install more EV charging stations. Electric vehicle charging station deployments varies in the USA, with "greener" states, such as California, deploying more EV charging stations than others. Analysts expected EV charging points to report approximately 50% growth globally between 2019 and 2026 (Data Bridge Market Research, 2021).

Technology

Unlike conventional vehicles powered by gasoline or diesel engines, EVs has motors powered through electricity generated from batteries or a fuel cell. The production cost of EVs was approximately USD 12,000 more than comparable internal combustion engine vehicles in the small- to midsize-car segment (Baik et al., 2019). Consequently, original equipment manufacturers lost money on almost every EV sold, apart from a few premium models, including Tesla (Baik et al., 2019).

DIVERSIFICATION OF GM INTO EVs [...]

In its effort to diversify into the EV market, GM is facing a number of challenges, which are discussed in some detail below.

Competencies

Historically, the chief area of competency of GM was in the engineering and technology of internal combustion engines, which it first installed in commercial cars in 1886. Over the years, attributes such as engine size and shape became core attributes in the automobile industry. Powertrain engineers almost enjoyed celebrity status in auto circles (Colias, 2021). In 1996, GM first ventured into the EV market with the launch of EV1, the first mass-produced electric vehicle. However, with several competitors entering the EV marketspace since that time, GM needed to develop a competitive advantage from scratch (Coren, 2021). To succeed in the EV market GM needed to develop competency in electric batteries, self-driving software, mobility networks, and more. In EVs, the brakes, steering, and air conditioner, and many other components were powered differently. New systems, from electromagnetics for the motors to onboard and off-board charging, required new development, all of which involved a learning curve. The engineers did not have established tests to follow. To start an electric car required finding a perfect sequence of electrical signals from more than a dozen modules. Pam Fletcher, GM's executive chief engineer for EVs, said, "Oh my God, it took us forever to get the first Volt [Chevrolet Volt] to start" (Davies, 2016). Chevrolet Volt was a plug-in hybrid technology car that GM launched in 2010 and discontinued in 2019 (Voelcker, 2019).

Next, lithium-ion batteries used in EVs were also a problem. Bill Wallace, GM's head battery engineer, said, "Batteries wear out just sitting there, and they wear out when you cycle them" (Davies, 2016). Lithium-ion batteries are also sensitive to temperature and easily change shape and catch fire. All these problems were new to the company, which prompted GM to collaborate with the University of Michigan to develop a program to train battery engineers. Barra, commenting on batteries for EVs, said, "For an electric vehicle, it's all about the battery" (Wayland, 2021a). She added, "I think keeping that technology close and leveraging the deep battery expertise we have at General Motors is the way we're going to accelerate that value creation." To develop competency for battery development. General Motors also formed in 2019 a joint venture with LG Chem. Gaining this competency was also critical as the price of EVs was primarily affected by the cost of batteries (Mason, 2021). Developing a new EV model cost approximately USD 455 million, and converting production lines to build EVs cost between USD 90 and USD 135 million per factory. Batteries accounted for 40%–50% of production costs (Morris, 2021). Barra decided to decrease dividend payments and stock buybacks and use that money to invest in EVs. In 2020, Barra invested USD 27 billion in research and development on EVs, with the expectation of increasing the contribution of EVs to total automobile sales (Mason, 2021).

Barra also adopted a two-pronged approach to address price differences in mainstream and luxury markets primarily due to battery technologies (Wayland, 2021b). For the mainstream market, in 2017, GM released two Chevrolet Bolt models. General Motors priced the all-electric Chevrolet Bolt under USD 34,000 (Wayland, 2021b). The batteries in Chevrolet Bolt models offered less driving range than GM's next-generation Ultium platform and batteries, which GM wanted to debut in the Hummer EV in late 2021 for the luxury market.

Previous Diversification Attempts by GM

General Motors had attempted to diversity into EVs several times before their most recent attempt in [2021…]. These attempts are briefly described below.

EV Launch

In 1996, with the launch of EV1, GM pioneered electric vehicle technology, which was many years before Tesla (Coren, 2021). General Motors priced EV1 at USD 35,000 and manufactured the vehicle for three years between 1996 and 1999. Lead-acid batteries powered EV1 (GM, 2021), giving drivers approximately 160 km range (Austermuhle, 2021). In a 1997 review of EV1, *Car and Driver* magazine mentioned,

> It is quiet, it performs well, and it emits no pollution, but the range problems, the recharging time, and the high purchase cost are obstacles that will have to be overlooked or overcome before the EV1 presents a viable alternative to gas-powered cars. Still, it's a start.
> (Austermuhle, 2021)

General Motors produced approximately 1,100 EV1 vehicles—and distributed to drivers only on leases in California and Arizona. Due to lack of demand, by 2003, GM discontinued its investment in EVs and actively recalled and destroyed the cars. However, GM also preferred that EVs fail because it held to the notion that it was an internal combustion engine company (Austermuhle, 2021).

Servitization Attempt

Servitization refers to "innovation of manufacturers' capabilities and processes to transform from selling products to selling integrated solutions that deliver value in use for customers" (Baines et al., 2009). As millennials were increasingly interested in car leasing, car rental, and car subscription services and not permanently owning a car, experts valued the global car-as-a-service at USD 122 billion in 2020 (Allied Market Research, 2021). Experts projected car-as-a-service to reach USD 226 billion by 2030, registering a compound annual growth rate of 6.8% (Allied Market Research, 2021). In 2016, GM diversified into this market through servitization projects such as Maven, which was a ride-sharing and long-term rental service program. Maven users could access the GM-owned fleet and perform random driving tasks such as short trips, which indirectly compete with Uber and Lyft (Willems, 2020). Users needed to tap the app, find the car, unlock it, drive off and abandon it once done. Maven Gig was another servitization program in which GM offered rental services for rideshare and delivery drivers.

In 2018, GM also launched peer-to-peer car sharing, where newer GM model vehicle owners could rent their cars to Maven customers. General Motors was also planning to add non-GM vehicles to its Maven program. However, after realizing that servitization required a different business model altogether, it abandoned the program during the COVID-19 pandemic (Willems, 2020).

Present EV Challenges Faced by GM

We present below GM's current attempts for diversifying into the EV market:

Battery Supply Chain Issues

Lithium-ion batteries, as with all non-plant-based products, consist of natural materials, including, in this case, lithium-rich minerals. These requirements imply mining, transporting, and chemically producing of materials. According to Mark Mills, a mining and energy specialist, a thousand-pound electric car battery requires the moving of 500,000 pounds of the earth in the course of mining (Yergin, 2021). Moreover, China dominated the lithium-ion battery production supply chain. In 2021, China controlled 80% of the lithium battery supply chain globally, which was not conducive for EV manufactures in the USA because of trade tensions between the two countries (Yergin, 2021). Barra wanted GM to rely less on outsourcing for EVs and reestablish jobs in the USA. She intended to establish four battery plants in the USA and not rely on low-cost countries such as China (Priddle, 2021) (see Figure 7.6 for the lithium-ion battery cost to EV makers). This implies looking for sources of lithium in the US instead of importing it from China so that trade tensions between the two countries do not impact lithium supply.

Labor Issues

Electric vehicles require less manpower as they are easier to build and need fewer parts without an engine (Shama & Wayland, 2019). Jennifer Kelly, research director of United Auto Workers, said, "EV powertrains are simple compared to internal combustion engines" (Shama & Wayland, 2019). She added, "The simplicity could reduce the amount of labor, and thus jobs, associated with vehicle production." Although simpler than gasoline engines, EV manufacturing required more skilled laborers, which would require additional training of workers or workers with more advanced technical skills than those who work on existing assembly lines.

In 2019, to increase capacity to build more electric and autonomous vehicles, Barra eliminated as many as 14,000 jobs and wound down five plants in North America. Approximately 48,000 GM workers went on strike. In 2020, GE had to debut its autonomous EV at the

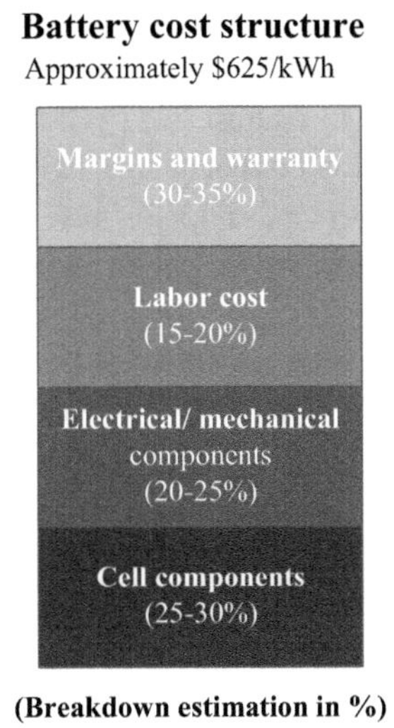

FIGURE 7.6 Battery Cost Structure

Source: Giffi, C., Vitale, J., Drew, M., Kuboshima, Y., & Sase, M. (2011). Unplugged: Electric vehicle realities versus consumer expectations. *Deloitte*. Retrieved from https://www2.deloitte.com/content/dam/Deloitte/global/Documents/Manufacturing/gx_us_auto_DTTGlobalAutoSurvey_ElectricVehicles_100411.pdf[22]

Consumer Electronics Show in Las Vegas. Due to the strike, its production was delayed, and GM had to cancel the debut of the EV (Chin, 2019). The strike that ended after 40 days of negotiation also caused production delays for the new Chevrolet Blazer and the C8 Corvette, which analysts considered GM's biggest launch.

Product Performance Issues

In 2021, GM had to recall Chevrolet Bolt three times due to fire incidents related to manufacturing defects in lithium-ion battery cells. The recalls resulted in an average cost of USD 800 million (Wayland & Kolodny, 2021). Consequently, GM shares plunged the most in more than a year. In early August 2021, Barra assured stakeholders that in newer vehicles, the battery problem would occur again, However, within two weeks, she made another announcement that even new EVs might have two manufacturing defects, a torn anode tab and folded separator, in the same cell, which increased fire risk (Bloomberg, 2021).

Such problems in EVs were industry-wide. In the past, even Tesla also reported fire issues with batteries (Blanco, 2021). In June 2020, *The J.D. Power Quality Study* on consumer problems with cars found that although the industry average for 2020 model-year vehicles was 166 problems per 100 vehicles, Tesla had 250 problems per 100 vehicles. However, it was the only EV in the car category, and the rest were conventional automobiles (Blanco, 2021).

Joint Venture Issues

Due to battery issues, as GM recalled Chevrolet Bolt's EVs multiple times over nine months (until August 2021), GM wanted its JV partner LG Chem to pay for the problem and its fix.

In contrast, LG Chem wanted GM to split the cost. LG Chem stated, "Together with our client and partners, LG is actively working to ensure that the recall measures are carried out smoothly" (Bloomberg, 2021). In August 2021, GM decided not to start repairs on the 141,000 recalled vehicles until it was confident that LG Chem was making defect-free EV batteries. Dan Flores, a GM spokesperson, said, "Because we are not confident that LG has the capability to build defect-free products, we've put the repairs on hold, and we are not building new Bolts" (LaReau, 2021).

LG Chem and GM have been partners since 2007. In 2015, when GM and LG Chem announced their joint venture for Chevrolet Bolt, they touted the quality of battery cells. However, the fires in Chevrolet Bolt electric cars and the challenges of finding a fix strained a 14-year relationship. This strain in the relationship also happened when GM and LG Chem started constructing two battery factories together in Ohio and Tennessee, each costing more than USD 2 billion (LaReau, 2021).

GM AND ITS RIVALRY WITH TESLA

As GM became more committed to producing EVs, a rivalry with Tesla was established. Factors that affected GM or aspects of this rivalry include GM market valuation, the diversification by Tesla of its revenues, the demands that the Tesla CEO places on his engineers, and the contrasting background and experience of GM and Tesla.

Market Valuation

Despite GM selling more than 14 times as many vehicles as Tesla in 2020 (Coren, 2021), by January 2021, Tesla's valuation was approximately USD 848 billion, whereas for GM it was USD 69 billion (see Table 7.1). In 2017, close to the time GM began to switch direction to become an EV company, GM shares traded at 5.5 times prospective earnings—i.e., approximately USD 5,000 for every car it sold in 2016—whereas for Tesla, with an almost identical market valuation, its shares traded at about USD 500,000 a car (Wilmot, 2017). David Keith, a professor at the MIT Sloan School of Management, noted that this happened as Tesla was less of an automobile company and more of a technology and robotics company with the potential of generating reoccurring revenue through multiple streams (Coren, 2021).

Tesla Diversifying Its Revenues

Lithium-ion batteries developed by Tesla for EVs were also used in Elon Musk's (founder and CEO of Tesla) space company, SpaceX, for use in spacecraft (Kolodny, 2020). Tesla also used its battery capabilities to introduce a line of home batteries, Powerwall, that served as energy storage systems in homes or businesses (Zucchi, 2021). Tesla also disrupted the traditional car industry business model. That is, Tesla was selling cars directly to customers rather than through franchises or dealers, as had been the custom for more than a century (Zucchi, 2021). Tesla also opted for a servitization strategy by offering several software upgrades to

TABLE 7.4 Bestselling Electric Cars in the US (2020)

Electric Cars	No. of Electric Cars Sold in 2020	Motor Trend Best Electric Car Score (Out of 10)
Tesla Model 3 & Model Y combined	442,511	9.3
Tesla Model S & Model X combined	57,039	8.3
Chevrolet Bolt EV	20,754	7.5
Nissan Leaf	9,564	7.3
Audi e-tron	7,202	8.3
Porsche Taycan	3,336	7.0

Source: Developed by the authors based on Stewart, B. (May 10, 2021). These are the ten bestselling EVs. *MarketWatch*. Retrieved from https://www.marketwatch.com/story/these-are-the-10-bestselling-evs-11620420651; Motor Trend. (2021). Best electric cars. Motortrend.com. Retrieved from https://www.motortrend.com/style/electric/

buyers through subscription services, including the autonomous or self-driving capability of the car-as-a-software platform. Generally known as software-as-a-service, or *SaaS*, by 2019, Tesla began to offer its Full Self-Driving Capability (FSD) as an optional software add-on. The company priced FSD at USD 6,000. The FSD updates enabled features such as automatic driving, lane changes, automatic parking, and a summon feature (such as a parked car reaching the owner on its own) (Trefis Team, 2019). Investors believed the FSD feature was popular among buyers (Trefis Team, 2019). With autonomous vehicles, Tesla also became an artificial intelligence (AI) company. Tesla intended to monetize on AI capabilities by offering robotaxis; i.e., robotic taxis for end consumers. Tesla was also able to innovate faster than competitors by deploying sensors in its EVs, providing it with real-time driving data (Marr, 2021). The company, using data analytics, was able to resolve car problems through software upgrades. Using data analytics, Tesla identified an engine overheating problem and solved it through software patches (Marr, 2021). Despite higher prices, Tesla EVs remained the best-selling in the US due to their superior performance (see Table 7.4 for the bestselling electric cars in the US).

Talent Management

Tesla was able to achieve these technological advancements as it was able to hire outstanding engineering talent. For engineering students, Tesla remained the most preferred automotive company to work despite Musk's expectations of 120-hour work weeks. On the positive side, Tesla was known for its agile approach and no-frills management style (Shiraishi & Fujino, 2020). On his strategies to achieve the vision of transforming the automotive industry, Musk said, "Nobody ever changed the world on 40 hours a week" (Coren, 2018).

Legacy Versus a New Modern Company

According to critics, the key hurdle for GM to compete against Tesla was that it was a legacy company that was trying to become a "new" modern corporation like Tesla (Mason, 2021). The "new" GM relied more on intellectual capital that focused on developing platforms and networks. The legacy business was more focused on highly specialized research efforts. Experts believed GM, as a "legacy" company, was comparatively in the early stages of building the new infrastructure needed for electric and autonomous vehicles, learning how to manage it while dealing with the "old" organization.

GM was also focusing on acquiring the new capabilities. For autonomous technology vehicles, GM acquired Cruise in 2016, a 40-person startup that by 2020 employed 740 people and was valued at USD 11 billion, ten times more than what GM paid for its acquisition (LaReau, 2018). By 2020, GM Cruise's fleet of 180 all-electric autonomous vehicles acted as a taxi-like service, but for its employees only. Barra did not disclose when these vehicles were expected to be available to consumers (Wayland, 2021c).

According to critics, workforce attitude was another challenge for GM, as legacy companies did not operate with the same urgency as "new" modern corporates. To compete against Tesla, GM must aim for where Tesla will be in three or five years rather than where it is at present (Wayland, 2021c).

In September 2020, Musk announced plans to develop Tabless batteries to improve the range and power of electric cars. Industry analysts expected Tabless batteries to reduce costs and make EVs available for the same price as gasoline-powered (Hawkins, 2020). In contrast, GM explored hydro-fuel technology (Wayland, 2021d). Hydrogen fuel cells were four times less expensive than the lithium batteries used by Tesla (D'Allegro, 2019). The transportation of hydrogen to refueling stations posed safety risks, but companies have not reported any serious incidents, and the industrial sector was transporting hydrogen for decades. For hydrogen fuel cell production, GM allied with Germany-based Liebherr-Aerospace (Wayland, 2021d). Due to infrastructure constraints of hydrogen fuel cells, GM was targeting commercial customers, as they had set routes and on-site fueling compared to end consumers (Wayland, 2021d). Other automotive companies were already offering hydrogen fuel cell cars—for example, Honda Clarity, Hyundai Nexo, and Toyota Mirai.

APPROACH TO EVs BY GM COMPETITORS

In the first half of 2021, GM remained one of the top global players in conventional automobiles sales. It was also a major automaker in the US (Carleir, 2021c). However, as GM focused more on EVs than profitable gasoline vehicles, its conventional competitors such as Toyota were pursuing an opposite approach (Welch & Coppola, 2021). Though GM competitors were investing in EV technology, they were innovating more in the profitable gasoline segment compared to GM. General Motors decided to replace only 14% of its annual sales volume with new gasoline models from 2022 to 2024. For Honda, it was 28%. Toyota decided to refresh 36% of its gasoline-running cars, and for Ford the target was 17% of the volume (Welch & Coppola, 2021). Analysts expected this strategy of GM would lower its market share in conventional vehicles, which GM was leveraging as a cash cow to fund EV business. Most traditional automobile companies perceived the low current demand for EVs and considered more seriously consumers' skepticism and unwillingness to embrace the EV technology quickly. Commenting on investments in EVs, Hau Thai-Tang, Ford's chief product development and purchasing officer, said, "We're trying to time this with the natural demand of consumers (so) we're not forced to do artificial things, and we don't violate the laws of economics" (Lienert, White, & Klayman, 2020).

Competitors were also following a partnership approach for competing against the EV industry leader Tesla. Such partnerships were intended to share the battery development and production costs. By August 2021, Nissan, Renault, and Mitsubishi allied to develop a common EV platform (Morris, 2021). They intended to share 70% of motors, batteries, and other EV components among the three brands. Toyota, Suzuki, and Daihatsu formed a partnership to develop electrified commercial vehicles. Volkswagen and Ford Motors also allied for electric and autonomous vehicle technology (Morris, 2021). Hyundai Motor Co. also intended to enter the electric vehicle future, and experts believed it would enter into an alliance with Apple for producing driverless EVs (Mason, 2021).

GLOBAL STRATEGY OF GM

General Motors sold more than 60% of its fleet overseas; still, most profits were derived from business in the US (LaReau, 2019) (see Table 7.5 for GM global sales). For GM, China was a critical market. General Motors sold more cars in China through joint ventures than in the US (Boudette & Davenport, 2021). In July 2020, GM, through its joint ventures in China, launched Wuling Hongguang Mini EV (Wuling). At USD 4,300, Wiling was a low-priced EV, primarily targeted at consumers in China's smaller and less affluent cities (Moss, 2020). In contrast, the Model 3 of Tesla was priced at USD 37,600 after subsidies and was targeted more toward wealthy metropolises in China (Moss, 2020). Within three months (July to September 2020), GM sold 55,781 units of Wuling in China against Tesla's sales of 35,283 units. General Motors was not expecting to make a profit from Wuling and was focusing on high-end

TABLE 7.5 Industry and GM Total Vehicle Sales (in Thousand) and GM Market Share (2019–2020)

	Industry Sales (2020)	GMSales (2020)	Market Share (2020) (%)	Market Share (2019) (%)
North America	17,722	2,924	16.5	15.9
Asia-Pacific, Middle East, and Africa	42,908	3,434	8	7.9
South America	3,158	470	14.9	15.5
Europe	14,795	1	0.006	n/a
Total of above regions	78,583	6,829	8.7	8.5
United Sates	14,824	2,547	17.1	16.5
China	24,922	2,901	11.6	12.2

Source: Stock Dividend Screener. (2021). Tracking GM global vehicle sales and market share. Stockdividendscreener.com. Retrieved from https://stockdividendscreener.com/auto-manufacturers/general-motors-vehicle-sales-and-market-share/

vehicles. Wuling primarily appealed to two-wheeler drivers in China who intended to switch to hatchback cars. Michael Dunne, chief executive of the consulting firm ZoZo Go, said, "GM can now say they're the market leader in EVs. That's quite an achievement." Pointing to a thin profit margin, he added, "The question is: How do you take those consumers to higher price points? It's really important they establish themselves at the high end" (Moss, 2020).

Nevertheless, as trade relations between the US and China worsened, GM was expected to experience a more difficult business climate. In 2019, in one of his tweets responding to increased tariffs by China, Trump mentioned, "Our great American companies are hereby ordered to immediately start looking for an alternative to China, including bringing your companies HOME and making your products in the USA. I will be responding to China's Tariffs this afternoon" (LaReau, 2019). However, the order did not materialize.

THE ROAD AHEAD

In the time period discussed in this case, leading up to early 2022, petroleum-fueled vehicles had a higher profit margin than mostly smaller, expensive-to-develop EVs (Lienert, White, & Klayman, 2020). As Barra decided to stop producing gasoline engines by 2035, she needed to ensure that GM had EVs that were better than gasoline equivalents and cost-competitive (Voelcker, 2021). Sam Abuelsamid, senior analyst at Navigant Research in Ann Arbor, Michigan, said,

> When you go from gas to electric, there's going to be a whole new set of problems you have to deal with, and we just have to figure out how to deal with those issues that you know that we haven't had to deal with in the past.
>
> (Wayland & Kolodny, 2021)

The learning curve with batteries was steep for traditional automakers, and battery technology remained challenging even for innovative companies like Tesla.

As GM was resolving issues with LG Chem over Chevrolet Bolt, by August 2021, it was also working with LG Chem on another battery platform, titled Ultium, that would be launched later in 2021. Barra mentioned that Ultium batteries were likely to be a "game-changer in driving down costs, increasing range and opening the design potential" of its EVs (GM Authority, 2020). However, industry experts were skeptical if GM would transform itself and become a rival to Tesla, given the latter's experience, agility, and learning curve with EVs. On the contrary, Tesla critics believed that competitors could replicate the capabilities of Tesla over time Tesla Business Analysis, 2018). Can Barra and GM dominate the EV market? What strategies should she pursue to achieve the goals she has set for GM?

DISCUSSION QUESTIONS

- How could GM use EVs to develop a sustainable servitization model
- Evaluate if GM's EV investment from the perspective of the effort-impact matrix. Evaluate if the investment creates any risk

- Is GM's diversification into EVs equivalent to Tesla's diversification into energy and software?
- Can GM benefit from sentiment analysis for its EV?

CHAPTER NOTES

1 https://www.weforum.org/stories/2020/11/what-is-servitization-and-how-can-it-help-save-the-planet/.
2 https://www.weforum.org/stories/2020/11/what-is-servitization-and-how-can-it-help-save-the-planet/.
3 https://www.weforum.org/stories/2020/11/what-is-servitization-and-how-can-it-help-save-the-planet/.
4 https://www.ecosystems.io/blog/thinking-of-adopting-a-usage-based-pricing-model-here-are-four-usage-metrics-you-should-consider.
5 https://images.philips.com/is/content/PhilipsConsumer/PDFDownloads/United%20Kingdom/CALI20160201_001-UPD-en_GB-CaseStudy_NUS_UK.pdf
6 https://www.oneplanetnetwork.org/knowledge-centre/resources/lighting-installation-service.
7 https://www.oneplanetnetwork.org/knowledge-centre/resources/lighting-installation-service.
8 https://www.simon-kucher.com/en/insights/mastering-tiered-pricing-strategy-revenue-maximization#:~:text=Diverse%20industries%2C%20one%20common%20strategy,Maximizing%20revenue%20opportunities.
9 https://www.simon-kucher.com/en/insights/mastering-tiered-pricing-strategy-revenue-maximization#:~:text=Diverse%20industries%2C%20one%20common%20strategy,Maximizing%20revenue%20opportunities.
10 https://www.impactanalytics.co/blog/decoy-pricing#:~:text=1.,Basic:%20$29/month.
11 https://www.impactanalytics.co/blog/decoy-pricing#:~:text=1.,Basic:%20$29/month.
12 https://subscribed.fyi/blog/is-netflix-a-cloud-based-application-understanding-digital-infrastructure/#:~:text=Netflix's%20cloud%2Dbased%20approach%20allows%20for%20efficient%20content,the%20streaming%20quality%20and%20overall%20user%20experience.
13 https://luxus-plus.com/en/how-the-prada-group-is-shaking-up-the-perfume-industry-with-loreal-this-fall/.
14 https://osuva.uwasa.fi/server/api/core/bitstreams/8b473abc-5449-4d1c-9768-e11e2e27fd5d/content.
15 https://www.sciencedirect.com/science/article/pii/S0019850122001481?via%3Dihub#bib448.
16 https://www.sprintwell.com/post/glossier-customer-feedback-loops#:~:text=4)%20Glossier%20uses%20feedback%20loops,rinse%2C%20repeat%2C%20and%20profit.
17 https://www.sprintwell.com/post/glossier-customer-feedback-loops#:~:text=4)%20Glossier%20uses%20feedback%20loops,rinse%2C%20repeat%2C%20and%20profit.
18 https://www.sprintwell.com/post/glossier-customer-feedback-loops#:~:text=4)%20Glossier%20uses%20feedback%20loops,rinse%2C%20repeat%2C%20and%20profit.
19 https://www.linkedin.com/pulse/social-value-secret-how-glossier-turned-0-buyers-shah-mohammed-m-tzbkc/.
20 YChart. (2021). Solutions. *Ycharts*. Retrieved from www.ycharts.com.
21 GM (2021). General Motors Company: Annual report. Investor.gm.com. Retrieved from https://investor.gm.com/static-files/f1b9d4ef-a7c1-4768-8789-c15985d72fab.
22 Giffi, C., Vitale, J., Drew, M., Kuboshima, Y., & Sase, M. (2011). Unplugged: Electric vehicle realities versus consumer expectations. *Deloitte*. Retrieved from https://www2.deloitte.com/content/dam/Deloitte/global/Documents/Manufacturing/gx_us_auto_DTTGlobalAutoSurvey_ElectricVehicles_100411.pdf.

FURTHER READINGS

Baines, T., Bigdeli, A. Z., Bustinza, O. F., Shi, V. G., Baldwin, J., & Ridgway, K. (2017). Servitization: Revisiting the state-of-the-art and research priorities. *International Journal of Operations & Production Management*, *37*(2), 256–278.

Baines, T. S., Lightfoot, H. W., Benedettini, O., & Kay, J. M. (2009). The servitization of manufacturing: A review of literature and reflection on future challenges. *Journal of Manufacturing Technology Management*, *20*(5), 547–567.

Eklund, J., & Kapoor, R. (2019). Pursuing the new while sustaining the current: Incumbent strategies and firm value during the nascent period of industry change. *Organization Science*, *30*(2), 383–404.

Foster, R. (1986). *Innovation: The attacker's advantage.* New York: Summit Books.

Kaplan, R. S., & Norton, D. P. (September 1, 2020). Having trouble with your strategy? Then map it. *Harvard Business Review*. Retrieved from https://hbr.org/2000/09/having-trouble-with-your-strategy-then-map-it

Kenton, W. (November 14, 2020). PEST analysis. *Investopedia*. Retrieved from https://www.investopedia.com/terms/p/pest-analysis.asp

CASE REFERENCES

Agnihotri, A., & Bhattacharya, S. (2023). *General motors creating shareholder value through diversification in electric vehicles: Can a legacy company win?* Sage Business Cases. https://doi.org/10.4135/9781529617221

Allied Market Research. (2021). Car-as-a-service market statistics 2021–2030. Alliedmarketresearch.com. Retrieved from https://www.alliedmarketresearch.com/car-as-a-service-market-A12371

Austermuhle, M. (August 24, 2021). A very rare electric car is sitting in a Howard University parking lot. dcist.com. Retrieved from https://dcist.com/story/21/08/24/a-very-rare-electric-car-is-sitting-in-a-howard-university-parking-lot/

Baik, Y., Hensley, R., Hertzke, P., & Knupfer, S. (March 8, 2019). Making electric vehicles profitable. *McKinsey*. Retrieved from https://www.mckinsey.com/industries/automotive-and-assembly/our-insights/making-electric-vehicles-profitable

Baines, T. S., Lightfoot, H. W., Benedettini, O., & Kay, J. M. (2009). The servitization of manufacturing: A review of literature and reflection on future challenges. *Journal of Manufacturing Technology Management*, *20*(5), 547–567.

Blanco, S. (April 21, 2021). Tesla fire in Texas crash was not how it was reported, says fire chief. Caranddriver.com. Retrieved from https://www.caranddriver.com/news/a36189237/tesla-model-s-fire-texas-crash-details-fire-chief/

Blink. (2021). Fact from fiction: Why consumers don't buy EVs. *Blinkcharging.com*. Retrieved from https://blinkcharging.com/fact-from-fiction-the-real-reason-why-consumers-dont-buy-electric-vehicles/?locale=en

Bloomberg. (August 29, 2021). Battery woes test GM, LG relationship. *Arkansas Democrat Gazette*. Retrieved from https://www.arkansasonline.com/news/2021/aug/29/battery-woes-test-gm-lg-relationship/

Boudette, N. E., & Davenport, C. (January 29, 2021). G.M. announcement shakes up U.S. automakers' transition to electric cars. *The New York Times*. Retrieved from https://www.nytimes.com/2021/01/29/business/general-motors-electric-cars.html

Business Wire. (May 28, 2015). Global EV charging stations to skyrocket by 2020, IHS report says. Businesswire.com. Retrieved from https://www.businesswire.com/news/home/20150528005122/en/Global-EV-Charging-Stations-to-Skyrocket-by-2020-IHS-Report-Says

Business Wire. (January 10, 2017). Acceptance and expectations of full-electric vehicles. Businesswire.com. Retrieved from https://www.businesswire.com/news/home/20170110005320/en/Acceptance-and-expectations-of-full-electric-vehicles

Carlier, M. (August 4, 2021a). Number of General Motors employees between FY 2010 and FY 2020. *Statista*. Retrieved from https://www.statista.com/statistics/239843/employees-of-general-motors/

Carlier, M. (August 9, 2021b). EV range of selected MY 2021 electric vehicles. *Statista*. Retrieved from https://www.statista.com/statistics/266633/ev-range-of-selected-plug-in-hybrid-and-electric-vehicles/

Carleir, M. (August 19, 2021c). Selected automakers' U.S. YTD market share in the 1st half of 2021, by key manufacturer. *Statista*. Retrieved from https://www.statista.com/statistics/343162/market-share-of-major-car-manufacturers-in-the-united-states/

Chin, C. (December 18, 2019). GM cancels debut of autonomous EV at CES 2020 due to strike-related delays: Report. *The Drive*. Retrieved from https://www.thedrive.com/news/31538/gm-cancels-debut-of-robotaxi-ev-at-ces-2020-due-to-strike-related-delays-report

Colias, M. (July 23, 2021). Gas engines, and the people behind them, are cast aside for electric vehicles. *The Wall Street Journal*. Retrieved from https://www.wsj.com/articles/gas-engines-cast-aside-electric-vehicles-job-losses-detroit-11627046285

Coren, M. J. (December 14, 2018). Former Tesla executive: "Everyone in Tesla is in an abusive relationship with Elon." *Quartz*. Retrieved from https://qz.com/1495131/former-tesla-executive-says-employees-in-abusive-relationship-with-elon-musk/

Coren, M. J. (January 30, 2021). GM just sped up the depreciation of everything it owns. *Quartz*. Retrieved from https://qz.com/1966116/electric-cars-will-speed-up-depreciation-of-everything-gm-owns/

D'Allegro, J. (February 23, 2019). Elon Musk says the tech is 'mind-bogglingly stupid,' but hydrogen cars may yet threaten Tesla. *CNBC*. Retrieved from https://www.cnbc.com/2019/02/21/musk-calls-hydrogen-fuel-cells-stupid-but-tech-may-threaten-tesla.html

Data Bridge Market Research. (January 30, 2021). Global electric vehicle charging stations market business growth statistics and key players insights. Openpr.com. Retrieved from https://www.openpr.com/news/1914570/global-electric-vehicle-charging-stations-market-business

Davenport, C. (August 26, 2021). G.M. agrees to tighter federal restrictions aimed at combating climate change. *The New York Times*. Retrieved from https://www.nytimes.com/2021/06/09/us/politics/gm-biden-fuel-economy-rules.html

Davies, A. (February, 2016). How GM beat Tesla to the first true mass-market electric car. *Wired*. Retrieved from https://www.wired.com/2016/01/gm-electric-car-chevy-bolt-mary-barra/

DeBord, M. (May 13, 2021). Mary Barra's $27 billion bet on making GM an electric-only vehicle company is the biggest swing an American automaker has taken in decades. *Business Insider*. Retrieved from https://www.businessinsider.com/mary-barras-bet-on-evs-biggest-swing-by-american-automaker-2021-5

General Motors: Rank 22. (2021). *Fortune*. Retrieved from https://fortune.com/company/general-motors/fortune500/

GM. (2021). GM Heritage Center. GM.com. Retrieved from https://www.gmheritagecenter.com/

GM Authority. (October 27, 2020). General Motors CEO Mary Barra says company has capability to 'put everyone in an EV.' Gmauthority.com. Retrieved from https://gmauthority.com/blog/2020/10/general-motors-ceo-mary-barra-says-company-has-capability-to-put-everyone-in-an-ev/

Hawkins, A. J. (September 22, 2020). Tesla announces 'tabless' battery cells that will improve range of its electric cars. *The Verge*. Retrieved from https://www.theverge.com/2020/9/22/21449238/tesla-electric-car-battery-tabless-cells-day-elon-musk

Inside Factory Zero, Where GM Is Betting Big on Electric Vehicle. (April 6, 2021). *CBS News*. Retrieved from https://www.cbsnews.com/news/general-motors-electric-vehicles-factory-zero/

Jenkins, L. M. (February 9, 2021). The electric car consumers want: Lower cost, higher mileage. Morningconsult.com. Retrieved from https://morningconsult.com/2021/02/09/energy-efficiency-series-electric-vehicles-consumers-polling/

Kane, M. (February 24, 2021). All-electric car price comparison for U.S. Insideevs.com. Retrieved from https://insideevs.com/news/490438/electric-car-price-comparison-us-20210224/

Kolodny, L. (April 8, 2020). Here's how Tesla and SpaceX worked with and paid each other in the past year. *CNBC*. Retrieved from https://www.cnbc.com/2020/04/28/heres-how-tesla-and-spacex-worked-with-and-paid-each-other-in-the-past-year.html

LaReau, J. L. (August 3, 2018). How General Motors is leading the race for self-driving cars. *Detroit Free Press*. Retrieved from https://www.freep.com/story/money/cars/general-motors/2018/07/19/general-motors-cruise-av-autonomous-car/782570002/

LaReau, J. L. (August 28, 2019). Trump would cost General Motors billions if he actually orders business out of China. *USA Today*. Retrieved from https://www.usatoday.com/story/money/cars/2019/08/27/trump-china-talks-general-motors-would-lose-billions-if-ordered-out/2128709001/

LaReau, J. L. (August 30, 2021). GM 'not confident' LG Chem will build defect-free Bolt batteries. *Detroit Free Press*. Retrieved from https://www.freep.com/story/money/cars/general-motors/2021/08/30/gm-lg-chem-bolt-batteries/5652862001/

Lienert, P., White, J., & Klayman, B. (March 26, 2020). Detroit's near future based on SUVs, not EVs, production plans show. *Reuters*. Retrieved from https://www.reuters.com/article/us-autos-emissions-suvs-insight/detroits-near-future-based-on-suvs-not-evs-production-plans-show-idUSKBN21D1KW

Mahy, E. (May, 2021). Car buyers still sceptical about going electric, says Ford boss. *BBC*. Retrieved from https://www.bbc.com/news/business-57200593

Marr, B. (July 13, 2021). The amazing ways Tesla is using artificial intelligence and big data. Bernardmarr.com. Retrieved from https://bernardmarr.com/the-amazing-ways-tesla-is-using-artificial-intelligence-and-big-data/

Mason, J. M. (January 8, 2021). General Motors: The problems facing a legacy company. *Seeking Alpha*. Retrieved from https://seekingalpha.com/article/4397951-general-motors-problems-facing-legacy-company

Mishkin, S. (November 12, 2020). EVs are the future, GM's Mary Barra says. Where the CEO sees growth. *Barrons*. Retrieved from https://www.barrons.com/articles/evs-are-the-future-gms-mary-barra-says-where-the-ceo-sees-growth-51605218949

Morris, C. (September 18, 2021). Can automakers team up to catch Tesla? Cleantechnica.com. Retrieved from https://cleantechnica.com/2021/09/18/can-automakers-team-up-to-catch-tesla/

Moss, T. (November 13, 2020). Tiny GM car Zips past Tesla to lead China's electric vehicle market. *The Wall Street Journal*. Retrieved from https://www.wsj.com/articles/tiny-gm-car-zips-past-tesla-to-lead-chinas-electric-vehicle-market-11605278148

O'Kane, S. (September 9, 2021). The Chevy Bolt recall is burning up what's left of GM's EV good will. *The Verge*. Retrieved from https://www.theverge.com/2021/9/19/22677539/chevy-bolt-recall-gm-electric-vehicles-fire-tesla-competition

Priddle, A. (June 30, 2021). GM CEO doesn't want electric cars available only to the rich. Motortrend.com. Retrieved from https://www.motortrend.com/news/gm-ceo-electric-vehicle-equity-affordability/

Rott, N., & Ludden, J. (March 31, 2020). Trump administration weakens auto emissions standards. *NPR*. Retrieved from https://www.npr.org/2020/03/31/824431240/trump-administration-weakens-auto-emissions-rolling-back-key-climate-policy

Shama, E., & Wayland, M. (September 30, 2019). GM strike highlights how shift to electric cars puts future auto jobs at risk. *CNBC*. Retrieved from https://www.cnbc.com/2019/09/30/gm-strike-highlights-how-shift-to-electric-cars-puts-future-auto-jobs-at-risk.html

Shiraishi, T., & Fujino, I. (August 8, 2020). Tesla looks to make its China operation as nimble as its cars. Asia.nikkei.com. Retrieved from https://asia.nikkei.com/Business/Automobiles/Tesla-looks-to-make-its-China-operation-as-nimble-as-its-cars

Trefis Team. (September 13, 2019). Tesla has a software business and it's big! *Forbes*. Retrieved from https://www.forbes.com/sites/greatspeculations/2019/09/13/tesla-has-a-software-business-and-its-big/?sh=436553b84d7c

Voelcker, J. (March 28, 2019). Retrieved from 1o lessons from the short life of the Chevy Volt, 2011–2019. Greencarreports.com. Retrieved from https://www.greencarreports.com/news/1122269_10-lessons-from-the-short-life-of-the-chevy-volt-2011-2019

Voelcker, J. (January 30, 2021). GM 'Aspires' to sell only EVs by 2035. Here's how to understand what that really means. *The Drive*. Retrieved from https://www.thedrive.com/tech/39016/gm-aspires-to-sell-only-evs-by-2035-heres-how-to-understand-what-that-really-means

Wayland, M. (June 16, 2021a). Despite pressure from investors, GM CEO insists the company is more valuable keeping its EV battery group. *CNBC*. Retrieved from https://www.cnbc.com/2021/06/16/gm-ceo-mary-barra-says-company-is-worth-more-keeping-ultium-ev-battery-unit-in-house.html

Wayland, M. (March 1, 2021b). GM's electric vehicle plans begin to take shape with new lower-priced Chevy Bolts. *CNBC*. Retrieved from https://www.cnbc.com/2021/03/01/gms-ev-plans-begin-to-take-shape-with-new-lower-priced-chevy-bolts.html

Wayland, M. (May 5, 2021c). GM expects to offer personal self-driving vehicles to consumers this decade. *CNBC*. Retrieved from https://www.cnbc.com/2021/05/05/gm-expects-to-offer-self-driving-vehicles-to-consumers-this-decade.html

Wayland, M. (June 21, 2021d). By 'land, sea and air,' GM plans to expand fuel-cell business beyond EVs. *CNBC*. Retrieved from https://www.cnbc.com/2021/06/21/by-land-sea-and-air-gm-to-expand-fuel-cell-business-beyond-evs.html

Wayland, M., & Kolodny, L. (August 20, 2021). Fires, probes, recalls: The shift to electric vehicles is costing automakers billions. *CNBC*. Retrieved from https://www.cnbc.com/2021/08/19/fires-probes-recalls-automakers-spend-billions-in-shift-to-evs.html

Welch, D., & Coppola, G. (June 11, 2021). GM's EV gamble could be Toyota's gain as carmakers place bets. *Bloomberg*. Retrieved from https://www.bloomberg.com/news/articles/2021-06-10/gm-s-ev-gamble-could-be-toyota-s-gain-as-carmakers-place-bets

Willems, S. (April 21, 2020). An experiment in error? Maven bites the dust, GM lauds 'insights' gained. Thetruthaboutcars.com. Retrieved from https://www.thetruthaboutcars.com/2020/04/an-experiment-in-error-maven-bites-the-dust-gm-lauds-insight-gained/

Wilmot, S. (May 5, 2017). How GM might unlock a Tesla-like valuation. *The Wall Street Journal*. Retrieved from https://www.wsj.com/articles/how-gm-might-unlock-a-tesla-like-valuation-1493980884

Yergin, D. (August 31, 2021). The major problems blocking America's electric car future. Politico.com. Retrieved from https://www.politico.com/news/magazine/2021/08/31/biden-electric-vehicles-problems-yergin-507599

Zucchi, K. (September 6, 2021). What makes Tesla's business model different? *Investopedia*. Retrieved from https://www.investopedia.com/articles/active-trading/072115/what-makes-teslas-business-model-different.asp

CHAPTER **8**

Global Business Strategy

Learning Objectives

After completing this chapter, students should be able to:

- Examine ways of international market entry;
- Evaluate ways of managing international markets;
- Comprehend theories guiding modes of internationalization;
- Utilize data analysis for choosing the mode of entry in international markets.

GLOBAL STRATEGY

Firms may pursue a global strategy in four ways: export strategy, standardization strategy, multidomestic/nation strategy, and transnational strategy.

- *Export Strategy.* An export strategy implies sales in a foreign market without establishing a subsidiary in that country.[1] In exports, the product is generally not customized to meet the needs of local markets, except to comply with the regulatory requirements of the host country.[2]
- *Standardization Strategy*. In this global strategy, firms maintain a standardized approach to managing value chain activities as they internationalize.[3] Thus, a firm maintains a standard approach to managing its products, services, marketing, and operations across international markets, and does not adapt these value chain activities to tailor to the needs of the local market.[4] Firms use a standardization strategy for product categories that have unique needs across different countries. Firms can sell products that have universal appeal, limited local variation, and minimal cultural or regulatory differences across different markets by employing a standardization strategy.[5] Several hardware and software products, such as those of Apple, are sold with a standardization strategy.[6] Apple makes only minor adjustments needed for language or power requirements, apart from which its iPhones are standardized globally.[7] Similarly, in the B2B sector, a firm may easily pursue

DOI: 10.4324/9781003568100-8

a standardization strategy. Products used in manufacturing, such as machinery, computer chips, or raw materials, have universal and standardized technical specifications and are primarily sold based on their functional appeal rather than cultural appeal; thus, firms may sell them using a standardization strategy.[8]

- *Multidomestic/Nation Strategy*. This strategy entails a business approach where firms tailor products, marketing, and operations to the distinct needs and preferences of local markets.[9] Firms prioritize local responsiveness over global integration.[10] Decision-making in multidomestic businesses is decentralized, allowing for tailored offerings and strategies that accommodate local culture, competition, and regulations.[11] Nestlé customizes its vast portfolio of food and beverage brands to local preferences in 186 countries. In the service industry, players such as Netflix also localize their content and apps for viewers across 190 countries.[12] McDonald's also customizes its menu and marketing to cater to local tastes and cultures.[13] Since the food industry is largely influenced by cultural variations across different countries, firms in the food sector largely follow a multidomestic strategy. For example, as a large number of people practice Jainism in India, Heinz offers tomato sauce without onion and garlic, as the Jain community does not consume these ingredients.[14]
- *Transnational Strategy*. This strategy entails maintaining global efficiency through the central coordination of certain value chain functions, while also allowing for local responsiveness of other value chain functions, such as marketing and R&D, through decentralized structures.[15] R&D is decentralized to reduce customized product development time and adapt quickly to changing local demands. However, other value chain functions, such as finance and procurement, are more centralized. Transnational companies rely on global suppliers for specific components, depending on the product category, to ensure uniform quality and benefit from economies of scale.[16] However, transnational companies may procure components that require customization from local suppliers.

Similarly, even for R&D knowledge, transnational companies invest in mechanisms for the global integration of R&D knowledge, thereby avoiding duplication of efforts across multiple geographies. Moreover, transnational companies also decentralize R&D to take advantage of different talent across different locations, apart from just serving the local markets.[17] For instance, several Asian emerging markets, such as India and China, are becoming preferred R&D hubs for transnational companies. These countries offer a varied pool of STEM-qualified talent at a much lower cost compared to developed countries, and their governments also provide tax advantages.[18] Overall, the integration of R&D efforts can be categorized based on the level of technology complexity as well as the degree of interconnectedness required between different departments.

Best-Cost Country Service Center. Some of the most cost-effective countries include India, Vietnam, and certain countries in Eastern Europe and South America, as they offer lower costs and talented employees simultaneously. For instance, R&D in India is 35% cheaper than in the US.[19] Therefore, if a company seeks to develop and test new, more efficient manufacturing processes for reducing waste and enhancing speed, India can serve as an R&D center.

- *Center of Excellence*. Nestlé has 22 R&D sites globally. The location of Nestlé's central "Nestlé Research" department is at its headquarters, namely Switzerland, which provides the basic scientific foundation for other sites to innovate in specific product categories.[20] One of its research centers in Lausanne, Switzerland, provides a scientific foundation for conducting R&D across all Nestlé businesses, which are spread across the US, China, Japan, and Chile.[21]

- *Global Network of Centers*. This implies that where technological complexity is high, the level of interaction with local customers and suppliers is also high. Given high local activity, having multiple R&D centers across multiple countries could be required for local adaptation of the product. Given the high technological complexity, scientists are likely to benefit from knowledge sharing with their peers in different countries, thereby establishing formal and informal channels of communication between R&D centers. Thus, multinational firms would benefit by connecting R&D centers through formal and informal networks. IBM has closely connected R&D units across India, the US, China, and European countries for knowledge sharing.[22]
- *Centers Serving Local Markets*. In such centers, technological complexity is low, and each country requires high interaction with local markets. Centers serving local markets are R&D units in specific countries aimed at adapting products and services to local needs. For example, Caterpillar's R&D center in China aimed at product adaptation for the Chinese market.[23]

LEVEL OF INTERNATIONALIZATION

The Uppsala model explains how firms incrementally enhance their resource commitment in international markets, starting from the low-resource commitment phase of sporadic exports to making direct investments in international markets through the establishment of production facilities to cater to the needs of international markets strategically.[24] Furthermore, advising firms on countries where they should make their first international move, the Uppsala model explains that managers select countries based on psychic distance in relation to the foreign market.[25]

Psychic distance refers to the cultural and linguistic differences between a person's home country and the host country.[26] The greater the psychic distance, the higher the informational and knowledge barriers, as per the model.[27] Thus, firms first enter proximate markets that have less psychic distance and uncertainty, and after gradually gaining knowledge about international markets, make larger-scale investments in host countries. IKEA, a Swedish company, for instance, after capturing the domestic market, began exports to nearby Nordic countries. Next, it expanded into neighboring European markets.[28] This expansion occurred as the psychic distance between Nordic countries and other European countries was low, due to cultural similarities, geographic proximity, strong institutional ties between the countries, and common linguistic roots.[29] Then, IKEA expanded to the American market and then to emerging markets like China, where the psychic distance was high. Psychic distance inhibits managerial ability to internationalize.[30] This inhibition occurs because, as the distance increases, familiarity with the distant market also increases, and accordingly, the perceived risk of doing business in an unknown territory, especially when cultures are dissimilar and the business environment is different, also increases.[31]

MODES OF ENTRY IN INTERNATIONAL MARKETS

Export is the most common and low-risk method that firms use to enter international markets. In this entry mode, a firm sells its goods or services to customers in a foreign market, using either intermediaries in the home country to manage shipping and marketing in host countries (indirect export) or selling directly to intermediaries or customers in foreign countries (direct export).[32] An Export Management Company (EMC) or an Export Trading Company (ETC) generally undertakes indirect exports for a firm.[33] These companies are typically responsible for finding overseas buyers, managing product shipping, and receiving payments. Alternatively, for indirect exports, companies can engage with online marketplaces such as eBay and Amazon, which have distribution centers in other countries and handle all administrative tasks, including customs and logistics, for a fee.[34] Then there are non-equity (contractual) methods of expanding in foreign countries. These include licensing, franchising, strategic alliance, joint venture, and establishing a wholly owned subsidiary.

- *Licensing*. In licensing, a firm grants a foreign company the right to use its intangible assets, such as patents, trademarks, or production methods, for a specified fee.[35] Multinationals such as Coca-Cola, PepsiCo, and Microsoft all used licensing to enter international markets.[36] These companies granted rights to local companies for producing and distributing their products or using their brands in exchange for royalties.
- *Franchising*. In this mode of entry, a firm permits a foreign franchisee to leverage its entire business model, including its brand name, in return for which the franchisee pays fees and royalties.[37] Franchising is widespread across the global restaurant industry. Fast food chains such as McDonald's, Subway, KFC, and Domino's follow a franchising model.[38] These food chains leverage their operational expertise and business models to train local entrepreneurs. Local entrepreneurs are then required to follow standard operating procedures when using the brand names of fast food chains and pay royalties in return. This way, fast food chains can scale faster in international markets with lower resource commitment and financial risk.[39]
- *Strategic Alliance*. In a strategic alliance, a firm intending to go international forms a partnership, i.e., a given firm and a foreign firm join hands to share risks, resources, and knowledge that helps the given company to smoothly enter foreign markets, without the need to form a new company, something that is typical of a joint venture.[40] In 2022, the world's six leading telcos—Bouygues Telecom, Cellnex, KPN, MTN, Telefónica, and WINDTRE—formed a non-equity consortium named Alaian. With this alliance, the telcos connected their open innovation ecosystems, effectively reaching 50 countries and 700 million customers.[41]
- *Joint Venture*. In a joint venture, a firm enters international markets via equity investment, where the joint venture partner in the host country shares financial risk with the firm.[42] Generally, the equity arrangement is 50% for each partner; however, contributions may vary. A company can opt for a joint venture either to reduce its risk in a foreign market or to comply with regulatory requirements, as some countries' governments do not allow 100% foreign direct investment in specific sectors. For example, in India, 100% FDI (Foreign Direct Investment) is not permitted in the retail sector. Accordingly, when Walmart decided to enter the Indian market, it formed a joint venture with Indian partner Bharti.

Bharti not only provided Walmart with local market knowledge and an understanding of Indian consumer behavior but also helped to comply with the complex Indian regulatory system. Walmart was not only able to reduce risks but also navigate the complex local conditions of the Indian market smoothly.

- *Establishing a Wholly Owned Subsidiary*. Instead of making a partial equity investment in the host country, a firm decides to make a 100% equity investment in the host country through a wholly owned subsidiary. A firm may use two methods to form a wholly owned subsidiary: Greenfield Investment or Acquisition. In *greenfield investment*, a company starts its operations in the host country from scratch and sets up a fresh subsidiary. In an acquisition, a company acquires an existing company in the host country, rather than starting from scratch. Tesla developed a Gigafactory in Shanghai, China, from scratch through a greenfield investment, rather than acquiring an existing facility, allowing it to customize its production and operational facilities for improved operational efficiency and control. In the retail sector, German retailers such as Aldi and Lidl have also leveraged greenfield investments for their expansion into the UK and the US. Accordingly, they developed stores and infrastructure from scratch rather than acquiring local companies.[43]

  Firms also leverage *acquisitions* to enter international markets. UK-based Vodafone acquired German industrial conglomerate Mannesmann, gaining access to key European markets in Germany, Italy, and other countries. In these countries, Mannesmann had a strong market share. Similarly, Anheuser-Busch InBev acquired SABMiller in 2016 with the motive of enhancing its presence in emerging markets, specifically in Africa and Latin America, where SABMiller had a strong market share.[44] This acquisition resulted in the creation of the world's largest beer company.[45]

Entry Mode Choice Theories

Transaction Cost Theory

According to the transaction cost theory, a firm should decide the international market entry mode based on the overall transaction cost. A firm may prefer exporting over FDI when the total transaction costs related to operations, transportation, tariffs, monitoring, uncertainty, and communication are lower compared to direct investment abroad. However, if these costs increase, then FDI might become a more cost-efficient mode. Uncertainty in international markets increases when countries have an underdeveloped institutional environment. Exporting, in this case, allows firms to serve the host country without the need to establish a costly and vulnerable local presence.

Ownership, Location Advantage, and Internalization Paradigm

According to the OLI (Ownership, Location Advantage, and Internalization) theory, a firm prefers FDI over other low-risk commitment entry modes, such as licensing or exports, for several reasons.

A firm may have an *ownership advantage* pertaining to some of its intangible assets, such as a brand, managerial skills, or patents, that it can best retain and protect when it opts for FDI rather than exports or licensing. In the oil industry, multinationals often possess specialized management and technical skills, including advanced geological analysis, drilling techniques, and project management expertise. It is not only challenging but also risky to transfer these skills and techniques to third parties through licensing. Thus, to retain ownership advantages, an oil company may enter a foreign market through FDI, then licensing or exports. It is due to these ownership reasons that oil companies, such as Shell, Saudi Aramco, and Sinopec, leverage FDI to enter international markets.[46]

Location advantage drives FDI over exports when the benefits of manufacturing goods or services within a host country outweigh the costs and risks associated with exporting finished products from the home country.[47] A location advantage arises when demand in the host country is enormous. When the target market has ample opportunities, FDI helps avoid missing sales opportunities due to long transport times.[48] Again, suppose a firm operates in an industry that requires significant customer interaction, such as the case with service firms. In that case, FDI becomes a more viable option because a firm with a local presence can better understand customer needs and respond more effectively to them.[49] Thus, firms opting for a transnational or multidomestic strategy are likely to enter international markets through FDI.

With *internalization*, a firm can control a value chain activity more effectively than exporting or licensing to a third party. In emerging markets, where the institutional environment is weak, internalization can reduce transaction costs and uncertainties associated with negotiating and enforcing contracts with licensees or third-party exporters in the host country. The risk of opportunistic behavior related to quality control and intellectual property leakage by third parties is also reduced. Thus, with increasing uncertainty in the host country, internalization through FDI can offer a better advantage. As countries with a poor institutional environment have poorly implemented laws, internalization can help firms protect their technology, patents, and know-how, which third parties could otherwise expropriate. Challenging this in courts can be complex and time-consuming in emerging countries.

CAGE Framework

The CAGE framework, developed by Pankaj Ghemawat, helps managers understand and evaluate differences between countries based on four factors: Cultural, Administrative, Geographic, and Economic distance. Managers can decide on an entry mode based on these factors.[50] The CAGE framework proposes that higher the cultural, administrative, geographic, and economic distance between the focal and host countries, the less the resource commitment the manager should make in the host country, and hence should opt for a less resource-intensive entry mode. We typically explain the choice between joint ventures and greenfield investments through wholly owned subsidiaries.[51]

Cultural Distance.[52] Cultural Distance reflects differences in culture, economic systems, and business practices between home and host countries.[53] The most common framework used to explain cultural differences is Hofstede's cultural dimension, which has six dimensions: power avoidance, individualism-collectivism, masculinity-femininity, uncertainty avoidance, long-term orientation, and indulgence.[54] Power distance implies the degree of inequality that exists—and is accepted—between people who have power and those who do not.[55] In a collectivist society, people remain loyal to their group and take responsibility for each other's well-being.[56] Motivation toward achievement implies the distribution of roles between men and women. In masculine societies, men and women have fewer overlapping roles. For instance, men in masculine society must be assertive, demonstrate success, and be strong and bold.[57] In feminine societies, gender roles have significant overlap. Both men and women value modesty.[58] Feminine societies emphasize maintaining relationships and cooperating. In societies that score high on uncertainty avoidance, individuals attempt to make life as predictable and controllable as possible.[59] Long-term orientation implies "society has to maintain some links with its own past while dealing with the challenges of the present and the future."[60] Societies or countries that score low on this dimension "prefer to maintain time-honored traditions and norms while viewing societal change with suspicion," while those countries that score high on this dimension "encourage thrift and efforts in modern education as a way to prepare for the future."[61] Finally, indulgence "stands for a society that allows relatively free gratification of basic and natural human drives related to enjoying life and having fun. Restraint stands for a society that suppresses gratification of needs and regulates it by means of strict."[62]

Managers may use Hofstede's cultural dimension tool to assess the cultural distance between two countries qualitatively. This tool allows the selection of countries for comparison. Let us consider two countries: the US vs. India. The power distance in the US is 40, while in India, it is 77. These scores imply that India has a higher power distance than the US. For individualism, the US scores 91, while India scores 48.[63] These scores suggest that the US is highly individualistic, whereas India is more collectivistic. Therefore, in India, an individual's decisions are influenced by the opinion of all family members. The employer/employee relationship is also based more on relationship management. Even firms base their hiring and promotion decisions on relationships, which is crucial in a collectivist society. In the US, employees tend to be more self-reliant and show initiative. Hiring and promotion decisions are based on merit and evidence, rather than relationships. Again, for India, the masculinity score is 56, while for the US, the masculinity score is 62.[64] Thus, both countries are high on masculinity, and the two countries do not differ much on this dimension. The same is true for uncertainty avoidance. For India, the score is 40, and for the US, 46, indicating that both countries are low in uncertainty avoidance.[65] Overall, there is a moderate cultural difference between India and the US, implying significant adaptations of work practices as an employer expands from India to the US or vice versa.

There is a vast cultural distance between the US (with a score of 40 on power distance and a score of 46 on uncertainty avoidance) and South Korea (with scores of 60 on power distance and 85 on uncertainty avoidance) in terms of power distance and uncertainty avoidance. This has significant implications for the use of makeup and cosmetics by people. For instance, if women are not into bold makeup, most will avoid any uncertain outcomes (societal comments, etc.). Similarly, even if they personally like bold makeup but adults make it taboo, they may stop using it, given the high-power distance.

Impact of Cultural Distance on the Choice between Greenfield Investment and Joint Venture Mode of Entry in the Host Country

Cultural differences could create barriers between partners trying to operate together in the host country through greenfield investment or joint ventures.[66] However, given the higher equity stake in greenfield investments, companies may be more cautious about risking equity.

This view may arise because cultural differences exacerbate the challenges of achieving synergies with greenfield investments and integrating the operations of an acquired unit with a parent company[67]—for example, cultural differences could increase the costs of interpreting information flows between firms from different countries. As misinterpretation occurs, conflicts between acquiring and acquired firms increase, resulting in greenfield investment failure. For firms, joint ventures may be a better option to avoid futile investments through failed greenfield ventures when cultural distance is high. This is because the parent firm from the home country, through its equity stake, will have a say in management decision-making and will be able to better guide on cultural nuances of the host country—for example, the cultural preferences of consumers in the host country. With increasing cultural differences, the risk of a firm's failure to understand consumer psychology and other tastes and preferences in the host country increases, implying the need for a partner with a say in decision-making, which is more feasible through a joint venture than a greenfield investment.

Administrative Distance. Administrative distance refers to the legal and political differences that exist between two countries. Administrative disparities encompass aspects such as corruption, colonial treaties, and trade agreements. Some of the significant administrative differences include the absence of a unified currency, a reduced possibility of participation in international trade due to a lack of membership, limited connections, corruption, and political hostility between the two countries.[68] Similarly, administrative distance decreases if the home and host countries are members of a common association, such as the Commonwealth Association, a voluntary organization comprising 56 independent countries across Africa, Asia, the Americas, Europe, and the Pacific. Administrative distance refers to the legal and political differences that exist between two countries. Administrative disparities encompass aspects such as corruption, colonial treaties, and trade agreements.[69] Some of the significant administrative differences include the absence of a unified currency, limited participation in international trade due to a lack of membership, inadequate connections, corruption, and political hostility between the two countries. Similarly, administrative distance decreases if the home and host countries are members of a common association, such as the Commonwealth Association, a voluntary organization comprising 56 independent countries across Africa, Asia, the Americas, Europe, and the Pacific.

Impact of Administrative Distance on the Choice between Greenfield Investment vs. Joint Venture Mode of Entry in the Host Country

In the case of a low administrative distance, there is a high likelihood that the manager of a firm attempting to internationalize in the host country will be familiar with the bureaucratic patterns and institutional idiosyncrasies of the host country's location. This familiarity stems from the likelihood that the institutional environments of both countries are likely to resemble each other.[70] Consequently, the manager will be able to utilize accumulated knowledge of legal requirements and regulations to operate effectively within the institutional context of the host country. A firm internationalizing in a host country with similar administrative traits could exploit knowledge about combating bureaucratic operations, dealing with political uncertainties, and adapting through pro-market reforms.[71] A firm would be more competent in overcoming such challenges and may not need the help of local partners through joint ventures. Given the existing capabilities that a firm may leverage to overcome administrative challenges in the host country, a firm has a good chance of success by maintaining complete control over operations through greenfield investment.[72]

Suppose a firm is accustomed to operating in an institutionally poor environment, for example, in India,[73] where bribing government officials or overlooking specific legal requirements, such as paying overtime to workers, is common. Suppose this firm expands to an international country with a strong political and legal environment, characterized by a robust institutional framework that strictly prohibits bribery and severely penalizes law infractions. In that case, the internationalizing firm may need to adopt new operating practices in the host country. Forming a joint venture or acquiring another firm in the host country may be a better option than establishing a wholly owned subsidiary. As administrative distance increases, firms are likely to benefit from collaborative modes of entry, such as joint ventures, rather than greenfield investments, to mitigate the adverse effects and complexities arising from increased distance. This applies both ways, i.e., a firm internationalizing from a country with low governance quality to one with high governance quality, and vice versa.

Geographic Distance. Geographic distance refers to the distance in kilometers between the capital city of a country and the capital city of the focal host country.[74]

Impact of Geographic Distance on the Choice between Greenfield Investments vs. Joint Venture Mode of Entry in the Host Country

Managers prefer greenfield investments for geographically proximate countries.[75] This is because control of operations could be favorable owing to the relatively low costs of coordination activities of the acquired company. However, as geographic distance increases, the transaction and coordination costs increase—with increasing geographic distance, communication frequency decreases, and time zone difference increases. Consequently, information flow remains inadequate, and urgent problems are not resolved adequately. Establishing greenfield investment in such an environment could be risky. Under such conditions, joint ventures with local actors who can provide immediate insights might be more feasible.[76]

Economic Distance. Economic distance implies a difference in the home country's economic development with the host country where the manager plans to expand their firm. The country's economic level is usually reflected in consumer purchasing power, labor cost, and macroeconomic stability.[77]

Impact of Economic Distance on the Choice between Greenfield Investments vs. Joint Venture Mode of Entry in the Host Country

Parameters of economic distance affect the kind of competencies a firm develops to operate in a market.[78] For instance, if the purchasing power parity of consumers is low, then a product cannot be priced high, implying superior quality products may not be successful in a given country. Furthermore, if the price of a product is to be kept low, then production costs also have to be controlled to a great extent, implying a firm's expertise in managing economies of scale and scope.[79] However, suppose a firm has competencies in developing superior quality products or does not focus too much on efficient production. In that case, it may not be successful in developing countries, where the general purchasing power of consumers is low. The vice versa is also true, i.e., if a firm has competency in developing low-priced products implying average quality products, it may not succeed organically in countries with high purchasing power parity (i.e., developed economies). In both cases, a firm may need to rely on the decision-making of local host country partners to render expertise in operating in less or more advanced economies. Thus, joint ventures over greenfield investments might be preferred.

BORN GLOBAL COMPANIES

Born global companies are firms that generally start as a startup and internationalize within the first ten years of their inception.[80] Their competitive advantage arises from their global presence, which they achieve by virtue of operating in multiple countries from the inception. Traditional multinationals typically began to internationalize after they had fully captured demand in their home country.[81] This typically takes several years, and once the domestic market has matured, they then enter international markets to enhance their revenue stream. However, born globals perceive different international markets as important as the home country market, and without waiting to capture market share within the home country, they begin the internationalization process with the aim of capturing the global market.[82] These companies typically leverage digital platforms for faster expansion into other markets. Firms like Netflix, Airbnb, and Spotify are all born globals.[83]

ASSIGNMENT QUESTIONS

1. Examine different ways in which transnational/ multinational firms manage their R&D.
2. Explain how the CAGE framework and the OLI paradigm guide international market entry modes.
3. Critically analyze how exports, licensing, and franchising can be used as international market entry modes strategies.
4. Conduct data analysis on the following case to inform a decision on international market entry modes.

CASE STUDY **8.1**

Choosing the Right Entry Mode

Applying the CAGE Framework and Logistic Regression at Glowmytique

In June 2025, Charles Smith, CEO of Glowmytique (a hypothetical US-based startup cosmetic retailer), planned to enter Asian markets. While exploring international expansion, Smith observed that Sephora had struggled in the South Korean market but had performed successfully in India. Initially, he attributed the difference to country-level factors. However, further investigation revealed that Sephora had used different entry modes in the two countries. In South Korea, the company entered through a wholly owned subsidiary (WOS), whereas in India, it largely operated through a joint venture (JV).

Seeking clarity, Smith hired a strategy consultancy firm to guide his foreign market entry decision. The consultants introduced him to the CAGE framework and explained that firms can use CAGE distance between countries to determine whether to adopt a JV or a WOS. However, Smith questioned the framework's predictive validity and requested empirical support. In response, the consultants conducted a data-driven analysis to examine whether the framework consistently predicts entry mode choices across industries.

REPORT ON SEPHORA

Sephora's US divisional CEO entered South Korea in 2019 and appointed Kim Dong-Ju as CEO. Sephora established operations as a WOS. The South Korean cosmetics industry was highly competitive, with strong domestic retailers such as Olive Young, Lotte-owned LOHBs, and Lalavla. CHICOR, often referred to as "the Sephora of Korea," also competed aggressively in the market.

South Korean consumers demonstrated strong demand for international, particularly Western, cosmetic brands. Many consumers viewed brands such as M.A.C., NARS, YSL, Chanel, and Bobbi Brown as status symbols. Sephora's Korean stores offered these global brands alongside dedicated K-beauty sections. The company hired social media influencers to promote product usage and strengthen brand appeal.

Despite strong initial store traffic, Sephora's South Korean operations failed to generate sustained profitability. Customers visited stores enthusiastically during the launch phase, but gradually grew dissatisfied with the product selection. Industry experts observed that Sephora introduced standardized products similar to those sold in the US without fully adapting to Korean consumer preferences. Korean consumers preferred lighter, more natural shades, while Sephora emphasized bold, solid color palettes. Ultimately, Sephora exited the South Korean market, closing both its physical stores and digital operations.

EMPIRICAL ANALYSIS CONDUCTED BY THE CONSULTANCY FIRM

To test the validity of the CAGE framework, the consultancy firm collected data on US-based service firms that internationalized in 2023. The researchers obtained a sample of 380 firms from a commercial database. All sampled firms completed their foreign market entry in 2023 through either a greenfield WOS or a JV. The data used by the consultancy firm is given in the Data.xlsx file in www.routledge.com/9781032938912.

Refer to Data Files in Online Support Material available in www.routledge.com/9781032938912

Because entry mode represents a categorical dependent variable (JV vs. WOS), the consultants applied binomial logistic regression. They coded entry mode as 0 for JV and 1 for WOS. The CAGE framework dimensions, cultural distance (CD), administrative distance (AD), geographic distance (GD), and economic distance (ED), served as independent variables. The binary logistic regression output is given in the Output.xlsx file in www.routledge.com/9781032938912. Figure 8.1 presents the steps of binomial logistics regression that the consultant followed.

Refer to Output Files in Online Support Material available in www.routledge.com/9781032938912

Go to Analyze → Regression → Binary Logistic → Click on Binary Logistic → Select the outcome variable (EntryMode, coded as "1" =acquisitions and "0" = joint venture and place in the Dependent variable list box → Select the predictor variables (CD, AD, ED, and GD) and the control variables (Firm Age, Firm Size, and Firm Cash Holding) and place them in the Covariate list box → Click on Options tab → Check (Tick) Classification plots, Correlations of estimates, Hosmer-Lemeshow goodness-of-fit, CI for Exp(B): 95%, Include constant in model → Click Continue → Click Ok

FIGURE 8.1 Steps of Binary Logistics Regression

Note: CD, AD, ED, and GD refer to cultural distance (CD), administrative distance (AD), geographic distance (GD), and economic distance (ED).

Source: Developed by the Authors

CI refers to Confidence Interval

The consultants measured CD using Hofstede's cultural dimensions theory and obtained country-level cultural data from Theculturefactor.com. Although a formula exists for calculating cumulative Hofstede distance, this case emphasizes the interpretation of regression output rather than computational procedures; therefore, the calculations are not presented. The consultants obtained GD data from Distancefromto.net. The consultant dummy coded the entry mode: JV as 0 and WOS as 1. The consultant included firm age, firm size, and firm cash holdings as control variables and transformed these variables using natural logarithms. They conducted the binomial logistic regression analysis using SPSS (Version 31.0). CD, AD, GD, and ED represent cultural, administrative, geographic, and economic distances, respectively. CI refers to confidence interval.

THE ROAD AHEAD FOR SMITH

After completing the empirical analysis, the consultancy firm reviewed the regression output with Smith. The consultants demonstrated that the CAGE framework possesses empirical support and systematically predicts entry mode choice across industries. The evidence strengthened Smith's confidence in using structured distance-based analysis rather than relying solely on intuition.

Using insights from the regression results, Smith evaluated potential Asian markets and ultimately chose to enter South Korea, given the country's growing cosmetic and beauty industry. Based on the consultancy firm's output, he now faced a strategic choice that would significantly shape Glowmytique's long-term international positioning.

The binomial logistic regression results appear in Sheet 2 of the attached data file and form the basis for Smith's final entry mode decision.

DISCUSSION QUESTIONS

1. How does the CAGE framework guide Smith's entry mode decision for South Korea?
2. How should Smith interpret the odds ratios from the binary logistic regression from a managerial perspective?
3. What overall conclusion can Smith draw from the binary logistic regression results regarding the appropriate entry mode for South Korea?

CHAPTER NOTES

1 Wang, W., & Ma, H. (2018). Export strategy, export intensity and learning: Integrating the resource perspective and institutional perspective. *Journal of World Business*, *53* (4), 581–592.

2 Wang, W., & Ma, H. (2018). Export strategy, export intensity and learning: Integrating the resource perspective and institutional perspective. *Journal of World Business*, *53* (4), 581–592.

3 Benito, G. R., Petersen, B., & Welch, L. S. (2019). The global value chain and internalization theory. *Journal of International Business Studies*, *50* (8), 1414–1423.

4 Benito, G. R., Petersen, B., & Welch, L. S. (2019). The global value chain and internalization theory. *Journal of International Business Studies*, *50* (8), 1414–1423.
5 Benito, G. R., Petersen, B., & Welch, L. S. (2019). The global value chain and internalization theory. *Journal of International Business Studies*, *50* (8), 1414–1423.
6 https://phrase.com/blog/posts/global-standardization/.
7 https://www.accelingo.com/apples-global-strategy/.
8 https://processnavigation.com/insights/product-standardization-a-comprehensive-analysis/.
9 https://localizejs.com/articles/what-is-a-multidomestic-strategy-what-every-global-business-should-know.
10 https://localizejs.com/articles/what-is-a-multidomestic-strategy-what-every-global-business-should-know.
11 https://localizejs.com/articles/what-is-a-multidomestic-strategy-what-every-global-business-should-know.
12 https://localizejs.com/articles/what-is-a-multidomestic-strategy-what-every-global-business-should-know.
13 https://localizejs.com/articles/what-is-a-multidomestic-strategy-what-every-global-business-should-know.
14 https://www.heinz.com/en-IN.
15 https://www.sciencedirect.com/science/article/pii/S1075425324000814.
16 Kotabe, M., & Murray, J. Y. (2004). Global sourcing strategy and sustainable competitive advantage. *Industrial Marketing Management*, *33* (1), 7–14.
17 https://www.nber.org/system/files/working_papers/w31724/w31724.pdf.
18 https://www.nber.org/system/files/working_papers/w31724/w31724.pdf.
19 https://isid.org.in/wp-content/uploads/2023/06/WP266.pdf.
20 https://www.nestle.com/about/research-development/organization.
21 https://www.nestle.com/sites/default/files/asset-library/documents/media/events/stc%20orbe%202013/ff%20randd%20%28march%202013%29_en.pdf.
22 https://nahr.shrm.org/sites/default/files/IBM_Global_Talent_Management.pdf.
23 https://govt.chinadaily.com.cn/s/201808/17/WS5bac9650498ebfcd07bee90f/caterpillar-research-development-center-china-co.html#:~:text=Caterpillar%20Research%20&%20Development%20Center%20(China)%20Co%20(CRDC%2C,have%20passed%20the%20training%20program.
24 Johanson, J., & Vahlne, J.-E. (2003). The internationalization process of the firm—A model of knowledge development and increasing foreign market commitments. In P. Buckley (Ed.), *International business* (1st ed., pp. 83–101). Routledge. https://doi.org/10.4324/9781315199689
25 Håkanson, L., & Ambos, B. (2010). The antecedents of psychic distance. *Journal of International Management*, *16* (3), 195–210.
26 Blomkvist, K., & Drogendijk, R. (2013). The impact of psychic distance on Chinese outward foreign direct investments. *Management International Review*, *53* (5), 659–686.
27 https://www.emerald.com/ebr/article-abstract/28/1/96/36942/Examining-knowledge-gap-and-Psychic-Distance?redirectedFrom=fulltext.
28 https://stptrans.com/ikea-how-swedish-home-furnishing-conquered-the-global-market/#:~:text=In%201963%2C%20a%20full%20decade,were%20all%20extremely%20valuable%20lessons.
29 https://www.researchgate.net/publication/226824280_Psychic_Distance_its_Impact_and_Coping_Modes.
30 https://link.springer.com/article/10.1057/palgrave.jibs.8490137#:~:text=Companies%20tend%20to%20begin%20their,improve%20the%20psychic%20distance%20concept.
31 https://link.springer.com/article/10.1057/palgrave.jibs.8490137#:~:text=Companies%20tend%20to%20begin%20their,improve%20the%20psychic%20distance%20concept.
32 https://www.researchgate.net/publication/346618618_Home_country_institutional_impact_on_the_choice_of_direct_vs_indirect_exports_an_emerging_markets_perspective.
33 https://beta.trade.gov/article?id=Approaches-to-Exporting.
34 https://beta.trade.gov/article?id=Approaches-to-Exporting#:~:text=If%20the%20wholesaler%20only%20sells,in%20the%20selected%20overseas%20markets.
35 Wang, K. C. A., Wang, Y. J., & Liang, W. J. (2016). Intellectual property rights, international licensing and foreign direct investment. *Asia-Pacific Journal of Accounting & Economics*, *23* (3), 291–305.

36 https://www.ewadirect.com/proceedings/aemps/article/view/6224#:~:text=Abstract,ensuring%20sustained%20growth%20and%20success.
37 https://www.franchise.org/franchising-overview/what-is-a-franchise/#:~:text=While%20from%20the%20public's%20vantage,the%20franchisor%20a%20franchise%20fee.
38 https://www.delightree.com/post/top-5-food-franchise-brands-with-the-largest-global-presence.
39 https://www.delightree.com/post/top-5-food-franchise-brands-with-the-largest-global-presence.
40 https://www.researchgate.net/publication/371542951_JOINT_VENTURE_AND_STRATEGIC_ALLIANCE.
41 https://www.telefonica.com/en/communication-room/press-room/alaian-is-born-a-global-alliance-for-innovation/.
42 Korbi, F. B., Ben-Slimane, K., & Triki, D. (2021). How do international joint ventures build resilience to navigate institutional crisis? The case of a Tunisian-French IJV during the Arab-Spring. *Journal of Business Research, 129*, 157–168.
43 https://www.europeanceo.com/business-and-management/how-lidl-and-aldi-found-the-ingredients-for-success/.
44 https://www.brookings.edu/articles/africa-in-the-news-anheuser-busch-buys-south-africas-sabmiller-kenya-announces-sez-implementation-plan-and-us-sends-noncombat-troops-to-cameroon/#:~:text=On%20Tuesday%2C%20Anheuser%2DBusch%20InBev,produced%20by%20the%20same%20company.
45 https://www.brookings.edu/articles/africa-in-the-news-anheuser-busch-buys-south-africas-sabmiller-kenya-announces-sez-implementation-plan-and-us-sends-noncombat-troops-to-cameroon/#:~:text=On%20Tuesday%2C%20Anheuser%2DBusch%20InBev,produced%20by%20the%20same%20company.
46 https://www.reuters.com/markets/commodities/over-year-making-aramco-stake-sale-brings-rare-foreign-investment-saudi-2024-06-11/.
47 https://www.sciencedirect.com/science/article/pii/S1925209924003218.
48 https://www.sciencedirect.com/science/article/pii/S0304387822001596.
49 https://www.sciencedirect.com/science/article/abs/pii/S2110701721000627.
50 https://www.ebsco.com/research-starters/business-and-management/cage-framework.
51 Moalla, E., & Mayrhofer, U. (2020). How does distance affect market entry mode choice? Evidence from French companies. *European Management Journal, 38* (1), 135–145.
52 Mariadoss, B. J. (2017). Global market opportunity assessment – CAGE analysis (Chapter 6.3). *Core Principles of International Marketing* [Pressbooks edition]. Creative Commons Attribution-NonCommercial-ShareAlike 4.0 International License. Retrieved from https://opentext.wsu.edu/mktg360/chapter/6-3-selecting-target-markets-and-target-market-strategies.

The Culture Factor. (August 28, 2024a). Intercultural management what you need to know: What is the Hofstede model of National Culture? Theculturefactor.com. Retrieved from https://www.theculturefactor.com/intercultural-management.

The Culture Factor. (2024b). Country comparison tool. Theculturefactor.com. Retrieved from https://www.theculturefactor.com/country-comparison-tool?countries=india%2Cunited+states.

53 Harzing, A. W., & Pudelko, M. (2016). Do we need to distance ourselves from the distance concept? Why home and host country context might matter more than (cultural) distance. *Management International Review, 56* (1), 1–34.
54 Gallego-Álvarez, I., & Pucheta-Martínez, M. C. (2021). Hofstede's cultural dimensions and R&D intensity as an innovation strategy: A view from different institutional contexts. *Eurasian Business Review, 11* (2), 191–220.
55 Daniels, M. A., & Greguras, G. J. (2014). Exploring the nature of power distance: Implications for micro-and macro-level theories, processes, and outcomes. *Journal of Management, 40* (5), 1202–1229.
56 Ahuvia, A. C. (2002). Individualism/collectivism and cultures of happiness: A theoretical conjecture on the relationship between consumption, culture and subjective well-being at the national level. *Journal of Happiness Studies, 3* (1), 23–36.
57 https://pmc.ncbi.nlm.nih.gov/articles/PMC10689301/.
58 https://pmc.ncbi.nlm.nih.gov/articles/PMC10689301/.
59 Lawrie, S. I., Eom, K., Moza, D., Gavreliuc, A., & Kim, H. S. (2020). Cultural variability in the association between age and well-being: The role of uncertainty avoidance. *Psychological Science, 31* (1), 51–64.

60 The Culture Factor. (August 28, 2024a). Intercultural management what you need to know: What is the Hofstede model of National Culture? Theculturefactor.com. Retrieved from https://www.theculturefactor.com/intercultural-management
61 The Culture Factor. (August 28, 2024a). Intercultural management what you need to know: What is the Hofstede model of National Culture? Theculturefactor.com. Retrieved from https://www.theculturefactor.com/intercultural-management.
62 The Culture Factor. (August 28, 2024a). Intercultural management what you need to know: What is the Hofstede model of National Culture? Theculturefactor.com. Retrieved from https://www.theculturefactor.com/intercultural-management.
63 The Culture Factor. (2024b). Country comparison tool. Theculturefactor.com. Retrieved from https://www.theculturefactor.com/country-comparison-tool?countries=india%2Cunited+states.
64 The Culture Factor. (2024b). Country comparison tool. Theculturefactor.com. Retrieved from https://www.theculturefactor.com/country-comparison-tool?countries=india%2Cunited+states.
65 The Culture Factor. (2024b). Country comparison tool. Theculturefactor.com. Retrieved from https://www.theculturefactor.com/country-comparison-tool?countries=india%2Cunited+states.
66 Mariadoss, B. J. (2017). Global market opportunity assessment – CAGE analysis (Chapter 6.3). *Core Principles of International Marketing* [Pressbooks edition]. Creative Commons Attribution-NonCommercial-ShareAlike 4.0 International License. Retrieved from https://opentext.wsu.edu/mktg360/chapter/6-3-selecting-target-markets-and-target-market-strategies; The Culture Factor. (August 28, 2024a). Intercultural management what you need to know: What is the Hofstede model of National Culture? Theculturefactor.com. Retrieved from https://www.theculturefactor.com/intercultural-management.
67 Mariadoss, B. J. (2017). Global market opportunity assessment – CAGE analysis (Chapter 6.3). *Core Principles of International Marketing* [Pressbooks edition]. Creative Commons Attribution-NonCommercial-ShareAlike 4.0 International License. Retrieved from https://opentext.wsu.edu/mktg360/chapter/6-3-selecting-target-markets-and-target-market-strategies; The Culture Factor. (August 28, 2024a). Intercultural management what you need to know: What is the Hofstede model of National Culture? Theculturefactor.com. Retrieved from https://www.theculturefactor.com/intercultural-management.
68 Mariadoss, B. J. (2017). Global market opportunity assessment – CAGE analysis (Chapter 6.3). *Core Principles of International Marketing* [Pressbooks edition]. Creative Commons Attribution-NonCommercial-ShareAlike 4.0 International License. Retrieved from https://opentext.wsu.edu/mktg360/chapter/6-3-selecting-target-markets-and-target-market-strategies.
69 Mariadoss, B. J. (2017). Global market opportunity assessment – CAGE analysis (Chapter 6.3). *Core Principles of International Marketing* [Pressbooks edition]. Creative Commons Attribution-NonCommercial-ShareAlike 4.0 International License. Retrieved from https://opentext.wsu.edu/mktg360/chapter/6-3-selecting-target-markets-and-target-market-strategies
70 Mariadoss, B. J. (2017). Global market opportunity assessment – CAGE analysis (Chapter 6.3). *Core Principles of International Marketing* [Pressbooks edition]. Creative Commons Attribution-NonCommercial-ShareAlike 4.0 International License. Retrieved from https://opentext.wsu.edu/mktg360/chapter/6-3-selecting-target-markets-and-target-market-strategies.
71 Mariadoss, B. J. (2017). Global market opportunity assessment – CAGE analysis (Chapter 6.3). *Core Principles of International Marketing* [Pressbooks edition]. Creative Commons Attribution-NonCommercial-ShareAlike 4.0 International License. Retrieved from https://opentext.wsu.edu/mktg360/chapter/6-3-selecting-target-markets-and-target-market-strategies.
72 Mariadoss, B. J. (2017). Global market opportunity assessment – CAGE analysis (Chapter 6.3). *Core Principles of International Marketing* [Pressbooks edition]. Creative Commons Attribution-NonCommercial-ShareAlike 4.0 International License. Retrieved from https://opentext.wsu.edu/mktg360/chapter/6-3-selecting-target-markets-and-target-market-strategies.
73 Palepu, K. G., & Khanna, T. (1998). Institutional voids and policy challenges in emerging markets. *The Brown Journal of World Affairs*, *5* (1), 71–78.
74 Mariadoss, B. J. (2017). Global market opportunity assessment – CAGE analysis (Chapter 6.3). *Core Principles of International Marketing* [Pressbooks edition]. Creative Commons Attribution-NonCommercial-ShareAlike 4.0 International License. Retrieved from https://opentext.wsu.edu/mktg360/chapter/6-3-selecting-target-markets-and-target-market-strategies.

75 Mariadoss, B. J. (2017). Global market opportunity assessment – CAGE analysis (Chapter 6.3). *Core Principles of International Marketing* [Pressbooks edition]. Creative Commons Attribution-NonCommercial-ShareAlike 4.0 International License. Retrieved from https://opentext.wsu.edu/mktg360/chapter/6-3-selecting-target-markets-and-target-market-strategies.
76 Mariadoss, B. J. (2017). Global market opportunity assessment – CAGE analysis (Chapter 6.3). *Core Principles of International Marketing* [Pressbooks edition]. Creative Commons Attribution-NonCommercial-ShareAlike 4.0 International License. Retrieved from https://opentext.wsu.edu/mktg360/chapter/6-3-selecting-target-markets-and-target-market-strategies.
77 Mariadoss, B. J. (2017). Global market opportunity assessment – CAGE analysis (Chapter 6.3). *Core Principles of International Marketing* [Pressbooks edition]. Creative Commons Attribution-NonCommercial-ShareAlike 4.0 International License. Retrieved from https://opentext.wsu.edu/mktg360/chapter/6-3-selecting-target-markets-and-target-market-strategies.
78 Mariadoss, B. J. (2017). Global market opportunity assessment – CAGE analysis (Chapter 6.3). *Core Principles of International Marketing* [Pressbooks edition]. Creative Commons Attribution-NonCommercial-ShareAlike 4.0 International License. Retrieved from https://opentext.wsu.edu/mktg360/chapter/6-3-selecting-target-markets-and-target-market-strategies.
79 Mariadoss, B. J. (2017). Global market opportunity assessment – CAGE analysis (Chapter 6.3). *Core Principles of International Marketing* [Pressbooks edition]. Creative Commons Attribution-NonCommercial-ShareAlike 4.0 International License. Retrieved from https://opentext.wsu.edu/mktg360/chapter/6-3-selecting-target-markets-and-target-market-strategies.
80 Cavusgil, S. T., & Knight, G. (2015). The born global firm: An entrepreneurial and capabilities perspective on early and rapid internationalization. *Journal of International Business Studies, 46* (1), 3–16.
81 Chetty, S., & Campbell-Hunt, C. (2004). A strategic approach to internationalization: A traditional versus a "born-global" approach. *Journal of International Marketing, 12* (1), 57–81.
82 Cavusgil, S. T., & Knight, G. (2015). The born global firm: An entrepreneurial and capabilities perspective on early and rapid internationalization. *Journal of International Business Studies, 46* (1), 3–16.
83 Etemad, H. (2022). The emergence of international small digital ventures (ISDVs): Reaching beyond Born Globals and INVs. *Journal of International Entrepreneurship, 20* (1), 1–28.

FURTHER READING

Mariadoss, B. J. (2017). Global market opportunity assessment – CAGE analysis (Chapter 6.3). *Core Principles of International Marketing* [Pressbooks edition]. Creative Commons Attribution-Non-Commercial-ShareAlike 4.0 International License. Retrieved from https://opentext.wsu.edu/mktg360/chapter/6-3-selecting-target-markets-and-target-market-strategies

Palepu, K. G., & Khanna, T. (1998). Institutional voids and policy challenges in emerging markets. The *Brown Journal of World Affairs*, *5*(1), 71–78.

Ricart, J. E., Enright, M. J., Ghemawat, P., Hart, S. L., & Khanna, T. (2004). New frontiers in international strategy. *Journal of International Business Studies*, *35*, 175–200.

CHAPTER 9

Turnaround Management

Learning Objectives

After completing this chapter, students should be able to:

- Understand different types of turnaround management;
- Evaluate how stakeholders or firms may predict the likelihood of bankruptcy;
- Analyze strategies that firms could consider for conducting different types of turnaround management;
- Explore how traditional CEO differs from turnaround specialists in making and implementing turnaround strategies.

DIAGNOSING THE TURNAROUND MANAGEMENT SITUATION

Managers need to identify the root causes or drivers of poor performance. Turnaround management refers to the process of restoring a firm to profitability or achieving growth. While evaluating reasons, firms need to examine both internal weaknesses and external threats. As a firm evaluates reasons, the following questions can be explored for evaluating the market scenario:

How has the market share of the firm varied and performed in the past few years.
How the overall industry has been performing in terms of growth rate.
Is the firm's growth rate aligned with the market/industry growth rate, or is it below average or below that of its direct competitors?

By evaluating industry growth rates, managers can gauge whether the industry is in the maturity or growth stage. Thus, if the growth rate has been declining or worse, the growth rate is negative, i.e., sales are declining every year, then the industry has probably touched its decline stage, and more drastic strategic actions such as radical innovation or diversification need to be pursued for revival. Firms may ask questions such as

DOI: 10.4324/9781003568100-9

- At what rate are new entrants entering the market, and at what rate are existing players exiting the market?
- How consumer tastes and preferences have been changing: if sales of frozen food are declining, they are being replaced by other kinds of food, such as organic or fresh food.

Apart from external market/environment evaluation, evaluating the internal work environment and its weaknesses is also important. Firms should examine all value chain activities and evaluate whether they are performed efficiently. For instance, manufacturing management may have become technologically obsolete, and competitors using the latest technologies have been able to reduce their manufacturing costs, while the focal firm with obsolete technology still bears a heavy manufacturing cost. Similarly, a firm should evaluate how effective its R&D is; internal conflicts between the R&D and marketing teams may be causing a communication gap, leaving the R&D team unable to appropriately respond to customer needs. In that case, change interventions with HR or an organizational development consultant might be needed.

Executives could conduct internal evaluations using survey instruments, prior company records, reported problems, or benchmarking their practices against best practices in the industry/across other comparable industries. Alternatively, a firm may use more formal diagnostic tools, such as the McKinsey 7S Framework. This framework was developed in the 1970s and first published in a book in 1982 by then McKinsey consultants Thomas J. Peters and Robert H. Waterman. The 7S Framework helps to understand the complex relations between different internal elements of the organization, namely Strategy, Structure, Systems, Shared Values, Skills, Style, and Staff.

- *Structure* implies a chain of command and reporting relationships in the organization, i.e., how hierarchical or flat they are.
- *Strategy* refers to the overall direction of the organization, as determined by top management.
- A *system* implies a technical infrastructure that supports the workflow and operational activities of the organization.
- *Skills* imply the capabilities and competencies of employees.
- *Style* refers to the leadership style of different managers, including top management.
- *Staff* refers to the human resource management (HRM) practices employed by the organization's HR department, including recruitment, training, and performance management.
- *Shared values* refer to the organizational culture and ideologies established by top management and shared among employees. This guides the decision-making.

Turnaround may require several remedial actions, such as reformulating the product market strategy, modernizing plant and machinery, and reducing manpower.

FINANCIAL TURNAROUND MANAGEMENT

As a firm incurs financial losses, the priority is to reduce and stop them in the short term. Given that launching new products or improving a firm's value chain activities to save costs may take time, the prompt action that managers need to take to stop losses is restructure its financial assets and liabilities. For instance, if a firm is debt-laden and repayment is nearing, the manager should opt for debt restructuring, in which they negotiate with banks to reduce interest rates and extend repayment terms. Several financial tools and instruments can be used as part of financial restructuring, as explained below.

Debt Restructuring

Debt restructuring is a process in which a company renegotiates its debt payment terms with banks and other financiers. This helps preserve short-term liquidity, as the firm uses cash holdings to improve operations rather than repaying debt.

Firms can also exchange their debt for equity as part of debt restructuring. Thus, if financiers have confidence in the firm's revised business model and are hopeful that the firm will be able to revive itself in the future through different strategic and operational activities, they may be willing to buy equity in exchange for debt. This is because, if the firm is publicly listed, chances are high that, after a successful turnaround, the firm's market valuation would rebound and debtors would be able to earn more than the interest obligation by selling the firm's equity.

Managers can also opt for debt consolidation, which combines multiple debts into a single, larger loan. As a new banker buys previous loans in an integrated manner, they can offer the suffering firm better repayment terms and interest rates, thus helping managers increase short-term liquidity again. Then, forbearance is also an option, where the financier postpones repayment on a temporary basis, but the interest rate and overall repayment schedule remain the same.

Equity Restructuring

Sometimes, shareholders may vote against current management and allow another firm to take over a financially underperforming firm. However, management might believe in their new business plan and may not want to sell the business. In this case, the foremost thing managers need to do is repurchase their shares from the open market through an equity restructuring. As shareholders sell their shares in an equity buyback program, managers gain more control over operations. However, equity buybacks should be undertaken only to avoid firm sales, not as a defense against shareholder pressure or expectations of a rapid firm revival. This is because, with an equity buyback, managers are making payments to shareholders, thereby reducing their already limited cash reserves.

Asset Sales

Yet another immediate action to release cash and increase liquidity that can be taken by managers is to sell off their non-performing assets. For instance, if a firm is operating in a non-core business where it is not even generating much revenue (recall dogs and question marks from the BCG matrix), then selling such divisions would help it realize immediate cash. For instance, GE, while reviving its multi-division business under Welch's leadership, sold all the business units that were not number 1 or 2 in their respective industries.

OPERATIONAL TURNAROUND MANAGEMENT

Once liquid cash is realized from financial restructuring, the next step is to use this cash to improve the firm's efficiency, enabling further cost savings. This can be done in several ways, as discussed below.

Lean Production System

Japanese firms have excelled at operational efficiency, and firms globally have learned from Japanese manufacturing techniques to improve operational efficiency, irrespective of whether a turnaround was needed. Bearing extra, inefficient costs is never a source of creating shareholder value. However, when firms are seeking turnaround management, these efficiency-increasing operations management tools become even more important. A lean production system is achieved by reducing waste, such as Just-in-time inventory, so that the inventory pile does not sit in the manufacturing plant, adding to cost, and the Kaizen system, i.e., removing waste such as unnecessary steps in manufacturing operations.

Retrenchment Strategy

A *retrenchment strategy* involves cutting costs by selling off non-performing assets. It can be carried out in two ways. *In Cost retrenchment,* managers focus on reducing the cost of different value chain activities, such as outsourcing non-core tasks. This could be legal and HR for a manufacturing firm. Or a firm may decide to temporarily stop big-budget advertising on national television and other expensive outlets.

Alternatively, to reduce costs, managers may lay off excess manpower, as declining revenues imply that demand is less than supply, so firms need to first reduce their supply, implying the need for less manpower. For technology infrastructure as part of the value chain, a firm may reduce costs in the long run by introducing more efficient industrial 5.0 technologies, such as generative AI that can diagnose consumer sentiment, thereby reducing the need for market research employees, which again leads to layoffs.

Hallmark, for instance, as part of its cost restructuring program, consolidated its plants and laid off employees. It also closed, underperforming 2,000 stores to save costs. Hallmark also invested in information technology modernization by outsourcing IT management to Tata Consultancy Services, an IT firm based in India.

STRATEGIC TURNAROUND MANAGEMENT

Strategic turnaround means making strategic changes to the firm's business philosophy and core value proposition. This is usually done through innovation and by reinventing the business model to generate more revenue. The main goal of strategic turnaround is to improve long-term revenue, not just to achieve short-term cost savings.

Thus, after conducting market analysis as the first step in diagnosing the problem, if managers realize that consumer demand has shifted, then, for strategic turnaround, top management will need to innovate to adapt to the change. Alternatively, if top management realizes that the industry has entered a decline phase, they may decide to diversify into related industries where their core competencies in existing technologies can be applied, or to reinvent the industry with an innovative business model and products. For instance, in the 1990s, when Apple faced bankruptcy risk due to increasing competition from Windows, it introduced more innovative product lines, such as the iMac.

If managers decide to pursue a strategic turnaround through diversification, it can be implemented in several ways.

First is vertical diversification, where managers can decide to integrate backward or forward in the industry value chain. For instance, if managers believe that by focusing on higher-quality, lower-priced products they can revive a given industry, they can bypass retailers and opt for a direct-to-consumer model, thereby integrating forwardly, with distribution to consumers handled directly by the firm, then by wholesalers, and finally by retailers. Today, several firms, in addition to retail channels, also have a D2C channel as part of their distribution strategy. Forward integration/vertical integration would imply managers invest more heavily in D2C distribution, making next-day delivery possible and taking their products off retailers' shelves in pursuit of cost savings and passing those benefits to consumers through lower prices. Similarly, retailers who are largely distributors of national brands can decide to integrate backward and sell their in-house-developed products, known as private label brands. For instance, Target and JCPenney are focusing more on private label brands as part of their turnaround efforts. It should be noted that private label brands were part of their product SKUs; however, as these retailers needed to turn around, their emphasis on backward integration increased, making it a core strategy. They also rationalized stores and store positioning, with greater emphasis on private label brands. Rather, for JCPenney, as of 2025, half of its sales are contributed by its owned brands such as St. John's Bay, Stafford, etc.

A firm may also pursue horizontal diversification, where the firm diversifies into a related product line. For instance, a textile company that manufactures garments could diversify horizontally to offer accessories such as shoes, belts, etc. This is because the segment of customers who buy clothes is also likely to buy matching shoes, belts, etc.

Firms can also pursue concentric diversification, where they leverage current technological know-how to develop a different product base for the same set of customers. For instance, a retailer repairing broken phones is likely to have the know-how to repair broken laptops and computers, since they are all electronic gadgets.

Diversification implies developing new products for completely new markets, which could be new geographies or new customer bases. For instance, an automobile company may decide to venture into the paper industry, implying entering a completely new product category (for the automobile firm) and a new customer base. If retailers are considered first-tier customers, then the distribution channel for automobiles is completely different from that for paper. Automobiles are sold via dealers, while paper is sold in retail outlets. When Coke and Pepsi launch health and functional beverage drinks, such as body armor or Gatorade, it makes case of diversification, though related diversification in terms of product category, but unrelated in terms of customer base, as its most likely niche category of customers such as athletes who would be buying energy drinks, in contrast to mass customers who buy soda based beverages.

THE SAF MATRIX FOR EVALUATING THE FEASIBILITY OF TURNAROUND MANAGEMENT OPTIONS

When managers develop several options for turnaround, they can select the best option using the SAF (Suitability, Feasibility, and Acceptability) matrix as explained below:

- *Suitability* implies the extent to which strategic action can help managers to achieve turnaround goal. For instance, to increase revenues, a firm should target new geographical areas or further penetrate the market. With a suitability assessment, managers can assess which is better.
- *Acceptability* implies gaining acceptance from stakeholders, such as employees, shareholders, and others. When Disney was moving more toward streaming platforms with Disney+, there was resistance from theatrical distributors as Disney reduced its theatrical releases. However, if Disney had not invested in Disney+, it would have led to further deterioration in shareholder value and heightened shareholder activism. Thus, a trade-off has to be considered. Disney gauged that investing in a streaming platform was more acceptable to the majority of stakeholders than investing in cinematic platforms.
- *Feasibility*. Here, managers need to decide if they have the appropriate resources to implement their strategic turnaround plan. For instance, when Bed Bath & Beyond (BBB) was trying to invest in private label brands to achieve an effective turnaround, it faced financial challenges because suppliers refused to offer any credit terms for the procurement of raw materials. Thus, though private label brand investment could have helped BBB avoid bankruptcy, the private label brand was not a feasible option.

Firms can select strategic options based on the SAF analysis using an arbitrary scoring method as explained below. Table 9.1 presents the corresponding scores.

TABLE 9.1 SAF Scoring to Achieve Operational Turnaround

Option	Suitability Scores Out of 10	Acceptability Scores Out of 10	Feasibility Scores Out of 10	Total Score
Employee lay offs	9 (Effective cost)	7 (Possible resistance from unions)	6 (Turnaround specialist missing to convince union for lay off)	21
Divest noncore assets	8 (Effective cost-cutting measure releasing cash)	10 (A firm taking over sold off unit will manage layoffs, least resistance to be faced by current management)	10 (Ample buyers' interest in buying non-core unit)	28
Purchase more cost-efficient machinery	8 (This will help to manage operations effectively)	7 (Less resistance from workers, given less chances of layoffs and shareholders may not completely support somewhat more investment in already poorly performing firm)	5 (Require financial resources, which may not be available)	20

Source: Developed by the Author.

As shown in Table 9.1, divesting low-performing businesses is the most effective strategic option, followed by acquiring efficient machinery and layoffs.

TURNAROUND SPECIALISTS

Although CEOs can manage successful organizations, returning a firm to profitability after losses requires different skill sets. These differ from those needed to manage or grow profit-making organizations. This is similar to how an entrepreneur's required skills shift from the start-up phase to managing a mature, stable organization. Firms achieve better turnaround management when they hire a specialist, someone skilled in diagnosing root causes of performance decline and in creating tailored business plans for financial, operational, and strategic turnarounds. Turnaround specialists follow the necessary steps more effectively thanks to their specialized training. They can delve deeply into financial statements, operational issues, market position, and employee relations to pinpoint causes of decline. When developing a turnaround plan, these specialists are better equipped to choose suitable financial restructuring tools. For example, they know when to consolidate debt or use forbearance to quickly improve liquidity. They also implement cost-efficiency measures effectively. Staff layoffs can create a culture of fear and demotivation, but turnaround specialists handle these situations more effectively than traditional CEOs. When creating strategic plans, specialists can better determine if diversification or business model innovation is needed. They apply diversification tests—such as the "attractiveness," "cost of entry," and "better-off" tests, to ensure the move creates and captures value. For instance, although not as part of a turnaround but as part of growth, Honda leveraged its core engine-building competencies to diversify into four-wheelers, such as cars, as well as aircraft engines, while leading in the motorcycle sector.

A turnaround specialist needs strong skills in evaluating a firm's financial performance. They must understand the balance sheet, cash flow statement, and other key reports. Operational knowledge is also important. Specialists should understand core technology, supply chains, and operational issues across the value chain. They must also excel at strategic thinking, including business model modification. Finally, they need cultural skills to improve employee relations and overhaul organizational culture.

FILING FOR BANKRUPTCY

Bankruptcy implies a firm declaring itself insolvent and signaling its inability to continue operating. Typically, when financial restructuring fails, such as when banks deny debt consolidation or equity exchange or forbearance, and managers have liquidity crisis to pay suppliers, operations may come to a halt. *Bankruptcy* filing is a legal process in which a firm files a petition with the court, disclosing all its outstanding debts as well as the company's assets. After declaring bankruptcy, the firm's assets could be sold to pay its creditors and suppliers the amounts they are due. The bankruptcy risk of a firm facing financial struggles can be predicted using the Altman Z-score model, as explained below.

Altman's *Z*-Score Model

Z-Score Model is based on the following equation:

$$Z = 0.012 \times Y_1 + 0.014 \times Y_2 + 0.033 \times Y_3 + 0.006 \times Y_4 + 0.999 \times Y_5 \tag{9.1}$$

where,

Z = Overall Index or Score
Y_1 = Working Capital/Total Assets
Y_2 = Retained Earnings/Total Assets
Y_3 = Earnings before Interest & Tax/Total Assets
Y_4 = Market Capitalization/Total Liabilities
Y_5 = Sales/Total Assets

The prediction rule is

If Z score is greater than 2.99, then the firm is less likely to file for bankruptcy.

When Z score is less than 1.81, then likelihood of firm going bankrupt in the near future is high.

Z score between 1.81 and 2.99 is considered to be a gray zone where it is difficult to predict with certainty if a firm file bankruptcy or not. Following example explains the same.

Consider the below given financial metrics

Y_1 = Working Capital/Total Assets = 0.25
Y_2 = Retained Earnings/Total Assets = 0.57
Y_3 = Earnings before Interest & Tax/Total Assets = 0.26
Y_4 = Market Capitalization/Total Liabilities = 1.02
Y_5 = Sales/Total Assets = 1.57

Based on Equation 9.1, the *Z*-score is 1.59, less than 1.81, implying high chance of filing for bankruptcy.

ASSIGNMENT QUESTIONS

1. Explain different types of turnaround management conducted by managers. Give recent examples of each kind of turnaround management.
2. Examine whether turnaround specialists are better able to make and implement turnaround strategies.
3. A successful coffee shop chain, "Daily Café," operates in major cities in the USA. Its target market is working professionals. It was uniquely located at busy locations only. It had earned a strong brand reputation. However, observing the market potential, many new entrants were opening similar types of coffee shops, giving them tough competition. Consequently, Daily Café's sales growth began to decline, and it needed a strategic overhaul of its business to create a unique position for itself. The management of a financially

struggling firm wanted to predict its chances of going bankrupt based on the performance of the past year. The financials of the firm are:

X_1 = Working Capital/Total Assets = 0.28
X_2 = Retained Earnings/Total Assets = 0.46
X_3 = Earnings before Interest and Tax/Total Assets = 0.45
X_4 = Market Capitalization/Total Liabilities = 2.01
X_5 = Sales/Total Assets = 2.06

What are the chances of Daily Café's bankruptcy?

CASE STUDY **9.1**

Bed Bath & Beyond Inc

Effectiveness of Turnaround Management

Agnihotri, A., & Bhattacharya, S. (2024). *Bed Bath & Beyond Inc: Effectiveness of turnaround management.* Sage Business Cases. https://doi.org/10.4135/9781071928769

INTRODUCTION

Bed, Bath & Beyond (BBB) was co-founded in 1971 by Warren Eisenberg and Leonard Feinstein, two veterans of discount retail in Springfield, New Jersey. An omnichannel retailer, the company sold an assortment of merchandise in one convenient location. As the chain expanded across the US, it grew in size, locations, and inventory options, and after going public in 1992, the stock hit a high of USD 70 per share in 2014 (Kaushal & Schafer, 2023).

Despite the former strength of the nationwide chain of retail stores, BBB's performance began to weaken over the years and the company experienced a revenue decline of 25% in 2022 when the home-furnishings market reported overall growth of 4% (Wahba, 2022). As a result of plunging sales and a fast cash burn the company filed for bankruptcy protection in April 2023.

Prior to its bankruptcy move, BBB had hired Mark Tritton to turnaround declining sales in 2019. He turned to strategies he had employed at Target, and established private label brands at BBB. That strategy failed, as consumers continued to favor online and other retailers, and Tritton was replaced by Sue Gove, a BBB board member. Gove became the interim CEO y in June and then the CEO in October 2022, and was tasked with trying to revive the brand. Under Gove's leadership, BBB focused on reversing Tritton's strategies, abandoning most of the private brands initiated by Tritton and pivoting back to national brands (Wahba, 2022). Gove believed that BBB had the trust of vendors—the big national brands on whom the retailer's survival depended—though critics believed that was not the case as vendors tightened their procurement terms and conditions with BBB (Wahba, 2022). Critics questioned BBB's strategy as well as its leadership team, but BBB forged ahead, trying to win back the trust of vendors with interim and fluctuating leadership.

However, industry experts like Mark Cohen, director of retail studies at Columbia Business School and a former CEO of Sears Canada, doubted BBB's survival (Wahba, 2022). Cohen said, "They've got no senior leadership, they've got no strategy, and they're trying to swing the pendulum back to where it was, and that was a pretty crappy place" (Wahba, 2022).

The fall of Bed, Bath & Beyond offers rich opportunities for learning. What went wrong with Tritton's strategies? Could Gove have harnessed back the trust of vendors to avoid BBB's bankruptcy? There are many lessons to be learned from considering what went wrong at BBB and what could have been done to turn the company around.

SUCCESSFUL BEGINNINGS

Established in New Jersey in 1971 as "Bed n' Bath," the company sold products such as bed linens, bath items, and kitchen textiles. It expanded to become BBB in the 1980s, offering a greater range of inventory including home furnishings, giftwares, health and beauty care items, food goods, and infant and toddler merchandise. In June 1992, the company became public, and the omni-channel retailer went on to operate additional stores, including Christmas Tree Shops, Harmon, and buybuy BABY.

Operating with an "everyday low price" philosophy, BBB was able to win over consumers in suburban markets, particularly females in the middle- to upper-middle class income level, aged 35–50 years old (Boyar, 2014). Spreading throughout the US in the 1980s and 1990s, BBB leveraged its price competitiveness and merchandise range to gain consumer loyalty. It became known for its mailed big blue coupons, and its great product assortment and presentation, and in-store customer service set it apart from other retailers (Boyar, 2014).

MOUNTING CHALLENGES

In the US, during the 1980s and 1990s, BBB was a beloved retailer that attracted mass-market and slightly trendy consumers (Kaushal, 2023; Wahba, 2022). It was also known for triggering impulse buys with 20%-off coupons (Wahba, 2022). Beginning in 2014, competition from players like Wayfair and other online platforms, like Walmart and Amazon, began challenging BBB's leadership position in home goods (Bowman, 2022). Although BBB had been able to underprice Amazon in 2013, the market share of BBB became stagnant in 2014 and then began falling, with Wayfair rising, and by early 2020, Wayfair overtook BBB in terms of market share (Bowman, 2022; Boyar, 2014).

In 2017, the company shifted its management strategy, reducing department and assistant store manager positions to simplify store management structure to meet customer needs with staffing focused on customers (Bed Bath & Beyond, 2017). In 2017 and 2018, BBB also shifted its store strategy to compete with ecommerce retailers and improve profits. Running over 1,500 stores at the time, BBB was locked into leases that cost a great deal and sales remained stagnant. As of 2018, instead of being able to find items consumers wanted in BBB stores, they would find products for sale in store as well as a range of merchandise on display that they could order online. This strategy aimed to optimize store layouts with a wide array of displays that created an experiential environment.

The stores offered many versions of the same product that confused consumers and BBB remained overly reliant on coupons that did not seem to meet evolving consumer needs.

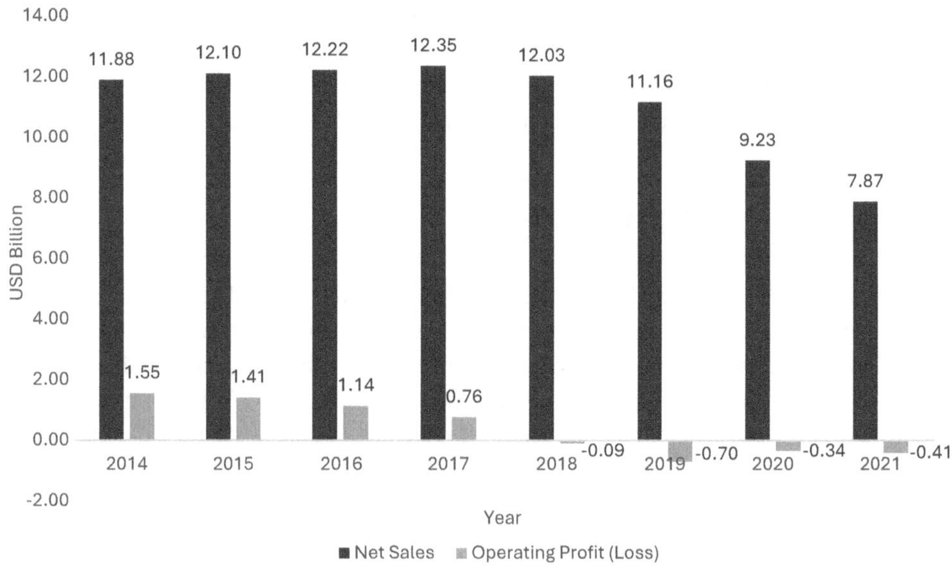

FIGURE 9.1 BBB: Net Sales and Operating Profit (Loss)

Source: Statista Research Department (2023) and Sabanoglu (2023)

Investors and customers did not respond well to the changes and criticized BBB for its cluttered stores and late response to e-commerce evolution that had not begun until 2018 (Bowman, 2022). Those criticisms were reflected in BBB's financial issues, with the company reporting operating losses since 2018 and declining net sales since 2019 (Sabanoglu, 2023) (see Figure 9.1).

TRITTON'S TURNAROUND INITIATIVES

Despite its efforts, BBB continued to see a decline in a sales and made changes to the COO, CAO, and CFO positions in 2018. In response to the falling financial performance, BBB also hired Mark Tritton as the CEO (Bowman, 2022). According to critics financial performance was falling as BBB was late to digitalize their stores and shift to hybrid model i.e. offering services both online as well as through physical retail stores.[1] In October 2019, when BBB announced Tritton as the CEO, investors were delighted. Tritton has worked as Target's chief merchandising officer and oversaw the creation of several of the retailer's highly successful store brands (Wahba, 2022). He also engineered 30 private label launches at Target in less than three years. These strategies were responsible for Target's successful turnaround (Wahba, 2022).

To begin, Tritton fired BBB's executive management team. Tritton said, "They were expensive, and they were ineffective" (Wahba, 2022). Soon the COVID-19 pandemic struck, which temporarily relieved BBB's declining revenues, as there was a surge in home goods spending—as people began more work from home (Wahba, 2022). By November 2020,

Tritton further shaped his turnaround plans by closing 200 stores and reducing product selection that confused shoppers (Wahba, 2022). This strategy released a cash flow of USD 2 billion and improved BBB's balance sheet (Wahba, 2022). Tritton said

> As part of its strategic growth plans, Bed Bath & Beyond will launch a clear customer value proposition to deepen connections with five core customer segments: the nester; the minimizer; the juggler; the innovator; and the creative. In addition, the Company will develop an enterprise-wide strategy to unlock value across its core brands in the Home, Baby, Beauty & Wellness markets, including plans for a reinvented loyalty program to deepen its customer relationship and motivate increased shopping across categories, channels and banners.
>
> (Bed Bath & Beyond, 2020)

Tritton leveraging his experience at Target, Nordstrom, and Nike, also decided to launch private label brands for BBB with the aim of generating 30% of sales from them. He believed BBB did not entice young customers because it did not have an ample "opening price point," a retail parlance for cheaper goods (Wahba, 2022). For example, the retailer's once-dominant wedding registry business had declined, signaling that young shoppers were doing wedding-related shopping elsewhere (Wahba, 2022). Although consumers remained price conscious, Tritton abolished the chain's coupon system, which issued weekly discount offers to customers regardless of whether they asked for them (Wahba, 2022). Chief Merchandising Officer Joe Hartsig explaining the reason said "We have an overreliance on the coupon"[2]

BBB also required a better inventory management system and an adequate supply chain that Tritton needed to fix. As part of an attempt to address these issues, BBB adopted a digital-first strategy that worked to "personalize the shopping experience for customers, enhance fulfillment capacity, and optimize merchandise planning and demand forecasting" (Bed Bath & Beyond, 2020). For the same in 2021, BBB selected Oracle as its Enterprise Resource Planning (ERP) technology partner. BBB was expected to receive real-time financial, supply chain and merchandising information, that was expected to enhance its inventory planning capabilities.[3]

Impact of Turnaround Initiatives

After being buoyed by pandemic-driven online sales in 2020, BBB's sales began declining again by mid-2021 (Wahba, 2022). In 2021, BBB had net sales of USD 7.87 billion, a 14.75% decline over the previous year (Statista Research Department, 2023) (see Figure 9.1). In the first nine months of 2022, the company reported net losses greater than USD 1.12 billion, more than analysts expected (Repko, 2023).

Although it was hoped that producing private labels in-house would help BBB cut costs if implemented effectively, that was not the case for the company. BBB executed the strategy unsystematically, launching several private brands in a relatively short period after having to build internal departments from scratch during the pandemic (Shoulberg, 2022). These new private label brands were then criticized for being bland and lower quality than national brands (Shoulberg, 2022). For example, Stacey Widlitz, president of SW Retail Advisors, commenting on the private label textiles like sheets or throws, noted that they were of low quality and not worth the price, especially if compared with deals that shoppers got for similar items at Amazon Basics. Widlitz said, "The playbook from Target did not transfer to Bed Bath & Beyond, and the customer walked in and felt they weren't providing private label products that were distinctive and at a better price" (Wahba, 2022). The strategy ended up filling stores with unknown private label products instead of the well-known national brands that consumers had come to associate with BBB.

In addition to being disappointed by these new offerings, consumers were not excited by BBB's deals anymore either. Despite hiring new leaders to helm BBB's strategic marketing, launching a digital marketplace to offer third-party brands, and launching a strategic partnership with brands like The Kroger Co., the core problem remained: BBB stores had become more cluttered, confusing, and hard for shoppers to navigate (Bed Bath & Beyond, 2021; Wahba, 2022). BBB added products on its store shelves that were readily available online, such as a massive assortment of household cleaning products, and offered too many options for the same products (Wahba, 2022). As shelf space was filled with more unnecessary products, customers often left the store buying just one item (Wahba, 2022). Many consumers also missed the coupons that Tritton had cut. Retail industry experts also criticized BBB for abolishing coupons, which many shoppers remained fond of even though they did not drive the same level of loyalty.

BBB's deterioration was further fueled by the supply-chain crisis related to the COVID-19 pandemic, which led to labor and product shortages and shifts in demand (Morgan, 2022). BBB heavily depended on its vendors for product development and supply chain fulfillment and struggled to maintain inventory. BBB's supply chain was below par even before the COVID-19 pandemic, and during the pandemic, the supply chain became even more catastrophic (Wahba, 2022). The company reported losing USD 175 million in revenue as its Asian factories' shipments did not arrive on time (Shoulberg, 2022). By September 2022, BBB was aiming to reduce inventory of private label brands from 50% to 30% and increase inventory for national and emerging direct-to-consumer brands.[4]

BBB's long-term debt in 2022 was about USD 1.4 billion and Tritton shut down 200 BBB stores to help raise USD 2 billion. The company then used USD 1 billion to repurchase BBB shares instead of repaying its debt. Neil Saunders, managing director of GlobalData, said this move was intended "to appease investors and to throw them something while the turnaround plan was taking place. But all it succeeded in doing is leaving the business in a very, very weak position."

GOVE'S COMEBACK ATTEMPTS

In June 2022, BBB fired Tritton due to his inability to enhance the financial performance of the company and announced Gove as BBB's interim CEO (CISION, 2022). Previously Gove had served as BBB's chair of the board's strategy committee (Lodewick, 2022). Gove believed that the key to reducing financial losses was doing away with Tritton's private label strategies. As she planned a turnaround, she had only a few top management team members to support her as several members including the operations officer, had left and vacancies still needed to be filled (Wahba, 2022). However, Gove had interim officers like the interim chief financial officer to support her (Wahba, 2022). A BBB spokesperson commenting on the lack of talent in the company said, “the board is very confident that Bed Bath & Beyond Inc. has the leadership team to execute our plans” (Wahba, 2022). However, critics like Cohen doubted BBB’s survival. He said, “They’ve got no senior leadership, they’ve got no strategy, and they’re trying to swing the pendulum back to where it was, and that was a pretty crappy place” (Wahba, 2022).

Under Gove’s leadership, BBB decided to abandon most of its private brands and pivot back to a strategy focused on the sale of national brands in an attempt to turn BBB around (Wahba, 2022). In 2022, Gove closed about two-thirds of the private label brands launched by Tritton including Wild Sage, a private brand of bedding, decor, and furniture (Repko & Thomas, 2022). This move was supported by Widlitz, president of SW Retail Advisors, who noted that shoppers preferred national brands over store brands in home goods, unlike apparel brands, where they liked to be more adventurous (Wahba, 2022). Gove commenting on support for national brands, said, “One of the most telling pieces to me, in terms of their receptivity, is how they are parroting back to us our strategy,” and “That’s come in the form of thank-you notes.” She added that there was “wide, open-armed embrace” of BBB’s old-is-new strategy by the vendors (Wahba, 2022).

However, the media believed vendors were possibly polite to BBB despite declining sales because they believed BBB could get sizable number of customers (Wahba, 2022). Most vendors also tightened their financing terms with BBB (Wahba, 2022). Vendors who decided to continue doing business with BBB were unlikely to send their best merchandise or any exclusive deals to BBB (Wahba, 2022). Saunders said, “If you’re a national brand, why on earth would you decide to launch exclusive things with Bed Bath & Beyond given the state that they’re in?” (Wahba, 2022). Vendors became even more skeptical after Chapter 11 bankruptcy filings of rivals J.C. Penney, Pier 1 Imports, Sears, and Linens ‘n Things between 2017 and 2022. BBB’s vendors were more interested in sending their best merchandise to growing retailers such as Amazon. Cohen said, “Vendors always get slammed, and they never get any kind of reasonable recovery” (Wahba, 2022).

Consumers were also facing inflationary pressure post the COVID-19 pandemic and other economic uncertainties that caused them to withdraw from discretionary spending (Jansen, 2022). Tim Derr, a partner in the consumer practice division of Kearney, said,

> People are tightening their purse strings. There’s obviously a little bit of pressure and stress on the way consumers are spending money in general, especially as you start to think about the impending or potential recession that some would argue we’re already in,

and “There’s going to be a little bit more apprehension to spend in these other discretionary categories like investments in their home” (Jansen, 2022). To help consumers, BBB added cash funds.[5] It also introduced consumer friendly app so that online buying experience could become more pleasant for consumers.[6]

Experts also believed that bringing back coupons or offering more national brands would not guarantee a successful revival of BBB. Saunders said, “The market is very crowded, and it's hard to see where they fit in." Saunders addefd, "They need to be a very innovative retailer, a place of discovery. But they really aren't that good at those things anymore" (Wahba, 2022). BBB had lost their loyal customer base, was struggling to fit into the ecommerce space that customers had gravitated toward, and was working to reestablish its national brand strategy as part of that struggle. Although BBB remained focused on customers, employees, and partners, their turnaround efforts were note going smoothly. In a January 2023 press release, BBB noted:

> Our plan has two anchors: the first enables us to refocus merchandising and inventory, operate more efficiently, and grow our digital and omni-capabilities, and the second focuses on strengthening our financial position. Transforming an organization of our size and scale requires time, and we anticipate that each coming quarter will build on our progress. … The Company continues to consider all strategic alternatives including restructuring or refinancing its debt, seeking additional debt or equity capital, reducing or delaying the Company's business activities and strategic initiatives, or selling assets, other strategic transactions and/or other measures, including obtaining relief under the U.S. Bankruptcy Code. These measures may not be successful.

LEARNING LESSONS

In January 2023, in a securities filing, BBB said it did "not have sufficient resources to repay the amounts under the Credit Facilities and this will lead the Company to consider all strategic alternatives, including restructuring its debt under the U.S. Bankruptcy Code" (Fonrouge & Rizzo, 2023). That prophecy was fulfilled in April 2023, when BBB filed for Chapter 11 bankruptcy protection. With declining sales, inventory constraints, and failure to move with shoppers' changing habits, BBB's downfall did not shock the investor community. The company was on the brink of survival, and BBB tried to embrace strategies to undo the wrong strategies it had tried thus far. Exploring what went wrong and what needed to be fixed helps reveal how those needs could have been addressed.

DISCUSSION QUESTIONS

1. Explain if BBB needs a financial, operational, or strategic turnaround.
2. Evaluate Tritton's retrenchment and lean moves for turning around BBB.
3. Examine how national brands influenced the feasibility of Gove's turnaround strategy.

CHAPTER NOTES

1 https://diginomica.com/slow-digital-transformation-makes-it-hard-to-see-beyond-bed-bath-and-beyonds-troubles.

2 https://www.cnbc.com/2020/10/28/bed-bath-beyond-plans-to-scale-back-coupons-to-boost-profitability.html.

3 https://www.prnewswire.com/news-releases/bed-bath--beyond-selects-oracle-to-modernize-enterprise-resource-planning-and-accelerate-technology-transformation-301226757.html.
4 https://www.supplychaindive.com/news/bed-bath-beyond-supply-chain-component-turnaround-plan-inventory/631080/.
5 https://www.youtube.com/watch?v=JNEPNgZaAo8.
6 https://www.youtube.com/watch?v=JNEPNgZaAo8.

FURTHER READINGS

Bumgardner, M., Buehlmann, U., Schuler, A., & Crissey, J. (2011). Competitive actions of small firms in a declining market. *Journal of Small Business Management, 49*(4), 578–598.

CISION. (June 5, 2018). New research from acosta reveals the importance of national brands to retailer success. Prnewswire.com. Retrieved from https://www.prnewswire.com/news-releases/new-research-from-acosta-reveals-the-importance-of-national-brands-to-retailer-success-300660326.html

Dawar, N., & Stornelli, J. (2013). Rebuilding the relationship between manufactures and retailers. *MIT Sloan Management Review, 54*(2), 83–90.

Kenton, W. (March 20, 2022). What is PEST analysis? Its applications and uses in business. *Investopedia.com.* Retrieved from https://www.investopedia.com/terms/p/pest-analysis.asp

Oubiña, J., Rubio, N., & Jesús Yagüe, M. (2006). Relationships of retail brand manufacturers with retailers. *International Review of Retail, Distribution and Consumer Research, 16*(02), 257–275.

Parnell, J. A., & Dent, E. B. (2009). The role of luck in the strategy-performance relationship. *Management Decision, 47*(6), 1000–1021.

CASE REFERENCES

Agnihotri, A., & Bhattacharya, S. (2024). *Bed Bath & Beyond Inc: Effectiveness of turnaround management.* Sage Business Cases. https://doi.org/10.4135/9781071928769

Bowman, J. (September 4, 2022). The hidden reason behind Bed Bath & Beyond's demise. *The Motley Fool.* Retrieved from https://www.fool.com/investing/2022/09/04/the-hidden-reason-behind-bed-bath-beyonds-demise/

CISION. (October 26, 2022). Bed Bath & Beyond Inc. appoints Sue Gove President & Chief Executive Officer. Prnewswire.com. Retrieved from https://www.prnewswire.com/news-releases/bed-bath--beyond-inc-appoints-sue-gove-president--chief-executive-officer-301659383.html

Fonrouge, C., & Rizzo, L. (January 26, 2023). Bed Bath & Beyond defaults on credit line, warns it can't pay down debts. *CNBC.* Retrieved from https://www.cnbc.com/2023/01/26/bed-bath-and-beyond-warns-it-doesnt-have-cash-to-pay-debts.html

Jansen, C. (August 19, 2022). Bed Bath & Beyond is at risk of filing for bankruptcy. How did it get here? *Retail Dive.* Retrieved from https://www.retaildive.com/news/bed-bath-beyond-bankruptcy-risk-what-happened/630011/

Kaushal, T. (February 7, 2023). Bed Bath and Beyond timeline: The chaotic final years of a classic American retailer. *Yahoo! News.* Retrieved from https://news.yahoo.com/bed-bath-beyond-timeline-bankruptcy-equity-offering-181700694.html

Lodewick, C. (June 29, 2022). Bed Bath & Beyond is firing its CEO because Americans are done spending with a recession in the distance. *Fortune.* Retrieved from https://fortune.com/2022/06/29/bed-bath-and-beyond-mark-tritton-recession/

Morgan, J. P. (May 25, 2022). What's behind the global supply chain crisis? Jpmorgan.com. Retrieved from https://www.jpmorgan.com/insights/research/global-supply-chain-issues

Repko, M. (January 10, 2023). Bed Bath & Beyond reports wider-than-expected loss as possible bankruptcy looms. *CNBC.* Retrieved from https://www.cnbc.com/2023/01/10/bed-bath-beyond-bbby-q3-2023-earnings.html

Repko, M., & Thomas, L. (August 5, 2022). Bed Bath & Beyond is discontinuing a private brand as it tries to reverse declining sales. *CNBC.* Retrieved from https://www.cnbc.com/2022/08/05/bed-bath-beyond-discontinues-wild-sage-private-brand-as-it-tries-to-improve-sales.html

Sabanoglu, T. (January 31, 2023). Operating loss of Bed Bath & Beyond worldwide from fiscal year 2014 to fiscal year 202. *Statista.* https://www.statista.com/statistics/1362377/operating-loss-bed-bath-and-beyond/

Shoulberg, W. (April 14, 2022). Is private label the problem—Or the solution—For Bed Bath & Beyond? *Business of Home.* Retrieved from https://businessofhome.com/articles/bed-bath-and-beyond-private-label-program

Statista Research Department. (January 31, 2023). Net sales of Bed Bath & Beyond worldwide from 2008 to 2021. *Statista.* Retrieved from https://www.statista.com/statistics/1074085/net-sales-of-bed-bath-and-beyond-worldwide/

Wahba, P. (September 28, 2022). Bed Bath & Beyond aspired to be the next Target. But strategic mistakes made it the year's biggest retail train wreck. *Fortune.* Retrieved from https://fortune.com/2022/09/28/bed-bath-beyond-earnings-share-price-struggles-turnaround-plan/

CHAPTER 10

Acquisitions and Mergers

Learning Objectives

After reading this chapter, students will be able to:

- Examine the motives of mergers and acquisitions;
- Conduct valuation of M&A deals;
- Explore the significance of knowledge management in M&A deals;
- Critically analyze different ways of integrating the acquired unit into the corporate parent;
- Examine how firms conduct divestitures if acquisitions fail.

ACQUISITIONS AND MERGERS

When one company acquires assets or equity in another company such that the focal company becomes the new corporate parent for the acquired entity, the process is called an *acquisition.*[1] It can be willing or hostile in nature. In a *willing acquisition*, firms conduct the absorption of assets and equity in a friendly manner, where the board of directors of the acquired company willfully transfers the rights to the acquiring company.[2] However, in a *hostile takeover*, when the board of directors is unwilling to sell their company, but the acquiring company is able to convince the shareholders of the target company to sell by offering an enticing share price, the acquisition is hostile.[3]

In a *merger*, on the other hand, two companies combine their equity and assets to form a new entity altogether. Mergers typically occur between companies of similar size and scale. For example, Daimler-Benz and Chrysler merged, creating a new company, DaimlerChrysler.[4] In a merger, a corporate parent may first acquire another company and then merge it with one of its brands. In 2024, HBC, corporate parent of Saks Fifth Avenue, first acquired the Neiman Marcus Group and then merged it with Saks Fifth Avenue.[5] Amidst rising competition from e-commerce retailing, the two luxury retailers—i.e., NMG (which owns Neiman Marcus and

DOI: 10.4324/9781003568100-10

Bergdorf Goodman) and Saks—were losing ground in retail sales. With the merger of Saks and NMG, a single luxury retail brand, Saks Global, was created.[6]

MOTIVES OF MERGERS AND ACQUISITIONS (M&As)

Value Creation

The most common driver of M&As is better shareholder value creation.[7] This occurs when management determines that the wealth generated by combining the assets of two companies is likely to be greater than the value created by each company individually. When the value creation of a combined or integrated entity exceeds that of its individual units, it is called *synergy*.[8] This synergy can arise from revenues or costs.

- *Revenue synergies* imply that companies are able to generate more sales as a combined or acquired entity than they would by selling their own products.[9] When Disney acquired Pixar, Pixar was already popular among viewers; however, it could not scale.[10] Disney, on the contrary, was exploring ways to increase its sales. With the acquisition of Pixar, Disney released Pixar's popular motion pictures more frequently through its expanded distribution network.[11] As a separate entity, Pixar would not have had access to Disney's distribution network, and neither Disney would have benefited from the sales generated by Pixar. Some of the Pixar characters, such as Buzz Lightyear, were particularly popular among kids.[12] Accordingly, Disney, after acquiring Pixar, utilized these characters in its merchandise, which Disney sold globally through its stores. Once again, Pixar would not have gained access to Disney's distribution network to increase its sales, and Disney would not have been able to increase its sales either, as it would not have been able to use Pixar characters without ownership. The acquisition made this possible. Finally, Pixar characters were also promoted in Disney's theme parks, further increasing revenue opportunities. Clearly, in this case, after the acquisition, the sales potential for both firms increased compared to what they could have earned individually, making it a revenue synergy-driven acquisition. In 2006, Disney's Consumer Products segment had USD 2.1 billion in revenues, which increased to USD 5.2 billion by 2022—demonstrating how the acquisition helped Disney nearly double its revenues. Pixar also gained from the acquisition, albeit as part of the Disney group.[13]
- *Cost synergies* occur when joint operations following an acquisition result in lower costs compared to the expenses incurred by each company when operating independently.[14] For instance, acquiring a parent and a target both have human resources (HR), information technology (IT), and accounting teams; however, after the acquisition, headcount can be reduced, as fewer employees can manage the operations of both the parent and the acquired entity once the operations are integrated. In 2018, when Nine Entertainment Co. and Fairfax Media, the two Australian media giants, merged, they realized cost savings of USD 50 million by eliminating redundant IT, media sales, and corporate functions roles.[15]

Financial Synergy. Financial gains incurred by firms after M&As, which are reflected in the financial metrics of the combined or integrated entity, are known as financial synergy.[16]

As such, cost and revenue synergy gains are also reflected in financial metrics such as profitability, revenues, or return on assets. However, financial synergy is a broader term used to capture gains from the financial aspects of business, including taxation, credit, debt, and other related areas. For instance, if a firm can lower its tax rate after an acquisition or merger, it may be a motive for the acquisition or merger.

Similarly, if a firm can lower its debt cost or increase its creditworthiness, then it is again a financial synergy and could be a driver of mergers and acquisitions. However, financial synergy motives are difficult to realize as the regulatory authority may block the deals. Pfizer in 2016 wanted to acquire an Ireland-based company, Allergan. Ireland had a much lower tax rate, and with the "tax inversion" motive, Pfizer wanted to shift its headquarters to Ireland. However, the US government changed its rules, which did not allow Pfizer to avail of a lower tax rate in Ireland (35% in the USA vs. 12% in Ireland), and the deal could not be finalized.[17]

Target Valuation

For valuing a target and deciding offer price for acquisition different financial metrics can be used depending on type of acquisition happening. Figure 10.1 presents the financial metrics.

HOW TO DO THE VALUATION OF AN M&A DEAL?

According to research, synergies, especially revenue synergies, should reflect a 1%–2% increase in sales for the target firm. i.e., after M&As, there should be at least a 1%–2% increase in sales of the acquired firm's products.[18] This sales increase can occur through cross-selling or utilizing the distribution channel of a corporate firm, as seen in the case of Pixar, or through any other means. The acquiring firm needs to pay the target firm a share of the increased revenues resulting from the synergy. Typically, they receive 30% of the potential

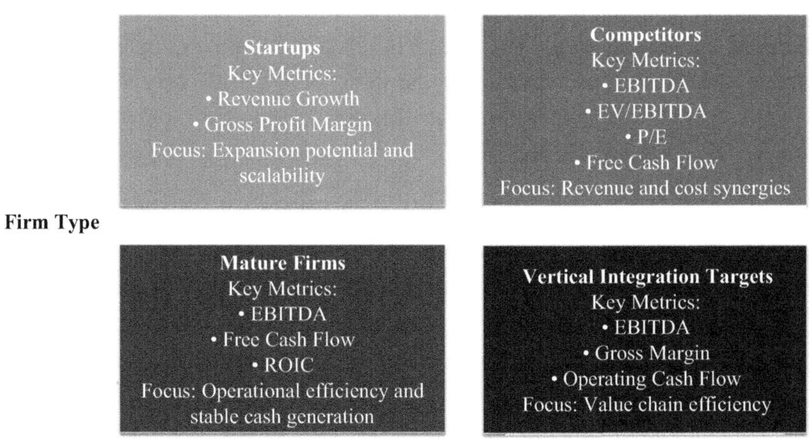

FIGURE 10.1 Strategic Evaluation of Acquisition Targets Here

Source: Developed by the Authors

TABLE 10.1 Valuation of a Target Firm in an M&A Transaction

Financial Metric	Data	Strategic Scenario	Standalone Scenario
Target Firm Annual Revenue (USD)	24,500,000	–	–
Estimated Synergy Potential (%)	6%	–	–
Total Potential Synergy (USD)	1,470,000	–	–
Share of Synergy Allocated to Target (%)	25%	–	–
Synergy Allocation to Target (USD)	367,500	–	–
Target Firm EBITDA (USD)	–	2,800,000	2,800,000
Synergy Contribution to EBITDA (USD)	–	367,500	0
Adjusted EBITDA (USD)	–	3,167,500	2,800,000
Enterprise Value Multiple (EV/EBITDA)	–	5.5	5.5
Estimated Enterprise Value (USD)	–	17,421,250	15,400,000
Value Created from Synergy (USD) (EV Strategic-EV Nonstrategic)	–	2,021,250	–
Implied EV Multiple After Synergy (New EV/Old Target EBIDTA)	–	6.22	–

Source: Developed by the Authors.

share, implying that the acquiring firm keeps the majority of the increased revenue share, i.e., 70%. Now, let us assume that the financial statements of the target firm indicate annual revenues of approximately USD 24.5 million and an EBITDA of USD 2.8 million. Suppose the acquiring firm estimates that operational synergies from the acquisition could increase revenues by approximately 6%, generating an additional USD 1.47 million in potential value. If 25% of the expected synergy gains are attributed to the target firm in the valuation process, the target would receive an incremental benefit of approximately USD 367,500, which increases its adjusted EBITDA to about USD 3.17 million. Assuming that the target firm is valued at an enterprise value multiple of 5.5 times EBITDA, the improved operating performance would lead to a higher enterprise value for the strategic acquisition scenario compared with the standalone case. The acquiring firm can therefore estimate the potential value creation from synergies as illustrated in Table 10.1.

Diversification

Another critical motive for M&A is diversification. In pursuit of growth, firms may sometimes decide to enter new markets, such as international markets, or introduce new product lines, including organic food products alongside standard food products that contain preservatives. When a firm or industry reaches a mature stage, managers may diversify their line of business to mitigate the risk of decline and enter an entirely new line of business.[19] However, when diversifying into unrelated businesses, shareholders may not approve the deal, as, rather than relying on a focal firm for earning profits and paying dividends in areas outside their core area, shareholders believe they can themselves invest in growing businesses where firms in that area already have expertise and better potential to give dividends.[20] Amazon has typically been an online retailer, but it decided to diversify into a brick-and-mortar retailer, which it did with the acquisition of Whole Foods. Similarly, Microsoft's acquisition of LinkedIn diversified its operations into the social media sector. However, this was not entirely unrelated, as Microsoft could utilize its software and productivity tools on LinkedIn's site, thereby creating synergy between its productivity tools and LinkedIn's professional networking platform.[21]

Acquisition of Assets

Sometimes firms are interested in acquiring new technologies to make their current product more relevant or better. Then, the acquisition of that asset, which would otherwise not be available (usually some technology), becomes a motive for the acquisition. Google acquired Android to establish its presence in the mobile market, where Apple was leading the race. Smartphones required a different operating system from laptops and PCs, and Android provided one.[22]

ACQUIRING BANKRUPT FIRMS

Acquiring bankrupt firms can be a good strategy to acquire an undervalued firm, as firms that have filed for bankruptcy are more likely to have their assets undervalued, and the acquiring firm can buy the target firm at a much lower price, without paying any acquisition premium, even when there is potential to realize revenue synergy.[23] Then, acquiring a parent can turn around the bankrupt firm, and the acquiring firm may benefit from the acquired bankrupt firm's assets and increased profitability, as it paid a lower price for the acquisition. Wilbur Ross of International Steel Group is known as "King of Bankruptcy." Ross's strategy involved acquiring only distressed assets. He acquired bankrupt companies at low prices, turned them around, and then sold the firm for a profit. Ross, a largely private equity player, formed International Steel Group (ISG) in 2002 by acquiring the assets of bankrupt steel firms, including LTV Corp. and Bethlehem Steel, among others.[24] The acquisition was cheaper than usual, as he eliminated the legacy costs associated with pension payments, retiree healthcare benefits, and other similar expenses. Given that steel firms declared bankruptcy, the federal government's Pension Benefit Guaranty Corporation fulfilled the obligations. Ross integrated the operations of the bankrupt steel mills to create the largest steel mill in the US. He turned the steel mill around using economies of scale and, within two years, sold ISG to Mittal Steel UK for 12.5 times the initial investment, generating USD 260 million from the deal.[25]

KNOWLEDGE MANAGEMENT IN M&As

Knowledge management is vital for the success of M&As, as it is a firm's crucial strategic asset, including both explicit and tacit knowledge. For instance, if a US-based firm acquires a firm in an international market to access new markets for its products, at a surface level, the firm may view synergy arising from access to the distribution channels of the target firm in international markets. However, employees in the target firm may have this additional information, that in their country, more than aggressive sales pitches, personal relations with customers help to increase sales. This tacit knowledge may lack documentation. Unless trust is established between employees and the target firm, they may be unwilling to share this knowledge, which can ultimately lead to the failure of the merger or acquisition. Thus, managing tacit knowledge is just as crucial as accessing explicit knowledge.[26]

Moreover, customer behavior differences may arise in the same country, and intracountry cultural differences are also widespread. For example, in Brazil, "Paulistas" from São Paulo are culturally distinct from "Gauchos" from Rio Grande do Sul in the southern part of Brazil.[27] "Paulistas" are more urban and nontraditional in their lifestyle, valuing material possessions such as wealth. For this reason, over the years, São Paolo has become a commercial hub in Brazil.[28] Portuguese influence is evident in their culture, and people have a slight Italian accent in São Paolo.

Gauchos, on the contrary, are believed to be more laid-back, less attached to material possessions of the world, and primarily rely on agriculture as an economic activity, in contrast to São Paulo, where manufacturing is the primary economic activity.[29] People in this region have a slightly Spanish accent.[30] Similarly, Bogotá and Cartagena have huge intracountry cultural differences in Colombia. Whereas people in Bogotá have an urban and rushed lifestyle, Cartagena offers a more enjoyable and playful vibe, thanks to its Caribbean and humid climate.[31] These social lifestyle differences across regions within the same country can have significant implications for acquiring customers across different regions. Thus, managing employees' tacit knowledge is critical.

Employees of the target firm may also have network-based tacit knowledge. They may know local suppliers and distributors who can help launch their products more quickly in the market or assist in managing seasonal demand trends. In the beverage industry, despite any brand having world-class information system based on data analytics, to inform bottling plant contract manufacturers about reorder quantity based on demand trends, yet what works more effectively is the regional sales manager's personal relations and networks with contract manufacturers, who, on the request of the regional sales executive, pulls resources and prioritize manufacturing for given brand.[32]

Additionally, knowledge management is also essential from the perspective of knowledge integration, facilitating innovation. General Motors integrated the assisted driving knowledge of its acquired firm, Cruise, to develop GM's own assisted driving and autonomous driving vehicles.[33]

Knowledge management failure in M&A can arise from three sources: a lack of understanding or information before acquisition, an inability to integrate tacit knowledge post-acquisition, and an inability to retain vital employees from the target firm post-acquisition. When HP acquired Autonomy Corporation in 2011, it failed to thoroughly understand Autonomy Corporation's accounting practices before the acquisition, suggesting an inadequate due diligence process.[34] In the software industry, deferred revenue (i.e., revenue earned but not yet realized) is generally high because software companies, such as SAP, earn upfront revenues for their software licenses (resulting in low receivables) as well as maintenance and support.[35] However, this customer service support typically occurs at a later stage, once the client has been using the licensed software for some time. Therefore, a firm may charge fees for the service but does not deliver customer service support until a need arises, resulting in high deferred revenue. Accordingly, they have low receivables. However, for Autonomy Corporation, as a software company, the case was just the opposite. This aspect, which HP did not fully comprehend during due diligence, is a key example of their failure in knowledge management.

Similarly, after an acquisition, especially when the acquisition is made to achieve cost synergies, employees become aware that some of them are likely to lose their jobs. In such a case, the employees of acquired firms may refuse to share critical knowledge with other employees of the target or acquiring company. Consequently, this could adversely affect the success of the acquisition. For instance, if there is any typicality in an accounting system that the accounting manager of the target company knows, but feels he is likely to lose his job after the integration of the accounting departments of the two companies, he may withhold that important information, leading to less realization of cost synergies.

Sometimes companies also fire executives after an acquisition, even if the objective is revenue synergy or diversification. In that case, they might lose access to critical knowledge that could have otherwise made the acquisition successful. For instance, after acquiring Skype, Microsoft fired several Skype executives as they believed their knowledge was not critical for integrating Microsoft's productivity tools with the corporate version of Skype. However, retaining them might have made the acquisition successful.[36]

Acquisition failures may also occur due to a lack of cultural similarities, which is crucial for gaining the trust of employees and senior management after a merger or acquisition. Several significant acquisitions failed due to cultural clashes, such as AOL and Time Warner, as well as Daimler and Chrysler. Daimler, for instance, as a German company, followed a more authoritarian approach in decision-making, involving employees minimally and communicating strategic decisions from top to bottom. Chrysler, being an American counterpart, believed in integrating junior-level employees' opinions and information received from them into strategic decision-making. Thus, after the merger, employees and senior executives faced setbacks in terms of how the firms made acquisition decisions and could not agree on common grounds due to differences in cultural values and philosophies that none of the parties were willing to change.

It is thus crucial to conduct a thorough cultural analysis before selecting a target firm for merger or acquisition. Generative AI makes this task much easier in today's world. Generative AI can summarize employee reviews from social media or review sites, such as Glassdoor and Indeed, and highlight the peculiarities of each organization.[37] For instance, in one organization, autonomy from managers may be dominant feedback, while micromanagement may be a dominant concern for employees in another organization. This is likely to result in a cultural clash as micromanagement and autonomy are two extreme ends of the same string. If an acquisition is necessary, both the acquiring and acquired firms may resolve cultural issues before the acquisition, allowing management from both companies to set expectations jointly. Similarly, generative AI can also assess human resource policies of both companies through employee handbooks, internal communications, and other sources, and report key insights.

INTEGRATION OF FIRMS POST-ACQUISITION

Firms can adopt different levels of integration of the acquired firm, depending on cultural differences and the type of synergy the acquiring firm wants to achieve. *Mentorship* is the least integrated strategy, where the target firm retains a high level of autonomy and operates as a largely standalone organization. The corporate parent that has acquired the target firm provides the resources needed to run the acquired organization with minimal day-to-day interference. They provide strategic guidance and bring no structural changes to the organization.[38] Generally, all employees of the acquired unit are retained, unlike in the case of an acquisition, where the corporate parent may fire some employees post-acquisition to reduce human resources costs.

The mentorship model works well when it is vital to preserve the brand identity of the acquired firm, or when independent operation offers better market responsiveness. When Tata Motors acquired the Jaguar and Land Rover brands from Ford, it retained the autonomy of the acquired brands. Tata Motors provided only the necessary resources and strategic guidance[39] because Jaguar Land Rover was an established brand, and its employees possessed all the technological knowledge required to turn around the brand. Moreover, the acquisition was not for the Indian market of Tata Motors, and it had less exposure to international markets, where these brands were dominant. So, mentorship was the most appropriate model. The acquisition was largely successful. Again, when the objective of acquisition is diversification through portfolio building, the mentorship model is more effective.[40] When cultures are dissimilar and acquisitions can provide greater revenue synergy, then again, the mentorship model is more suited.

A *limited or targeted integration* is appropriate when integrating certain functions can increase overall operational efficiency, but the acquired firm requires autonomy in managing other functions.[41] Suppose a regional player acquires another regional player, where cultural differences in the markets are high. In that case, the acquired and acquiring firms may integrate their backend functions, such as HR and finance. Still, the marketing team can be left as autonomous units, as they have a better understanding of regional dynamics. Integrating marketing in this case can put revenue synergy at risk. When Lenovo from China acquired the PC division of IBM, for the first few years, there was no integration of the IBM PC division's functions with those of Lenovo. Lenovo did the integration in phases, with some functions, such as marketing, retaining autonomy.

Complete integration is another level of integration, implying the integration of an acquired unit into the management processes and organizational structure of the corporate parent. Complete integration results in a combined business entity, where employees of the acquired unit are required to adapt themselves to the working practices and culture of the acquiring parent.[42] Unlike targeted integration, where employees of the acquired unit have some autonomy to complete work processes independently of the functions of the acquiring unit, complete integration results in the loss of such autonomy. The corporate parent opts for complete integration when an acquisition has been made to achieve cost synergies.[43]

DIVESTURE

Divestiture is the sale of a business unit that is no longer contributing value to the corporate parent. Divestiture occurs when a business unit is underperforming or is not aligned with the company's strategic goals. Sometimes a firm may need capital to grow business divisions that have the potential to perform well in the market or focus more on core competencies by launching new products through R&D. Divesting can free financial resources and raise shareholder value.[44] Divestiture is also a portfolio management technique for businesses. According to a McKinsey survey, firms that refresh their business divisions' portfolio through acquisitions and divestitures generate 5.2% more shareholder returns per year.[45] A firm may conduct a divestiture by selling a given business to another entity, spinning it off into an independent entity, or closing the division altogether.

However, divestiture is not a straightforward exercise. For instance, when Gap decided to divest Old Navy, several suppliers of Gap had a sense of resentment, as they had worked with Gap largely because of Old Navy (Chapter 9).[46] Given the complex intertwining of logistics and supply chains of various Gap brands, including Old Navy and other iconic brands such as Banana Republic, Athleta, and Janie and Jack, divestiture was eventually called off, despite the declining performance of Old Navy. Gap commented that "there would be "dis-synergies" from the split, given how many resources Old Navy and the rest of the company share in terms of buying fabrics, manufacturing facilities, and clout with landlords in negotiating rent."[47]

For intertwined businesses where resources are shared, businesses generally allocate resources to the better-performing business, which is also one of the key reasons why divestiture takes place. The divestiture happens because the business being divested is not performing well, which could be partly due to the maturity or decline phase of the industry life cycle. For instance, Motorola's cellular and enterprise solution division holds the patents for the technology, the "batwing" logo (that had significant brand recognition among customers), and cash. As Motorola's cell phone business was declining amid intense industry competition, and the enterprise solutions business was known for its innovative capacity, Motorola allocated all these shared resources to Motorola Mobility at the time of the separation.

In contrast to divestitures, when Honeywell divested Resideo as a spinoff unit, it continued selling certain products under the brand name "Honeywell Home." However, this happened after Resideo signed a trademark licensing agreement with Honeywell. As per the agreement, Resideo received an exclusive license to use the Honeywell Home name for 40 40-years. Honeywell received royalties of 1.5% of the net sales of trademarked products.[48] In spinoffs, there is always a risk that the spun-off unit will accuse the corporate parent of allocating too significant a share of corporate expenses and liabilities to the spun-off unit, especially if the spun-off unit is unable to succeed after the spinoff. For instance, Tronox, Paragon Offshore, and Garrett Motion filed lawsuits against their respective corporate parent companies, Kerr-McGee (now Anadarko), Noble, and Honeywell, respectively, accusing them of allocating larger shares of debt, liabilities, pension obligations, and other liabilities.[49]

ASSIGNMENT QUESTIONS

1. What are the differences in mergers and acquisitions? Give examples.
2. What motivates managers to engage in mergers and acquisitions? Give recent examples.
3. As a manager, what significance do you think knowledge management in mergers and acquisitions holds? Elaborate.
4. Examine different approaches to post-acquisition integration of the acquired firm. Give examples of each kind of integration approach.

CASE STUDY **10.1**

Smucker's Diversification into Indulgence Food

Will It Pay Off?

Agnihotri, A., & Bhattacharya, S. (2025). *Smucker's diversification into indulgence food: Will it pay off?* Sage Business Cases. https://doi.org/10.4135/9781071986639

INTRODUCTION

In 2023, contrary to the growing trend of diversification of food companies into healthy alternatives, J M Smucker Co (Smucker's) acquired for USD 5.6 billion Hostess Brand Inc (Hostess), a leader in the sweet baked goods and indulgent snacks categories (Coleman, 2023). Smucker's provides customers healthy alternatives for everyday snacking (Newman & Thomas, 2023). Mark Smucker, CEO of Smucker's commented on the Hostess acquisition saying, "This expands and transforms their portfolio of items to bring them into a completely different market (convenience stores)" (Gelski, 2023a). The CEO added that Smucker's and Hostess have complementary capabilities to drive further growth and innovation (Gelski, 2023b). Some of the expected innovations were new products where jelly might appear in chocolate cupcakes or chocolate could appear in Smucker's Uncrustables (pre-made frozen sandwiches) (Gelski, 2023a). Geoff Coltman, vice president of client engagement for Chicago-based Catena Solutions, a merger and acquisition consultant, said, "In my opinion, you're going to start to see the Hostess items through innovation start to merge with other SKUs and brands (owned by J.M. Smucker)" (Gelski, 2023a).

However, industry observers believe the US health and wellness market has better growth prospects. Smucker's, on the contrary, was driven by a 20% faster growth of indulgence snacks between 2020 and 2023 compared to healthy alternatives (Harvey, 2023)

In 2023, Hostess reported a 14% compound annual growth rate (CAGR) between the years 2020 and 2023. Alexia Howard of Alliance Bernstein, commenting on Hostess's CAGR, said this is not likely to be a predictor of future performance (Cooke, 2023). According to her indulgent snacking experienced growth during the pandemic years because of affordability reasons and as post-pandemic economy improves and prices of healthy food items stabilizes, consumers would switch to healthy snacking. (Cooke, 2023). However, according to Mark

Smucker consumers were likely to snack in multiple ways including both health and indulgent snacking depending on occasion. (Harvey, 2023). According to Howard, how well Smucker's could innovate by mixing its brands with Hostess brands would likely determine the acquisition's success. Howard said, "The big question here is whether Hostess will continue to deliver strong top-line growth in coming years under Smucker's ownership: it seems that this growth is predicated mainly on continued strong innovation" (Cooke, 2023). Did Mark Smucker make an appropriate decision to diversify into the indulgence snacks category? How can he create Smucker's synergy with Hostess?

COMPANY BACKGROUNDS

Smucker's

Jerome M. Smucker founded Smucker's in 1897 (Case Western Reserve University, 2019). Smucker's manufactures and markets food products globally, and its main products include peanut butter and fruit spreads, coffee and pet food, shortening and oils, canned milk, baking mixes and ready-to-spread frostings, flour and baking ingredients, juices and beverages, frozen sandwiches, dessert toppings, etc. (DiPalma, 2023). Smucker's portfolio has more than 40 brands, like Smucker's®, Folgers®, Jif®, and Milk-Bone®, and its products can be found in more than 90% of US households (Smucker's, 2023). Smucker's has more than 7,000 employees (Smucker's, 2023). Mordor Intelligence predicted that in the US, the jam, jelly, and preserves market would grow at only 1.7% given the high sugar content and the death of baby boomers due to age-related factors—implying a decline in the core customer base of Smucker's (Poinski, 2018). Moreover, the jam, jelly, and preserves market is highly competitive, with several local and regional players (Mordor Intelligence, 2023).

Hostess

Hostess, an iconic American brand for generations, focused on growing indulgent snacking (Hyslop, 2022). Its brand portfolio consists of Twinkies®, Ding Dongs®, and Donettes®. It also produces cookie and creme wafer products, including sugar-free varieties under its Voortman® brand, acquired in 2020 (Hostess Brands, 2022). Dolly Madison®, Cloverhill®, and Big Texas® are also part of its branded products. Hostess reported revenues of USD 1.39 billion between October 2022 and September 2023, with 5.63% growth year-over-year (Stock Analysis, 2023).

In 2022, Hostess introduced the Hostess Bouncers product line targeting student lunch boxes and after-school treats at home. Hostess believed that adult shoppers were exploring convenient bite-size snacks for their kids to eat that were also easy to clean up. This need drove Hostess to launch a mini snack version of Twinkies under the Hostess Bouncers brand (Doering, 2022). In this case, Hostess was innovating by introducing new flavors of an existing product and capturing additional occasions where consumers could eat them (Doering, 2022). As vice president of Hostess's Marketing Center of Excellence, Tina Lambert said, "We're betting big behind Bouncers because we believe this is a big idea" (Doering, 2022).

Commenting on innovation capabilities of Hostess, Mark Smucker said, "Offering the consumers different sizes and smaller products, lower calories, whatever it might be, has been one of the ways that [Hostess has] innovated, and we liked that idea" (DiPalma, 2023) He further added "Hostess has done such a nice job creating single-serve small portions that allow people to have snacking, sweet snacks, in moderation" (Coleman, 2023).

CONSUMER ATTITUDE'S TOWARD INDULGENCE AND HEALTHY SNACK OPTIONS

A 2020 study by the Hartman Group in the US found that 43% of consumers asserted that snacking helped them cope with boredom or frustration. For 55% of respondents, snacking comforted them, reflecting a nine-point increase in that same timeframe in previous year (Oller, 2021). Brad Schwan, vice president of category marketing for Archer Daniels Midland, had this to say about snacking: "It provides a variety of benefits, but one of them is the ability to manage their perceived stress and help with their [consumers'] mood and kind of provide this emotional comfort" (Oller, 2021).

Experts believe that the growth of indulgence snacks was driven by economic challenges consumers faced during the COVID-19 pandemic (like job losses and stimulus payments) and post-pandemic (like inflation) (Hamstra, 2022). As inflation shot up, post-pandemic prices for products ranging from gas to groceries increased, and consumers observed pastries and doughnuts as more affordable than healthy organic food options (Hamstra, 2022). Smucker's also conducted a consumer survey in 2022 to understand how consumers planned to cope with the inflation-stuck economy scenario and found that consumers would be exploring new indulgence-snacking options (Straughn, 2022). Andrew Callahan, Hostess's president and CEO, said, "Eighty-two percent say that sweet snacks bring them joy, especially during times of uncertainty." In 2023, Dan O'Leary, chief growth officer at Hostess, said, "We are often asked if indulgence is a sustainable trend relative to better-for-you, and our short answer is absolutely" (Crawford, 2023).

According to O'Leary, indulgent and healthy snacking were non-competing categories as consumers sought ways to increase the occasion of snacking and follow a balanced approach to both healthy and indulgent snacking. (Crawford, 2023). Thus, consumers relished both healthy and indulgent snacking during different times of the day. While for health reasons, consumers relished healthy snacking; however, when they wanted to reward themselves for healthy lifestyle choices, they also relished indulgent snacking (Rydings, 2023).

General Mills, in 2020, also announced the return of a 1990s snack, Dunkaroos, targeting Gen Z, the cohort of 30 million consumers born between 1990 and 2000 (PYMNTS, 2023). Jeff Caswell, president of snacks at General Mills, said, "For those who grew up in the '90s, the original cookie-frosting combo represents the taste, color, and fun of being a kid during that decade" (PYMNTS, 2023). He added, "We know there's a lot of love for Dunkaroos, and fans everywhere have been asking for it. We're excited to help '90s kids relive all the best parts of childhood." Alyssa Hangartner, consumer insights analyst of flavor and ingredient trends at Mintel, explained how COVID-19 pandemic increased indulgence snacking, as consumers wanted nostalgic flavors and products to bring a sense of comfort in a time driven by stress (PYMNTS, 2023).

Generational Gap in Snacking Attitude

Commenting on growth of snacking market over different generations, Schwan said "Snacking used to be, three decades ago, seen as something that was to be avoided, and seen as something that was in many ways for kids." He added, "And we've seen a multidecade evolution in the snacking category to a place where consumer attitudes are super different, and they see snacking as something that can contribute to a healthy way of life" (Oller, 2021). Baby boomers preferred three square meals a day. He explained, "They're less inclined to use snacking as a conscious strategy to achieve their health goals." Emotions of stress and boredom were also not found to be drivers of snacking for boomers. Their prime objective for eating was to support physical and mental alertness, compared to other age groups (Oller, 2021).

Schwan said, "Flexibility is pretty important to this particular group" (Oller, 2021). He added, "You start to see more and more snacking to cope with stress, or to [meet] some of what we call 'the optimization needs'—so managing alertness, managing focus starts to show up a bit more for millennials." This appears confirmed in a 2020 survey by the Hartman Group, where they found that 60% of millennials snacked to cope with stress, compared to only 23% of baby boomers (Oller, 2021). Households with children under the age of 18 years also turned to snacks to manage alertness and focus (Oller, 2021). Stress-driven snacking was also prominent among Gen Z. Seventy-two percent of Gen Z consumers snacked for comfort, compared to only 42% of baby boomers (Oller, 2021). As Schwan emphasizes, "There is among this age cohort just a general higher level of stress and anxiety" (Oller, 2021). This might explain why 70% of Gen Z consumed at least two sweet snacks per day as a reward for following a healthy lifestyle (Gelski, 2023b).

SMUCKER'S DIVERSIFICATION THROUGH ACQUISITION

Smucker had extensive acquisition experience and applied them "acquisition filter" to identify if the target company for the acquisition was a strategic fit that included criteria; this filer asked question such as, "Does it provide Smucker's with a leading brand? Is it in an attractive category? Does it have a center-of-the-store presence? Is it North America-focused?" (Schroeder, 2013). Smucker's characterized its acquisitions as one of three types: transformational, enabling, or bolt-on (Schroeder, 2013).

As part of the "transformation acquisition," which is acquisition enabling focal firm entry into new markets, channels or category (Facenda, 2019), Smucker's entered the coffee category with the acquisition of the Folgers Coffee brand in 2008 (Facenda, 2019). Folgers was the top-selling retail (i.e., grocery and mass market) coffee brand in the US, with USD 1.5 billion in sales in 2008. Smucker's coffee portfolio later also included the Dunkin' Donuts Coffee at Home brand, the heritage Café Bustelo brand, and the in-house 1,850 brand, which it launched in April 2018 (Facenda, 2019). The company commented on diversification into coffee: “Coffee is the perfect complement to breakfast or dessert, two areas we know a lot about” (Bhattarai, 2008). After Folger’s acquisition, by 2009, Smucker’s reported sales of USD 3.8 billion, 49% more than in 2008 (Smucker’s, 2009).

“Enabling acquisitions” are those that “were typically smaller in size, but presented opportunities for new products, capabilities and technologies, where Smucker’s could capitalize on its current resources” (Schroeder, 2013). For example, in 2013, Smucker’s acquired Enray, a leading manufacturer and marketer of premium organic and gluten-free ancient grain products (Schroeder, 2013). Enray generated net sales of approximately USD 45 million (Food Processing, 2013) in the organic food category, where Smucker’s was already present before the Enray acquisition.

To expand its presence in a given product category through smaller acquisitions, Smucker’s followed a “bolt-on acquisition” approach, which involves “add-on” or “follow-on”) acquisition of a typically smaller company to expand market presence in already existing product category (UHY, 2020). … Accordingly, in 2012, it acquired Rowland Coffee. Rowland Coffee’s products, namely Cafe Bustelo® and Cafe Pilon brands, were the leading producers of espresso coffee in the US (The J. M. Smucker Company, 2011). Vince Byrd, president and chief operating officer at Smucker’s, said, “This is an exciting bolt-on transaction and a good strategic fit for our Company” (The J. M. Smucker Company, 2011). He added, “The acquisition is expected to provide our coffee business with greater scale and reach.” By acquiring several coffee brands, Smucker’s intended to leverage its existing coffee infrastructure and expand distribution and marketing support of the acquired brands. The combined manufacturing operations of all coffee brands was expected to have offered cost synergies to the company (The J. M. Smucker Company, 2011).

In 2016, Smucker’s also had its foray into the pet food category by acquiring Big Heart Pet Brands for USD 5.8 billion (Gerrard, 2015). Big Heart Pet Brands was the US’s largest standalone producer and marketer of premium-quality, branded pet food and pet snacks. Big Heart Pet Brands included brands like Meow Mix, Milk-Bone, Kibbles’n Bits, 9Lives, and Natural Balance (Gerrard, 2015). Richard Smucker, the CEO of the company, commenting on the acquisition, said, “The acquisition of Big Heart Pet Brands supports our purpose of ‘helping to bring families together to share memorable meals and moments,’ as we recognize that pets are cherished members of the family” (Gerrard, 2015). He added, “With approximately two-thirds of U.S. households having at least one family pet, we will now be able to serve the mealtime and snacking needs of the whole family.” Smucker’s, in total, acquired 17 companies by 2023 and divested 8 (Mergr, 2023).

Smucker’s Hostess Acquisition

Smucker’s expected that Hostess’s acquisition would help it diversify its product offerings and reduce its reliance on its core brands (Witt, 2023). Analysts considered the acquisition of Hostess as a strategic move to ensure growth through diversification, as some analysts expected indulgence snacking to grow, and Smucker’s was largely absent in this category (Witt, 2023). The Hostess snack brand was expected to contribute about USD 1.5 billion of annual net sales to Smucker’s (Gelski, 2023b).

The Hostess acquisition gave Smucker's access to a completely different market, i.e., convenience stores (Gelski, 2023a). Commenting on better access to alternative distribution channels such as C-stores, Mark Smucker said, "The acquisition will also add significant exposure to our business in the perimeter of retail stores and the highly complementary and strategic convenience channel as 40% of Hostess sales are in the c-store channel" (Gelski, 2023b). Smucker's already had a strong presence in traditional grocery retail, while Hostess offered a strong presence in convenience stores (O'Marah, 2023). Through the acquisition, Smucker's saw the potential to cross-sell and use mixing centers for consolidating shipments to chase growth (O'Marah, 2023).

A 2022 survey by NCSolutions, which provides advertising effectiveness measurement solutions and services, suggested that 92% of Gen Z consumers enjoyed convenience store shopping experience, in contrast to 77% of "all other generations" (Dworski, 2022). Gen Z was also 49% more likely to receive products from C-stores (i.e., convenience stores) than other generations (Dworski, 2022). NCSolutions encouraged consumer packaged goods brands to leverage Gen Z consumers' preferences as they explore market expansion strategies (Dworski, 2022).

Smucker's and Hostess Seem Complementarity

Smucker's expected the acquisition to help it expand its snack offerings, given that the two brands were complementary (Coleman, 2023). Mark Smucker said, "We complement each other so well." He added, "And we have great strength in our core grocery channels as well as our expertise in marketing, so there's a lot of complementary capabilities that are really going to allow both businesses to continue to grow here" (Coleman, 2023). Further commenting on complementary capabilities, Mark Smucker said, "They don't invest a lot in consumer marketing, and we do." Smucker believed there was an opportunity to amplify the Hostess brand recognition with consumers through marketing and advertising capabilities of Smucker (DiPalma, 2023). A study conducted by Hostess in 2022 revealed that although 95% of people knew of the Hostess brand, 60% did not buy it as it was not top of mind (Doering, 2022). Commenting on the need for advertising, Lambert said, "This is a huge opportunity for us as we think not just about innovation, but also our marketing to really drive that top-of-mind awareness among those younger parents and bring the next generation into Hostess" (Doering, 2022). She added, "It's not because they don't know what Hostess is [or] they don't have positive associations with Hostess, it's just that they've forgotten."

Integration of Hostess with Smucker's

Smucker was confident about its ability to integrate the Hostess brand. Mark Smucker said, "Smucker's history demonstrates our ability to successfully integrate large acquisitions" (Gelski, 2023b). Around 3,000 Hostess employees were expected to join Smucker's brand without any layoffs (Dairy Foods, 2023). However, integrating the two companies was likely to take time. Coltman said, "I don't think you're going to see employment change for a while" (Gelski, 2023a). Mark Smucker expected cost synergy of USD 100 million worth of costs post-acquisition integration within two years (Moreno, 2023). For brands, analysts expected Hostess brands and products to merge with Smucker's Brands through innovation. Creating new strategic divisions was also expected to smoothen innovation (Petrak, 2023).

Challenges in Achieving Synergy

Despite its belief in the growth potential of indulgent snacks, Smucker faced a challenging category due to the rising health consciousness among consumers. The company's past M&A success was mixed, adding to the complexity. Undeterred, Smucker made a significant investment of USD 7.7 billion to enter the pet food market, acquiring Big Heart Pet Brands in 2015 and Ainsworth Pet Nutrition in 2019 (McClay, 2019). Smucker's performance in the pet category was impressive, however yet it sold 60% of acquired business in this segment for approximately USD 1.3 billion between 2021 and 2023 (Hooper, 2023).

THE ROAD AHEAD

Acquisitions played a vital role in Smucker's growth strategy, where it aimed for category leadership and scale by acquiring large iconic brands. Smucker's wanted to pursue bolt-on acquisition opportunities to explore new categories, channels or geographies in packaged consumer products retail (MarketScreener, 2023). By acquiring Hostess in particular, Smucker's was expected to increase its presence in convenience shops, dollar stores, and other venues (Bomey, 2023).

Mark Smucker was not worried that consumers would lose interest in sweet snacks and become more and more health-conscious (Coleman, 2023). He said,

> We view that people are always going to want to snack. And there are different times of day when somebody might want a protein-based snack like peanut butter with celery, but other times, people want something a little more indulgent.
>
> (Coleman, 2023)

However, according to food industry experts, with the advent of the U.S. Food and Drug Administration–approved weight loss drugs, demand for indulgent snacking was likely to decrease (Cooke, 2023). Howard said,

> While snacking is likely to remain on a higher growth trajectory than meal-based foods, there is the question of whether indulgent snacks will lose out to better for you snacking in future years, especially with the uncertain impact of the new GLP-1 weight loss drugs which may curb purchases from some high consumption individuals.
>
> (Cooke, 2023)

Whether or not it was wise for Smucker's to venture into indulgence snacking is yet to be seen.

DISCUSSION QUESTIONS

1. Would you classify the Hostess deal as diversification-oriented or consolidation-oriented, and why?
2. What kinds of synergies are expected from the acquisition of the Hostess brand?
3. What is the nature of Hostess acquisition: Transformational/Bolt?

CHAPTER NOTES

1 https://online.hbs.edu/blog/post/mergers-and-acquisitions.
2 https://www.fbb.com/business-transactions-101-mergers-acquisitions-business-takeovers/.
3 https://corporatefinanceinstitute.com/resources/valuation/hostile-takeover/.
4 https://group.mercedes-benz.com/company/tradition/company-history/1995-2007.html#:~:text=Taking%20advancing%20globalisation%20into%20account,incorporated%20into%20the%20corporate%20portfolio.
5 https://lawreview.law.miami.edu/the-saks-neiman-marcus-merger-the-future-of-luxury-retail-from-a-legal-business-perspective/.
6 https://lawreview.law.miami.edu/the-saks-neiman-marcus-merger-the-future-of-luxury-retail-from-a-legal-business-perspective/.
7 Campa, J. M., & Hernando, I. (2004). Shareholder value creation in European M&As. *European Financial Management*, *10* (1), 47–81.
8 Tantalo, C., & Priem, R. L. (2016). Value creation through stakeholder synergy. *Strategic Management Journal*, *37* (2), 314–329.
9 Chatterjee, S. (1986). Types of synergy and economic value: The impact of acquisitions on merging and rival firms. *Strategic Management Journal*, *7* (2), 119–139.
10 https://www.nytimes.com/2006/01/25/business/disney-agrees-to-acquire-pixar-in-a-74-billion-deal.html.
11 https://www.filmsite.org/pixaranimations.html#:~:text=(Although%20Disney%20has%20only%20owned,Soul.
12 https://www.rollingstone.com/tv-movies/tv-movie-lists/best-pixar-movies-characters-164982/.
13 https://www.wallstreetoasis.com/resources/skills/deals/synergistic.
14 Hennart, J. F., & Reddy, S. (1997). The choice between mergers/acquisitions and joint ventures: The case of Japanese investors in the United States. *Strategic Management Journal*, *18* (1), 1–12.
15 https://www.afr.com/companies/media-and-marketing/nine-lifts-cost-savings-target-in-fairfax-merger-to-65-million-20181207-h18v7x.
16 Chatterjee, S. (1986). Types of synergy and economic value: The impact of acquisitions on merging and rival firms. *Strategic Management Journal*, *7* (2), 119–139.
17 https://www.wallstreetoasis.com/resources/skills/deals/financial-synergy#:~:text=Proven%20Track%20Records.-,Financial%20Synergy%20Examples,amount%20of%20people's%20smartphone%20time.
18 https://www.cfo.com/news/are-buyers-fudging-the-synergies-of-ma-deals/658629/.
19 Goold, M., & Luchs, K. (1993). Why diversify? Four decades of management thinking. *Academy of Management Perspectives*, *7* (3), 7–25.
20 David, P., O'Brien, J. P., Yoshikawa, T., & Delios, A. (2010). Do shareholders or stakeholders appropriate the rents from corporate diversification? The influence of ownership structure. *Academy of Management Journal*, *53* (3), 636–654.
21 https://www.linkedin.com/pulse/analyzing-benefits-microsofts-acquisition-linkedin-nitesh-shrivas-uxeyf/.
22 Wen, W., & Zhu, F. (2019). Threat of platform-owner entry and complementor responses: Evidence from the mobile app market. *Strategic Management Journal*, *40* (9), 1336–1367.
23 Ellias, J. A., & Stark, R. J. (2020). Bankruptcy hardball. *California Law Review*, *108* (3), 745–787.

24 https://prospect.org/labor/wilbur-ross/#:~:text=One%20of%20Ross's%20private%20equity,20%20percent%20of%20the%20industry.
25 https://prospect.org/labor/wilbur-ross/#:~:text=One%20of%20Ross's%20private%20equity,20%20percent%20of%20the%20industry.
26 https://www.sciencedirect.com/science/article/pii/S0148296301003149.
27 https://www.sciencedirect.com/science/article/pii/S0148296301003149.
28 https://www.sciencedirect.com/science/article/pii/S0148296301003149.
29 https://www.sciencedirect.com/science/article/pii/S0148296301003149.
30 https://www.sciencedirect.com/science/article/pii/S0148296301003149.
31 https://www.sciencedirect.com/science/article/pii/S0148296301003149.
32 https://www.linkedin.com/jobs/view/sales-director-domino-s-at-the-coca-cola-company-4296649450/.
33 https://investor.gm.com/news-releases/news-release-details/gm-acquire-cruise-automation-accelerate-autonomous-vehicle/#:~:text=We%20intend%20to%20invest%20significantly,://www.gm.com.
34 https://skillgigs.com/business-insights/leadership/it-leadership/a-detailed-timeline-of-an-ma-disaster/.
35 https://skillgigs.com/business-insights/leadership/it-leadership/a-detailed-timeline-of-an-ma-disaster/.
36 https://www.seattletimes.com/business/skype-fires-executives-avoiding-payouts-after-microsoft-buyout/#:~:text=Joseph%20Galante-,Skype%20Technologies%2C%20the%20Internet%2Dcalling%20service%20Microsoft%20is%20buying%2C,at%20Boyden%2C%20a%20search%20firm.
37 https://www.anecdoteai.com/blog/how-to-analyze-glassdoor-customer-reviews-with-ai#:~:text=Understanding%20AI%20and%20Its%20Role,before%20proceeding%20with%20this%20step.
38 https://www.kearney.com/service/mergers-acquisitions/article/-/insights/to-integrate-or-not-to-integrate#:~:text=Full%20integration:%20the%20acquirer%20and,A%20functional%20lens.
39 https://www.reuters.com/article/world/tata-motors-completes-acquisition-of-jag-land-rover-idUSBMA000842/#:~:text=By%20Reuters,continuing%20in%20the%20coming%20years.%22.
40 https://www.kearney.com/service/mergers-acquisitions/article/-/insights/to-integrate-or-not-to-integrate#:~:text=Full%20integration:%20the%20acquirer%20and,A%20functional%20lens.
41 https://www.kearney.com/service/mergers-acquisitions/article/-/insights/to-integrate-or-not-to-integrate#:~:text=Full%20integration:%20the%20acquirer%20and,A%20functional%20lens.
42 https://www.kearney.com/service/mergers-acquisitions/article/-/insights/to-integrate-or-not-to-integrate#:~:text=Full%20integration:%20the%20acquirer%20and,A%20functional%20lens.
43 https://www.kearney.com/service/mergers-acquisitions/article/-/insights/to-integrate-or-not-to-integrate#:~:text=Full%20integration:%20the%20acquirer%20and,A%20functional%20lens.
44 Chen, S., & Feldman, E. R. (2018). Activist-impelled divestitures and shareholder value. *Strategic Management Journal*, *39* (10), 2726–2744.
45 https://www.mckinsey.com/capabilities/strategy-and-corporate-finance/our-insights/whats-keeping-you-from-divesting.
46 Feldman, E. R. (2022). *Divestitures: Creating value through strategy, structure, and implementation.* New York, NY: McGraw Hill Professional.
47 https://fortune.com/2020/01/17/gap-inc-old-navy-spin-off/.
48 Feldman, E. R. (2022). Divestitures: Creating value through strategy, structure, and implementation. New York, NY: McGraw Hill Professional.
49 Feldman, E. R. (2022). Divestitures: Creating value through strategy, structure, and implementation. New York, NY: McGraw Hill Professional.

FURTHER READINGS

Anand, J., & Singh, H. (1997). Asset redeployment, acquisitions and corporate strategy in declining industries. *Strategic Management Journal*, *18*(S1), 99–118. Retrieved from https://www.jstor.org/stable/3088212

Bauer, F., & Friesl, M. (2024). Synergy evaluation in mergers and acquisitions: An attention-based view. *Journal of Management Studies*, *61*(1), 37–68. https://doi.org/10.1111/joms.12804

Ginsberg, A. (1989). Construing The Business Portfolio: A cognitive model of diversification. *Journal of Management Studies*, *26*(4), 417–438. https://doi.org/10.1111/j.1467-6486.1989.tb00737.x

UHY. (2020, September 30). What is behind the increasing trend of bolt-on acquisitions in recent periods. Uhy-us.com. Retrieved from https://uhy-us.com/insights/2020/september/cf-qa-what-is-behind-the-increasing-trend-of-bolt-on-acquisitions-in-recent-periods

Ural, A. (2019, May 10). Whether M&A contributes to shareholder value creation has been an ongoing debate for decades. Ey.com. Retrieved from https://www.ey.com/en_us/strategy-transactions/bolt-on-acquisitions-are-better-poised-for-value-capture-in-life-sciences

CASE REFERENCES

Bhattarai, A. (June 5, 2008). Smucker to pay $3 billion for Folgers Coffee. *The New York Times.* Retrieved from https://www.nytimes.com/2008/06/05/business/05folgers.html

Bomey, N. (September 11, 2023). Once-bankrupt Hostess completes comeback, thanks to J.M. Smucker. Axios. Retrieved from https://www.axios.com/2023/09/11/hostess-smucker-twinkie-deal

Case Western Reserve University. (November 6, 2019). Encyclopedia of Cleveland history: The J. M. Smucker Company. Case.edu. Retrieved from https://case.edu/ech/articles/j/j-m-smucker-company

Coleman, J. (September 11, 2023). Smucker CEO on merger with Hostess: 'We complement each other so well.' *CNBC.* Retrieved from https://www.cnbc.com/2023/09/11/smucker-ceo-on-hostess-merger-we-compliment-each-other-so-well.html

Cooke, E. (September 13, 2023). Signal: With Hostess, Smucker gambles on continued growth of indulgent snacks. Just Food. Retrieved from https://www.just-food.com/news/smucker-gambles-on-continued-growth-of-convenient-indulgent-food/

Crawford, E. (March 3, 2023). Hostess Brands: Indulgent, better-for-you snacks are additive, not competitive as consumers adopt 'this and that' stance. *Food Navigator USA.* Retrieved from https://www.foodnavigator-usa.com/Article/2023/03/03/hostess-brands-indulgent-better-for-you-snacks-are-additive-not-competitive

Dairy Foods. (September 11, 2023). Smucker buys Hostess Brands. *Dairy Foods Magazine.* Retrieved from https://www.dairyfoods.com/articles/96706-smucker-buys-hostess-brands

DiPalma, B. (September 11, 2023). J.M. Smucker CEO: 4 Reasons why buying Twinkies maker Hostess makes sense. *Yahoo! Finance.* Retrieved from https://finance.yahoo.com/news/jm-smucker-ceo-4-reasons-why-buying-twinkies-maker-hostess-makes-sense-204248390.html

Doering, C. (October 5, 2022). Hostess brands 'betting big' on smaller versions of classic treats to catch snacking competitors. Retrieved from https://www.fooddive.com/news/hostess-bouncers-bite-sized-snacks/631964/

Dworski, B. (November 4, 2022). Gen Z consumers enjoy the c-store experience more than other generations, study finds. *C-Store Dive.* Retrieved from https://www.cstoredive.com/news/gen-z-consumers-enjoy-c-store-experience/635775/

Facenda, V. L. (June 4, 2019). Smucker is getting bolder. *Tea and Coffee.* Retrieved from https://www.teaandcoffee.net/feature/22864/smucker-is-getting-bolder/

Food Processing. (August 22, 2013). J.M. Smucker buys enray. Foodprocessing.com. Retrieved from https://www.foodprocessing.com/business-of-food-beverage/business-strategies/news/11338250/jm-smucker-buys-enray

Gelski, J. (September 12, 2023a). Smucker receives mixed reviews on Hostess acquisition. Bakingbusiness.com. Retrieved from https://www.bakingbusiness.com/articles/59932-smucker-receives-mixed-reviews-on-hostess-acquisition

Gelski, J. (September 12, 2023b). Smucker gives 'convenient food' as reason to acquire Hostess. Bakingbusiness.com. Retrieved from https://www.bakingbusiness.com/articles/59904-smucker-gives-convenient-food-as-reason-to-acquire-hostess

Gerrard, J. (February 4, 2015). JM Smucker diversifies into pet foods with Meow Mix owner. *Food Engineering.* Retrieved from https://www.foodengineeringmag.com/articles/93459-jm-smucker-diversifies-into-pet-foods-with-meow-mix-owner

Hamstra, M. (August 12, 2022). Consumers torn between health and indulgence in snack foods. *Supermarket News.* Retrieved from https://www.supermarketnews.com/center-store/consumers-torn-between-health-and-indulgence-snack-foods

Harvey, S. (September 12, 2023). J.M. Smucker rebuffs concerns over indulgent snacks in wake of Hostess buy. *Just Food.* Retrieved from https://www.just-food.com/news/j-m-smucker-rebuffs-concerns-over-indulgent-snacks-in-wake-of-hostess-buy/

Hooper, O. (June 9, 2023). $30 million: The future of J.M. Smucker's divested pet food portfolio. *GlobalPets.* Retrieved from https://globalpetindustry.com/article/30-million-future-jm-smuckers-divested-pet-food-portfolio

Hostess Brands. (December 31, 2022). Hostess Brands Inc: Form 10K. Hostessbrands.com. Retrieved from https://www.hostessbrands.com/investors/sec-filings/annual-reports##document-1026-0001644406-23-000013-2

Hyslop, G. (May 5, 2022). Exceptional results from Hostess 'underscores favorable sacking behavior.' *Bakery & Snacks.* Retrieved from https://www.bakeryandsnacks.com/Article/2022/05/05/Exceptional-results-from-Hostess-underscores-favourable-snacking-behaviour

MarketScreener. (2023). The JM Smucker Company. Marketscreener.com. Retrieved from https://www.marketscreener.com/quote/stock/THE-JM-SMUCKER-COMPANY-14400/news/The-J-M-Smucker-to-Seek-Acquisitions-39573348/

McClay, R. (June 25, 2019). JM Smucker to acquire Ainsworth for $1.7B. *Investopedia.* Retrieved from https://www.investopedia.com/news/jm-smucker-acquire-ainsworth-17b/

Mergr. (2023). J. M. Smucker Mergers and acquisitions summary. Mergr.com. Retrieved from https://mergr.com/the-j.-m.-smucker-acquisitions

Mordor Intelligence. (2023). US jam jelly and preserves market size & share analysis – Growth trends & forecasts (2024–2029). Mordorintelligence.com. Retrieved from https://www.mordorintelligence.com/industry-reports/us-jam-jelly-and-preserve-packaging-market

Moreno, J. E. (September 11, 2023). Twinkies and jam to mix as Smucker buys Hostess for $5.6 billion. *The New York Times.* Retrieved from https://www.nytimes.com/2023/09/11/business/smucker-twinkies-hostess-brands-deal.html

Newman, J., & Thomas, L. (September 11, 2023). Smucker sets sights on snacks with $4.6 billion Twinkies deal. *The Wall Street Journal.* Retrieved from https://www.wsj.com/business/deals/jm-smucker-buy-hostess-twinkies-maker-6924a82

Oller, S. (April 11, 2021). How the pandemic is reshaping the snacking occasion. *Food Dive*. Retrieved from https://www.fooddive.com/news/how-the-pandemic-is-reshaping-the-snacking-occasion/597757/

O'Marah, K. (September 14, 2023). Smucker's + Twinkies = Brand driven growth in a TikTok supply chain world. *Forbes.* Retrieved from https://www.forbes.com/sites/kevinomarah/2023/09/14/smuckers--twinkies--brand-driven-growth-in-a-tiktok-supply-chain-world/?sh=72e29a333f8d

Petrak, L. (November 8, 2023). Smucker makes internal changes following Hostess acquisition. *Progressive Grocer.* Retrieved from https://progressivegrocer.com/smucker-makes-internal-changes-following-hostess-acquisition

Poinski, M. (August 21, 2018). Smucker sales roll over into the black after Nutrish acquisition. *Food Dive*. Retrieved from https://www.fooddive.com/news/smucker-sales-roll-over-into-the-black-after-nutrish-acquisition/530571/

PYMNTS. (Febraru24, 2023). Hostess CEO says stressed millennials turn to Twinkies. Pymnts.com. Retrieved from https://www.pymnts.com/earnings/2023/hostess-ceo-says-stressed-millennials-turn-twinkies/

Rydings, M. (March 6, 2023). Consumers balance indulgent and BFY snacks, says Hostess. *Commercial Baking.* Retrieved from https://commercialbaking.com/consumers-balance-indulgent-and-bfy-snacks-says-hostess/

Schroeder, E. (September 10, 2013). Smucker outlines acquisition strategy. Bakingbusiness.com. Retrieved from https://www.bakingbusiness.com/articles/25661-smucker-outlines-acquisition-strategy

Smucker's. (2009). The J.M. Smucker Company: Annual report-2009. Annualreports.com. Retrieved from https://www.annualreports.com/HostedData/AnnualReportArchive/t/NYSE_SJM_2009.pdf

Smucker's. (2023). About Smucker's. Smuckers.com. Retrieved from https://www.smuckers.com/about-us

Stock Analysis. (November 7, 2023). Hostess Brands, Inc. (TWNK). Stockanalysis.com. Retrieved from https://stockanalysis.com/stocks/twnk/revenue/

Straughn, S. (November 9, 2022). Slideshow: Hostess brands sees success in sweet snacking. *Food Business News*. Retrieved from https://www.foodbusinessnews.net/articles/22599-slideshow-hostess-brands-sees-success-in-sweet-snacking

The J. M. Smucker Company. (May 16, 2011). The J. M. Smucker Company acquires leading Hispanic brands from Rowland Coffee Roasters. *PR Newswire*. Retrieved from https://www.prnewswire.com/news-releases/the-j-m-smucker-company-acquires-leading-hispanic-brands-from-rowland-coffee-roasters-121947483.html

Witt, R. (September 11, 2023). Smucker's strategic move. *Yahoo! Finance*. Retrieved from https://finance.yahoo.com/news/smuckers-strategic-move-165648079.html

CHAPTER 11

Strategic Alliances

Learning Objectives

After reading this chapter students will be able to:

- Comprehend what strategic alliances are and the different types of strategic alliances;
- Evaluate how to identify an appropriate partner for alliances;
- Explore different types of strategic alliance partners;
- Critically analyze the dynamics of strategic alliances.

STRATEGIC ALLIANCE

A strategic alliance refers to a cooperative strategy in which a given firm collaborates with another firm to achieve strategic objectives.[1] Firms may apply this collaboration to any kind of value chain activity, such as R&D, marketing, or operations. The ultimate objective is to either increase customer value or enhance operational efficiency, such as reducing the capital investment risk of failure in R&D investments associated with the development of new products, or reducing manufacturing costs through joint manufacturing or sharing of manufacturing facilities.

Sometimes, operational costs in the manufacturing sector can be heavy, and firms prefer to pool their resources so that the cost burden on each partner is reduced.[2] In 2022, Ford partnered with Volkswagen to utilize its manufacturing facility for electric vehicle (EV) production for a period of six years. Ford was exploring ways to expand its production of EVs without making an intense capital investment.[3] As R&D can be expensive and risky, owing to a high failure rate, companies sometimes ally to share their R&D costs as they develop innovative products for growth. In the emerging EV sector, Toyota and BMW have formed an R&D alliance to develop hydrogen fuel cell systems as a potential replacement for lithium-ion batteries.[4]

DOI: 10.4324/9781003568100-11

One of the most popular type of marketing alliances are co-branding alliances. Here, companies from the same or even different industries ally to offer a branded and bundled product to consumers. Nike and Apple partnered to offer Nike+ipod, where Apple's iPod was equipped with additional software for tracking the sports activities of runners. Customers could listen to music and track their physical activity while wearing Nike shoes.[5] The alliance helped to increase sales for both Nike and Apple.

Alliances can be equity or non-equity-based. *Equity-based alliances* are referred to as joint ventures, where the equity contribution typically is 50% by each firm; however, it can vary depending on the contractual arrangements between the two firms. To enhance customer value, marketing or branding alliances are often formed, such as code-sharing agreements between different airlines or ingredient branding/co-branding alliances by laptop companies, like HP, which feature the label "Intel Inside." This ingredient/label indicates intel signals about high-quality microprocessors used in laptops, given the brand name Intel in the microprocessor field. In 2025, Intel revised the logo to "That's the power of Intel Inside".[6]

Identifying Alliance Partners

Several factors can influence the selection of alliance partners, such as complementary skill sets. An alliance partner must have *complementary skill sets*, allowing both parties to benefit. In the Panasonic and Tesla alliance,[7] Panasonic provided its advanced battery expertise, which Tesla required for EVs. Panasonic agreed to offer its battery technology to Tesla owing to Tesla's excellent electric vehicle design and vision for the EV market, which could have helped Panasonic grow rapidly in the EV market.[8]

Similarly, large pharmaceutical companies often ally with smaller biotech companies, as their resources complement each other. Due to their size and database, big pharma companies can conduct clinical trials alongside biotech companies, and in return, biotech companies offer their drug discoveries for curing diseases. For instance, Merck partnered with biotech company Ridgeback Biotherapeutics to commercialize *Molnupiravir*, an oral antiviral medicine. Although Ridgeback developed the drug, Merck provided its expertise for clinical development, regulatory approval, and commercialization of the drug.[9]

Once an alliance partner is selected, a due diligence process should be defined, including the duration of the alliance, decision-making processes, monitoring, and control mechanisms.[10] It should be clear who will make strategic versus operational decisions in the alliance. Will it be taken jointly by the senior management team of both companies, or will employees implementing the alliance have the authority to do so? If conflicts arise between the two parties regarding their opinions, how those conflicts are resolved. Despite strong governance mechanisms, several strategic alliances still fail due to poor communication between parties, a lack of trust between them, and cultural differences.[11]

Type of Strategic Alliance Partners

Strategic alliance partners could be firm suppliers, customers or competitors.

Alliances with Suppliers

Strategic alliances with suppliers are generally aimed at increasing supply chain efficiency, as suppliers are usually involved in supplying raw materials to focal firms.[12] Sometimes, contractual agreements with suppliers are also signed to control suppliers' ESG (Environmental, Social, and Governance) practices, as the firm wants to ensure that ESG practices are followed across the supplier end as well, rather than only inside the firm.[13] When suppliers have a weaker status compared to the focal firm, alliances also ensure that the focal firm provides training and resources to suppliers so as to enhance their resource status. For example, Nestlé has partnerships with farmers in developing countries for key ingredients such as coffee, cocoa, and milk as part of its "Creating Shared Value" program. This program is designed not only to ensure a consistent supply of ingredients but also to improve the livelihoods of farmers. Accordingly, Nestlé helps coffee farmers transition to regenerative farming practices, such as planting cover crops and enhancing soil health, in countries like Mexico, Côte d'Ivoire, and Indonesia. Nestlé collaborates with nonprofits such as Cargill and the Earthworm Foundation to support farmers in adopting regenerative agriculture and reforestation practices.

Alliances for ESG Practices

Sometimes firms form alliances with suppliers to ensure consistent ESG practices across the entire value chain. For instance, GSK takes responsibility for the ESG practices of its suppliers through its Sustainable Procurement Programme, which provides them with training and support. GSK took this initiative as studies revealed that supply chain activities contributed 40% of GSK's carbon emissions.[14]

Outsourcing

An outsourcing alliance implies a firm partnership with third-party organizations where a specific value chain function, such as HR or manufacturing, is delegated to third parties within the same or foreign countries. The objective is to enhance the value chain function more efficiently.[15] For instance, when manufacturing is outsourced to low-cost countries abroad (known as offshoring), the aim is to leverage low-cost labor in developing countries for more efficient manufacturing. As the cost of manufacturing is decreased by virtue of offshoring, a firm can save tremendous manufacturing costs incurred in in-house manufacturing in developed countries. This cost-saving benefit is typically passed on to customers in the form of lower prices. Figure 11.1 presents wage rate differences of countries with the US.

Although offshoring helps to reduce manufacturing costs, other costs may offset the savings, increasing the overall cost of overseas manufacturing. For instance, tariffs and import duties could significantly increase the cost of overseas manufacturing. Similarly, a firm may incur substantial international freight costs, especially for bulky items. Then, quality control could be challenging in offshoring locations. Apart from this, due to the poor legal environment in third-world countries, protecting intellectual property rights can also be a challenge. However, despite all these cost-benefit analyses, the firm ultimately benefits from offshoring. Suppose the cost of manufacturing an average sneaker in Asia is USD 15, compared to USD

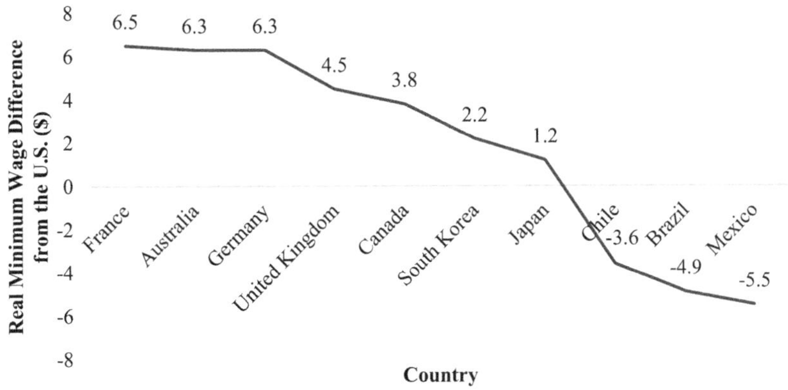

FIGURE 11.1 Country-wise Real Minimum Wage Difference from the US (USD) in 2022

Note: Real Minimum Wages in the US in 2022 was USD 7.30

Source: Developed by the Authors Based on Information Available at: Armstrong, M. (2024, January 18). How the United States' minimum wage compares. Retrieved from https://www.statista.com/chart/3501/the-countries-with-the-best-minimum-wages/

45 in the US.[16] This difference arises because US factory workers are paid USD 12–16 per hour on average, while workers in China, Vietnam, or Indonesia receive USD 3 and USD 1.50, respectively.[17] Then, labor laws are stringent in developed markets like the US, whereas they are lax in third-world countries, further raising the cost of manufacturing in the US.[18] Overall, sneakers made in the US cost almost double, or even more, compared to counterparts from China. For example, the iconic New Balance 990v5, manufactured in the US, costs about USD 199, while Nike's Air Monarch IV, made in China, is sold for USD 80 in the US market.[19] For cost-effectiveness, focal firms in developed countries, such as the UK and the US, prefer to form contractual alliances with third-party manufacturers in developing countries.

From the customer perspective, the most critical challenge is to avoid exploitative labor practices in foreign countries. One exploitative advantage of weak legal systems in third-world countries that third-party manufacturers and their focal clients in developed countries take advantage of is disregarding workers' rights and safety standards. Exploitative practices such as unsafe working conditions, child labor, wages below minimum wage rate, overtime, etc, are common in offshoring. In fact, sometimes offshoring manufacturing sites are also referred to as sweatshops.[20] *Sweatshops* refer to manufacturing facilities where working conditions are poor, characterized by substandard building construction, inadequate safety equipment, low wages, and widespread labor law violations.[21] Industries such as fast fashion, athleisure, electronics, and agriculture, which are labor-intensive by nature, are often associated with sweatshops.[22]

There have been protests calling for multinationals to take responsibility for the socially irresponsible behavior of their third-party outsourcing contractors. By 2024, Lululemon and Puma ensured that their outsourcing partners in developing countries adhered to all stringent labor laws and provided suitable working conditions to their workers.[23] Puma deployed 50 experts from around the globe whose task was to ensure that third-party contractors were following workplace standards. Puma conducted audits at factory premises, covering more than 1,200 suppliers, to ensure workplace standards at third-party contractors' premises.[24] Although such audits require a significant investment of resources in overseeing production in developing countries, these companies report double-digit revenue growth and profits.[25]

MAKING ECONOMICALLY EFFECTIVE OUTSOURCING DECISIONS

When a firm makes an outsourcing decision, it may not always result in cost savings, as transaction costs are involved, including contract negotiations and logistics. Moreover, as wage rates in developing countries increase, outsourcing may become economically ineffective. Firms may use the following method to decide on the feasibility of outsourcing.

Assume company ABC is seeking to outsource manufacturing for one of its products.[26]

- Fixed cost to make product in-house (plant overhead, depreciation, core staff): USD 50,000.
- Variable manufacturing cost per unit (materials, direct labor, per-unit overhead): USD 25/unit.
- Opportunity cost of making: Foregone rental income from using spare plant area = USD 5,000/year.
- Buy price from supplier (including logistics cost, i.e., freight & duties): USD 40/unit.
- Additional transaction costs associated with buying (contract negotiation, quality inspection, logistics overhead): USD 3/unit.
- Buying total unit cost, i.e., supplier price plus transaction cost: USD (40 + 3) = USD 43/unit.
- Expected demand scenarios: Low = 2,000; Base = 3,500; High = 5,000 units.
- Make total cost (including opportunity cost):

$$\begin{aligned} TC_{make}(Q) &= Fixed_{make} + Var_{make}\, Q + OppCost \\ &= \$50{,}000 + 25Q + \$5{,}000 = \$55{,}000 + 25Q, \end{aligned}$$

  where Q = required units per year.
- Buy total cost (including per-unit transaction costs)

  $TC_{buy}(Q) = (Buyprice + Trans.cost)\,Q = 43Q$ (since both cost varies with unit so buyprice × quantity + transaction cost × quantity implying (Buy price + Transaction cost) × Q.

Finding Critical Quantity i.e. Quantity at Which Both Make or Buy Are Equally Effective

Find the critical quantity (indifference point, Q^*)

- Set costs equal for buying and making

$$55{,}000 + 25Q = 43Q$$

  This gives Q as

$$55{,}000 = 18Q \Rightarrow Q^* = \frac{55{,}000}{18} = 3{,}055.56 \text{ per units}(\text{approx.})$$

Thus at approx. 3,056 units, total yearly cost is the same whether making or buying.

Calculate TC_{make} and TC_{buy} for Low (2,000), High (5,000) demand:

Low (2,000)

- $Q = 2{,}000$:
- Total cost make = 55,000 + 25 Q = 55,000 + 25 × 2,000 = 55,000 + 50,000 = 105,000
- $TC_{buy}(Q) = (\text{Buyprice} + \text{Trans.cost})Q = 43Q$, implying 43 × 2,000 = 80,000

Buying is cheaper.

High (5000)

- $Q = 5000$:
- Total cost make = 55,000 + 25 Q = 55,000 + 25 × 5000 = 55,000 + 125,000 = 18,000
- $TC_{buy}(Q) = (\text{Buyprice} + \text{Trans.cost})Q = 43Q$, implying 43 × 5000 = 215,000
  Making is cheaper than buying.

GLOBAL ALLIANCES WITH MULTIPLE SUPPLIERS

Some companies form alliances with a complex web of suppliers, and their supply chain is more global in nature. Such alliances occur when companies leverage the diverse competencies of different suppliers, particularly when advanced and complex technologies are involved in the production of a product. Boeing allies with about 2,100 "Tier 1" suppliers, who specialize in different unique manufacturing techniques.[27] These suppliers, based in countries such as Japan, Italy, and India, are responsible for designing and producing various sections of the aircraft, including the wings and fuselage.[28] Boeing, on the other hand, has expertise in the final assembly of aircraft, so it focuses on component integration.[29] However, suppliers faced issues with parts compatibility and engineering mismatches among themselves, owing to poor communication and weak control by Boeing over its globally dispersed suppliers, resulting in production delays.[30,31] Sometimes, suppliers submitted unreliable quality, resulting in retroactive testing by Boeing.[32] Eventually, Boeing acquired some of the suppliers, such as Vought and Global Aeronautica, for better control of operations.[33]

Sometimes alliances are not voluntary but are made to meet legal requirements. In some countries, specific industries are government-regulated, and to venture into that industry as an international player, a firm cannot make FDI directly, but must ally with a local partner.[34] This model is commonly used in Asian markets, such as China and India. For example, in India's retail sector, FDI was not allowed, so Walmart entered the Indian market after making a joint venture with Bharti Enterprises to offer cash-and-carry stores.[35] These stores were B2B in nature, as consumer retailing was not open for FDI at all. The joint venture sold retail goods in bulk to businesses and institutions.

Companies also form alliances for asymmetrical reasons, whereby the larger alliance partner may exploit resources from the smaller partner and then may dissolve the partnership. Small firms also form alliances with larger firms to leverage their asymmetry, as they seek resources that larger firms possess.[36] For instance, a larger firm may acquire specialized technology or intellectual property that a smaller firm possesses, learn the critical know-how, and then dissolve the partnership. A smaller firm, in the meantime, may also benefit as it gains financial resources for further R&D from a larger counterpart or can commercialize technology using the distribution channel of a larger firm.

FROM ALLIANCES TO CONSORTIA OR CONSTELLATIONS

Sometimes alliances are formed across multiple partners in the industry value chain, and then they are called a consortium or a constellation.[37] These can be formed for several motives, such as R&D or setting industry standards, as discussed below.

R&D Consortia

In such consortia, different industry participants, such as Corporations, universities, and laboratories, collaborate for R&D to share R&D costs, as R&D is inherently risky.[38] Leveraging their complementary knowledge, partners conduct novel research to accelerate technological development. One classic example is the case of the SEMATECH consortium.[39] With support from the US government, 14 US semiconductor manufacturers formed this consortium in 1987.[40] At that time, the American semiconductor industry was losing its competitive edge to other countries. Thus, instead of competing against each other, US manufacturers decided to collaborate and combat global competition to first protect the reputation of the US as the leading semiconductor industry. SEMATECH aimed to improve manufacturing processes and introduce new, advanced equipment for semiconductor fabrication.[41] To avoid friction between chipmakers and equipment suppliers, the consortia created a common ground for developing and testing next-generation tools. The manufacturing process was to be made more efficient by inventing cost-effective lithography (Using light to transfer patterns onto silicon wafers), deposition (Processes involved in growing or coating materials onto semiconductor wafers), and etching processes (processes through which materials are removed from the wafers).[42]

In the airline industry, three major global alliances currently operate: Star Alliance, SkyTeam, and Oneworld.[43] Airlines in these consortia offer a seamless travel experience to passengers, as they share lounges, code-sharing for luggage transfer, and reciprocal frequent flyer benefits. Star Alliance was established in 1997 as the largest airline alliance, including members such as Lufthansa, United, and Air Canada.[44] SkyTeam airline members include Delta Air Lines, Air France, and KLM, and the alliance has been in operation since 2000.[45]

Consortia for Establishing Industry Standard

Sometimes consortia are formed to establish industry standards and eliminate the lock-in strategy of vendors supplying proprietary technologies.[46] For instance, in the manufacturing industry, tens of thousands of individual instruments monitor equipment such as pumps, valves, and pressure gauges, ensuring smooth manufacturing. In the digital world, the underlying technology that runs smartphones or the internet is standardized. ExxonMobil advocated for the idea that, in the manufacturing sector, firms required standardized technology, and it became the first manufacturing company to adopt new technology known as Open Process Automation (OPA).[47] OPA integrates best-in-class components from multiple vendors and decouples software from hardware, ensuring that a single vendor cannot lock in industrial customers for technology support. OPA features a plug-and-play design that enables automatic upgrades of new technologies from various vendors.[48]

Consortia for Combating Competition

Apple is combating competition from Microsoft, which is allied with Motorola and one of its common rivals, IBM.[49] Microsoft's competitive advantage was in Wintel, i.e., Intel inside Windows (Intel being a microprocessor chip provider).[50] IBM was a diversified company that operated in multiple segments of the tech business, including chips, desktops, and servers. Instead of competing head-on with Apple in the PC market, IBM decided to focus on chips and compete against Intel by providing faster microprocessors for Apple PCs and laptops. Motorola joined the alliance to assist IBM in microprocessor development, leveraging its expertise in RISC architecture and chip design.[51] However, the duo failed to offer the same quality and speedy chips that Intel provided for Microsoft Windows.

Moreover, IBM gradually shifted its focus from the hardware market to the software market, such as cloud servers and analytics, as this was a more profitable business, and competing against Intel was becoming increasingly complex.[52] Motorola also shifted its focus from the chip business to the telecom equipment business.[53] Sometimes objectives are not fulfilled, as partner firms may decide to either change their area of core competency or focus on core competency. For Motorola, microprocessors were never the area of their core expertise.[54]

International Strategic Alliance

For access to newer markets, which are generally untested waters in international markets, a firm seeking growth can ally with an international partner in the foreign market that may market the company's product. Thus, a company need not make any capital investment in the newer market and yet achieve growth with the help of a local partner. For instance, Monday.com entered the South Korean market by partnering with SPH. The local knowledge and sales expertise of SPH helped Monday.com triple its revenue within nine months.[55] As an American company, understanding the local culture of South Korea was complex, and a local partner was a safe approach to test the market and eventually grow in that market.

ASSIGNMENT QUESTIONS

1. Explain how equity strategic alliances differ from non-equity alliances. Give examples.
2. Elaborate on different types of partners in strategic alliances. What are the specific challenges with buyer-supplier alliances and offshore or outsourced-based alliances?
3. Critically evaluate the performance of R&D consortia. How do they differ from traditional strategic alliances?
4. A firm is evaluating whether it should outsource car door manufacturing to an offshore unit. Please assume that the in-house variable cost of manufacturing doors by the company is USD 55, and the cost of outsourcing is USD 23. Assume in-house fixed cost of car manufacturing is USD 85,000. The opportunity cost is USD 6,000, and the transaction cost per unit is USD 96. A company forecasts that it will make 23,000 units of cars in 2025 and 50,000 units in 2026. Evaluate if it should outsource the manufacturing or not.

CASE STUDY 11.1

Shein's Fast Fashion at the Cost of Sustainability

Agnihotri, A., & Bhattacharya, S. (2025). *Shein's fast fashion at the cost of sustainability*. Sage Business Cases. https://doi.org/10.4135/9781071960400

INTRODUCTION

Singapore-based SheIn Group Ltd. (Shein) is one of the fastest-emerging fast fashion e-retailers (Rajvanshi, 2023). It took less than a decade to become the dominant player in fast fashion and a favorite shopping destination for low-cost fashion. Chris Xu is the CEO of Shein. The e-retailer made dresses available at prices as low as USD 10 for a dress and USD 5 for a top (Ndure, 2023). Shein rolled out hundreds of designs every week. Analysts also referred to Shein's business model as real-time retail, as designs were made available to consumers within a week (Peiyue, 2021). By early 2023, it was the second most downloaded shopping app in the US and had more followers on TikTok than any other apparel retail brand (Dawkins & Mayer, 2023).

Critiques mentioned that Shein's business model relied on tax loopholes, a negligent attitude toward intellectual property, and a lack of empathy toward social responsibility (Eley & Olcott, 2021). One of the fashion retailers' CEOs said, "I think it should be closed down" (Eley & Olcott, 2021). However, young consumers were hooked to Shein, given its rock-bottom price dominance, raising concern in Western fashion companies' boardrooms (Eley & Olcott, 2021).

To improve its sustainability score, Shein announced an investment in circular economy practices by encouraging customers to return the worn clothes instead of throwing them in the trash (Ewen, 2023). A circular economy encourages activities that can preserve the product's value through energy, labor, and materials used in manufacturing the product (Webster, 2019). Shein also began to source more organic cotton and implemented efficient energy programs. On the other hand, 3D printing was catching up in the fast fashion industry, and experts believed that it had the potential to disrupt it, though challenges remained. How did Xu make Shein a successful fast fashion e-retailer? Is Shien's success at the cost of sustainability? Has Xu taken ample steps for circular economy practices? How likely is Shein to be threatened by 3D printing?

BACKGROUND

Company

Shein, pronounced as "she-in," is a fast-fashion Chinese behemoth. Xu, a US-born entrepreneur, quit his marketing job and founded Shein in Nanjing, the capital of Jiangsu province, China, during the 2008 financial crisis (Eley & Olcott, 2021; Rajvanshi, 2023). Shein was initially a low-cost Chinese apparel merchant that rose to a global, online-only fashion powerhouse, with its sales reaching USD 100 billion from USD 10 billion between 2020 and 2022 (Rajvanshi, 2023). Within 12 years, Xu seized a quarter of the US fast-fashion market, and experts believed its rapid growth disrupted established global players such as Inditex and H&M (Eley & Olcott, 2021). During its initial days, Shein was an e-commerce platform that exported made-in-China wedding dresses to the Western market. In 2012, the e-retailer changed its name to SheInside.com and expanded into a broader range of women's apparel (Peiyue, 2021). In 2015, Xu decided to reinvent the business as a fast-fashion brand with a new name, Shein. He also shifted the company's headquarters from Nanjing to Guangzhou—China's leading clothing manufacturing hub (Peiyue, 2021). In 2022, the company completely shifted its headquarters to Singapore for regulatory, international expansion, and financial reasons—while keeping its supply chains and warehouses in China (The Economist, 2023). Shein had over 10,000 employees globally in 2023 (Shein, 2023).

History of Fast Fashion

The fast fashion business model was pioneered in the 1990s by Inditex, the parent company of Spanish retailer Zara (Hansen, 2012). Zara challenged the concept of fashion seasons, where the production cycle was an annual process, by introducing new designs every few weeks (Hansen, 2012). As Zara enticed customers with its fast fashion strategy, other Western designers and retailers, such as H&M and Forever 21, followed the lead and fast fashion became the norm (Chua, 2019). Companies began launching fast fashion designs every two weeks (Chua, 2019). This reduction in lead time was made possible by outsourcing the manufacturing process to low-cost countries, mainly in Asia, with poor labor laws implementation practices. Manufacturers made workers work overtime without additional pay, and fashion retailers profited from this (Chua, 2019).

By 2010 came the era of Fashion 2.0, i.e., ultra-fast fashion companies, including players like Asos, Boohoo, Fashion Nova, and Shein (Shadel, 2022). In Fashion 2.0, retailers opt for faster production cycles and trend churn. More than half of Fashion 2.0 garments are made from "virgin plastics that shed microfibers into waterways and the air," consequently affecting workers and the environment (Shadel, 2022). Investors threatened fast fashion companies who anticipated that fast fashion companies like Zara might be made extinct by Fashion 2.0 companies (Rajvanshi, 2023).

SHEIN'S ULTRA-FAST FASHION MODEL

Xu hired a team of in-house designers and developed an extensive supply network among local factories in China (Peiyue, 2021). He identified designs trending in the West and produced similar items for export in just six to seven days—resulting in "ultra-fast-fashion" (Peiyue, 2021). Shein's revealed its ultra-fast fashion model in 2021. It added between 2,000 and 10,000 individual styles to its app daily between July and December 2021 (Rajvanshi, 2023). The on-demand business model was one of the core traits of Shein's business (Ewen, 2023). According to this model, Shein first produced 10–100 copies of any garment and sold them on their website (Ewen, 2023). If Shein detected a demand signal through aspects such as people putting them in an e-shopping cart or buying rapidly, they interpreted the signal as a high-demand product and accordingly federated with their network of suppliers. Shien gave suppliers with large-scale capability mass production orders for that particular design. If those initial 100 copies of the design did not sell, Shein avoided the creation of an extensive inventory as mass production did not occur (Ewen, 2023). However, Shein relied extensively on polyester and the large consumption of oil, which together churned out CO_2 (carbon dioxide), equivalent to using 180 coal-fired power plants (Rajvanshi, 2023). Shein emitted 6.3 million tons of CO_2 a year, 45% more than the target level of global carbon emissions by 2030 for fashion companies as imposed by the United Nations (Rajvanshi, 2023). The fashion industry released approximately 10% of carbon emissions across all other industries (Rajvanshi, 2023).

SHEIN'S SUPPLY CHAIN

Unlike fast fashion retailers like Zara, Shein leveraged a multi-supplier system (van Wyk, 2022). Shein owned no manufacturing units and relied on an extensive network of contract manufacturers, mainly in southern China (Liao, 2022). Its clothing orders were distributed among hundreds or thousands of Chinese manufacturers through subcontracting, though most contractors' location was in Guangzhou Province. Although the small-batch system increased production costs for suppliers, given that Shein paid them instantly and did not require any deposit or commissions, it enticed suppliers to bear this cost (van Wyk, 2022). George Chiao, head of Shein's operations in the US, said, "It took 10 years to build these supply chains because most suppliers don't want to sell you only 100 pieces" (Eley & Olcott, 2021). Payment terms were one way of convincing suppliers that Shein used. Chiao added, "We started with 30 days, unheard of at the time. We were able to get buy-in for Shein's way of sourcing." Standard payment terms for garment companies were up to 90 days (Eley & Olcott, 2021). However, Shein was co-located with their vendor base in Guangzhou, so it could directly work with the manufacturers, eliminating the need for agents, traders, or middlemen. Eliminating intermediaries also reduced overall product costs and offered direct and immediate access to any innovation through their supply chain and with quick decision-making (Kathiala, 2023). The lead times for Shein's orders were just seven days, whereas other retail clothing companies allowed two weeks (Peiyue, 2021).

However, margins were thin, and manufacturers had to complete the order by very short deadlines, which resulted in long working hours for workers in these manufacturing units (Liao, 2022). Workers had to work approximately 75 hours a week and were not even given employment contracts (Roshitsh, 2021). The workshops where Shein's contractors subcontract manufacturing are jokingly called "handshake buildings" as different towers almost touch each other.

There were also fire risks, and several businesses were illegal with no formal contract with Shein. These illegal businesses made it difficult for Shein to verify whether workers were well-treated (Peiyue, 2021). In one factory, workers made a daily base salary of USD 20, which would reduce to USD 14 if garments did not pass quality checks (Rajvanshi, 2023). Shein's spokesperson denied the allegations of labor exploitation, saying it paid its contract manufacturers 45% more than the national average salary (Eley & Olcott, 2021). However, an investigation by Sixth Tone, a Chinese online magazine, found that several of Shein's manufacturers cut their costs by further outsourcing to small workshops (Eley & Olcott, 2021). These workshops incurred exploitative practices, paid their workers less, and broke labor laws. Critics raised similar complaints against competitors like the UK's Boohoo (Eley & Olcott, 2021). Even in Shein's warehouses, workers faced an adverse work environment, as rest breaks were short and were within walking distance of dozens of kilometers (Peiyue, 2021). Shein also had a bad reputation for extreme secrecy, with one investor dubbing it "China's most mysterious billion-dollar company" (Peiyue, 2021).

Shien, in the wake of allegations against its supply chain practices, decided to invest in responsible sourcing where "all contracted manufacturing suppliers agree to comply with the Shein Code of Conduct, which is aligned to International Labor Organization's core conventions, and local laws and regulations" (Liao, 2022). Shein also set up a feedback system through which workers of the manufacturing units could "anonymously submit complaints, feedback, and suggestions via email, phone or WeChat, to support the company's efforts in monitoring and managing compliance to its Code of Conduct and upholding the labor rights of workers" (Liao, 2022). On Shein's announcement about the worker condition investigation, Zofia Zwieglinska, a fashion journalist, commented: "I'm not quite sure how he's going to be able to change anything for the brand because a lot of the supply chain issues that are there depend on their business model and the other way around" (Roshitsh, 2021).

However, industry skeptics believed that Shein's investment in responsible sourcing and managing workers' rights is going to be at loggerheads with the value proposition it offered to customers, i.e., affordable ultra-fast fashion, as sustainability initiatives would raise the cost of manufacturing (Liao, 2022).

SHEIN'S CUSTOMER FOCUS

Gen Z customers in the US prefer shopping from Shein to Amazon (Daxu E-Consulting, 2022). Shein targets Gen Z as they are most price-conscious and are used to online shopping from any place in the world (Daxu E-Consulting, 2022). A 2017 fashion clothing survey by Hubbub, an environmental charity with 10,000 respondents, found that 41% of all 18–25-year-olds felt pressured to wear a different outfit every time they went out, with 47% being women (Bowman, 2017). Shien invested in big data analytics to gain accurate insight into customer needs. It developed a tracking system that captured products of all kinds on clothing retail websites (Zhang & Gou, 2021). The tracking system analyzed popular colors, price changes, and usage patterns (Zhang & Gou, 2021).

Shein also leveraged the help of Google Trends Finder to evaluate trending words in different countries in terms of color, fabric, style, etc. For example, in the summer of 2018, using Google Trends, Shein predicted the trend in US fashion of lace and Indian cotton. This data helped Shein conduct an appropriate R&D level for fashion designs to differentiate itself from competitors (Zhang & Gou, 2021). Due to data analytics, Shein had live access to customer data to explore new designs within three days (Nguyen, 2021). Matthew Brennan, a Beijing-based writer, and analyst of Chinese technology, said, "Each new design is basically a bet because Shein can estimate how well a product is going to do, but it doesn't know for sure until it sells" (Nguyen, 2021).

Regarding Shein's advantage, Brennan added, "Compared to its fast fashion competitors, Shein can take more bets, but at a lower risk. It's able to place very small initial orders with factories, about 100 or even smaller." Zara and other ultra-fast fashion retailers, like Boohoo, ordered at least 300–500 units per style. If any design went viral on social media, Shein boosted production for that garment (Nguyen, 2021).

Shein's promotional strategy involved micro-influencer marketing (Daxu E-Consulting, 2022). Micro-influencers refer to individuals with a few hundred to thousands of social media followers. These micro-influencers, who Shien delivered garments free of cost, posted the clothing on different social media platforms, including Instagram, YouTube, or TikTok (Daxu E-Consulting, 2022). Shien also gave micro-influencers 10%–20% of commission on referral sales (Daxu E-Consulting, 2022). By Jan 2022, 10% of the traffic on Shein's website was through influencer recommendations (social and referrals), and 45% came from direct organic searches. Direct access to their website exceeded 38%, implying that customers were returning to Shein (Daxu E-Consulting, 2022) (see Figure 11.2).

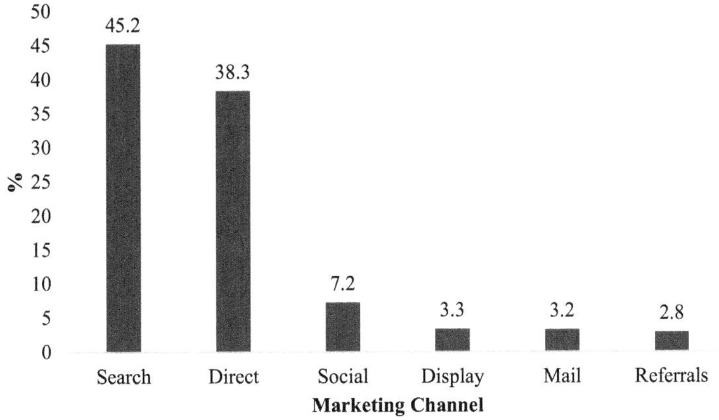

FIGURE 11.2 Shein's Marketing Channels

Source: Daxu E-Consulting. (July 6, 2022). Shein's market strategy: How the Chinese fashion brand is conquering the West. Retrieved from https://daxueconsulting.com/shein-market-strategy/

The 2017 study by Hubbub also revealed that one in six young respondents felt they could not wear the same outfit again, if they have worn the same previously and an image of their with the outfit is on social media. In this study, 79% of the respondents admitted that their buying of clothes and accessories was influenced by social media, especially when they saw influencers unpacking their shopping bags to reveal their loot to the camera (Bowman, 2017). This enticed them to make purchases, and they were willing to take debt to keep pace with fast-moving fashion (Bowman, 2017). However, in reality, these micro-influencers were being gifted clothing and accessories from garment companies so that influencers benefit these companies with their PR (Bowman, 2017). When Drew Afualo, a TikTok influencer with over 6 million followers, faced online backlash for partnering with Shein, she defended the partnership and said, "Not everyone can afford to shop sustainably" (Rajvanshi, 2023).

ACCUSATIONS AGAINST SHIEN

Violation of laws

By early 2023, critics accused Shein of law violations and opaque sustainability practices. Under the US trade law, goods valued under USD 800 are considered "de minimis," and customs duty does not apply to these goods (Ludwikowski & Christensen, 2023). This law gives e-commerce retailers a significant cost advantage if the packages are shipped directly to the customer instead of in bulk in shipping containers that require customs clearance and duty payment (Ludwikowski & Christensen, 2023). According to critiques, Shein taking advantage of this US trade law was debatable, as it could be considered a disruption in fashion retail or an unfair advantage of the law (Ludwikowski & Christensen, 2023).

Furthermore, Shien's ultra-fast-fashion model leveraged several hazardous chemicals that resulted in environmental destruction and health hazards (Greenpeace International, 2022). A Greenpeace Germany report suggested that on randomly testing 47 of Shein's products, it found widespread usage of hazardous chemicals in 15% (or 7) products that broke the European Union regulatory limits, and five out of seven products broke the limits by 100% or more (Greenpeace International, 2022). See Table 11.1, which reveals some of the hazardous chemicals used in clothing.

Critics also accused Shien of copying designs from multinationals such as Dr Martens and Levi's and individual designers such as UK-based entrepreneurs Deborah Breen and Sarah Vaughan (Eley & Olcott, 2021). Against these allegations of intellectual property theft, Shien said they would respond "promptly and fairly to any accusations of intellectual property theft" (Eley & Olcott, 2021). Chiao claimed that Shein was supporting independent fashion designers such as Reia Toombs. Toombs, in support of Shein, said, "The cost of running my brand was too high. But now the company pays for my manufacturing and marketing costs" (Eley & Olcott, 2021).

TABLE 11.1 Chemical in Clothing and Long-Term and Short-Term Health Impacts

Chemicals	Flame Retardants	PFAS (Per- and Polyfluoroalkyl Substances)	Lead	Chromium	Phthalates	Chlorine Bleach	Azo Dyes	VOCs
Probable carcinogens	X	üX	X	X	X	üX	X	X
Skin irritants	ü	Ü	X	X	ü	üX	X	X
Hormone disruptors	X	X	X	X	X	X	X	X
Environmental degradation (water pollution)	üX	üX	X	X	üX	X	X	X

X: Prolonged or extensive exposure may lead to health impact.

ü: Short-term or acute exposure may lead to health impact.

Source: Wilson, J. (November 4, 2022). TOXIC TEXTILES: The chemicals in our clothing. Earthday.org. Retrieved from https://www.earthday.org/toxic-textiles-the-chemicals-in-our-clothing/.

Sustainability Practices

Due to Shein's nontransparent supply chain practices, as per the Fashion Transparency Index report of 2021, the e-retailer received a total score of 1 out of 100—on supply chain traceability (Peiyue, 2021). The e-retailer received a score of 0 out of 100 in 2023 (Fashion Revolution, 2023). A factory owner said, "Shein called us recently and reiterated that we shouldn't share any company information with outsiders, as a lot of business spies are out there trying to copy Shein" (Peiyue, 2021). See Table 11.2 for Shein's overall performance on Fashion Transparency Index in 2023 compared to other brands.

In response to these criticisms and to enhance compliance with the US laws and its traceability system, in February 2023, Shien's manufacturing suppliers were only allowed to source cotton from the US, India, Brazil, Australia, and other approved regions, such as Bangladesh, Tanzania, and Pakistan (Shein Newsroom, 2023). By 2023, cotton from the US, India, Brazil, and Australia made 95% of all cotton sourced for Shein branded products. Shein also developed a proprietary material traceability information management system that integrated supply chain documentation required from yarn, fabric, and finished product suppliers (Shein Newsroom, 2023). As an environmental initiative, Shein also intended to spend USD 7.6 million in partnership with the nonprofit Apparel Impact Institute (Rajvanshi, 2023). This nonprofit helps manufacturers to implement energy efficiency programs. Shein aimed to reduce its supply chain emissions by 25% by 2030 through reliance on renewable power sources for manufacturing (Rajvanshi, 2023).

Shein also decided to increase sustainability through circular economy initiatives, as per which Shien was to manufacture with shallow waste on the pre-production side (Ewen, 2023). Shein reported less than 2% of unsold inventory (Ndure, 2023). After post-production, Shein also encouraged consumers to contribute to circular economy initiatives by either reselling

TABLE 11.2 Brands' Overall* Transparency Score (2023)

Brand	Transparency Score	Range	Brand	Transparency Score	Range
Van Heusen	0	0%–10%	Chloé	43	41%–50%
Reebok	1		New Balance	46	
Pepe Jeans	2		Zara	50	
Shein	7		Nike	50	
Macy	7		Lululemon	52	50%–60%
Costco	10		Adidas	56	
Chanel	11	11%–20%	Levi Strauss & C	60	
Fossil	16		Timberland	66	61%–70%
Victoria's Secret	19		Puma	66	
Walmart	23	21%–30%	The North Face	66	
Boohoo	24		H&M	71	71%–80%
Amazon	26		Gucci	80	
Louis Vuitton	29		OVS	83	81%–90%
Dior	29				
John Lewis	32	31%–40%			
Columbia Sportswear	37				
Marks & Spencer	38				
Primark	40				

* Overall score is the average final score a brand receives across parameters like policies and commitments, governance, traceability, etc.

Source: Fashion Revolution. (July 12, 2023). Fashion Transparency Index 2023. Fashionrevolution.org. Retrieved from https://issuu.com/fashionrevolution/docs/fashion_transparency_index_2023_pages.

their garments through the retailer's exchange process so that garments could be reintroduced for resale or reintroduced through recycling of fabrics (Ewen, 2023). Caitrin Watson, Director of Sustainability at Shein, commenting on sustainability, said,

> Since Shein's business model is to create products on demand, we don't accumulate excess fabric liability, which is one of the biggest financial and sustainability challenges for the fashion industry. We are poised to purchase high-quality surplus materials, helping us to reduce the environmental impact of our products and become a circular solution for other businesses.
>
> (Shein Group, 2023)

TECHNOLOGY INNOVATION IN THE FASHION INDUSTRY

3D printing in the fashion industry was typically limited to art pieces or haute couture (BCN3D, 2020). Artists and designers created complex and unique geometric designs primarily displayed during fashion shows and art exhibitions (Buckley, 2023). Israel-based Danit

Peleg was the first fashion designer to experiment with 3D printing in 2015. Peleg created an entire collection using desktop 3D home printers. The printed clothes were part of her graduate project. She used a new kind of filament called FilaFlex, a new technology that "is a flexible TPU filament (thermoplastic polyurethane), which through an innovative manufacturing process, is able to obtain a filament of unparalleled elasticity and texture capable of being printable in an FDM 3D printer" (Recreus, 2022). Printing each outfit took Peleg 400 hours (Buckley, 2023). Critics believed that Peleg gave rise to a new wave of sustainable fashion (Buckley, 2023).

Since 2015, several architects, engineers, and researchers have been teaming up with fashion designers globally to sustainably reshape the future of fashion (Buckley, 2023). Iris Van Herpen was yet another designer to pioneer 3D fashion printing. She hailed from the Netherlands. Teyana Taylor, Winnie Harlow, and Fredrik Robertsson wore her designs at the Met Gala 2022 (Buckley, 2023). Both Peleg and Van Verpen were even looking at the possibility of developing smaller printing machines that designers could install in homes for printing purposes. In 2018, Nike also developed the world's first running shoe with 3D-printed uppers. Athlete Eliud Kipchoge wore these in the London Marathon (Buckley, 2023).

3D printing in the fashion industry has several benefits. Manufacturers wasted 10%–20% of textiles in garment production due to weaving, coloring, and prototyping errors (Buckley, 2023). Making one t-shirt requires 2,700 liters of water, and prevention of 10%–20% of wastage implied tons of water saving (Buckley, 2023). With 3D printing technology, manufacturers generate less waste, given the precision of the technology. The Danish clothing brand *Son of a Tailor* tackled production waste through 3D technology (Buckley, 2023). The brand developed a 3D knitted, made-to-order pullover using 3D technology and eliminated unnecessary pre-consumer waste. Son of a Tailor also promoted the upcycling of material (Buckley, 2023). In upcycling, firms improve a garment to make it functional again that consumers would otherwise bin for landfills.

Fashion brands had the choice of making 3D-printed clothes from recyclable and biodegradable materials. They could melt clothes after use and reuse the material for the next outfit (Buckley, 2023). It reduced the requirement for raw materials. 3D-printed clothes have the potential to save 90% of natural resources. Manufacturers could also source materials from plastic bottle waste (Buckley, 2023). An American brand, Ministry of Supply, transformed 1.2 million water bottles into 3D filaments, preventing 21 tonnes of CO_2 from being emitted into the atmosphere (Buckley, 2023).

3D printing was customizable and did not require mass production. The risk of being out of stock was also low, given that fashion brands could create a product when an order was placed (Buckley, 2023).

3D printing also gave designers more creative freedom, as they could manufacture what would have been otherwise very expensive (Buckley, 2023). However, one of the 3D printing problems was that only a few fabrics were compatible with 3D printers (Buckley, 2023). The most compatible material had plastics that could affect human health if vaporized at room temperature (Buckley, 2023).

Moreover, the 3D printed fabric did not offer the same comfort and flexibility as traditional casual wear, though the technology was being researched for this issue (Buckley, 2023). Industrial-grade 3D printer machines were expensive and cost USD 180,000, making them unaffordable for smaller brands (Bain, 2017). According to industry experts' production costs of 3D-printed knitwear could not compete with conventional clothing due to low market compatibility (Mikahila, 2022). Thus, players like the Ministry of Supply were still operating in the luxury segment in terms of price, where customers were willing and able to spend a lot for personalization, sustainability, and quality (Mikahila, 2022).

However, experts also believe that in the future, 3D printing will play a more significant role in the fashion sector as technologies further revolutionize it. Rosanne van der Meer, a knitwear designer, and developer, said, “Changes in the textile industry are slow. Yes: in the future, we will find more additively manufactured clothing, but how far this progress is in the future cannot be said” (Mikahila, 2022). Before the 2020s, a fashion designer to own a commercial grade 3D printer required USD 50,000–100,000. However, by the early 2020s, high-end desktop 3D printers were available for under USD 5,000 (Welson-Rossman, 2018).

THE ROAD AHEAD

Shein became one of the few Chinese consumer brands to disrupt the US and European markets while not selling in China (Eley & Olcott, 2021). Chiao said, “It has been difficult for Chinese brands to go to the West and make a name for themselves.” The tendency of Chinese companies is generally to concentrate on manufacturing and to shun publicity (Eley & Olcott, 2021). He added,

> Chinese people have been very good at manufacturing. Why? Because they lock themselves up in a factory and make products westerners ask them to make. It’s a cultural thing. Chinese people don’t like to talk about themselves and take away from what the business has built.
>
> (Eley & Olcott, 2021)

In 2021, Shein renamed its high-end offering, Shein Premium, to MOTF, a more upmarket label that used better quality fabrics, but the company still priced below mass-market equivalents (Eley & Olcott, 2021). However, Shien remained unapologetic about accusations of evoking demand for disposable clothing. Chaiso said, “This is what consumers want” (Eley & Olcott, 2021). Analysts valued Shein at an estimated USD 15 billion, and by 2021, it was the US’s top-selling fast-fashion retailer, surpassing H&M and Zara (Walk-Morris, 2021). In April 2023, Shien announced its plans to focus more on sustainability and not just be concerned about affordability (Ndure, 2023). However, this raised concerns about its profitability. Its net profit margin in 2021 was approximately 6%; however, due to an increase in procurement cost that made 20% of gross merchandise value and marketing cost, which made 8% of gross merchandise value, its net profit margin decreased marginally in 2022 (van Wyk, 2022). Is Shein’s success at the cost of sustainability? How can Xu improve Shein’s sustainability practices?

DISCUSSION QUESTIONS

1. Explain whether Shein's relationships with its several small contract manufacturers resemble a strategic alliance or a purely arm's-length supplier arrangement. What are the motives of the buyer-supplier alliance in the case of Shein?
2. Evaluate why Shein would choose small, flexible factories instead of large, more professional manufacturers as alliance partners.
3. Examine the main governance failures in Shein's supplier network. How can these failures be reduced?

CHAPTER NOTES

1 Contractor, F. J., & Lorange, P. (1992). Competition vs. cooperation: A benefit/cost framework for choosing between fully-owned investments and cooperative relationships. In F. R. Root & K. Visudtibhan (Eds.), *International strategic management: Challenges and opportunities* (1st ed.). New York, NY: Routledge.
2 Zahoor, N., Khan, Z., Marinova, S., & Cui, L. (2024). Ambidexterity in strategic alliances: An integrative review of the literature. *International Journal of Management Reviews, 26* (1), 82–109.
3 https://www.cnbc.com/2022/03/14/ford-volkswagen-electric-vehicle-partnership-expanded-in-europe.html#:~:text=Volkswagen%20is%20expanding%20its%20electric,and%20autonomous%20vehicles%20in%202019.
4 https://www.press.bmwgroup.com/global/article/detail/T0444790EN/hydrogen-pioneers:-bmw-group-and-toyota-motor-corporation-take-collaboration-to-the-next-level-to-offer-fuel-cell-electric-vehicle-fcev-options-for-passenger-cars?language=en.
5 https://electronics.howstuffworks.com/gadgets/fitness/nike-ipod.htm.
6 https://newsroom.intel.com/corporate/postcard-from-vision-a-refreshed-intel-brand-takes-center-stage#:~:text=in%20Las%20Vegas.-,Leading%20with%20%E2%80%9CThat's%20the%20power%20of%20Intel%20Inside%C2%AE%2C%E2%80%9D,Vision%202025.
7 https://www.globalfleet.com/en/manufacturers/global/analysis/massive-production-and-price-cuts-how-did-tesla-panasonic-alliance-thrive-over-years?t%5B0%5D=Tesla&t%5B1%5D=Electrification&curl=1#:~:text=The%20alliance%20now%20enters%20maturity,overall%20price%20drop%20for%20Tesla.
8 https://www.globalfleet.com/en/manufacturers/global/analysis/massive-production-and-price-cuts-how-did-tesla-panasonic-alliance-thrive-over-years?t%5B0%5D=Tesla&t%5B1%5D=Electrification&curl=1#:~:text=The%20alliance%20now%20enters%20maturity,overall%20price%20drop%20for%20Tesla.
9 https://www.merck.com/news/merck-and-ridgebacks-investigational-oral-antiviral-molnupiravir-reduced-the-risk-of-hospitalization-or-death-by-approximately-50-percent-compared-to-placebo-for-patients-with-mild-or-moderat/#:~:text=Molnupiravir%20was%20invented%20at%20Drug,split%20between%20the%20partners%20equally.
10 Hanisch, M. (2025). Strategic alliance governance through termination provisions: Safeguard and incentive, flexibility and commitment. *Journal of Management*, *51* (7), 2852–2880.
11 Ryan-Charleton, T., Gnyawali, D. R., & Oliveira, N. (2022). Strategic alliance outcomes: Consolidation and new directions. *Academy of Management Annals*, *16* (2), 719–758.
12 Khan, S. A., Mubarik, M. S., Kusi-Sarpong, S., Gupta, H., Zaman, S. I., & Mubarik, M. (2022). Blockchain technologies as enablers of supply chain mapping for sustainable supply chains. *Business Strategy and the Environment*, *31* (8), 3742–3756.
13 Wang, S., Hu, H., & Wang, X. (2024). Green entrepreneurship orientation and environmental, social, and governance performance: Do contractual strategic alliances matter? *Corporate Social Responsibility and Environmental Management*, *31* (6), 5275–5295.

14 https://www.esgtoday.com/gsk-sets-sustainability-requirements-for-suppliers/#:~:text=GSK%20Unveils%20Sustainability%20Requirements%20for,goals%20on%20climate%20and%20nature.%E2%80%9D.

15 Gambal, M. J., Asatiani, A., & Kotlarsky, J. (2022). Strategic innovation through outsourcing—A theoretical review. *The Journal of Strategic Information Systems*, *31* (2), 101718.

16 https://finance.yahoo.com/news/much-sneakers-made-us-cost-153919903.html.

17 https://finance.yahoo.com/news/much-sneakers-made-us-cost-153919903.html.

18 https://finance.yahoo.com/news/much-sneakers-made-us-cost-153919903.html.

19 https://finance.yahoo.com/news/much-sneakers-made-us-cost-153919903.html.

20 https://www.oxfam.org.au/what-we-do/economic-inequality/#:~:text=Donate%20today,related%20disasters%20become%20more%20common.

21 https://www.oxfam.org.au/what-we-do/economic-inequality/#:~:text=Donate%20today,related%20disasters%20become%20more%20common.

22 https://www.oxfam.org.au/what-we-do/economic-inequality/#:~:text=Donate%20today,related%20disasters%20become%20more%20common.

23 https://www.cnbc.com/2024/02/01/clothing-brands-failing-to-eradicate-forced-labor-risk-in-supply-chains-research-finds.html#:~:text=Over%2020%25%20of%20the%20companies,/100)%20came%20in%20third.

24 https://www.cnbc.com/2024/02/01/clothing-brands-failing-to-eradicate-forced-labor-risk-in-supply-chains-research-finds.html#:~:text=Over%2020%25%20of%20the%20companies,/100)%20came%20in%20third.

25 https://www.cnbc.com/2024/02/01/clothing-brands-failing-to-eradicate-forced-labor-risk-in-supply-chains-research-finds.html#:~:text=Over%2020%25%20of%20the%20companies,/100)%20came%20in%20third.

26 Canez, L. E., Platts, K., & Probert, D. (2000). Developing a framework for make-or-buy decisions. *International Journal of Operations and Production Management*, *20*, 1313–1330. https://doi.org/10.1108/01443570010348271.

27 https://www.boeingsuppliers.com/awards#programs.

28 https://simpleflying.com/boeing-problem-outsourcing-787/#:~:text=Boeing%20transformed%20aircraft%20manufacturing%20with,Boeing's%20facilities%20in%20the%20US.

29 https://simpleflying.com/boeing-problem-outsourcing-787/#:~:text=Boeing%20transformed%20aircraft%20manufacturing%20with,Boeing's%20facilities%20in%20the%20US.

30 https://simpleflying.com/boeing-problem-outsourcing-787/#:~:text=Boeing%20transformed%20aircraft%20manufacturing%20with,Boeing's%20facilities%20in%20the%20US.

31 https://simpleflying.com/boeing-problem-outsourcing-787/#:~:text=Boeing%20transformed%20aircraft%20manufacturing%20with,Boeing's%20facilities%20in%20the%20US.

32 https://simpleflying.com/boeing-problem-outsourcing-787/#:~:text=Boeing%20transformed%20aircraft%20manufacturing%20with,Boeing's%20facilities%20in%20the%20US.

33 https://simpleflying.com/boeing-problem-outsourcing-787/#:~:text=Boeing%20transformed%20aircraft%20manufacturing%20with,Boeing's%20facilities%20in%20the%20US.

34 Kim, J. (2019). Does foreign direct investment matter to domestic entrepreneurship? The mediating role of strategic alliances. *Global Economic Review*, *48* (3), 303–319.

35 Sharma, G., & Anurag, P. (2024). Walmart in India: Crafting competitive advantage using joint venture and acquisition. *Journal of Information Technology Teaching Cases*, *15* (2), 20438869241239668.

36 Yang, H., Zheng, Y., & Zhao, X. (2014). Exploration or exploitation? Small firms' alliance strategies with large firms. *Strategic Management Journal*, *35* (1), 146–157.

37 Gomes-Casseres, B. (2003). Competitive advantage in alliance constellations. *Strategic Organization*, *1* (3), 327–335.

38 Gibson, D. V., Kehoe, C. A., & Lee, S. Y. (1994). Collaborative research as a function of proximity, industry, and company: A case study of an R&D consortium. *IEEE Transactions on Engineering Management*, *41* (3), 255–263.

39 Grindley, P., Mowery, D.C., & Silverman, B. (1996). The design of high-technology consortia: Lessons from SEMATECH. In M. Teubal, D. Foray, M. Justman, E. Zuscovitch (Eds.), *Technological infrastructure policy. Economics of science, technology and innovation* (vol. 7). Dordrecht: Springer. https://doi.org/10.1007/978-94-015-8739-6_7

40 Grindley, P., Mowery, D.C., & Silverman, B. (1996). The design of high-technology consortia: Lessons from SEMATECH. In M. Teubal, D. Foray, M. Justman, E. Zuscovitch (Eds.), *Technological*

infrastructure policy. Economics of science, technology and innovation (vol. 7). Dordrecht: Springer. https://doi.org/10.1007/978-94-015-8739-6_7
41 Helms, C. R. (2003, September). Semiconductor technology & manufacturing status, challenges, and solutions—A new paradigm in the making. In D. G. Seiler (Ed.), *AIP Conference Proceedings* (Vol. 683, No. 1, pp. 63–73). Melville, NY: American Institute of Physics.
42 Helms, C. R. (2003, September). Semiconductor technology & manufacturing status, challenges, and solutions—A new paradigm in the making. In D. G. Seiler (Ed.), *AIP Conference Proceedings* (Vol. 683, No. 1, pp. 63–73). Melville, NY: American Institute of Physics.
43 Czipura, C., & Jolly, D. R. (2007). Global airline alliances: Sparking profitability for a troubled industry. *Journal of Business Strategy, 28* (2), 57–64.
44 Fan, T., Vigeant-Langlois, L., Geissler, C., Bosler, B., & Wilmking, J. (2001). Evolution of global airline strategic alliance and consolidation in the twenty-first century. *Journal of Air Transport Management, 7* (6), 349–360.
45 Sorge, A., Noorderhaven, N., & Koen, C. (2015). Integrative case: Airlines—A global industry and exemplary enterprises. In A. Sorge, N. Noorderhaven, & C. Koen (Eds.), *Comparative international management* (pp. 430–449). New York, NHY: Routledge.
46 Weiss, M., & Cargill, C. (1992). Consortia in the standards development process. *Journal of the American Society for Information Science, 43* (8), 559–565.
47 Trevathan, M. M. T. (2020). *The evolution, not revolution, of digital integration in oil and gas* (Doctoral dissertation, Massachusetts Institute of Technology).
48 https://corporate.exxonmobil.com/news/corporate-news/pioneering-a-new-automation-technology#Lowercostsmoreinnovation.
49 Den Hartigh, E., Ortt, J. R., Van de Kaa, G., & Stolwijk, C. C. (2016). Platform control during battles for market dominance: The case of Apple versus IBM in the early personal computer industry. *Technovation, 48*, 4–12.
50 Hawker, N. W. (2009). Wintel under the antitrust microscope: A comparison of the European Intel Case with the US Microsoft Cases, Updated as of May 12, 2009. https://www.antitrustinstitute.org/wp-content/uploads/2018/08/working-paper-09-02_061120092140.pdf
51 Dittrich, K., Duysters, G., & de Man, A. P. (2007). Strategic repositioning by means of alliance networks: The case of IBM. *Research Policy, 36* (10), 1496–1511.
52 Dittrich, K., Duysters, G., & de Man, A. P. (2007). Strategic repositioning by means of alliance networks: The case of IBM. *Research Policy, 36* (10), 1496–1511.
53 Hagedoorn, J., Carayannis, E., & Alexander, J. (2001). Strange bedfellows in the personal computer industry: Technology alliances between IBM and Apple. *Research Policy, 30* (5), 837–849.
54 Slater, M. (1996). The microprocessor today. *IEEE Micro, 16* (6), 32–44.
55 https://insider.crossbeam.com/entry/strategic-alliance-definition-types-examples?b2bd8d91_page=4.

FURTHER READINGS

Brydges, T. (2021). Closing the loop on take, make, waste: Investigating circular economy practices in the Swedish fashion industry. *Journal of Cleaner Production, 293*, 126245.

Zhang, L., & Gou, Y. (2021). Value-creation strategy of Nanjing SHEIN. *International Journal of Frontiers in Sociology, 3*(20), 89–94.

CASE REFERENCES

Bain, M. (April 5, 2017). Brands see the future of fashion in customized 3D-knitted garments produced while you wait. *Quartz*. Retrieved from https://qz.com/949026/brands-including-adidas-uniqlo-and-ministry-of-supply-see-the-future-of-fashion-in-on-demand-3d-knitting

BCN3D. (June 8, 2020). 3D printing in fashion: How are 3D printers used in the fashion Industry? Bcn3d.com. Retrieved from https://www.bcn3d.com/3d-printed-fashion/

Bowman, L. (November 15, 2017). One in six young people won't wear an outfit again if it's been seen on social media. *Metro*. Retrieved from https://metro.co.uk/2017/11/15/one-in-six-young-people-wont-wear-an-outfit-again-if-its-been-seen-on-social-media-7078444/

Buckley, S. (May 2023). Is 3D printing the future of fashion? *Fibre 2 Fashion*. Retrieved from https://www.fibre2fashion.com/industry-article/9632/is-3d-printing-the-future-of-fashion

Chua, J. M. (September 12, 2019). The environment and economy are paying the price for fast fashion—But there's hope. *Vox*. Retrieved from https://www.vox.com/2019/9/12/20860620/fast-fashion-zara-hm-forever-21-boohoo-environment-cost

Dawkins, J. O., & Mayer, G. (Aug 24, 2023). Shein's rise: How the wildly popular brand became the most feared fast-fashion retailer in the world and now could be sold in Forever 21 stores. *Business Insider*. Retrieved from https://www.businessinsider.com/what-is-shein-billion-dollar-fast-fashion-company-explained-2023-7?r=US&IR=T

Daxu E-Consulting. (July 6, 2022). Shein's market strategy: How the Chinese fashion brand is conquering the West. Retrieved from https://daxueconsulting.com/shein-market-strategy/

Eley, J., & Olcott, E. (December 9, 2021). Shein: The Chinese company storming the world of fast fashion. *The Financial Times*. Retrieved from https://www.ft.com/content/ed0c9a35-7616-4b02-ac59-aac0ac154324

Ewen, L. (July 6, 2023). Shein exec talks transparency, sustainability and the afterlife of clothing. *Fashion Dive*. Retrieved from https://www.fashiondive.com/news/shein-Peter-Pernot-Day-global-head-of-strategy-q-and-a/654139/

Fashion Revolution. (July 12, 2023). Fashion Transparency Index 2023. Fashionrevolution.org. Retrieved from https://issuu.com/fashionrevolution/docs/fashion_transparency_index_2023_pages

Greenpeace International. (November 23, 2022). Taking the shine off SHEIN: Hazardous chemicals in SHEIN products break EU regulations, new report finds. Greenpeace.org. Retrieved from https://www.greenpeace.org/international/press-release/56979/taking-the-shine-off-shein-hazardous-chemicals-in-shein-products-break-eu-regulations-new-report-finds/

Hansen, S. (November 9, 2012). How Zara grew into the world's largest fashion retailer. *The New York Times*. Retrieved from https://www.nytimes.com/2012/11/11/magazine/how-zara-grew-into-the-worlds-largest-fashion-retailer.html

Kathiala, R. (January 20, 2023). How supply chain advantage has helped Shein dominate cross border e-commerce and fashion. *SCMR*. Retrieved from https://www.scmr.com/article/how_supply_chain_advantage_has_helped_shein_dominate_cross_border_e_co

Liao, R. (December 7, 2022). As its fashion empire booms, Shein wants an ESG makeover. *Tech Crunch*. Retrieved from https://techcrunch.com/2022/12/06/as-its-fashion-empire-booms-shein-wants-an-esg-makeover/

Ludwikowski, M., & Christensen, K. (July 13, 2023). Proposed legislation could alter e-commerce purchases of low-value items and shift competition among retailers. *Reuters*. Retrieved from https://www.reuters.com/legal/legalindustry/proposed-legislation-could-alter-e-commerce-purchases-low-value-items-shift-2023-07-13/

Mikahila, L. (December 6, 2022). 3D knitwear: How 3D printing is revolutionizing the fashion industry. 3D Natives. Retrieved from https://www.3dnatives.com/en/3d-printing-knitwear-220720215/!

Ndure, I. (April 26, 2023). Fast fashion giant Shein to increase focus on sustainability. *Just Style*. Retrieved from https://www.just-style.com/news/fast-fashion-giant-shein-to-increase-focus-on-sustainability/

Nguyen, T. (August 10, 2021). Shein is the future of fast fashion. Is that a good thing? *Vox*. Retrieved from https://www.vox.com/the-goods/22573682/shein-future-of-fast-fashion-explained

Peiyue, Wu. (September 17, 2021). The shady labor practices underpinning Shein's global fashion empire. *Sixth Tone*. Retrieved from https://www.sixthtone.com/news/1008472

Rajvanshi, A. (January 17, 2023). Shein is the world's most popular fashion brand—At a huge cost to us all. *Time*. Retrieved from https://time.com/6247732/shein-climate-change-labor-fashion/

Recreus. (January 24, 2022). Filaflex. Recreus.com. Retrieved from https://recreus.com/gb/content/35-filaflex

Roshitsh, K. (December 20, 2021). Shein hires an ESG exec, spurring mixed reactions. *Women's Wear Daily*. Retrieved from https://wwd.com/feature/shein-esg-exec-hire-december-2021-fashion-sustainability-online-shopping-1235021888/

Shadel, J. D. (February 25, 2022). What is ultra-fast fashion? Investigating why it's ultra bad. *Good on You*. Retrieved from https://goodonyou.eco/ultra-fast-fashion/

Shein. (June 17, 2023). Shein- Singapore. *LinkedIn*. Retrieved from https://sg.linkedin.com/company/shein

Shein Group. (May 10, 2023). SHEIN sets ambition to become global leader in rescuing industry's excess inventory through circular economy technology in partnership with Queen of Raw. Sheingroup.com. Retrieved from https://sheingroup.com/protecting-the-environment/shein-sets-ambition-to-become-global-leader-in-rescuing-industrys-excess-inventory-through-circular-economy-technology-in-partnership-with-queen-of-raw/

Shein Newsroom. (February 8, 2023). SHEIN's multi-layer approach to supply chain management & customs compliance. Sheingroup.com. Retrieved from https://sheingroup.com/corporate-news/sheins-multi-layer-approach-to-supply-chain-management-customs-compliance/

The Economist. (March 7, 2023). How China Inc is tackling the TikTok problem. *The Economist*. Retrieved from https://www.economist.com/business/2023/03/07/how-china-inc-is-tackling-the-tiktok-problem

van Wyk, B. (September 6, 2022). SHEIN's fast-fashion sales machine earns billions as new competitors launch. *The China Project*. Retrieved from https://thechinaproject.com/2022/09/06/sheins-fast-fashion-sales-machine-earns-billions-as-new-competitors-prepare-to-enter-the-fray/

Walk-Morris, T. (July 12, 2021). Shein surpasses H&M, Zara in US fast fashion sales. *Retail Dive*. Retrieved from https://www.retaildive.com/news/shein-surpasses-hm-zara-in-us-fast-fashion-sales/603160/

Webster, K. (May 20, 2019). The circular economy in detail. *Ellen Macarthur Foundation*. Retrieved from https://ellenmacarthurfoundation.org/the-circular-economy-in-detail-deep-dive

Welson-Rossman, T. (February 7, 2018). 3-D printing poised to revolutionize the fashion industry. *Forbes*. Retrieved from https://www.forbes.com/sites/traceywelsonrossman/2018/02/07/3-d-printing-poised-to-revolutionize-the-fashion-industry/

Zhang, L., & Gou, Y. (2021). Value-creation strategy of Nanjing SHEIN. *International Journal of Frontiers in Sociology*, *3*(20), 89–94.

Index

Note: **Bold** page numbers refer to tables and *italic* page numbers refer to figures.

For Product Safety Concerns and Information please contact our EU representative GPSR@taylorandfrancis.com Taylor & Francis Verlag GmbH, Kaufingerstraße 24, 80331 München, Germany

Batch number: 10726306

Printed by Printforce, the Netherlands